Philanthropy and the Hospitals of London

Edward VII (then still Prince of Wales) at Marlborough House, 1897

Philanthropy and the Hospitals of London

The King's Fund, 1897–1990

F. K. PROCHASKA

With a Foreword by
HRH the Prince of Wales

CLARENDON PRESS · OXFORD

1992

Oxford University Press, Walton Street, Oxford OX2 6DP

Oxford New York Toronto
Delhi Bombay Calcutta Madras Karachi
Petaling Jaya Singapore Hong Kong Tokyo
Nairobi Dar es Salaam Cape Town
Melbourne Auckland
and associated companies in
Berlin Ibadan

Oxford is a trade mark of Oxford University Press

Published in the United States
by Oxford University Press, New York

British Library Cataloguing in Publication Data
Data available

Library of Congress Cataloging in Publication Data
Prochaska, F. K.
Philanthropy and the hospitals of London : the King's Fund,
1897–1990 / F.K. Prochaska.
Includes bibliographical references and index.
1. King Edward's Hospital Fund for London. 2. Hospitals,
Voluntary—Great Britain—London—Finance—History. I. Title.
[DNLM: 1. King Edward's Hospital Fund for London. 2. Charities—
history—London. 3. Economics, Hospital—history—London. 4. Fund
Raising—history—London. 5. Hospitals—history—London. WX 11
FE5 P9p] R988.L7P76 1992 362.1′1′09421—dc20
DNLM/DLC for Library of Congress 91-27174
ISBN 0-19-820266-0

Typeset by Best-set Typesetter Ltd., Hong Kong
Printed and bound in
Great Britain by Bookcraft Ltd,
Midsomer Norton, Bath

FOREWORD

As President of the King's Fund, I am delighted to contribute a foreword to this history. The Fund is an institution with which my family has been associated since its foundation, when HM King Edward VII (then The Prince of Wales) launched the charity to celebrate Queen Victoria's Diamond Jubilee. At a time of rapidly advancing medical science and of reforms in clinical and nursing practice, the voluntary hospitals of London were constantly in financial difficulty as they struggled to keep up with ever greater demands from their patients. The Prince (advised by Sir Henry Burdett, among others) wanted both to help them financially and to see that they were subject to proper financial discipline.

Like other medical charities, the Fund had to adjust to the Welfare State after the Second World War. It shifted its priorities and developed a variety of new services. While it continued to provide grants to individual London hospitals, it gave increasing prominence to projects which contributed to the development of the National Health Service more broadly. Today its interests include standards of care, nursing practice, homelessness and hospital design. Wherever it turns its attention, the King's Fund has always put a premium on the particular, on treating patients as individuals, and on seeing hospitals as part of their communities. These humane priorities are as necessary today as they were in the High Victorian England of the Fund's creation. I like to think that my great-great grandfather would be proud of the Fund's continuing ability to respond to the pressures, and rise to the challenges, of health care in modern times.

PREFACE

As a historian of British philanthropy, I was initially attracted to the idea of writing a history of the King's Fund because it was an influential charity in a field with which I was unfamiliar: twentieth-century hospital administration. I believed that it was sufficiently central to the subject to be a vehicle for a rather wider study than is usual for institutions. I was pleased to discover that the Fund's officials had a 'life and times' approach in mind as well. I hope that they will be happy with the result.

The history of hospital provision in Britain, like the history of social policy generally, has been distorted by collectivist perspectives. This book, though primarily about London, is an attempt to counter this distortion by looking at the subject from the voluntary point of view. Approached from this angle, hospital provision over the last 100 years looks rather different from the picture that is often presented. At a time when charities are being pressed on all sides to make a greater contribution to health provision, not least to hospitals, a history of philanthropy and the London hospitals may be of some interest.

The historian of Victorian England, G. M. Young, said that publishing with the Oxford University Press was like sleeping with a duchess: 'It was a greater honour than a pleasure.' The same sentiments have been held about writing institutional history. But in writing this book and preparing it for publication, I have found it both an honour and a pleasure. The Press has given me every assistance, including the satisfaction of dining at its expense, and the King's Fund every facility, short of sleeping with a duchess. (It is less richly endowed with duchesses these days.)

This work has been financed by the King's Fund and by a number of other organizations, including Bond Street Bureau, Buck Paterson Consultants Ltd., CASPE, Clerical Medical Investment Group, C. J. Bossey and Sons Ltd., Cluttons, J. W. Falkner and Sons Ltd., Furness Houlder (Insurance) Ltd., Hillier Parker May and Rowden, Intercon Computers Ltd., W. A. Lidgate Ltd., MCP Management Consultants, Macmillan Magazines, Reed Executive plc, and Turner Kenneth Brown.

My thanks are due to all those who assisted my research at the following institutions: the British Library, the Public Record Office, the Institute of Historical Research, the Wellcome Institute for the History of Medicine, the Bodleian Library, Oxford, Baring Brothers and Co., Ltd., the Family Welfare

Association, the Sunday Fund, the BBC Written Archives Centre, the National Film Archive, the Imperial War Museum, and the Greater London Record Office. I owe a special debt to Bridget Howlett of the GLRO for so skilfully compiling the list of the Fund's papers. By gracious permission of Her Majesty The Queen, I have been able to make use of material from the Royal Archives at Windsor and to reproduce certain pictures from the Royal Collection.

Many individuals have contributed to this volume. I am much indebted to Lindsay Granshaw and Bill Bynum of the Wellcome Institute, where I have been a Research Fellow while writing this history. I would like to thank Miss E. M. Gwyer for the loan of papers in her possession from her grandfather, Sir Henry Burdett, and for permission to quote from these and other of his papers in the Bodleian Library. Early on in my researches, Christopher Maggs and John Orbell guided me to sources which I would have missed if left to my own devices. The Fund's librarians, in particular Nancy Black and Gaynor Messenger, have assisted me throughout. I inherited various taped interviews with retired officials of the Fund from Betty Lucas, formerly head of the Fund's publishing office, for which I am most grateful. On other points of detail I am indebted to G. D. Black, Kathleen Burk, John Campbell, and Sarah Pallot. At the Oxford University Press, Ivon Asquith, Kim Scott Walwyn, and Tony Morris, not to mention their expert readers, have made a great difference to the final product. So too has my wife and fellow historian, Alice Prochaska, who read the manuscript with her customary charity.

Several of the Fund's officials, some now retired, have given generously of their time, particularly A. G. L. Ives, Sir Francis Avery Jones, Sir Andrew Carnwath, and Leslie Paine. The present management and staff of the King's Fund have been invariably helpful, from the Treasurer, Robin Dent, who advised me on financial and other matters, to the catering staff, who have convinced me that there is such a thing as a free lunch, and a good one. Jean Shill arranged my office with efficiency and unearthed documents from parts of the Fund known only to herself. Victor Morrison and Barbara Regis read the manuscript with a sharp editorial eye. Finally, I would like to thank the Secretary, Robert Maxwell, for his unwavering support and telling criticism. I suspect that he would not altogether agree with my interpretation, but he and his colleagues have provided me with the context in which I could write the history of this peculiar and fascinating institution with a sense of complete freedom.

F.K.P.

London, 1990

CONTENTS

LIST OF ILLUSTRATIONS

(*between pp. 148 and 149*)

LIST OF ABBREVIATIONS

BMA	British Medical Association
BMJ	*British Medical Journal*
COHSE	Confederation of Health Service Employees
COS	Charity Organisation Society
CVO	Commander of the Royal Victorian Order
DHSS	Department of Health and Social Security
EBS	Emergency Bed Service
EMS	Emergency Medical Service
FCM	Finance Committee Minutes (King's Fund)
FRCP	Fellow Royal College of Physicians
FRCS	Fellow Royal College of Surgeons
GCM	General Council Minutes (King's Fund)
GCVO	Knight Grand Cross of the Royal Victorian Order
GLRO	Greater London Record Office
HMC	Hospital Management Committee
HSA	Hospital Saving Association
KCB	Knight Commander of the Order of Bath
KCVO	Knight Commander of the Royal Victorian Order
KF	King's Fund
LCC	London County Council
MCM	Management Committee Minutes (King's Fund)
MCP	Management Committee Papers (King's Fund)
MH	Ministry of Health
MRC	Medical Research Council
MVO	Member of the Royal Victorian Order
NCVO	National Council for Voluntary Organisations
NPHT	Nuffield Provincial Hospitals Trust
NHS	National Health Service
NSPCC	National Society for the Prevention of Cruelty to Children
NUPE	National Union of Public Employees
PRO	Public Record Office
RA	Royal Archives
RAWP	Resource Allocation Working Party
RSPCA	Royal Society for the Prevention of Cruelty to Animals

I

Victorian Values

IN the high-Victorian surroundings of the King's Fund in Palace Court, Bayswater, hangs a copy of Sir Arthur Cope's portrait of Edward VII in Garter robes and chain.[1] This image of the king, dignified, benevolent, and sure of his place in history, has been cultivated by the institutions which he founded. None has nurtured it more assiduously than the King Edward's Hospital Fund for London, which is arguably Edward VII's most significant permanent memorial. But to fill out the background and early history of the King's Fund (as it is always known), we need to set Cope's varnished portrait alongside less-celebrated photographs of Edward at his desk. One picture shows him at Marlborough House in the year of the Fund's creation, cigar and papers in hand, dressed for business (see Frontispiece). If Cope depicts the dignified part of monarchy, here we have the efficient part. Both the presence and the capacities of Edward, first as Prince of Wales and then as King, had a near-mystical significance when brought to bear on the charitable establishment.

When the young Prince of Wales entered upon the charitable scene in the middle of his mother's reign, philanthropists were in expansive mood. One contemporary historian called it 'the age of charitable societies'.[2] The pressures of industrialization, rapid population growth, and blighted cities had enlivened charitable enterprise. So too had religious revival, which had inspired a phenomenal growth in voluntary institutions, especially among women.[3] Conditioned by Christian individualism, with its high moral seriousness, the Victorian mind ascribed social ills to individual inadequacies or exceptional circumstances, not to structural faults in the economy. Solutions to the evils of poverty, disease, and unemployment thus required personal discretion rather than bureaucratic intervention by the State.

This is not to say that the State was uninterested or uninvolved in the social sphere. The precise boundaries of state action in health, welfare, and education had long been subjects of public debate. And by the mid-nineteenth century there was a body of interventionist legislation in areas such as public health and factory life. But it was widely assumed that industrial growth and economic prosperity flowed from the creative energies of unfettered individuals. Many concluded that unfettered voluntary action was the most wholesome remedy for the pains of an industrial society. Not least among its advantages, it produced benefits for the charitable themselves; for in choosing between the objects of benevolence, they received a moral training and lessons in self-discipline.

As befitted a nation which believed that philanthropy was the most effective remedy for its ills, there was a phenomenal growth of charitable funds. Behind the systematic campaign to pick the public's purse was the assumption that everyone not on charitable relief was a potential subscriber, young and old, rich and poor. Well into the twentieth century, the amount of money contributed each year to charity constituted a massive redistribution of wealth, which far exceeded the gross expenditure on poor relief. By the 1890s, the charitable receipts of the thousand most prominent London charities alone, put at over £7,000,000, came to more than the national budgets of several European nations and most of the British colonies.[4] Widely reported in the press, such details were a source of national and imperial pride and fuelled Podsnap's boast to his foreign guest in *Our Mutual Friend* that 'there is not a country in the world, sir, where so noble a provision is made for the poor'.[5]

In our highly administered world of large-scale health and social services, the nineteenth-century belief that philanthropy could cope with the dimensions of distress is baffling. But in their less-administered world, in which pressures were typically local and individual, Victorians saw few alternatives beyond benevolence and self-help. They assumed that the individual as fellow sufferer, not as ratepayer, was responsible for the cares of the world. A sense of duty to the community outstripped the assertion of rights on the part of the deprived. The particular mix of Victorian evangelicalism and liberalism heightened and redirected philanthropic impulses and put a check on other forms of self-expression. As that eminent twentieth-century Victorian G. M. Young remarked, 'Evangelical discipline, secularised as respectability, was the strongest binding force in a nation which without it might have broken up.'[6]

Even for those without religious enthusiasm, philanthropy was a sign of social standing and social ambition. In the prevailing liberal ethos, in which Christianity and commerce neatly joined, religious virtues resembled those of successful businessmen, with an echo of the Calvinist's suspicion of wealth, which encouraged giving some of it away. With few restrictions placed on charitable enterprise, it was an expression of the human face of capitalism, addressing the social and individual ills which capitalism often created or exacerbated. The peculiar mix of sectarian social conscience and *laissez-faire* doctrine encouraged competition for sinners and distresses between institutions. And in a society splintered by class, religious, and local allegiances, charities proliferated. The results were sometimes disproportionate to the need of the recipient, but proportionate to the need of the giver.

To the Victorian mind, philanthropy was a form of enlightened self-interest. Voluntary action not only provided moral and social benefits to the giver, but it acted as a guard against the State's standardizing tendencies. Nonconformists, of course, had good historical reasons for distrusting the State, and their emphasis on the freedom of religious sects evolved naturally in the direction of independent voluntary institutions. 'The diffusion of intelligence, activity, and public spirit among the governed,' wrote John Stuart Mill, was 'the only check against political slavery.' Without the habit of spontaneous voluntary action, he added, citizens 'have their faculties only half developed'.[7] Such views reconciled the liberal belief in Treasury restraint with the conviction that social ills were removable. They were commonplace among civil servants whose admiration for personal accountability went hand in hand with a passion for retrenchment.

The ideal of personal service had nobility, but charitable institutions had the unhappy tendency to fall out of repair or into dispute. Given the philanthropic world's love of local autonomy and *ad hoc* remedies, and its tendency to sectarian rivalry and self-interest, muddle and confusion proliferated. Across the spectrum of charitable activity, competition was rife. In the medical field, there were at least six eye-hospitals in London in the 1860s, most of them north of the Thames.[8] In the 1870s, there were five national charities campaigning 'to reduce Sunday Gloom'.[9] Proud of their distinctive origins and chary of centralized authority, such agencies offered choice to the public, and a local voice, but many of them worked in the same field without co-operation and with little knowledge of each other's activities. Their rivalries and overlapping services aroused critics of charity and worried sympathizers. Paradoxically, the individualist nature of voluntary activity was to create demands for reform which would lead to an erosion of charitable convictions.

The persistence of poverty and disease was acutely embarrassing in a society of obvious wealth which prided itself on social improvement. Rising charitable revenues excited expectations of their successful application. Under the sway of social science, which became the rage among philanthropists in the mid-Victorian years, the co-ordination and rationalization of charitable resources became a pressing issue. Few before the 1880s dissented from the view that the State's role in health and welfare should be limited to public health, that is 'sanitary reform', and a responsibility for those cases administered by the Poor Law. But how best could the morality and health of the poor be promoted? How were the respective spheres of voluntary and public provision to be co-ordinated? And what administrative reforms would increase the utility of the voluntary health and social services? These were

issues at the heart of the nineteenth-century debate on the condition of
England and particularly relevant to those agencies established for poor-relief
and medical provision.

In the nineteenth century a wealth of charitable initiatives emerged,
including the development of branch societies and the use of working-class
missioners as social workers. Among the most important was the growth of
agencies for charitable co-ordination and the dissemination of practical
information. Geared to urban, industrial life, these 'organizing' institutions
sought to bring a measure of fruitful co-operation through the application of
the principles of political economy and empirical method to social conditions.
Unsentimental, they sought to put philanthropy's house in order before its
abuses aroused the public to favour increased state intervention in social
policy. They did not challenge the conventional wisdom which guided
Victorian social policy: that social ills were removable by personal service. As a
late-Victorian co-ordinating charity, the King's Fund would inherit and
extend these traditions to hospital provision.

It is impossible to pin down the origin of the idea of charitable co-
ordination with precision, but it was well-established by the mid-Victorian
years. Institutions such as the Liverpool Central Relief Society (1863), and
the formidable Charity Organisation Society (1869), now known as the Family
Welfare Association, took the lead. Most of the co-ordinating charities dealt
with poor-relief. They promoted self-help schemes, provided useful
information, and attacked malpractices, especially indiscriminate almsgiving.
On the wider front they sought co-ordination between charities and Poor Law
officials. By the application of social science to parochial administration, they
encouraged more sophisticated approaches to welfare provision. While they
did not bring about the hoped-for revolutionary improvement in the condition
of the poor, they did have a measure of success in reducing casual almsgiving
and training social workers and, eventually, hospital almoners. By these and
other means they hoped to invigorate Christian family life and neighbourly
service and thereby keep ministerial control at bay.

Nineteenth-century voluntary institutions promoted an understanding with
statutory authorities that the reformation of the individual was their concern.
By the mid-nineteenth century a division of responsibilities emerged which
had been endorsed by the Poor Law Amendment Act of 1834. Charity was to
assist those deserving cases which could be aided by preventive or remedial
action. The Poor Law was to deal with undeserving paupers in workhouses,
where the authorities imposed hard work and spartan conditions on the
able-bodied. There was to be little, if any, overlapping of services; charity was
to begin where public relief ended. Though it did not always relate to
conditions on the ground, this conventional wisdom was espoused by the

organizing charities throughout the nineteenth century and was to become deeply ingrained in the ethos of the King's Fund.

Applied to medical care and administration this view fostered a division of services suited to the prejudices of the voluntary hospitals, which prided themselves on running a premier service. Sick paupers, fever cases, the mentally ill, and patients with venereal disease and other chronic disorders increasingly found themselves accommodated in Poor Law institutions, where the pressure to expand facilities increased. The voluntary hospitals accelerated this process because they traditionally turned away these patients. This was especially so in London, where the problems of poor-relief were severe. Infectious cases and aged paupers made 'uneconomical' use of beds and were of little interest to teachers and researchers in the medical schools. Acute cases, on the other hand, gave a better return in terms of cure. Hospital fund-raisers knew full well that a quick recovery of acute patients impressed subscribers with the immediate and tangible benefits of their generosity.[10] But by such means the voluntary hospitals circumscribed the scope of charity and encouraged the expansion of state medicine.

What might be described as an explosion of hospital facilities took place in Britain in the second half of the nineteenth century. This growth was most pronounced in the voluntary sector, where the number of charitably financed general hospitals rose from 130 to 385 between 1861 and 1891. There was also a dramatic increase in the number of specialist voluntary hospitals in these years, many of them built in London. Not a few of them were for the treatment of tuberculosis, which qualifies any assumption that the charitable hospitals were only interested in acute cases. (There were seventy-nine voluntary hospitals for the treatment of tuberculosis by 1919.)[11] Building-schemes in the public sector did not lag far behind the charitable sector. The passing of the Metropolitan Poor Act of 1867 made provision for Poor Law infirmaries independent of workhouses. The Poor Law Amendment Act of the following year authorized provincial authorities to establish separate infirmaries. One result of statutory planning was a dramatic increase in public hospitals for infectious diseases. By 1891, there were over 350 of them.[12]

The reasons for the rapid expansion in hospital accommodation between 1861 and 1891 were various, but they had little to do with improvements in medical treatment. The wish to isolate cases of infectious disease and the campaign against outdoor relief fuelled the demand for in-patient care.[13] The expansion of specialist hospitals had its own logic, not unconnected with the personal ambition of medical men. Many commentators lamented the growth of specialist institutions, which they saw as a threat to the general hospitals. In 1860, the *British Medical Journal* said that to establish one, all it took was an aspiring surgeon with a spare house, aristocratic patronage, and a 'striking speciality' such as the treatment of 'inverted eyelashes'.[14] By the end of the nineteenth century, however, specialist hospitals were much more respectable, and doctors increasingly exploited them as 'stepping-stones' to private practice, or became more specialized themselves.[15]

The late nineteenth century was a period of ferment in medical science, unparalleled since the seventeenth century, but scientific breakthroughs took time to find practical application. A. G. L. Ives, a former Secretary of the King's Fund, wrote that at the turn of the century the hospitals were becoming 'released from their ancient handicaps by the threefold advance—in anaesthetics, in antiseptics and in nursing'.[16] Diagnostic techniques improved, surgery expanded, and new specialties emerged. E. W. Morris, the Secretary of the London Hospital, saw dramatic progress in fighting disease beginning in the 1890s. In his view the introduction of X-rays and the electrification of hospitals, which made treatment possible round the clock, were of special significance.[17]

The immediate importance of such advances for patients' prospects should not be overstated. Moreover, the pace of reform varied from one institution to another. But by the 1890s, as a leading scholar argues, 'the hospital began to be transformed into an expensive scientific clinical, highly mechanised, research organisation—the prototype of the hospital of the present'.[18] By the time the King's Fund came into existence, therefore, the public was beginning to have somewhat greater expectations of the efficacy of hospital treatment, a process which the Fund would do much to encourage.

Altered perceptions and social changes resulted in the appearance of middle-class patients in hospital pay-beds in the Victorian years. It was not unknown for them to dress up in ragged clothes to get past the hospital almoner and into a charity-bed. But as voluntary hospitals remained essentially for the deserving poor, the middle classes preferred to be looked after at home or in private nursing-homes, which were developing in parallel to hospitals taking paying patients. Wealthy patrons who paid for improvements in medical care avoided their beloved hospitals when they were sick. Perhaps they felt it an indignity to enter institutions which concentrated on disease at the expense of individuality and which had the stigma of charity. Few of them had any experience of hospital life from the patient's point of view. One who had, Lord Mount Stephen, who became the Fund's premier patron, was not cheered by his stay in the Aberdeen Royal Infirmary. 'I was mighty glad to get out of it', he recalled.[19] As far as it can be determined, none of the original committee men of the King's Fund died in hospital.

With the ferment in institutional care, co-ordinating bodies like the Charity Organisation Society found much to criticize when they came into the orbit of the hospital world. Indeed, any advances in medical practice made deficiencies in administration more apparent and the co-ordination of services more urgent. In the atmosphere of expanding but unrestrained charitable provision, many of the hospitals had little regard for local need. The mania for building, which blinded hospital managers, decoyed funds from legitimate projects. Some institutions could be taken for 'sleazy boarding houses'. A few were 'blatantly fraudulent'.[20] As one hospital governor put it, 'we have a competition between rival charities, a fictitious demand for new institutions, a hawking about of gratuitous medical service amongst classes who do not require it, and a total number of medical charities larger than the public can be induced to support'.[21]

London was richly endowed with hospitals, but they were distributed unequally. Like the churches, with which they often had close links, most of them were concentrated in the wealthy, historic centre of the capital. (The interplay of hospital and religious provision tells us a lot about Victorian values.) In the 1880s, nine-tenths of all hospital beds in the metropolis were within walking distance of Charing Cross.[22] Ten years later, there were eight general and twenty-six special hospitals within a mile of the Middlesex Hospital (see Plate 2).[23] Thus the residents of Westminster had an ample supply of hospital beds while the poor in the rapidly expanding suburbs were ill-served. Even in densely populated Camberwell there was no general hospital, and the sick had to travel a long way to reach one. The desire of general practitioners to be within hailing distance of a hospital exacerbated the shortages in medical provision in parts of the metropolis. Perhaps more importantly, they desired to be near wealthy patients. In Bethnal Green at the turn of the century there was only one doctor for every 3,000 residents. In Kensington there was one for every 480 of the population.[24]

The need for hospital reform and planning in London began to be widely discussed in the mid-Victorian years. Among the more vociferous in support of reform was the Charity Organisation Society, which sought to bring medical charity into closer partnership with charity generally. In 1871, its medical subcommittee reported on medical philanthropy, with particular reference to overcrowded out-patient departments and their encouragement of 'medical pauperism'. With the years, the COS reported increasingly on the chaotic world of hospital provision: the wasteful overlapping of services; the lack of uniform policies, not least in hospital accounts; the uncertain administrative procedures; and the numbing chaos of out-patient departments, which reminded Somerset Maugham, a medical student at St Thomas's, of Daumier's grimmer drawings.[25] Under the able leadership of Charles Loch, who was said to combine the heart of Dickens and the head of Bismarck, the Society eventually called for an inquiry into hospital administration and persuaded others, from the Royal Colleges and hospital committees, to do likewise.

In 1890, under pressure from the COS, the House of Lords set up a select committee. Chaired by Lord Sandhurst, it investigated the condition of all the London hospitals, charitable institutions, and public dispensaries for the treatment of the sick poor. The British Medical Association welcomed the inquiry; others, worried about a fall in subscriptions, doubted the wisdom of putting the voluntary hospitals under the glare of public scrutiny. Among those opposed to the investigation was Henry Burdett. A leading authority on hospital management, with powerful allies in the City of London, he had been calling for years for a Royal Commission to look into hospital provision.[26] But what the hospitals now needed, he argued, was 'more cash and less criticism'.[27] The involvement of the COS itself was a major cause of anxiety to Burdett and others, for it had a reputation as a charitable killjoy bent on extending its power into medical philanthropy.

The final report of the select committee, published in 1892, was far from revolutionary. As with all such inquiries, interested parties saw what they wanted to see in the findings. To the delight of some, it criticized the London medical world for its lack of system, wasteful rivalries, and concentration of facilities north of the Thames. Others took comfort in the judgement that the voluntary hospitals were generally well run. The report's chief recommendation was the need to establish a central board to co-ordinate the management of hospitals in the capital. This idea had done the rounds before. Not wishing to be ignored, Burdett wrote to *The Times* to say that he had originated it.[28] The report of the select committee ended with the warning that if voluntarists did not put their own house in order 'it will be necessary for hospitals to have recourse either to government aid or municipal subvention'.[29]

The recommendations in the select committee's report, though widely discussed, did not have any direct results. The COS, among others, continued to press for a central board in the mid-1890s, but there was little agreement on how it was to be constituted. Several schemes appeared, one from the COS, another from Sydney Holland, Chairman of the London Hospital. All of them found critics, who saw them variously as deficient in medical representation, retrogressive, or unworkable.[30] The strong-minded men who ran London's voluntary hospitals, tenacious in defence of their respective institutions, were not easily to be bullied into reform or co-operation with their rivals. Some of them translated the call for co-ordination, overseen by a central board, into a threat to the autonomy and individuality of their institutions.[31] Nor were they to be reasoned out of their humanity by the COS gospel of scientific charity, inclined to penny-pinching and red tape, which many of them did not recognize as charity at all.

Though it did not conform to medical needs, the haphazard growth of hospital facilities in London, as elsewhere, had its own dynamic. Doctors and hospital administrators cherished their proximity to wealth, medical resources, and private practices. They valued no less their traditional sub-scribers and local committees of management, which London's prosperous neighbourhoods had always provided. What would persuade them to re-organize, to amalgamate, or to remove their institutions to the expanding working-class hinterlands? It took a selfless devotion to the sick poor for a Harley Street physician with a consultancy at the Middlesex to uproot himself from such endearing connections, not to mention his rich private patients, and pack his bags for Neasden or Bethnal Green. Not unlike today's civil servant in Whitehall asked to remove to Wales, he thought such a proposition laughable.

Given the centrifugal tendencies in voluntarism, the co-ordination of medical services in the metropolis looked a hopeless cause to some, undesirable to others. But the spectre of state intervention and that endemic problem of medical provision, the financial deficit, gave reformers an opportunity. By the end of the nineteenth century, hospital care was seen by a growing number of people as an integral part of the social economy of London. As perceptions gradually began to change about the benefits of hospital treatment, the need to open new beds became fixed in the public mind, and remains so to this day. But how were London's medical institutions to meet the needs of a population of over four million, who were attending hospitals in ever larger numbers?[32] As promoters of the voluntary hospitals argued, the greater complexity of treatment required more sophisticated equipment, greater space, new teaching-facilities, and alterations in the surroundings of the patients—all of which cost money. Institutional rivalries added to the expense and pushed up the deficits.

In the mid-1890s these deficits, coupled with the imbalances in hospital accommodation, created a periodic crisis familiar in hospital affairs. Against the background of the depression in trade, *The Times* published an article 'Is Charity in extremis?' on Christmas Day 1894.[33] Burdett, self-appointed 'Chancellor of the Exchequer for the British Charities', said no, yet the phrase summed up widespread unease.[34] According to Burdett's figures, the voluntary hospitals of London treated 1,696,276 patients in 1893 at a cost of £790,229. The total income of the hospitals in that year was £766,245.[35] This represented a deficit of only seven pence in the pound, but several prominent institutions, including the Westminster, Charing Cross, and King's College hospitals desperately needed large sums to defray running-costs. Guy's Hospital, though richly endowed, had suffered financial embarrassment from the 1880s owing to the collapse in the value of its agricultural estates. Extension schemes were postponed and economies enforced, including the closure of wards.[36] By 1895, the hospital's financial position was dire, at a time when public expectations of its resources were growing. Across the voluntary hospital world, the cry was for more money.

But where was the money to come from? Public funds were unavailable. Philanthropists were chary of accepting state money in any case; they likened it to the curly-haired boy's feelings of revulsion in *Nicholas Nickleby*, as his mouth opened before Mrs Squeers's brimstone-and-treacle spoon.[37] Statistics compiled by Burdett showed that legacies and income from invested property, 'the dead hand' as he put it, provided over half the income of the London voluntary hospitals. More was needed from 'the living hand'. Burdett had particularly in mind the many new middle-class citizens who sprang from the old artisan élite. They were unused to formal subscription-lists, and the hospitals must adjust their appeals to reach them. 'Money must now be collected not from the few, but from the many, and everyone must be interested in the process.'[38] This approach was well-established in other charitable campaigns, most notably the foreign and domestic missions. To Burdett, it needed to be systematically applied to medical provision.

There were already in existence institutions dedicated to the support of London's voluntary hospitals. The Metropolitan Hospital Sunday Fund, the London version of the Sunday Fund set up in Birmingham in 1859, raised money through special church-collections each year in June. Instituted in 1872, it was inspired by Dr James Wakley and put on its feet by its Secretary, Sir Sydney Waterlow. Traditionally, the offertory benefited hospitals. The Sunday Fund simply co-ordinated collections and distributed it more effectively. Fashionable among the wealthier classes, it acted along the lines of a central hospital board. It collected information, made hospital visits, and gave the money to those institutions thought to be doing beneficial work. By the mid-1890s it was bringing in about £40,000 a year from over 1,800 congregations. The ubiquitous Burdett, a long-standing friend of the Sunday Fund, campaigned vigorously on its behalf in 1895 and helped to raise the figure to £60,000 in that year.[39] But he was the first to recognize that it was not enough.

The other leading collecting-agency for London hospitals was the Saturday Fund, established in 1874. It raised money from the working classes largely through workshop, factory, and street collections on payday. Such schemes were well-established by the 1860s in the provinces, where some hospitals received more than half their income from working-class subscriptions.[40] In London, Saturday Fund receipts came to about £20,000 a year in the 1890s. Though it lacked the Sunday Fund's social connections and its knowledge of hospital administration, it developed a method of allocating grants based on hospital efficiency and expected to have a say in the running of those institutions it supported. Unlike the Sunday Fund, it was widely seen by its benefactors as a provident scheme, in which introductions for treatment, 'hospital letters', were distributed in exchange for grants.[41]

The Saturday Fund aroused opposition. In so far as it was seen as a form of insurance, it alienated those with essentially charitable motives. Though diplomatic about its rival, the Sunday Fund recognized that to some extent it was in competition with it for subscribers. Predictably, the COS worried about the Saturday Fund's potential to encourage pauperism. For their part, some socialists attacked the Saturday Fund as a capitalist dupe.[42] Never happy with its management and practices, Burdett called for it to be wound up in January 1896. If it were, he wrote, 'contributions from the working classes to hospitals would double or quadruple their present amount in a few years'.[43] These remarks were not impartial, for in early 1896 Burdett was turning his mind to an altogether grander project than workshop and church collections to rescue London's voluntary hospitals.

Henry Burdett (1847–1920) was a man to watch.[44] The son of a Leicestershire clergyman, he began his career in a Birmingham bank, but at 21 joined the administration of the Queen's Hospital in that city. In 1873 he entered Guy's Hospital as a medical student; but for reasons which are not altogether clear he did not complete the course. Having resigned his post in Birmingham, he became House Governor to the Seamen's Hospital in Greenwich, where he transformed the institution's management and finances. Astonishingly energetic, he compiled comparative statistics on medical provision in his spare time and wrote widely on hospital affairs. In an exceptional change of career, he joined the Stock Exchange as Secretary to the Shares and Loan Department in 1881, where he remained for seventeen years. There he found time to publish numerous books and edit the *Hospital*, a weekly journal of administrative medicine, all the while making connections which would help to bring to fruition the various schemes his fertile mind devised. An avid sportsman and gambler, he was said to have broken the bank at the Casino in Monte Carlo. Characteristically, he gave the winnings to the Prince of Wales.[45]

Sanguine and 'a little noisy', Burdett had the genius to persuade, indeed compel, others to join in his ambitious plans. Combative, he steamrollered anyone audacious enough to disagree with him. To those who shared his outlook and kept pace with his exhausting demands, he could be the soul of kindness. He was on the best of terms with the caged birds in his study, if not always with his wife and colleagues. To royalty, in the accepted Edwardian manner, he was obsequious. This was partly due to his ingrained sense of social hierarchy, widely shared by his contemporaries, but also due to the importance he attached to the voluntary cause, which he admired, above all, for its humanity. His motto, which he never tired of repeating, was 'personal service to the sick in the days of health'.[46] But no innocent, he acted on a fundamental truth about organized charity: it was not simply the nature of the campaign that determined its success, but who could be found to support it.

By the mid-1890s, Burdett had been cultivating the royal family for years.

In 1889, he recruited the Prince and Princess of Wales as patrons of his Royal National Pension Fund for Nurses.[47] In his book *Prince, Princess, and People*, published in the same year, he chronicled the philanthropic activities of the royal couple in flattering detail and with the same thoroughness he applied to charitable institutions. To Burdett, the Prince and Princess *were* charitable institutions. The ostensible purpose of the book was to study 'how far the heir to a constitutional monarchy may influence the development and administrations of the various institutions and social movements in the British Empire at the present day'.[48] Very far indeed, thought Burdett, or he would not have expended his energy. As hoped, the book enhanced his reputation at court and prepared the royal couple for his future entreaties.

The reputation of the Prince of Wales had undergone something of a transformation by the 1890s. Years before, Walter Bagehot, a friend of the monarchy, had described him as an 'unemployed youth'.[49] More damningly, the Prince had been criticized for bringing the royal family into disrepute by his unseemly associations. In the early 1870s, the Prime Minister, William Gladstone, felt obliged to remind the Queen, who was rarely seen in public, of 'the vast importance . . . of the social and visible functions of the monarchy'.[50] As Bagehot put it: 'to be invisible is to be forgotten . . . To be a symbol, and an effective symbol, you must be vividly and often seen.'[51] The gradual retirement of the royal family from political life, a trend which accelerated in the reign of Victoria, and the behaviour of the youthful Prince of Wales, had eroded the prestige of the monarchy.

But as the monarchy's political power waned, its ceremonial function filled the vacuum and helped to retrieve its prestige. In the late nineteenth century, it has been argued, 'there was a fundamental change in the public image of the British monarchy, as its ritual, hitherto inept, private and of limited appeal, became splendid, public and popular'.[52] Promoted by a growing electorate, imperial pride, and an increasingly sensational press, the royal family became 'a unifying symbol of permanence and national community' in a time of social dislocation.[53] With astute handling by his aides, the Prince of Wales gradually turned into the benevolent patriarch depicted by Cope. It would not have been possible, of course, without the Prince's love of pageantry and his willingness to harness royal rituals to popular campaigns.

There is much to recommend this analysis, yet Edward VII is ill served by it. Some biographers, obsessed by gossip, have given the impression that he had little sense of social obligation.[54] Historians of high politics, on the other hand, undervalue his capacity for public usefulness by extra-political means. Those who emphasize the expansion of the royal family's ceremonial role see it essentially as a reflection of monarchical decline. Ensnared in a conventional view of politics, they ignore the influence that the royal family exercised through the voluntary movement. This social power had been wielded for centuries by the monarchy, but in the late Victorian years the word 'duty' resounded up and down the social order. The pre-eminence of voluntarism in British life made it a compelling vehicle for social advancement to all sections of the community. Allied to prominent philanthropic causes, the monarchy raised its prestige and reaffirmed its importance in a time when it was retiring from national politics.

Arguably, the royal family's influence on the day-to-day life of the nation, its health and happiness, increased as its influence in national politics waned and more of its attention was given over to charity, often local in character. Whatever his political ambitions, the Prince of Wales could do little more than create an atmosphere with a state visit or a reception. Given the favourable climate for philanthropic enterprise and his own liberal impulses, he was easily persuaded that voluntarism was superior to state social action. In the charitable world he was free to initiate and to control policy. Indeed, his patronage of voluntary causes had political implications of some significance. As the nation's premier philanthropist, he discouraged, perhaps postponed, state intervention in social policy. In the process, he contributed to making the monarchy a centre of quasi-political loyalty to citizens with traditional allegiances, a role which the royal family retains today through its support of voluntary causes. As it transpired, voluntary action was to prove the most effective means by which the monarchy averted the dangers posed to it by political democracy and the expanding State.

In the nineteenth century, as now, charities made every effort to get glamorous backers, preferably titled ones. Thriving on publicity, they merged philanthropy and fashion. If charitable attachments gave respectability and opportunities for public display to the monarchy, royal patronage was a life-line to innumerable charities, a virtual guarantee of prosperity. In a society deeply imbued with hierarchical views and social snobberies, an institution which received royal support had achieved the highest accolade. It was the philanthropic equivalent of a royal warrant to business, with similar effects.

Across the country, voluntary bodies, from mechanics' institutes to homes for cats and dogs, inundated the royal family with requests for support. As with companies granted royal warrants, they were scrutinized with care, for the choice of recipient reflected upon the monarchy as well as the institution. The number of charities which had royal patronage increased with the years.[55] By the end of the century, the Prince of Wales alone supported over 200 institutions, including seventy-five hospitals.[56] (Today, the Queen lends her support to 2,000 charities.)[57] Royal connections not only added to funds and prestige, but reassured many societies worried about losing their independence to centralized authorities.

The monarchy was well aware of the reciprocal benefits of charitable attachments, and with the years the Prince and Princess of Wales wove them into an ever more elaborate tradition of commemoration. There was hardly a cause which went without some form of assistance. Despite the criticism of Prince Edward's social rounds in the press, he carried out about forty-five official philanthropic functions each year by the 1890s, and supplemented these with unofficial visits to favoured institutions.[58] With fewer distractions, Princess Alexandra was more active. The charitable work carried out by the Prince of Wales at his desk was considerable, but he preferred the ceremonial side of the work: the opening of new buildings, chairing annual meetings, and attending anniversary dinners.

Improvements in medical and surgical practice were of great interest to the Prince of Wales, perhaps because of his own serious illness, diagnosed as typhoid, in 1871. Some of the activities of the King's Fund would later derive from his concerns about his own health and that of his family. As a boy he had attended Faraday's public lectures on natural science and, influenced by his father, sought to encourage the practical application of science. With a growing sympathy for the sick poor and for the medical profession, he cultivated the society of leading physicians and surgeons and kept himself informed of the latest research. In 1881 he opened the International Medical Congress in London, and in 1888 hosted a meeting to found a National Association for the Prevention of Consumption. When he discovered that Joseph Lister, the pioneer of antisepsis, sought to promote bacteriological research, he lent his support to the foundation of the British Institute of Preventive Medicine, established in 1891. In appreciation of his services to the medical profession, the Royal College of Physicians offered him an honorary fellowship in 1897, which he accepted.[59]

All the leading London voluntary hospitals had royal patronage. (The fact that it did not extend to the Poor Law infirmaries confirmed their low public standing and exacerbated the divisions between charitable and state provision.) Hospital officials, and patients too, eagerly anticipated visits from their premier patrons. Such occasions loom large in the histories of metropolitan hospitals; they invariably resulted in a rise in subscriptions. The Prince of Wales took the lead. Eventually patron of thirty-five London hospitals, he made hundreds of visits to them over his lifetime.[60] At the London Fever Hospital, for example, he became patron in 1863, laid the foundation stone in 1864, visited the institution in 1878, presided at a dinner in 1882, and opened a new building in 1887. At St Bartholomew's, where he became President in 1867, he was a frequent visitor, presided at annual dinners, and opened new buildings.[61] The Princess of Wales had her own favourite institutions, such as the Hospital for Women, Soho Square and the London Hospital. On one occasion she pulled £2,000 out from under her sofa-cushion and gave it to Sydney Holland for the London Hospital.[62]

The latter years of Queen Victoria's reign presented philanthropic institutions with splendid opportunities to benefit from royal celebrations. In the Jubilee Year, 1887, voluntary causes of all descriptions took advantage of the royal landmark. Several were initiated as a result of the celebrations, including various homes, almshouses, and Queen Victoria's Jubilee Institute for District Nurses. The Prince of Wales, anxious that a major institution be built to link the imperial pageant with a scheme of permanent public usefulness, promoted the Imperial Institute, now transformed into the Commonwealth Institute in Holland Park. But the scheme proved a disappointment to the Prince, for it never raised funds sufficient to realize his ambitions for it as a showpiece of imperial resources. Extremely conscious of his exalted status, he became more hesitant in lending his name to subsequent appeals which might fail to meet financial targets.

Around the country, hospitals took what advantage they could of the celebrations in 1887. In Britain and the colonies charitable donations established several Jubilee hospitals. In London, there was concern in the medical world that the public, distracted by the Imperial Institute and other campaigns, would withhold hospital subscriptions. This certainly worried Burdett. The idea of a Jubilee fund for London hospitals had been suggested to him in early 1887, but he felt there was little point in approaching the Queen or the Prince of Wales when they were already committed to other appeals. He lamented that many of these were of little public benefit compared to the hospitals, which urgently needed £100,000 a year.[63] When the Diamond Jubilee came round in 1897, he would be better prepared to take advantage of the occasion. The publication of the House of Lords report on London's hospitals in 1892 and the subsequent discussions about a central board helped to concentrate his mind. So did the growing popularity of the Prince of Wales, which he assiduously promoted.

The precise origins of the Prince of Wales's (later King Edward's) Hospital Fund for London are somewhat obscure, owing partly to the destruction of relevant correspondence. The idea that a permanent central agency for the support of London hospitals could be established by means of a royal appeal had an obviousness about it; it must have dawned on various people during the Jubilee celebrations of 1887 or soon after. Certainly, Burdett saw possibilities along these lines as early as 1887. Sir Francis Knollys, the Prince of Wales's Private Secretary, was in no doubt that it was Burdett who 'initiated the idea'.[64] We may therefore dismiss the claim of the philanthropic timber-merchant Harold Boulton MVO, who said he first suggested the idea at court in July 1896.[65] Nor can we credit the view that the Prince of Wales himself originated it.[66]

It is likely that Burdett had been biding his time after 1887, ingratiating himself with the royal family and waiting for the right moment to approach the Prince of Wales with a scheme for London hospitals. He was much in favour at court in the mid-1890s. The Prince habitually consulted his work for information on worthwhile causes and asked for his advice when in doubt. If Burdett raised a query about any particular institution, it could lead to an inquiry and the withdrawal of royal patronage. Institutions favoured by Burdett received special attention. The Sunday Fund, for example, was able to recruit the Prince of Wales as Vice-Patron in early 1896, an event which reinvigorated the institution and Burdett's support for it. Precisely when Burdett first suggested an appeal on behalf of a new central fund for the London hospitals is unclear, but he had various meetings with the Prince in late 1895 and early 1896, when the opportunity would have presented itself.

The mistress of the Prince of Wales, Frances, Countess of Warwick, hosted some of these meetings.[67] Born into a world of wealth and privilege, she was a highly individual example of aristocratic social conscience. Then going through her 'lady bountiful' phase, she had persuaded the Prince to sign workhouse visitors' books, visit aged cottagers, and support other of her pet projects. Through her charitable connections she had become a friend and correspondent of Burdett. (He later advised her on financial matters.) In December 1895, he had written to her asking about the business capacities of the Prince of Wales, presumably with the view to his personal involvement in an important charitable scheme. A royal mistress, uncertain of her status at court, is not inclined to be critical of a future king. In her reply to Burdett, the Countess lavished praise on the Prince, particularly for his administrative flair, his attention to detail, his 'genius for letter writing', and his remarkable memory. Perhaps Burdett was reassured most by her remark that 'his friendship is very loyal, and he rarely changes his opinions about men'.[68]

At meetings between Burdett and the Prince of Wales, attended by the Countess of Warwick, the subject of hospital finances came under discussion. The Countess wrote in her autobiography years later that at one of these meetings 'Henry [Burdett] and I talked it all out with the Prince and we had the joy of being the means of his founding the Prince of Wales's Hospital Fund.'[69] The influence of the Countess, who had a liking for publicity, should not be exaggerated, yet the King's Fund can claim the novel distinction of being promoted by a royal mistress, who later became a socialist. In the spring of 1896, discussions between Burdett and the Prince were well under way. In a letter dated 6 July, Alfred Harmsworth, the proprietor of the newly established *Daily Mail*, mentioned to the Countess: 'I happen to be engaged with Sir Henry Burdett in furthering a small part of the Prince of Wales' Hospital scheme.'[70] As proposed, the scheme was to be part of any Diamond Jubilee celebrations to be held the following year.[71]

Whatever the hopes that Burdett and the Prince of Wales entertained for their project, much depended on factors outside their control. Would the ageing Queen Victoria be alive in 1897 and, if so, would she wish to celebrate her Jubilee with commemorative appeals? Would she sanction one on behalf of London hospitals? Would one of the other 4,000 appeals under consideration dash its prospects?[72] *Punch* pointed to the compassion-fatigue induced by the stream of begging-letters received for worthy causes such as 'Self Supporting Orphans' and 'Homes for the Affluent', which no one had heard of before but which sought to take advantage of the auspicious occasion.[73] More to the point, the Prince of Wales wanted to be reassured that there would be sufficient public enthusiasm to guarantee the success of a hospital appeal. On this issue, Burdett, with his contacts in the City and knowledge of trade, was hopeful, perhaps too hopeful. In 1896–7, the British economy was expanding after the set-backs in exports earlier in the decade, and the South African war was not yet under way.

At the time when they were organizing their central hospital scheme, other fund-raising drives were in progress that would have repercussions for it. Having recruited the Prince as its Vice-Patron in early 1896, the Sunday Fund was in buoyant mood. On 8 June, it organized a special meeting at the Mansion House as a tribute to Burdett, who had been instrumental in adding so substantially to its revenues in 1895. Making his first appearance in aid of the charity, the Prince of Wales spoke most warmly of his friend: 'I venture to say', he concluded, '. . . that for what Mr Burdett has done for the great charitable institutions of this country his name will go down to posterity as it is at present—a household word'.[74] The enthusiasm of the two men for the Sunday Fund at this particular time was probably not unconnected with their plans for the Prince of Wales's Hospital Fund, for they did not want the Sunday Fund to feel imperilled by a powerful rival on the hospital scene.

Another major fund-raising drive was on the horizon in early 1896 as well, which would have important implications for the Prince of Wales's Fund. An ambitious scheme had been proposed for Guy's Hospital. This was the Endowment Appeal, which was to culminate in a festival dinner in June 1896. The official history of Guy's gives the impression that the appeal was a straightforward success. Invited by Guy's to attend the dinner, the Prince of Wales accepted, in part in tribute to his friend A. D. Fripp, a member of the hospital staff, who had formerly treated the Prince's eldest son, the Duke of Clarence. On 10 June, the Prince, 'fresh from his triumph with Persimmon on Derby Day', chaired the banquet at the Imperial Institute. Upon the retirement of Lord Aldenham, he also had accepted the presidency of the Hospital. Thus, the official history concludes, Guy's Endowment Fund began with a spectacular success and eventually reached its ambitious financial target.[75]

The events surrounding the festival dinner were rather more complicated. A memorandum left by Burdett, now in the possession of his granddaughter, tells a different story of the events leading up to the festival dinner.[76] It points to problems common in Victorian hospital management and the way in which they could be resolved by royal intervention. That the memorandum is in accord with the surviving Guy's Hospital records for 1896 gives it the ring of truth. So too does the Prince's festival-dinner speech, in which he paid special tribute to Burdett 'to whom they were indebted for the trouble he had taken to make that hospital dinner a success'.[77] For some, this tribute must have left a bitter taste, only a little sweetened by the vast sum, put at £150,000, raised on the hospital's behalf.

According to the memorandum, the Prince of Wales sought Burdett's advice in regard to the invitation from Guy's Hospital to preside at a festival dinner. Burdett candidly told the Prince that 'there was a strong feeling in the City that the management of Guy's Hospital was effete or unsatisfactory' owing to the age of the President, Henry Hucks Gibbs, Lord Aldenham, and the inertia of the Treasurer, Edward Lushington.[78] When Aldenham called on Burdett at the Stock Exchange, he was presented with a proposal, which had the backing of the Prince of Wales. If he and Lushington were prepared to resign, the Prince would replace Aldenham as President, preside at the festival dinner, and guarantee a successful appeal. 'Everything should be done to save the front and feelings' of the two resigning gentlemen, Burdett added. A few days later the two men lunched with Burdett at the Bank of England, reluctantly accepted his conditions and approved a letter intimating their retirement from office.[79]

The Prince of Wales's Fund did not grow out of the Guy's Endowment Appeal, as some have suggested.[80] But the success at Guy's enhanced its prospects, for it confirmed that together Burdett and the Prince wielded unrivalled power in the hospital world. Moreover, it reassured them of their ability to open City purse-strings. From the outset, they took the view that their proposed central fund, if it were to become something more than a mere collecting and distributing charity, would have to be lavishly financed. And to be a worthy memorial to the Queen, it would have to transcend political and sectarian rivalries and carry the diverse hospital boards with it. Unspoken, was the knowledge that in time the fund would be seen as a memorial to the Prince of Wales. Having brought the Prince into the scheme, Burdett and his colleagues could not contemplate failure.

In the summer of 1896, few people knew very much about the plans for a hospital fund sanctioned by the Prince of Wales, apart from intimates at court and a few of Burdett's contacts. At the time, some leading philanthropists with an entrée at Marlborough House took the view that there would be no Diamond Jubilee appeals because it was too soon after 1887.[81] Only when the Queen gave her blessing to an appeal could the Prince and his colleagues proceed. When the Prince of Wales spoke to her in late 1896, the Queen wanted to know whether his scheme would encroach upon the Lord Mayor's

Indian Famine Fund. Reassured on this point, she told the Prince that she was 'quite agreeable' to a hospital fund set up in association with Jubilee year.[82]

Before the new society could be launched, other hospital schemes had to be considered and placated. It was suggested that the Prince of Wales's Fund, to avoid possible conflict with the Sunday Fund, should be secularized and should exclude clerics from its management.[83] The Prince vetoed this. Perhaps he assumed that his patronage of the Sunday Fund would moderate any anxieties that it might have. Nor was it desirable to alienate the Saturday Fund, despite Burdett's hostility to it. The scheme proposed by Burdett and amended by the Prince was to be comprehensive, including leaders of various religious denominations and political parties. If the Prince of Wales was to be closely identified with the institution, clearly he could not be seen to favour one section of the community over another. Diplomacy, for which the Fund became a byword, was essential to its success. This helps to explain why Burdett, impatient of dissenting opinion, played a rather less visible part in the new society than might have been expected.

Having received the Queen's blessing, the Prince of Wales summoned a host of leading churchmen, financiers, politicians, and medical men to Marlborough House on 21 January 1897. Twenty-two men in all, their number restricted by the size of the dining-room table. Among them were the Lord Mayor of London, Sir George Faudel Phillips; the Earl of Strafford; the Bishop of London, Dr Mandell Creighton; the Chief Rabbi, the Reverend Dr Adler; the Governor of the Bank of England, Albert G. Sandeman; Lord Rothschild; President of the Royal Society, Lord Lister; President of the Royal College of Physicians, Dr Samuel Wilks; President of the Royal College of Surgeons, Sir William MacCormac; John Aird, MP; and Henry Burdett.[84] As he entered the room, the Prince of Wales, fully aware of the gravity of the proposed undertaking, turned to Burdett and one or two other confidants, expressed his earnest support for the project, and reminded them of his reliance on their judgement.[85]

In his preliminary remarks, the Prince of Wales told the gathering that the Queen approved of his proposed hospital appeal, but that should a society be established it must take care to avoid competition with other charities, particularly the Indian Famine Fund.[86] Having cleared the ground, a discussion of medical provision in the metropolis ensued. It was then unanimously agreed that the Diamond Jubilee offered, as an earlier historian of the Fund has put it, 'an unique opportunity for launching an enterprise capable of providing a bulwark equally for the voluntary system and for London's hard-pressed hospitals, while at the same time doing worthy honour to a great occasion'.[87] Those present then constituted themselves a General Committee, the forerunner of the Fund's General Council. In turn, it

appointed a Special Committee, soon to become the Executive Committee, to
settle the details of setting up the new institution. Consisting of ten men, it
included the Earl of Strafford,[88] Lord Rothschild, Lord Lister, Sir Savile
Crossley, and Burdett.

While rumours circulated about a Prince of Wales's Fund, rival plans for a
central hospital board were still under discussion. On 25 January, four days
after the meeting at Marlborough House, the Charity Organisation Society
hosted a meeting to discuss its own scheme. Sir William Broadbent, while
proposing the establishment of a Central Hospital Board for London, fuelled
speculation in the hospital world when he mentioned the 'possibility of there
being a gigantic scheme for the benefit of hospitals, inaugurated by the Prince
of Wales'.[89] Press comment regarding the anticipated project varied. Burdett
had lined up various newspapers on behalf of the Prince's scheme. But more
than one warned of the risks. The successful dinner for Guy's Hospital was
one thing, said *The Times*, the establishment of a permanent endowment for
all London's voluntary hospitals was another.[90] Nor was the COS amused, for
it had been hammering away at its own plan for years. But whatever the merits
of this plan, it lacked the vital ingredient: the Prince of Wales.

On 28 January, at the Earl of Strafford's house in St James's Square, the
Special Committee discussed the formal name of the new institution. They
decided that the title had to avoid the use of 'London Hospitals' because of
the possible confusion with the 'London Hospital'. The Committee thus
recommended that the new institution be called 'The Prince of Wales's
Hospital Fund for London to Commemorate the Sixtieth Year of the Queen's
Reign'.[91] That the Jubilee year appeared in the title suggested just how
important the royal occasion was in the minds of those in charge of the new
institution. But would a charity so intimately tied to a passing royal celebration,
which depended on perennial public support, be able to sustain itself in the
years to follow? A leader in *The Times* put it another way: 'enthusiasm, even
when most glowing, is not always convertible into a satisfactory equivalent in
cash'.[92] This worry was not limited to the press. Lord Lister, who was to play
a prominent role in the Fund's early history, had expressed it to his family.[93]

At a meeting of the General Committee on 3 February chaired by the
Prince of Wales, the title recommended by the Special Committee was
adopted. By this time Lord Rothschild, buttonholed by the Prince, had
consented to become Honorary Treasurer, Sir Savile Crossley and C. Stuart
Wortley Honorary Secretaries, and John G. Craggs and Ian Malcolm,
Honorary Assistant Secretaries. With a small paid staff, including a clerk and
a shorthand writer, the Fund set up offices in rooms provided by the Bank of
England. It dispatched its agents. Committee men alerted their constituencies
and pulled those strings at their disposal. More specifically, Albert Sandeman
arranged further office-space at the Grocers' Company; Lord Rothschild,

who opened an account in the Fund's name at the Bank of England, lobbied
the financial district; the Bishop of London rallied the clergy; Burdett im-
portuned the press. Meanwhile, the Prince of Wales, more anxious than ever
about the prospects of his scheme, had a word with some of his friends.[94]

A letter addressed to the inhabitants of London, signed by the Prince of
Wales and published in all the leading newspapers on 6 February 1897, made
the appeal public.[95] Closely identifying the new institution with his own
charitable preferences and the Queen's Jubilee, the Prince outlined the
financial anxieties of London's voluntary hospitals. The solution was a combined appeal to raise between £100,000 and £150,000 in annual subscriptions.
Targeted groups included ground landlords, railway companies, banks, trade
associations, and, above all, the innumerable householders who were not
already found in hospital subscription-lists. Though he recognized the difficulties in distributing the monies raised, he was satisfied that public opinion
favoured the voluntary system for the maintenance of hospitals. 'It is obvious,
however, that if these institutions are to be saved from the State or parochial
aid, their financial condition must be secured.'[96] To do so would require the
creation of a unique institution and the launch of a most ambitious charitable
appeal.

Royal Appeals and Arrangements

'THE right cause, the right method, and the right man' proclaimed a friend of the Prince of Wales's Fund at its foundation.[1] Such encomiums fuelled a belief that the institution would soon rank among the premier charities in Britain. If it could raise over £100,000 a year it would dwarf the Saturday and Sunday Funds and rival the great missionary societies and the Royal National Lifeboat Institution in income. But benighted heathens and drowning mariners pulled on British heart-strings. Would something as abstract as the co-ordination of London's hospital services do likewise? The founders did not worry on this score. Given the modest level of bureaucracy in Victorian hospitals, they could equate better hospital administration directly with improvements in health. The Fund's anxieties about hospital deficits lay behind its astute campaign to draw on public compassion for the sick and helpless. By the same means, subscriptions to the Fund would become symbols of 'love and loyalty to the throne' (see Plate 1). In a society fascinated by the royal family, and with an increasing demand for hospital provision, the Fund had every hope of success.

To achieve its large ambitions, the Fund developed an unusual financial policy, which has greatly influenced the institution's character and administration ever since. As its President, the Prince of Wales insisted that the charity create a sizeable capital reserve, which wisely invested would yield £50,000 a year. At an early meeting of the General Council he remarked, 'I should deplore, if for the sake of making a great effect before the public by giving a large sum of money away, we should encroach upon our capital.'[2] The Fund's reluctance to release capital to needy hospitals was controversial, both inside and outside the institution. It led to the need for a new constitution in 1907 and increased the authority of those in charge of investments. In its hierarchy the Treasurer stands higher than the Chairman.

The Fund's financial policy thus differed from that of other distributing charities, which operated out of annual revenue.[3] An endowment income, it was argued, would not only give permanence to the institution as a memorial to Queen Victoria, but would enhance its authority over London's hospitals. While it was undesirable to give the impression of hoarding capital, the last thing the Prince of Wales wanted was to fritter away the Fund's income on transitory objects. As he made clear to Burdett, he did not wish to feel under pressure to go cap in hand to the public each year.[4] But as he soon discovered, raising a substantial endowment was more difficult than his advisers had led him to believe.

Only when the Fund was on a solid financial base itself could it hope to reduce the deficits of hospitals and bring the anticipated improvements in London's health care. The first step was to appoint established, sympathetic men to the Council and the committees. (It was exclusively men. The Council did not include women until 1920; the first female joined the Management Committee in 1948; no woman has ever sat on the Finance Committee.) Many of them were hand-picked by the Prince of Wales from among his personal friends and advisers. They represented a wide range of social, religious, political, commercial, and professional interests. Some of the thirty seats on the original Council pertained to offices. Presidents of the Royal Colleges, the Governor of the Bank of England, and the Bishop of London were invited to serve, and they added to the Fund's respectability and authority. As membership of the Council and the prominent committees was by royal appointment, it bestowed prestige in turn. Active hospital managers were excluded. So was the British Medical Association, whose social status was much lower than that of the Royal Colleges.

The Fund's Council and committees were an expression of what the Victorians called a representation of the 'best interests'. In keeping with an institution described by one of its Secretaries as 'a surprisingly autocratic body, a sort of limited monarchy', the Fund did not feel the need for elections.[5] Instead, it recruited a cross-section of the Establishment, a policy that was intended to reassure contributors. The more active committee men tended to be Conservatives with a keen interest in imperial affairs. Several, including Lord Rothschild and Sir Savile Crossley, were members of the group of Liberal Unionists who, under the sway of Joseph Chamberlain, had split from the Liberal Party over Irish Home Rule and by 1895 had allied themselves with the Tory Party. Burdett was a supporter of Chamberlain's radical imperialism from his days in Birmingham and stood for Parliament in 1906, unsuccessfully, as an Independent Conservative.

To the Conservative mind, democratic authority is immanent in institutions. While the Fund had a liberal outlook, in line with the views of the Prince of Wales, it placed a premium on recruiting individuals to its committees who embodied a spectrum of institutional opinion reconcilable with its aims. By attracting a range of opinion and experience, the Fund hoped to keep sectarian critics at bay and to reassure the divergent London hospitals it wished to serve. As an unelected body, it was open to the charge of influencing hospital provision without being answerable to the public for its interventions. As we shall see, the most pointed criticism of the Fund in its early years came from those it excluded from its committees.

The management of the Fund was at first rather ill-defined. The direction of policy and its administration were vested in the Council, and this formidable body was never more active than when under the guidance of its first President. The Executive Committee took responsibility for much of the administration. Its immediate task was to ensure that the institution raised sufficient funds to survive in the highly competitive charitable sector. There was no finance committee before 1906; investments stood in the names of Lord Rothschild, the Treasurer, and Hugh Smith, Governor of the Bank of England. Smith also took over the chairmanship of the Executive Committee in December 1897 from the ailing Lord Strafford, who died the following year. The other important committee formed in 1897 was the Distribution Committee, chaired by Lord Lister, which dealt with the administration of grants to hospitals. It was complemented in 1898 by a Convalescent Homes Committee, established to administer £1,000 a year contributed to the Fund by the London Parochial Charities. These two committees acted on information provided by a team of lay and medical visitors, who inspected institutions which applied for grants.

The Fund took little action in the early years without the authority of the Prince of Wales. Burdett kept him informed about sensitive issues such as methods of fund-raising and the distribution of income.[6] For their part, the Honorary Secretaries submitted all recommendations of the Executive Committee regarding policy and appointments to him for approval through Sir Francis Knollys. Moreover, the Prince's participation at meetings of the Council, which he never missed as President, kept him in touch, while it lifted morale and guaranteed publicity. The records of these meetings demonstrate that the Prince was informed, involved, and strong-minded. His views, however, were not always translated into policy.

In a charity so dependent on the active support of the royal family, an important initial appointment was Sir Savile Crossley (later Lord Somerleyton) as an Honorary Secretary. He was the first in a line of unpaid staff for whom the institution became a way of life. For over thirty years he provided a crucial link between the Fund and its royal presidents and between members of the various committees. As he also served as Chairman of the Saturday Fund for many years, he eased relations in that quarter as well. The grandson of the carpet-weaver John Crossley of Halifax, he was brought up as a country gentleman and educated at Eton and Balliol. A Liberal-Unionist MP for Halifax (1900–6) and High Sheriff of Suffolk, he was known at court for his shooting and his diplomatic skills. In the Fund, the former were an advantage, the latter indispensable.[7]

Given its royal associations and public nature, the Fund was jealous of its autonomy and hostile to criticism from outside. In this it mirrored many of the London voluntary hospitals it sought to reform. Given its dependence on effective advertising and faithful subscribers, the slightest hint of impropriety could bring a loss in funds. Continually in the public eye, it had to carry the public with it if a change in object were to be undertaken. Answerable to its supporters, it has to put on the best possible face. Thus it made the most of its royal connections, filled its committees with the great and the good, and chronicled its successes in its annual reports and its associated publicity. Administrative costs, the bane of all charitable institutions intent on raising funds, had to be seen to be kept to a minimum.

In setting up the Fund's administration, economy was the byword. The free legal services offered by the solicitors Freshfields and Williams helped.[8] So too did the waiving of fees by the honorary auditors, Deloitte, Dever, Griffiths and Co. The free use of committee rooms also helped to keep down costs in the early years. But meetings in the Bank of England, Marlborough House, and the House of Commons, to mention only a few of the addresses used, also added to the Fund's prestige. The original secretarial offices were in 1 Tokenhouse Buildings, EC (removed to 81 Cheapside in 1901). When they were fitted out, the Fund reminded contractors and suppliers that it was a charity and bills should reflect the fact.[9] Thus discounted linoleum lined the floors. Its telegraphic address was 'Solicitous'.

The ratio of administrative costs to sums received was low by the standards of many charities, though this was to be expected of a distributing society with modest staff-requirements. In the first decade, the working expenses, which included rent, salaries, and advertising, cost an average of under £2,300 a year. This was just 1.35 per cent of income, a figure which would delight any charity today, including the Fund itself.[10] Such economical running-costs were a point of pride and were celebrated in the annual reports.[11] They would not have been possible without the unpaid and unflagging services of the Honorary Secretaries and committee men. Crossley, who contributed £500 to the Fund each year, took work home with him when he returned to his estate in Suffolk, an unusual practice for a Victorian country gentleman.

In the early years, the paid staff, organized by the Honorary Secretaries Craggs, Crossley, and later Danvers Power, consisted of a clerk, William Gascoyne, and a shorthand writer. Others were taken on in emergencies or for particular projects on a temporary basis. Staff salaries were authorized by the Executive Committee on the advice of the Honorary Secretaries, who interviewed applicants and oversaw their work. Just as the Council and the committees were a male preserve, so too was the office. The first female employee, Miss Ethel Millns, a clerk, was not hired until 1916.[12] The Fund was unusual in the charitable world in not employing women. Other institutions saw it as a way of keeping morale up and wages down, which helps to explain the large number of women, estimated at over 20,000 in the 1890s, who worked as paid charitable officials.[13] Given its royal direction, the ethos of the Fund was patrician, even if many of its committee men were not. It was common for business to be transacted in London clubs, prominent among them the Athenaeum, Brooks's, and the City Carlton. The clubbable and conservative men who ran the Fund preferred to meet women in domestic settings.

The Fund was not overgenerous to its staff initially; indeed, it reduced their pay in 1898. But ten years later, by which time the permanent staff had increased to six, salaries were competitive with administrative positions outside the charitable world. Gascoyne retired in 1905, asked to resign because of ill health and the changing character of the work. In the following year H. R. Maynard joined the Fund. Because of the weight of his responsibilities, he was given the title Secretary. An Oxford graduate with experience at Toynbee Hall and the Central Unemployment Board for London, he had a background in voluntarism and social work. He accepted a salary of £500 a year, not an inconsiderable sum at the time for a man of 30 trained as an economic historian.[14] By the time of his arrival, the Fund had settled into a pattern of well-meaning paternalism in regard to staff, but it kept in mind the essential aims of the institution. These could only be achieved by domestic economies and the creation of a large capital reserve.

Given the interest rates at the turn of the century, the Fund's invested capital would have to reach a million pounds or more to return £50,000 a year. The issue was not whom to approach, but how to go about it. Here the Fund adopted well-established charitable ploys, some more subtle than others, and added a few variants of its own. It cleverly played on guilty consciences and social aspirations. For those who liked to see their name in print and to impress their friends, it announced all subscriptions in *The Times*, a tradition which continued until 1940. The format of the annual report also increased the pressure to be seen to contribute. Like the reports of other prominent charities, it gave over many of its pages to listing subscribers, a tradition ended only in 1942, when paper shortages dictated economies.

The first people to be solicited were the Fund's officials, many of whom were chosen for their wealth or their access to the wealth of others. The Prince of Wales took the lead by instituting a plan whereby he and each member of his family gave an annual subscription to the Fund by standing order. (Between them Edward VII and Queen Alexandra gave £2,000 before they died.)[15] Though several members of the original Council did not contribute, including Burdett, who was very sensitive about his charitable donations,[16] others proved very generous indeed. Over the years, the Treasurer, N. M. 'Natty' Rothschild, contributed £15,000 through his merchant bank; the Tory Edward Cecil Guinness, later the first Earl of Iveagh, gave £60,000 from the proceeds of the drink trade.

By comparison with the laymen, the Fund's medical men were relatively reluctant to part with their money.[17] Lord Lister was an exception. A political conservative imbued with a sense of *noblesse oblige*, he fitted in with the Fund's ethos; and sensitive to the need for reforms in hospital administration he fitted in with its aims. His connections with the institution were a way in which he could continue to exert influence and moral leadership over the medical profession after his surgical career was over. Like others in the Fund, he was appointed to lend respectability and to open up avenues to others. But Lister was the nation's most prominent medical man, and the Prince of Wales may have felt that not to have recruited him to the Fund would be seen as a singular omission. That he became an active committee man and a generous benefactor was a bonus. Though not a man of great wealth, he left the Fund £8,000 upon his death in 1912.

In line with the Prince of Wales's letter to the press, primary targets for raising money were institutions, including banks, railways, and other charities. Here, predictably, the Fund met with an uneven response.[18] With a modest annual subscription of £250, the Bank of England did not live up to Burdett's expectations of it. Most of the merchant banks, led by J. S. Morgan and Co. and N. M. Rothschild and Sons, and clearing banks, led by Lloyds, contributed to the initial appeal. Baring Brothers, which was to develop very close ties with the Fund, was not a prominent initial contributor. The London and North-Western Railway topped the list of railways, which generally disappointed. Other generous supporters were the Prudential Assurance Co., the City of London Corporation, and Moët and Chandon. The United Grand Lodge of Freemasons gave over £5,500 to the initial appeal, which may be seen as a tribute to Edward VII's zeal for the craft and his position as Grand Master of the Order in England.[19]

Given its connections, the Fund had high hopes of the City livery companies. With their traditions of buying places and patrimony, they also provided a model of organization. One of the first initiatives of the Organising Sub-Committee, which included Lord Rowton, formerly Disraeli's Private Secretary, Hugh Smith, Burdett, and Crossley, was to contact the city companies. Rowton, who combined tact and sociability in equal measure, was put up at the City Carlton Club the better to exploit his many Tory friends, among them Goldsmiths. Smith approached the Fishmongers, Merchant Taylors, Drapers, and Grocers; Burdett the Mercers; Crossley the Skinners. The Lord Mayor, Sir George Faudel Phillips, who as President of the

Saturday and Sunday Funds sat on the Fund's General Council, also agreed
to use his position with the city companies. According to Burdett, his
intervention backfired, for the city companies resented the view that he had
any influence over them.[20]

In the first year, the Fund's appeal to the livery companies produced little
result. Some companies, including the Goldsmiths, Ironmongers, and Salters
held back subscriptions until they were satisfied of the Fund's effectiveness.
The Grocers' Company offered temporary office-space in lieu of cash, though
it eventually contributed. The Skinners, among others, wanted to know more
about the Fund's policy on the distribution of its money before they would
commit themselves. A few wanted to have their donations earmarked for
particular hospitals. The Fund refused these requests and advised that the
money be sent directly to the hospitals in question. The Drapers wanted to
know if hospital letters would be provided to them in exchange for
contributions. But the Fund did not offer letters, a policy for which it paid a
price in lost subscriptions.[21]

For substantial donations, the Fund offered representation on the Council
or the Executive Committee. Burdett pressed this policy on the Prince of
Wales and also suggested that the twelve premier companies be invited to
send representatives to Marlborough House for a reception.[22] By the end of
the nineteenth century, the Merchant Taylors had a seat on the Executive
Committee for £1,000 a year; the Fishmongers and the Clothworkers had
seats on the Council for the same sum.[23] With the years, the links between
the Fund and particular companies matured, especially the Drapers, the
Fishmongers, and the Merchant Taylors. Such links proved rewarding.
Between 1897 and 1940 alone, twenty-one livery companies contributed a
total of £240,000 to the Fund, much of it in seven-year agreements to avoid
tax.[24] Though this was a considerable sum, it was dwarfed by several individual contributions.

Whenever an opportunity presented itself, the Prince of Wales nobbled the
wealthy on behalf of the Fund and brought them into a royal web of obligation
and expectation. He began by soliciting contributions from his own entourage
and those who wished to join it, especially that diverse group of financiers,
bankers, mine owners, and company promoters, many of whom were
German-Jewish in origin, who had yet to establish themselves in aristocratic
circles. That he put his own finances in the hands of such men, most notably
his friend the financier Ernest Cassel, aroused a mixture of pity and hostility
in some circles. The German Emperor once called his uncle Edward 'a
jobber in stocks and shares' because of his connections with Cassel.[25] The
members of Britain's landed society, who had fallen on hard times during the
agricultural depression of the late nineteenth century, could be just as cruel,
especially as they found it difficult to sustain their former social role. Behind

their complaints was an aristocratic code of conduct, whose sympathies did not extend, as one of their number put it, to 'Jew speculators'.[26]

In the expanding world-economy at the turn of the century, business magnates constituted a powerful plutocracy. Though socially obscure and not always free from the taint of scandal, they exerted a strong political influence. Despite their diversity, they had much in common and frequently found themselves rivals or partners in business transactions. Though extremely wealthy, they did not command much respect in landed society, despite their large houses in Park Lane and the country. Ambitious and socially conventional, they were anxious to pay, to work, or to marry their way into the landed élite. But imitating the English aristocracy could lead to embarrassment. Cassel, for example, could not keep his seat on a horse. He found that sitting on charitable committees proved a less hazardous means of improving his social standing. The more such men sought social respectability the more likely they were to wish to be seen to be philanthropic. Thus the Prince's association with self-made businessmen, which had excited criticism, could be turned to the Fund's advantage.

Many of the largest contributions to the Fund during Edward VII's lifetime came from this new plutocracy, not least the German-Jewish element in it. Consequently, it was well represented in the Council and the committees. Cassel, who served on the Council and the original Finance Committee, gave generously to many of Edward VII's charities, most notably £200,000 to the King Edward VII Sanatorium for Consumption, Midhurst. To the Fund he contributed £66,000 in all.[27] The Jewish financier Edgar Speyer, who along with Cassel and Alfred Beit founded the Anglo-German Union Club in 1905, gave the Fund £25,000 and became a member of both the Council and the Executive Committee. During the First World War he was arraigned for alleged pro-German sentiments, coupled with suspicions of corruption. He moved to the United States and consequently ended his association with the Fund.[28]

Arguably the man most closely identified with shady city dealings who contributed to the Fund, and sat on its original Council, was the very English Lord Farquhar. As Master of the Royal Household, he administered Edward VII's finances along with Cassel.[29] Like others at court, including Edward VII himself, Farquhar enjoyed a flutter on the Stock Exchange. But in 1907, he came under attack for recruiting members of the royal household, including Francis Knollys, to directorships of a Siberian goldmining company. Through clever trading Farquhar netted £70,000 as the shares bounced up and down. More than a few eyebrows were raised over the affair, for the royal household was expected to show the greatest restraint in its business dealings.[30] Neither Farquhar, nor Speyer, it should be said, was typical of the Fund's benefactors or officials.

The businessmen who came together at meetings of the Fund in Edward VII's lifetime oiled the wheels of the institution and gave it acumen and a hybrid character. They were a diverse mix of foreign-born and established British plutocrats. Cassel, Speyer, Julius Wernher, the diamond merchant, and Everard Hambro, the merchant banker, were among the former; Guinness, the brewer, Lord Revelstoke, the head of Barings, and John Aird, the civil-engineering contractor, were among the latter. The connections of these and other Councillors and committee men of the Fund can only be touched upon here, but they are intriguing.[31]

In the City, as in the Fund, public confidence and personal contacts were essential. When he wished to sell his family business to the public, Guinness approached Rothschild and then Barings. Hambro was an associate of the Barings and the Morgans, who were represented in the Fund by J. P. Morgan Jun. Hambros Bank eventually gave the Fund £7,000. Lord Revelstoke (1863–1929) was a close friend of most of the leading bankers and financiers associated with the Fund, especially Cassel, with whom he made some handsome profits in the first decade of the twentieth century.[32] As a Director of the Bank of England, he cemented the Fund's ties with that body. (He succeeded Lord Rothschild as the Fund's Treasurer in 1914.) It is worth noting that Burdett, from his years as Secretary to the Shares and Loan Department of the Stock Exchange, was friendly with many of these men. Indeed, he had had considerable financial backing for other of his charities from, among others, Rothschild, Hambro, and Junius Morgan.[33]

Cassel's connections are particularly interesting. A dominant figure in the City of London, he had extensive dealings with many of his colleagues at the Fund, most notably Edward VII, who ascended the throne free of debts because of his advice. Cassel was, if anything, more shrewd than his business rivals Revelstoke and Rothschild. In 1897 he agreed to provide the finance for the construction of the Aswan Dam, which was built by John Aird and Co., a firm which appeared among the Fund's more generous subscribers. He also invested heavily in the South African mines developed by Wernher, Beit and Co. The German-born diamond merchant Alfred Beit and his brother Otto eventually gave over £125,000 to the Fund. Cassel also had long-standing connections with the London merchant bank, Bischoffsheim and Goldschmidt. Mr and Mrs Bischoffsheim contributed £14,000 to the Fund between 1899 and 1906. It is not clear whether Cassel put pressure on his business associates to contribute to the Fund, or whether his own generosity aroused their interest. But as the closest male friend of the Prince of Wales and an initial contributor, his role in the Fund was significant. Every fund-raiser knows the value of starting a charitable campaign with a well-connected benefactor.

To what extent, if any, the Fund's meetings and social occasions promoted the business affairs of its band of Edwardian plutocrats can only be imagined. None of them relied on charitable connections to stimulate business. They often met socially elsewhere, as in 1906, when several of them came together at a dinner, hosted by Lord Revelstoke, in honour of the incoming Liberal, Herbert Asquith.[34] But certainly the Fund benefited enormously from their profits, especially those derived from expanding markets in the Americas, Egypt, and South Africa. It is unlikely that they would have been so generous without the knowledge that Edward VII desired it. His friends the Bischoffsheims were quick to admit as much.[35]

Edward VII, in turn, would not have been so quick to bring such people into his entourage and lavish honours on them without their contributions to his favoured causes. As honours are often awarded for unspecified good deeds, it is difficult to know just how many were given exclusively for services to the Fund. Still, the reciprocal benefits of charity were clearly felt, and deeply appreciated, by the Fund's principal supporters. Cassel collected honours and decorations, usually in return for government services, with the same enthusiasm that he collected dividends. He was made a Privy Councillor in 1902, and later received a KCVO and a GCVO. (Edward VII stood godfather to his granddaughter Edwina, who married Lord Louis Mountbatten, a great-grandson of Queen Victoria.) Speyer was given a baronetcy in 1906 and made a Privy Councillor in 1909 for his 'conspicuous generosity'. Burdett, who gave the institution time rather than money, probably owed his KCB, bestowed on him in the year of the Fund's foundation, to King Edward.[36] He received a KCVO in 1908. In other cases the honours preceeded large donations. Julius Wernher, a man of impeccable reputation who gave his measured counsel to the Fund, received a baronetcy in 1905 for his philanthropic work. He left a huge bequest of £390,000 to the Fund in 1912.[37]

As a cynic might say, nothing arouses a philanthropist more than the expectation of a knighthood. In the history of the Fund, tapping the honours system is a subterranean theme. Few charities have benefited more from it. As Burdett pointed out, a knighthood enabled the recipient to be more useful. Honours were given for faithful service, but also to keep good men at their posts. We should not conclude, however, that the Fund's officers served the institution simply, or primarily, in anticipation of honours. Charitable motives, though rarely pure, cannot often be explained simply by reference to self-interest. The Fund's officers and contributors had innumerable reasons for their charities. Sickness or a death in the family often triggered an interest in hospital work, as in the case of Edward VII himself. Others had religious or humanitarian motives. For others still, particularly the female fund-raisers, charitable work broke the monotony of domestic life and opened up possibilities of wider experience and usefulness.[38]

Most of the Fund's supporters were, of course, well-removed from the honours system. In keeping with an institution determined to raise money from rich and poor alike, the Fund complemented its royal persuasions with a range of standardized appeal-letters and thank-you notices, carefully graded to suit individual cases. Little was left to chance. Here, as elsewhere, the hand of the Prince of Wales could be seen, for he had a particular interest in the commemorative side of fund-raising.[39] Those who contributed £5,000 pounds or more received personal letters from him, and sometimes invitations to parties or royal events. Others who contributed time or money received gifts of game from Sandringham, in a hierarchy from pheasants to rabbits, with a tag attached headed 'From the Prince of Wales'.[40] Royal game was not in short supply, for the Prince increased the number of animals killed each year at Sandringham to 30,000.[41] But the survival of these tags reveals both the importance of royal gifts to their recipients and the subtlety with which the Prince of Wales graced the lives of his subjects while reaching into their pockets.

Smaller contributors to the Fund did not very often command the personal attention of the Prince of Wales, but he was no less interested in their participation. As the saying went, 'the privilege of giving is open to all'. In his letter to the public, the Prince had argued that there were as many as 500,000 households in London with the means to support their voluntary hospitals. But in the 1890s, only 50,000 of them did so. Many of those already contributing were part of the 'charitable ten thousand', privileged people well-known to hospital administrators and other writers of begging-letters. The Fund hoped to increase their contributions and not simply shift them from one institution to another. By an analysis of published subscription-lists, it monitored their donations and made appeals to those thought likely to contribute to the Fund. It also scoured the obituaries with a view to approaching surviving relatives, especially when money was left to undefined 'charitable purposes'.

Respectable families without traditions of giving regularly to hospitals were thought to be the most exciting prospects. In recruiting them, the Fund did not have to worry about taking subscribers from rival medical appeals. They included members of what Burdett called the new middle class, which sprang from the élite of workers, many of whom lived in the expanding suburbs. In the Fund's suspect analysis, influenced by Burdett's optimism, it was calculated that if only half of those outside the traditional fund-raising channels could be persuaded to part with 10s. each, the future of London's voluntary hospitals would be guaranteed. But reaching a quarter of million London households was more easily said than done. Such an enormous campaign had never been attempted before by a hospital charity and had rarely been attempted by other institutions, except those, like the National

Society for the Prevention of Cruelty to Children and the Bible Society, which had thousands of female volunteers collecting from door to door.[42]

The spring of 1897 saw the Fund's first mass appeal in full swing. By summer it had dispatched 200,000 appeal letters to a wide range of potential contributors. At a unit cost of 7*d*., each one contained a copy of the Prince of Wales's letter to the press, a banker's order form, and a return envelope. Names were culled from guides and directories, and some 5,000 shopkeepers and 100,000 middle-class suburban families were selected as special targets. The Fund also advertised widely in the London papers, placed collection boxes in clubs, and posted circulars to institutions. Street collections were not used, for Burdett and others thought them counter-productive; but a former military officer scoured offices in the City. Workshops and churches were not widely canvassed for they were assumed to be the terrain of the Saturday and Sunday Funds. The Post Office passed out circulars provided by the Fund to its own staff and arranged deductions from their salaries, but did not follow up the suggestion that it forward an appeal letter to each of its 1,500,000 depositors.[43]

The Post Office was approached about another ingenious idea, the Prince of Wales's Hospital Fund stamp. Though closely associated with Burdett, who was commissioned by the Executive Committee to deal with it, the idea was not his alone.[44] The object was to recruit small subscribers who might otherwise be missed. Confident that the Post Office would recognize the stamps, Burdett unwisely predicted that £58,000 would be raised by their sale. But when the Fund approached the Controller and Registrar of Stamps, and reserved a seat on the Council for him, he failed to give official sanction to the stamps. His appointment to the Council was not confirmed.

Burdett pushed ahead, encouraged by the willingness of the royal family to co-operate. The Prince and Princess of Wales saw the stamps being printed by De la Rue and Co., and the Duke and Duchess of York witnessed the ceremonial destruction of the plates. Based on a picture of Charity by Joshua Reynolds, they came in different colours and denominations, neatly packaged with a message from the Prince. The image of a woman surrounded by her children served as badge of innumerable Victorian charities and expressed an underlying theme of the Fund—the promotion of healthy family life. Widely advertised in hospitals and other public buildings, the stamps proved particularly popular with church- and chapel-goers. Sold through stationers, they raised £34,776 in 1897. A second issue the following year did far less well.[45]

The stamp was a variation on the truism in charity that subscribers may have to be approached indirectly, by means of gimmicks or entertainments. As one wit put it, a philanthropist is a person who can make you grin while picking your pocket. There was a superabundance of ideas. Among the more traditional were the contributions from bazaars, mothers' meetings, and benefit concerts. The Vienna Philharmonic and Dame Nellie Melba provided their talents. The sale of Jubilee Procession Programmes, which raised over £2,000, was less conventional, an early example of the Fund's clever use of its royal association in raising money. Another was the photograph album, in which 100,000 children were to have their pictures taken set beside a picture of the royal princes. Though supported by Princess Alexandra, who appealed for 'every child in the land to contribute to their poor afflicted brothers and sisters', this scheme came under attack.[46] As the *Daily News* put it, parents 'run the risk of turning their offspring into little snobs and hypocrites'.[47]

The Fund thus missed few opportunities to extract money from the public, from the proverbial widow's mite to the large sums donated by Edward VII's rich friends. Burdett estimated that over a million people contributed in 1897, more than half of them through the sale of stamps. Of those included in the formal list of subscribers, about 40 per cent were female (in purely financial terms their contribution was less).[48] One irate woman, Miss Honnor Morten, a member of the London School Board, wrote to *The Times* on this issue. Infuriated by hospitals run 'by busybodies and philanthropists whose main object was to get a peerage', she demanded that 'a fund so largely supported by women should be just enough to put women on its managing body. Nurses demand this.'[49] To this attack the Fund did not reply. The Prince of Wales and his colleagues were little interested in bringing the issue of women's rights to the attention of the public.[50]

One nursing leader who was conspicuous for her absence from the Fund's subscription list was Florence Nightingale. 'What am I to do?', she wrote when approached about a contribution in April 1897, 'people say it will diminish subscriptions to individual hospitals... I must subscribe to St Thomas's'.[51] Sydney Holland of the London Hospital advised her not to contribute to the Fund. By this time Holland had, in Nightingale's words, 'a wholesome horror of Burdett', who he thought was doing his best to keep the 'London' out of the Fund.[52] She too had a 'horror' of Burdett, for he was 'pushing' and one of her more dangerous rivals in the nursing field. When he had requested that he pose for a photograph with her ten years earlier for publicity purposes she remarked, 'the last person... I should sit for would be: Mr Burdett'.[53] Given her abhorrence of Burdett and her dislike of hospitals and competitors generally, it is not surprising that she took the view that the Prince of Wales's Fund would have to do without her support. Were she alive today, she would find it quite in order that the Fund generously supports the Florence Nightingale Museum Trust.

Florence Nightingale's reluctance to subscribe to the Fund was far from singular. Many of those so assiduously canvassed remained unconvinced of the Fund's usefulness, or simply had the courage to bear the misfortunes of

London's sick poor. But were the worries voiced in *The Times* about turning enthusiasm for the Jubilee into an equivalent in cash confirmed? What did all the Fund's arm-twisting, canvassing, and zeal add up to in revenue? And was it enough? The total receipts for 1897 amounted to £227,562, 75 per cent of which was invested. This was a considerable sum, which contributed to making 1897 an unusually prosperous year for the London hospitals. It was, however, much less than the amount needed to provide a return of £50,000 on invested capital.[54] To put the Fund's initial income into some context, it was the largest sum of money raised by any British charity in Jubilee year apart from the Church Missionary Society. (The unique subscription for the Indian Famine Fund, sponsored by Queen Victoria, raised over £2,000,000 nationally.)[55] Still, the Fund's receipts for 1897 were less than Edward VII's stables earned in stud fees over his lifetime.[56]

The Fund expected a drop in income after the initial liberality triggered by Jubilee year, but it had to put a brave face on what were disappointing receipts for 1898: £39,272. Indeed, this sum was less than the amount raised by the Sunday Fund that year.[57] The following year was little better. By the end of it the Boer War had broken out and the Fund interrupted its fund-raising in order to avoid clashing with the various war-appeals. The Fund's staff became increasingly anxious about the potential effectiveness of the institution; outside critics, never in short supply in the early years, began to remark that it was not living up to expectations.[58] The *Lancet* was cautious, though it did not disguise the fact that it thought the results of the first year 'undoubtedly disappointing'.[59] The *BMJ* noted with worry that most of the money raised seemed to come from those who were already hospital subscribers.[60] What was the point of giving to the hospitals with one hand what it had taken with the other? As one critic put it, the Fund's proceedings resembled 'that of the Paddy who is said to have cut a piece off the top of his blanket with which to keep his feet warm'.[61]

Despite small sums contributed by gypsies, labourers, and servants, the Fund recognized that its original appeal had failed to reach large sections of its potential support among the poorer classes. The disposable income of the working classes had been rising since about 1875 and their subscriptions were much sought after by Victorian charities. The Fund took the view that it was far better for poor citizens to contribute to health and hospitals than to throw their money away on the horses and drink. A fear of social unrest, heightened by the miseries of the poor in London, still haunted Burdett and others at the end of the century.[62] Working-class contributions would reduce the miseries. As importantly, they were a demonstration of self-help and active citizenship, a sign of respectability and a common culture. To the voluntary hospitals, they were also ammunition in the propaganda war against those who were beginning to call for municipalization or state control. The Fund looked forward to a time when people gave a hospital subscription as automatically as they paid their rates, but 'with all the difference in cheerfulness'.[63]

Disappointed by the Fund's receipts for 1897–8, Burdett came up with an innovation designed to tap the incomes of the respectable working class. This was the League of Mercy, a fascinating institution with a history of its own.[64] The League was devised as an auxiliary to the Prince of Wales's Fund, and its aim was to extend the Fund's tendrils into working-class districts of London and the Home Counties. Like other charitable auxiliaries, such as the NSPCC's League of Pity or the RSPCA's Band of Mercy, the League of Mercy was intended to bring local traditions of community service to bear on a wider cause, in this case the voluntary hospitals. Ideally, it would attract sorely needed cash and publicity to the Fund, but would also bear witness to the friendly, reciprocal relations between the hospitals and principal users of their services.

Burdett's proposal for a League of Mercy was not universally admired. Some saw it as unworkable and feared that it might embarrass the royal family. Charles Loch of the COS, unenthusiastic about the Fund itself, called it a 'bold measure' of 'a wrong type', which would congest an already overcrowded field of charitable provision.[65] Hoping to stop it in the planning-stages, he petitioned the Queen in October 1898.[66] The following month he requested an interview with the Prince of Wales on the issue. It was refused. His opposition to the scheme may be seen against the background of his proposals for a central hospital board, which the Fund had studiously ignored in its proceedings. And, like others, he was doubtful about any proposal associated with Burdett. Sydney Holland wrote reassuringly to Loch that the League would inevitably fail and hoped that this would end the Prince of Wales's 'admiration' for Burdett.[67]

Holland and Loch were to be frustrated. Far from dishing Burdett, the League enhanced his reputation. The Prince rallied to the idea. He wrote to his sister Victoria in December 1898 that a preliminary meeting to set up the League had been very promising. The following March he wrote to her again: 'I very successfully started my League of Mercy. We had a large meeting at Marlborough House and you will doubtless have seen an account of it in *The Times*.'[68] On 30 March 1899, the institution received a royal charter, which established it as an auxiliary to the Prince of Wales's Hospital Fund. Burdett remembered the occasion vividly, for the Prince handed him the document with the words: 'There is your charter; now go and work it.'[69]

Nominated Treasurer by the Prince, Burdett would be closely associated with the League of Mercy for the rest of his life, and though he had enormous difficulties getting it under way, his dogged determination paid off. In the early years, he lectured extensively to large meetings of working people, from Lambeth to Sevenoaks, whipping up support. Like a 'gigantic snowball', Loch lamented, the League just grew and grew. In 1904 Burdett set up a branch in Harrods after speaking to 2,500 employees in the Food Hall.[70] Each year he reported to the Fund on the money raised by the League and celebrated its successes in the press and the pages of the *Hospital*. To the relief of several of his colleagues at the Fund, it kept him occupied elsewhere.

The League takes us deeper into the social role of the royal family and the ways in which honours and royal occasions can be used to encourage participation in charity. It was designed to appeal to the sensibilities of the Prince and Princess of Wales, who became its first Grand President and Lady Grand President. As an institution based on social attraction, rich in ceremonial functions, it had a particular charm for the Prince. He delighted in the annual garden-parties or receptions at Marlborough House. Captivated by the decorative, and seductive, trappings of royalty, he awarded the 'Order of Mercy' to officials of the League for conspicuous service.[71] Within ten years, by which time another Prince and Princess of Wales hosted these occasions, there were about 20,000 officers and workers collecting money in London and the Home Counties.[72] Sir William Collins, the Chairman of the London County Council and a member of the Fund's Council, was among the League's more active officers. Burdett, whose relations with Collins soured, thought he received far too much credit for its success.[73]

The organizational model behind the League was a simple social pyramid. Below the Prince and Princess of Wales were Presidents and Lady Presidents. Ideally drawn from the royal family or titled aristocracy, each was appointed to head a district based on parliamentary divisions. Princess Victoria of Schleswig-Holstein, for example, was Lady President of Berkshire district. As royals and aristocrats were unavailable to fill all the sixty-five districts canvassed by 1902, MPs, senior churchmen, and friends of Edward VII, including Cassel and Hambro, were made to do. They nominated an upper-middle-class Vice-President and Lady Vice-President, who, in turn, enlisted middle-class members with local roots. In addition to making contributions themselves, they each secured twenty subscribers of 1s. or more. Tradesmen, artisans, and domestic servants came under particular pressure. Thus through an institutional hierarchy which mirrored the social order, the League extracted small sums from local communities.[74] Unlike the Saturday Fund, it was accomplished without the inducement of hospital letters, though humble subscribers were known to wear their League of Mercy badges around their necks just in case they found themselves unexpectedly in hospital.

The League depended on the power of social aspiration, particularly among the middle classes, and the willingness of women to come forward as volunteers. The hospitals were an attractive issue on which to campaign, but the League was further proof of the accuracy of Burdett's view that success in charitable fund-raising is largely determined by whom you can get to support it at the top. To the Fund, the League proved a useful ally and one of the principal means by which it extended its tendrils into neighbourhoods in London and beyond. It did much to placate those critics at the *BMJ* and elsewhere who complained in the early years that the Fund failed to attract small subscribers.[75] Before it was wound up in 1947, it had given over £600,000 to the Fund for the benefit of London's voluntary hospitals. It also awarded an additional £250,000 to hospitals outside London under its own name.[76]

The League may be seen as a gamble which Burdett and the Prince of Wales were willing to take to reach a section of the population which had not been reached by other means. Although its contribution to the Fund rose rapidly in its early years, it was never likely to bring in the sums needed. At the turn of the century, the creation of a sizeable endowment continued to elude the Fund. The pressure to distribute income limited the money available to invest on capital account. In general, only the larger donations were invested; subscriptions and income were distributed. Only £30 was added to the capital account in 1901, a sign of the public's suspicion of endowment funds. The assets in investments in the first five years came to just over £181,000, a figure which fell far short of expectations.[77] The initial investments, handled by Rothschild and Smith, were in Bank of England stock and British railway shares. But with the years, they broadened the Fund's portfolio to include Rio Tinto shares, Egyptian bonds, Transvaal Government 3 Per Cent Stock, and various American securities.[78] However wisely invested, the sums available could not produce very much return. In 1901, the combined interest from deposit and capital accounts came to under £6,000.

By a fortuitous turn of events, the Fund's prospects improved dramatically in 1902. Just as Queen Victoria's Jubilee had triggered the creation of the Fund, her death in January 1901 resulted in opportunities which, when acted upon, constituted its relaunch. As King, Edward could no longer serve as President of the Fund, and the office was taken up by his son George, the new Prince of Wales. In May 1901, at a meeting of the General Council chaired by the Duke of Fife, who had undertaken the interim duties of the President until they were assumed by the Prince of Wales later in the year, a telegram was read from King Edward expressing his unabated interest in the Fund.[79] Thereafter he would keep in touch with its activities largely through the Prince of Wales, whose enthusiasm for the institution proved no less than his own. His relations with George were exceptionally warm, 'unique in the annals of the royal family',[80] and he had prepared him for his responsibilities as President. This was among Edward's most important services to the Fund, whose fortunes were so dependent on its royal leadership.

One of Edward's last personal services to the fund was the appointment of a committee in 1901 to launch a 'Coronation Appeal'. The object of the appeal was to solicit fresh revenue and inform the public of the work of London's voluntary hospitals. To the public, it was loosely seen as a means of putting the hospitals in a position of financial security, which the Fund had not been able to accomplish in its early years. Chaired by Lord Duncannon (later Earl of Bessborough), the organizing committee also included Savile Crossley, John Craggs, and the Director of Bovril Ltd., George Lawson Johnston (later Lord Luke). They quickly realized that the Coronation offered the Fund a once-in-a-lifetime opportunity. As the Jubilee Appeal had shown, the public was more inclined to part with its money in the happy atmosphere of a royal occasion. As Edward VII's coronation was the greatest royal event since 1837, it could, with a little imagination, result in enormous benefits for those charities with royal associations, especially those sponsored by His Majesty.

Deeply attuned to the charitable advantages in royal commemoration, the Fund devised a scheme by which contributions would be collected for a 'Coronation Gift' to King Edward. The King, in turn, graciously declared his wish that the Gift should be devoted to the Fund. This elegant idea tied the institution ever closer to its royal founder, who oversaw the campaign in some detail, despite his new responsibilities.[81] The decision to rename the charity the King Edward's Hospital Fund for London as from January 1902, may be seen as part of this campaign. The King's willingness to consent to this change in name showed his esteem for the institution and his growing confidence in it. The willingness of the heir apparent to take over its reins was a guarantee of continuity and a further boost to the Fund's morale and its prospects. Continuing royal favour not only guaranteed additional funds; it restrained the critics, most of whom did not wish to be seen to be attacking the monarchy, if only by implication.

The Coronation Appeal drew on the traditions of the initial Jubilee appeal, but had a distinctive character suited to the particular royal occasion.[82] The Fund alerted the press to write supporting articles and took space for advertisements. A new twist, sanctioned by the King, allowed companies to associate themselves with the appeal. Thus Oxo and Bovril, Pears Soap, and Holbrook's Sauce took out advertisements with King's Fund notices included (see Plate 3). Here, as elsewhere, the Fund showed a strong sense of design, which was to become a feature of its campaigns. Among the collection boxes was an ingenious design in which a nurse popped out when the coin dropped in. Other attractions included a concert at the Albert Hall with Melba and Clara Butt, and the sale of a Coronation march and a limited edition of the royal book-plates. (The following year a hospital shopping-day caused some embarrassment when several leading stores refused to participate.) The sale of seats along the Coronation route proved particularly rewarding. The Fund was not the only institution to exploit this idea. St George's Hospital, with its prime site at Hyde Park Corner, raised £8,000 by the sale of Coronation seats, a sum its staff may have remembered when the hospital was put under pressure to remove to the suburbs.[83]

Coronation year may be seen as an *annus mirabilis* in the history of the Fund. The 'Coronation Gift' appeal alone raised over £118,000 in 1902. But when the accountants added up all the sums associated with Coronation year, the figure rose to over £600,000. This was one and a half times what had been raised in the previous five years combined. Numerous small sums from working-class contributors and shopkeepers, bazaars and church collections, were highly valued, but in financial terms the bulk of the money came from several large benefactors. Most notable among them were Lord Mount Stephen (George Stephen) and his cousin and business partner Lord Strathcona (Donald Alexander Smith). Of humble Scottish descent, both of them had become Canadian millionaires and well-known philanthropists. In a joint gesture, initiated by Mount Stephen, each gave £200,000 to the Fund in 1902, to be added to the endowment. 'These two donations', wrote Knollys to Burdett, 'have done much to place the undertaking on a sound foundation.'[84]

A feature of the 'Coronation Gift' was that it was thrown open to the whole of the Empire. The money from Mount Stephen and Strathcona was made in North America, most of it from railway speculation. From India came large donations from the Maharaja of Gwalior and the Maharaja of Jaipur. Other charitable institutions, from humble mothers' meetings to the great missionary societies, had imperialist sympathies. They were marked in the Fund, which was richly endowed with imperialists in its management. Burdett and others were quick to point out that the London voluntary hospitals treated patients from all over the world. As a vicar from South Devon wrote to him, the Fund 'must bring the whole English-speaking race into closer unity and sympathy'.[85] Contributions to it from abroad were a tribute to the high regard in which the London hospitals were held outside Britain, particularly the great teaching hospitals. They were also a reminder of the power of the royal family beyond the confines of the capital. Such large donations would inspire confidence in other potential contributors to the Fund, as the rise in the number of legacies over the next few years confirmed.

In raising money, as in other matters, the Fund was fortunate in its new President. George, Prince of Wales, was, unlike his father, a diffident man with little worldly experience; but his strong sense of social duty prompted him to take his charitable responsibilities very seriously. Like his father, who kept him informed of his charitable schemes, he recognized the reciprocal advantages in taking the lead in philanthropic campaigns. His appointment to the presidency of the Fund, an institution so closely associated with his father, was a boost to his morale, a sign of His Majesty's respect and esteem. It may be seen as an example of the way in which Edward VII fortified his son's self-confidence. The awe in which the Prince held his father reinforced his enthusiasm for the Fund.[86]

Just as his father had done before him, George brought his friends and contacts into the Fund, and nurtured their interest by rewards, honours, and his companionship. They fully appreciated that their expressions of social conscience increased his affection for them. Mount Stephen, who lived at Brocket Hall in Hertfordshire, was a frequent guest of the Prince and Princess of Wales.[87] His second wife had been a lady-in-waiting to the Princess's mother, the Duchess of Teck. A man of broad views and simple tastes, with business ambition spent, he inspired confidence. He appealed to the Prince's decided preference for down-to-earth, unpretentious country gentlemen, like himself. Mount Stephen had contributed modest sums to the Fund from 1899 to 1901, but with the accession of his friend Prince George to the presidency, his interest grew.

Long-associated with individual hospitals in Montreal, Aberdeen, and elsewhere, Mount Stephen believed that the King's Fund was the most appropriate means by which to improve medical provision in London and keep municipal control at bay. But he felt that the Fund's object was too great for the purse of the general public, a view shared by the new Prince of Wales and his Private Secretary, Sir Arthur Bigge (later Lord Stamfordham).[88] As the small contributions did not approach the desired £100,000 a year, they believed the very rich would have to relaunch the institution. With this in mind Mount Stephen gave the Prince a list of names of men who he thought would be worth cultivating; it included William Waldorf Astor, Alfred Beit, Andrew Carnegie, Sir Thomas Lipton, Julius Wernher, and the Duke of Westminster.[89] He saw his own contribution of £200,000 in 1902 as bait to attract others, though he was quick to give the credit for success, as in the case of Lord Strathcona, to the Prince of Wales.[90]

Mount Stephen chased up his rich friends on behalf of the Fund with more enthusiasm than success. In his New Year greetings to the Prince of Wales in 1904 he offered to contribute a further £100,000 if three others could be persuaded to do likewise within two months. When no one came forward, he gave the Fund £200,000 worth of Argentinian bonds, announced in the annual report for 1905, with a predicted yield of £11,000 per annum.[91] A philanthropic predator, he swooped down on potential contributors whenever they presented themselves as targets. He hoped to get a further instalment from 'the old fox', Strathcona, and extract £1,000,000 from 'little Andy'— Carnegie.[92] Carnegie did give the Fund £100,000 in 1907, and might have given more had he not had doubts about contributing to an endowment fund.[93] Mount Stephen himself did not disappoint. A man of quixotic generosity, with a dread of personal riches and no direct heir, he donated another £100,000 in 1908.

One other prominent benefactor cultivated by the Fund in these years was Ada Lewis. Her husband, Samuel Lewis, a Jewish money-lender of humble origins, had left the Fund £250,000 upon his death in 1901, subject to his wife's life interest in the capital. Anxious to extract the £10,000-a-year interest in the capital, the Fund asked Lord Farquhar, with the approval of the Prince of Wales, 'to manage' her. With the assistance of Mrs Lewis's solicitor, Algernon Sydney, who later became a member of the Fund's Council, he persuaded her to part with the £10,000 a year just before Edward VII's coronation. Mount Stephen followed the negotiations with the 'old lady', as he unflatteringly called her to the Prince, with a consuming interest. He wrote to Bigge, saying that her 'splendid gift' had 'set the pace' and added that it should be acknowledged in the press, for 'she is a woman'.[94]

Acknowledgment of Mrs Lewis's generosity had already been sent in the form of gracious letters from both the King and the Prince of Wales, a seat in Westminster Abbey for the Coronation and a Coronation medal, and the inevitable parcel of game from Sandringham. Given her husband's background and profession, such attentions were perhaps exceptional, but they reveal the Edwardian Court's openness to people with money, especially those willing to give it away. When she died in 1906, Ada Lewis left the King's Fund half the residue of the estate. By the time it was wound up decades later, the Lewises' contribution to the Fund came to over £565,000. In an address to the Fund's General Council in December, 1906, the Prince of Wales paid tribute to this 'charitable lady, who was one of our most liberal supporters'.[95] Sir Arthur Bigge remarked, with wry amusement and a hint of contempt, 'certainly the Hospital Fund have benefited by the money lending business'.[96] Only Mount Stephen's Great Northern Railroad of America, based in Minnesota, proved a greater source of King's Fund capital.[97]

Thanks to the Lewises, Mount Stephen, and Strathcona in particular, the Fund's finances were greatly improved after 1902. This had important implications not only for London's hospitals, but for the Fund itself. As more money was put into the capital account, over £400,000 in 1902 alone, the urgency of carefully considering financial administration grew. Given the magnitude of the Fund's invested property, in itself a sign of institutional perpetuity, the Prince of Wales appointed a Finance Committee, which met for the first time in November 1906. In setting it up, he had been prompted and guided by Lord Mount Stephen. Here, as elsewhere, the Prince was in no doubt as to Mount Stephen's singular importance. As his Private Secretary said at the time, that 'dear old man', was the Fund's 'most important donor, past, present, and future'.[98]

In September 1906, Bigge wrote a long letter to the Prince of Wales, in which he explained Mount Stephen's anxieties about the Fund's finances and his proposals for their future management. Mount Stephen had been annoyed at the way in which his gift of Argentinian bonds, which many in the City thought of dubious value, had been reinvested. In his opinion this was a costly mistake, indicative of a lack of zeal and financial control. He blamed Lord Rothschild. What was needed was a committee of capable financiers with a better understanding of American securities. His recommendations for the Finance Committee were: Hugh Smith, Chairman; Lord Rothschild; Lord Revelstoke; Sir Ernest Cassel; and his close friend the Scottish financier Robert Fleming. He was particularly keen to have the last three as they were all friends and 'pre-eminently fitted' to supply a knowledge of American securities. Mount Stephen had intimated his willingness to give further such securities to the Fund, but he did 'not want to see this capital dealt with by men who ... do not understand the business'. Preferring to work behind the scenes (he had earlier declined an invitation to join the Council), he excluded himself from the Finance Committee on the grounds of age.[99]

As in regard to all its committees, the object in setting up the Finance Committee was to assemble a group of people with broadly compatible views and personalities. The management structure of the Fund had a great advantage here, which proved useful on this and other occasions. This was that a decision made or authorized by the Prince of Wales would be accepted with good grace by all parties. In regard to the Finance Committee, he largely followed Mount Stephen's advice. His only alterations were to add the Honorary Secretaries Craggs and Crossley and to appoint Lord Rothschild as Chairman instead of Smith. Here he felt that he had no alternative because of Rothschild's long association with the Fund as Treasurer. Rothschild, according to Bigge, had reservations about Cassel, but the Prince appointed Cassel none the less, on the grounds that he was a friend of the King's and was a stand-in for Mount Stephen. Mount Stephen was well-satisfied with the arrangements.[100]

The Finance Committee took charge of all matters dealing with finance and investments in November 1906. But the growth in funds and the proposed change in their administration had already pointed out certain difficulties. It was not altogether clear whether the Fund's past investments, standing in the names of Lord Rothschild and Hugh Smith, were strictly legal. Much depended on the interpretation placed on Edward's letter of February 1897. Did His Majesty's delegation of the office of President to the Prince of Wales in 1901 alter the relationship between the Fund and its subscribers? Did those who acted for the Fund have the legal right to invest contributions at their own discretion without any restriction? Were they liable for any depreciation in the value of the securities invested? It was conceivable that Lord Mount Stephen could sue Lord Rothshild, and perhaps even the Prince of Wales, who authorized his actions, for the loss of income from the sale of those Argentinian bonds.[101]

The problems of financial management pointed out the Fund's amateurishness and raised fundamental questions about its organization. Though well-conceived, it needed to be put on a more businesslike footing. The upshot was an inquiry into constitutional issues in late 1906 by the Prince of Wales and his colleagues in the Fund, aided by teams of legal advisers.[102] The choice put before the Prince, who was an avid reader of official documents, was to have either a royal charter or an act of incorporation. After detailed discussions, it was decided to opt for an act of incorporation, on the advice of counsel, F. Vaughan Hawkins. Hawkins argued that this was the only way to ensure legal protection for past investments and give sufficient powers for future investment. It also ensured that the President could not be sued and kept the Charity Commissioners at arm's length.[103] Hawkins drew up a draft bill, which had the sanction of the Prince of Wales, at the end of 1906. The King was kept informed.

All was not smooth sailing. Controversial issues emerged in framing the Bill which would have considerable implications for the Fund. The most important of these was the question of financial control. The Prince of Wales was determined to retain 'the same complete control' over the Fund as he had enjoyed in the past. He took the view, put most forcefully by Mount Stephen, that there must be 'no representative control. . . . The money is given to the Prince of Wales and he appoints whoever he chooses to administer it.'[104] The reasoning behind this was simple. As a King's Fund memorandum of 1905 stated, the Fund 'expresses the loyal sentiment of the contributors towards our King and the Heir to the throne'.[105] And as Bigge wrote to Power in January 1907: 'If Parliament places restrictions on the President's power as to investments or disposals of money, many of the most liberal friends of the Fund will shut up their pockets.'[106] He recalled the words of Mrs Bishoffsheim, who said that the money she and her husband were giving to the Fund should 'be dealt with or invested as His Majesty may direct'.[107]

Both inside and outside Parliament, there was opposition to the proposed changes in the Fund's constitution, especially in regard to the President's powers. The BMA sent out an alarm. In September 1906, it had asked for representation on the Fund's Council and Distribution Committee, but was turned down on constitutional grounds.[108] The Birmingham surgeon Dr Henry Langley Browne, Chairman of the BMA, took particular exception to the Prince of Wales as sole trustee. The Prince took a look at his extract from the *Medical Directory* and decided that he was not distinguished enough to pose a threat.[109] There were also rumours of an 'anti-King's Fund society', emanating from certain London hospitals, led by the Nose and Throat Hospital. As the Harley Street physician who leaked this news to the Fund remarked, 'one can get no wrong righted it seems in medical circles without the "spilling of blood"'.[110]

Opposition in Parliament was more worrying. The Liberals had a parliamentary majority but they were not much in evidence in the Fund. Because of his good connections in the Liberal Party, Sir Savile Crossley was asked to steer the Bill through Parliament. It passed through all its stages in the House of Lords with minor modifications regarding the appointment of the President. As amended, any future President had to be either a son, brother, or grandson of the Sovereign. (Typically for the day, no one questioned the exclusion of women.) He could only be appointed on the recommendation of the Lord Chancellor, the Prime Minister, and the Governor of the Bank of England, and hold office only during the pleasure of the Sovereign. But doubts increased about the power vested in the President when the Bill came before the Select Committee of the House of Commons on Unopposed Bills in May, 1907. Various members took the view that it might not always be possible to have a President who enjoyed the same degree of public confidence as the incumbent and his father.[111]

It was in response to such criticism that a section of the Bill was amended. The Prince's strategy was to keep as much power as possible to himself as President of the Fund without endangering the passage of the Bill. As early as February, he and Sir Arthur Bigge noted the growing opposition to investing the entire control in the President. They yielded on this point at the last minute by conceding equal control of the management and finances of the Fund to the General Council. But as Bigge pointed out, the concession would give the Council 'an apparent, tho' not actual control. We must be careful to safeguard the power of the President to appoint and remove members of the General Council.'[112] The amended clause stipulated that all Councillors and members of committees were to be reappointed annually by the President. It was this clause, rewritten to appease parliamentary opposition to the Bill, which gave meaning to the view that constitutionally the Fund was a 'limited monarchy'.

The Bill came up for debate in the Commons on 1 July, 1907. The apparent concession did not allay everyone's fears. 'Where do the People come in?' asked one critic, who felt that subscribers required representation. Others argued that the medical profession and public bodies, including the London County Council, must be formally represented, thereby making obligatory what was already customary. The Attorney General, Sir John Walton, pointed out that the majority of subscribers did not wish to interfere with the discretion of the royal family and that it was almost impossible to specify a constituency to carry out election. The present Council, he added, was 'a representative council in the best sense of the term'.

The Prime Minister, Sir Henry Campbell-Bannerman, impressed by the Fund's low running-costs, called it a 'model' of management; and he reminded the critics that the King had created the institution and that 'it was to him that the money was given—money which would not have been obtained' otherwise. It was therefore not unreasonable to expect that the President wished to have some say in the management of the money. He concluded that the concession vesting an equal control in the Council went a long way towards providing representation. These arguments prevailed and the Bill received the royal assent on 26 July 1907.[113] As intended, it put the Fund on a legal footing, protected its past investments, provided wide powers in regard to its future investments, and gave the President extraordinary, if not absolute, control over the institution.

Well-pleased with the Act, the Fund's Council met on the day it was passed to reassess the constitution of the committees. While the direction and financial management of the Fund were vested in the President and General Council, the Act authorized them to delegate their respective powers to committees. The four permanent committees—Executive, Finance, Distribution, and Convalescent Homes—carried on much as before, with few changes in personnel. But with a greater income there was now more work to be undertaken, especially for the Distribution Committee, which advised the President and the Council about hospital grants and made rules to be observed by the hospitals which applied for them. The increase in administrative work required the setting-up of new offices; these were opened in 1907, at 7 Walbrook Street, EC4.

In the delegation of power to committees one issue in particular proved awkward. Its resolution was to have significant, long-term implications for the Fund and the voluntary hospitals. From the earliest days, there was a tension in the Fund, which surfaced during times of hospital crises, between those responsible for investments, who tended to be fiscal conservatives, and those who wanted to release more money for the pressing demands of London's sick poor. The treasury view was strengthened by the fact that its principal adherents, Rothschild and Smith, were on both the Executive Committee and the newly formed Finance Committee. Given their long-standing responsibility for investments, they were acutely aware that the sizeable endowment had taken a long time to build and that Edward VII did not want it frittered away.

By the Act of Incorporation, the Finance Committee had responsibility for the investment of funds and the transfer and control of property. But when established in 1906, it had sought the power to recommend to the Council the amount of money available for annual distribution. The Executive Committee, which had performed this important duty, rejected the proposal. Only the timely intervention of the Prince of Wales, who asked for the issue to be postponed, prevented a battle of wills between committee men.[114] To avoid internal dissension, which might lead to the President's embarrassment, the Finance Committee withdrew its proposal. Rothschild and Smith left the

Executive Committee in 1907 to concentrate on investments. The former Chairman of the Coronation Appeal, the Earl of Bessborough, who had been Secretary to Speaker Robert Peel, succeeded Smith as Chairman of the Executive Committee.

Prince George took the view that the more the work of the Fund became known, the more the public would support it; and the greater its annual distribution, the greater its power in restraining the spending-tendencies of the more profligate hospitals.[115] When he settled the issue of the responsibility for the sum to be annually distributed after the Act of Incorporation, he thus sided with the Executive Committee, which tended to recommend the release of more money. In practical terms, the decision meant that the London hospitals received £10,000 more in 1907 than they would have done had the financiers had their way.[116]

Edward VII lived to see his favoured institution surpass the financial goals which he had set it. The return on invested capital reached over £50,000 for the first time in 1907. In the year of the King's death, 1910, the Fund's total assets were over £1,800,000 and the income from investments stood at £77,000.[117] Though Burdett complained that the middle classes were still not paying their share, these figures were substantial and exceeded the aims of Lord Mount Stephen. But Mount Stephen had reason to be unhappy with the return on the trustee stocks and American securities handled by the newly formed Finance Committee. In a period of stable interest-rates, the interest on the Fund's overall investments dropped from 5.4 per cent in 1902 to 3.9 per cent in 1907.[118] Such figures were still above the rate of inflation, but taking note, the Bank of England reduced its commission charges to the Fund.[119]

In spite of the rather disappointing return on its investments, the Fund distributed the symbolic sum of £150,000 to London's voluntary hospitals and convalescent homes for the first time in 1909. As the report of the Council proudly announced, this was the sum mentioned by the King at the inauguration of the Fund. Unfortunately, £150,000 would not buy as much as it would have done a decade earlier.[120] Moreover, hospital deficits were on the rise at the turn of the century.[121] Whether such annual distributions were sufficient to satisfy the needs of London's ever more elaborate hospital provision was open to question, but they put the Fund at the centre of London's medical map and silenced many of the critics. Having raised such a massive sum, far more than any other co-ordinating charity, the Fund could devote more attention to its practical application.

The death of Edward VII marked the end of an era for the Fund and the hospitals of London generally. As Prince of Wales and King, he had been a special friend of the medical establishment. According to Burdett, his intervention at crucial moments had saved several London hospitals from closure.[122] It certainly improved their annual income and invigorated those associated with their appeals, from humble subscribers to hospital governors. The Fund and the London hospitals had the support of various members of the royal family, but they recognized that the enthusiasm, personal magnetism, and social power of King Edward were uniquely beneficial to their cause. The kindly, paternal image which the Fund cultivated was a reflection of his personal qualities and would be difficult to sustain without him.

His death had immediate practical implications for the Fund, not least for its appeals, which were so bound up with royal attachments. In 1910, the Fund lost both its Patron and its President. George V succeeded his father as Patron but his son, the future King Edward VIII, was too young to become President. In accordance with the Act of Incorporation, the Prime Minister, the Lord Chancellor, and the Governor of the Bank of England selected for recommendation to His Majesty three Governors. These were the Duck of Teck, Viscount Iveagh, and the Speaker of the House of Commons, the Rt. Hon. James W. Lowther. It was ironic that only three years earlier, the Act pressed on Parliament by the Prince of Wales had created an institution so dependent on an active royal President. Though its ties with King George V remained close, the Fund was moving into uncharted waters. But first, let us consider its aims, activities, and influence in the early years.

3

Edwardian Aims and Activities

THE King's Fund had come into existence to meet the new demands which public expectation was placing upon the hospitals. Although uncertainties about the economy threatened its perennial appeals, the times were propitious for its success. Advances in medical science and reforms in nursing and clinical practice, which were changing perceptions of the benefits of hospital treatment, also created a need for complementary reforms in hospital administration. The wider interest in health and welfare, which cut across party-political lines, also affected its policies. There was a particular anxiety over the physical condition of the poorer classes as a growing body of social data became available. The mass of evidence behind the select committee's report on metropolitan hospitals in 1892 bore sad testimony to the physical condition of London's poor. Charles Booth's inquiry, *The Life and Labour of the People in London* (1889–1903), brought an awareness of suffering in the capital to a wider public. The Boer War, which highlighted the wretched health of many recruits, added to the alarm and fuelled calls for action.

By the end of the century, discussion about national efficiency and imperial strength was a feature of the political landscape.[1] It was obvious that the British economy and military establishment could not remain competitive without a steady supply of fit workers and recruits. The many imperialists in the Fund, led by Edward VII and his colleagues, with their investments overseas, never doubted it. London is 'the metropolis of the Empire' said Burdett; and the health of 'our countrymen who have gone out to fight the battle of Empire all over the world' depended on the capital's medical men and facilities.[2] Such views were unexceptional in the Fund and found their way into the annual reports.[3] The Coronation Appeal exploited to advantage the relationship between London's hospitals and imperial well-being. The General Council reported in 1902 that 'those who live outside London may reasonably be expected to give something to the Hospitals of the Capital of the Empire, since twenty-five per cent of the patients in London hospitals come from outside the metropolis'.[4]

Ideas about imperial defence and national efficiency were part of the Fund's intellectual baggage, but they were not the cause of its creation. Fortuitously, the Jubilee that occasioned its birth coincided with the growing belief that the poor were in an advanced state of debility. The Fund thus profited from a highly topical issue. But if the decline of working-class health was as marked as people assumed, its task was formidable, all the more so as it wished the voluntary hospitals to institute reforms without government assistance. The Fund's own activities would add to the interest in the health and welfare of the working classes. But in time, other reformers would come to different political conclusions using the evidence that it supplied.

In exchange for grants and useful information, the Fund's officials expected a return in efficiency. But reform on the scale proposed would require an unrivalled knowledge of hospital affairs and an ability to bring diverse and sometimes competing institutions into line. The promise of an annual grant to a hospital in deficit was a powerful reforming tool, but inadequate if handled without sympathy and understanding. The co-ordination of London's voluntary hospitals could not be achieved painlessly, but if the Fund got a reputation for heavy-handedness, favouritism, or unwanted interference in medical affairs, it would struggle to survive. Hospitals were volatile institutions, which threw together officious patrons, aspiring professionals, and uninvited guests. The Fund's flair in raising money would have to be matched by judgement in spending it.

When the Prince of Wales inaugurated the institution in 1897, he was careful to avoid unnecessary exactness or hyperbole in defining its aims. He confined himself to a prosaic statement of the need to provide 'sufficient and permanent support' for the voluntary hospitals of London by reducing their deficits. Basing his calculations on audited accounts for 1895, he estimated these deficits to be in the region of £100,000 for 122 metropolitan hospitals and convalescent homes.[5] He further noted that, apart from their philanthropic work, 'we look to the voluntary hospitals for the means of medical education and the advancement of medical science'. But he did not say that the Fund would support the medical schools *per se*, an issue that eventually aroused considerable controversy. Nor was he precise in his definition of London's boundaries, though he called on those who lived in the metropolitan district to come forward as subscribers.

This calculated imprecision was deemed essential to give flexibility to an institution with claims to permanence. Furthermore, as an internal memorandum argued in 1905, the Fund's 'undefinable' associations preserved 'the valuable atmosphere of personal attachment to the throne'.[6] George, Prince of Wales, endorsed this view when he turned his mind to constitutional arrangements in 1906.[7] Consequently, the Act of Incorporation avoided putting the institution's aims into a strait-jacket. Given the Fund's sensitivity to the many changes taking place in medical provision, its objects were left as vague as practicable: 'the support benefit or extension of the hospitals of London or some or any of them (whether for the general or any special purposes of such hospitals) and to do all such things as may be incidental or conducive to the attainment of the foregoing objects'.[8]

The expression 'hospitals of London' was generously defined in the Act, in regard to both 'hospitals' and 'London'. As Sir Francis Avery Jones said to the Council in 1978: ' "the question is", quoting Alice, "whether you can make words mean different things" '. Whether by design or oversight, 'public' hospitals were not specifically excluded by the Act, though the Fund had no wish to assist them in its early years. The Fund's definition of a London hospital included

present or future hospitals, convalescent homes, nursing homes, nursing institutions, lying-in institutions, dispensaries, medical missions, societies for the provision of surgical or medical aid or appliances, and institutions for the rest, relief or cure of sick persons as shall be situate within the county of the city of London or the Metropolitan Police District as existing at the passing of this Act or as the same may be hereafter extended or being situate beyond such county or district shall afford medical or surgical treatment or rest relief or cure to patients all or some of whom are persons usually resident or carrying on their vocation in life within such county or district.[9]

The original Distribution Committee, chaired by Lord Lister, included two other medical men, Sir William Church and Sir Trevor Lawrence, and the laymen Burdett and Frederick Fry. They fully appreciated that until the Fund raised a substantial endowment its aims might appear too ambitious. This made it all the more important that its distribution policy command the confidence of the public and the medical profession. But how much money should be allocated and how was it to be most effectively administered? What institutions were to be the principal beneficiaries of the money distributed? What rules and guide-lines should be laid down for grants and applications? How could the inspection of hospitals by an independent body be made to result in greater efficiency? What benefits, apart from financial assistance, could the Fund provide? These were among the issues which needed to be resolved. Otherwise, as Lord Lister put it to the Prince of Wales, the Fund would 'dwindle and fail'.[10]

The Prince of Wales had strong views on the distribution of the Fund's hard-won money. As mentioned, he wished to avoid dipping into capital to make a great initial effect, a principle buttressed by his belief in the paramount importance of investigating the state of hospitals before awarding grants indiscriminately. It did not take a large income to initiate debate over the sum to be annually distributed. Muted arguments began soon after the initial contributions arrived. The need to build up an endowment and the lack of independent machinery to evaluate applicants encouraged caution; the need to satisfy subscribers and expectant hospital governors encouraged liberality.

Some members of the Executive Committee wanted £100,000 set aside for distribution in 1897; Burdett recommended £80,000; the Prince of Wales thought such large figures altered the terms of the Fund and was reluctant to consider any sum above £50,000.[11] The division of opinion left the Distribution Committee with a dilemma, but a compromise was struck that was acceptable to the Prince. With £227,551 received by the end of the year, the Council settled on a sum of just under £57,000 to be awarded. After deducting for expenses, the remaining £167,000 was invested. Some hospital secretaries criticized this decision, for they felt that it was a mistake to withhold money when thousands of deserving patients were being turned away for want of cash.[12]

Without the capacity to investigate applications in detail in its first year, it was necessary for the Fund to rely on information from the Sunday Fund. It was decided to make awards to the ninety-seven hospitals and convalescent homes already in receipt of Sunday Fund grants which were within a seven-mile radius of Charing Cross. Given the money available, a wider catchment-area was not at first feasible. The initial awards were divided into annual grants and special Jubilee donations. Virtually all the ninety-seven institutions received a special donation, but most of this money went to the larger hospitals.[13]

The Executive Committee rejected a uniform system of awards based on the number of beds occupied or patients treated. In the early years it concentrated on the larger hospitals with medical schools, but it divided their awards in proportion to their 'needs and usefulness'. Given the Fund's connections, the decision to look favourably on the well-established institutions was unexceptional; it would have long-term implications for health provision in London and for the Fund itself after 1948. The application of this policy in the Fund's first distribution saw the £22,000 from subscriptions divided among thirteen of those seventeen London hospitals which had 100 beds or more in constant occupancy. Guy's Hospital (423 beds) topped the table with an annual grant of £6,600, followed by the London Hospital (634 beds) with £5,000, and St Thomas's (375 beds) with £1,800.[14] Only St Bartholomew's failed to receive either a grant or a donation, on the grounds that it was richly endowed. (It began to receive money from the Fund in the 1920s).

The Fund's distribution policy came in for a measure of criticism from those who wanted a lower level of grant to a larger number of charities.[15] It was not always appreciated that the Fund's object was to do the greatest good to the greatest number of the sick, not to do the greatest good to the greatest number of hospitals. But when studying the initial list of annual grants, managers of the smaller institutions could be forgiven for recalling the saying 'unto every one that hath shall be given'. At least one hospital secretary complained of 'the fallacious and partial basis of the awards'.[16] Nor was Sydney Holland, the 'Prince of Beggars', happy with the Fund's distribution. He grumbled about Guy's Hospital getting a larger grant than the London, which did more work.[17] In 1899 the *Lancet* applauded the Fund for its 'worthy' distributions and observed that 'there are always undeserving establishments as well as undeserving individuals and they are both apt to think that they are the contrary'.[18]

The inclusive definition of what constituted a London hospital created difficulties as well as opportunities. Religious charities, hospitals for needy gentlefolk, and convalescent homes outside the capital all asked for and expected support. In many cases it was given. Non-sectarian, the Fund was at pains to publicize that its grants were made on humanitarian, patient-centred lines.[19] This was necessary to attract a wide range of subscribers. But it was also in keeping with its belief in scientific medicine and research, which were important to the Prince of Wales and to Lord Lister, who as Chairman of the Distribution Committee had a considerable influence on the Fund's policy. On this score, a few institutions were beyond the pale, including the National Anti-Vivisection Hospital, which began to apply for grants in 1905. It is surprising that this hospital bothered to apply, for anti-vivisectionists were decidedly suspicious of the Fund. The feelings were mutual. (Lister himself carried out numerous animal experiments.) The Fund declined to visit the institution on the grounds that its work was not sufficiently concerned with the welfare of patients, and it refused to receive a deputation from it.[20]

More contentious were applications from the homoeopathic and temperance hospitals, whose practices were highly suspect to the medical profession. Invited by the Prince of Wales to comment on problems of distribution in early 1898, Lord Lister specifically warned the Prince about these institutions. The homoeopathic hospitals came in for his particular castigation: 'All that is highest and best in the Medical Profession repudiates homoeopathy as a grievous error in principle; and I can assure your Royal Highness that this is not due to any spirit of narrow-mindedness, but to conviction which sound technical knowledge makes inevitable.'[21] He advised the Prince that if the Fund offered grants to temperance and homoeopathic hospitals it would 'entirely' alienate the medical profession. To support his case, he recommended that the Fund call on the advice of the Central Hospital Council, a body recently set up by men known to him in the teaching hospitals.

Undaunted by Lister's letter, the Prince rejected the suggestion that the Fund seek outside advice; and he pressed for the London Homoeopathic Hospital to be given a grant. 'I am not a homoeopath myself' he argued, 'nor are any of my family homoeopaths. Yet I do not see that there is any reason why it should be struck out.'[22] Here Edward showed his independence of mind, for Lister was not the only one critical of homoeopathy; so were Burdett and Sir Francis Knollys.[23] In the next distribution, the London Homoeopathic Hospital received a grant of £200 and the Temperance Hospital £600. By 1948 the former had been given £71,000 by the Fund, the latter £128,000.[24] The reason for these significant awards may have been that the Distribution Committee, as Lister feared, was open to domination by its lay members, who did not always share the views of medical members.

All charities with money to distribute are subject to charges of favouritism from disgruntled claimants. But such complaints against the Fund were relatively few and then often based on a misunderstanding. As we shall see, the shape of the Distribution Committee and the rules regarding visitors kept doubtful practices to a minimum. Still, the Fund was susceptible to certain pressures. When in 1899, for example, the Princess of Wales asked that a grant be given to the Mary Wardell Convalescent Home in Stanmore, Middlesex, the Convalescent Homes Committee took notice, and it became the unlikely winner of the largest award given to such an institution that year.[25] In later years Queen Alexandra continued to press the claims of this home on the Fund, but with less obvious effect.[26] Considering the weighty private interests involved, the degree of discernment and fairness displayed by the Fund in its distribution of grants was remarkable. Even if its officials had not been so high-minded, the very rivalry between hospitals which aroused complaints against the Fund encouraged impartiality.

Disputes over individual grants did not alter the Fund's priorities, the first of which was to open closed wards. The Prince of Wales and Burdett insisted that any wards reopened by the Fund should remain open, but the Prince's suggestion that they might be renamed 'Queen Victoria wards' was quietly dropped.[27] The Fund questioned the chairmen of London's leading hospitals on the number of vacant beds in their institutions; its grants in 1897 brought 185 of them back into permanent use.[28] As a sweetener, the Fund distributed 100 cases of champagne in 1898, donated by Heidsieck, among the institutions receiving grants, excluding the Temperance Hospital, in proportion to the number of charity-beds occupied.[29] Always a convivial institution itself, it passed out massive quantities of brandy in later years. But when the wine-merchants of Bordeaux offered a thousand cases of claret to distribute in 1902, Crossley, inexplicably, turned the offer down.[30]

The identification of a hospital bed with medical progress was ingrained in the Fund; and it announced in the annual reports the number of additional beds it had helped to open and to maintain, a figure which rose to a total of 433 in 1902.[31] A hospital bed is no longer invested with such significance by the Fund, for in-patient care has become increasingly expensive and institutionalization less fashionable. But in the late nineteenth century, endemic disease and general standards of health put an awesome pressure on hospital facilities. The poor patients who reached the beds often lived in such cramped, unsanitary conditions at home that a hospital ward looked inviting. Preventive medicine, which might have kept them out of hospital, was not a priority in the Fund, for it was not a priority in the institutions it was set up to support.

The Fund assumed that the first responsibility of the voluntary hospitals was to fulfil their charitable duty in treating the sick poor. Thus its distribution of money was conditional on hospitals opening beds for poor patients. Appeals from institutions which turned the poor away in favour of necessitous gentlefolk, such as St Saviour's Hospital, Osnaburgh Street, tended to be refused.[32] The Fund was not hostile to pay-beds for middle-class patients in voluntary hospitals. Burdett, who promoted the growth of pay-hospitals, argued that pay-beds were far preferable to control by local government—what he called 'municipalization'.[33] But the essential thrust of the Fund's activities was to provide for the 'deserving poor'. Ideally, with some assistance, they would get back on their feet and lead independent, productive lives again. This policy was in accord with that of the charitable hospitals. By a greater use of almoners, they were increasingly selective in their choice of patients, if only to avoid the accusation of providing treatment free to those who could afford to pay for it.

The initial grant to Guy's Hospital illustrates the nature of the agreement struck between the Fund and the institutions it persuaded to open charity-beds. Guy's management was anxious to oblige the Fund, especially as it saw the award as a gift from its new President, the Prince of Wales. Its recently appointed Treasurer, Cosmo Bonsor, accepted that to qualify for further grants the money must be spent along the lines requested, just as the Fund desired. Guy's therefore placed forty-seven of its 'guinea beds', which had been reserved for the 'better class' of patient, at the disposal of the sick poor.[34] Thus among the first effects of the Fund's intervention in hospital affairs was a reduction in middle-class provision. Before long, middle-class pressure for inexpensive hospital care became an ineradicable feature of British life. This would pose a dilemma for all the charities, including the Fund, dedicated to the sick poor.

The Fund's officials had various reasons for opening beds for poor patients, from social and religious motives to the defence of Empire, but the Distribution Committee had other objects in mind as well. After a study of hospital finances, the Committee took the view that large-scale improvements to buildings and sanitation in the great hospitals should come from their own capital reserves. The Fund's grants, in addition to opening closed wards, should be applied to the reduction of debts, the supply of special needs, increased aids to general maintenance, and the amalgamation of small hospitals.[35] It was thought that such assistance, though perhaps unglamorous, was sufficiently important to persuade hospital administrators of the Fund's usefulness and the need for economy and co-operation. The Act of Incorporation did not prohibit support for the clinical side of hospital work and various small grants were given for special needs such as X-ray equipment and operative appliances.

Support for medical research was altogether more sensitive. Stephen Coleridge, the Treasurer of the Victoria Street Society for the Prevention of Vivisection, wrote to the Prince of Wales in March 1897 with the request that money contributed to the Fund should not be used for the purposes of medical research. The Prince replied that the main principle of his scheme was the collection of money for the purpose of relieving suffering humanity but declined to enter into any 'collateral considerations'.[36] Coleridge was not placated, for he noted that the Prince, in opening Guy's new medical-school laboratory in 1897, had said that animal experiments were humanely carried out and beneficial. Moreover, in inaugurating the Fund, the Prince had referred to the important role the voluntary hospitals played in medical education.

Turning his inquisitorial eye to hospital accounts, Coleridge satisfied himself that money from the Fund found its way to the medical schools, and he assumed that hospital subscribers did not wish to see their money spent on destroying animals. In letters to *The Times*, he complained of Lister's support for vivisection and challenged Crossley's assertion that none of the Fund's money went to medical schools.[37] Crossley took a dim view of anti-vivisectionists, who he thought were out for publicity at the Fund's expense, and he must have recalled these letters when the National Anti-Vivisection Hospital, with which Coleridge was associated, applied for grants a few years later.

In 1900 the Metropolitan Radical Federation, which represented some 50,000 working-class members, joined the debate in a Memorial to the Prince of Wales. The sick poor appreciated the 'good and noble work' of the voluntary hospitals, said the 'Memorialists', but they worried that doctors and medical students looked at them 'as so much material for experiment'. What guarantee was there that money from the Fund would not be diverted to medical schools and consequently to animal experiments? 'Medical schools are hotbeds of vivisection. Down with them! Every penny given to them is an outrage on humanity.'[38] Behind the criticism was the implication that the Fund was insufficiently democratic and needed representation on its committees from the poor it assisted.

In its reply, the Fund denied that human experiments were carried out in the manner suggested and rejected the argument that the Fund's money financed medical research, though it admitted that 'some minute unascertained portion of a grant for general purposes may have percolated under the administration of the hospital concerned into a medical school or laboratory'. It concluded loftily that there was 'no reason to believe that the eminent authorities who are associated with the large and important hospitals that have medical schools have done otherwise than act to the best of their ability in promoting the highest interests of the hospital patients'.[39] Unimpressed, the Radical Federation replied that it was 'one of the greatest scandals of our time' that charitable subscribers should finance laboratories licensed for vivisection. It profoundly regretted that the Prince of Wales should be so misled by his own committee.[40]

The criticisms of Coleridge and the Metropolitan Radical Federation were easier to ignore than to discredit. Among many others in the Fund, Burdett thought anti-vivisectionists tiresome and Coleridge 'unscrupulous', but he nevertheless accepted that some hospitals had foolishly allowed money given for the sick poor to be transferred to their medical schools.[41] This, he felt, resulted in a loss of hospital subscriptions, especially from those working-class Londoners he was at such pains to recruit. He was not alone in his worries about subscriptions being shifted from patient care to medical research. But the complicated financial relations between hospitals and their medical schools made it very difficult to find out where the money ended up.

The matter might have remained unresolved but for the intervention of Lord Mount Stephen, who raised the issue in a letter to the Prince of Wales in March 1904. After offering further securities to the Fund, he expressed 'a hope that your Royal Highness, as President of the King's Hospital Fund, may see your way to prevent any portion of the Funds subscribed for the relief of the Sick Poor being diverted to purposes of medical education'.[42] This was a request the Prince could not overlook given his view of Mount Stephen's importance, and he appointed a committee, chaired by Sir Edward Fry, a former Lord Justice of Appeal, to look into the financial administration of the teaching hospitals.

On 29 March 1905, the Prince of Wales (later HM King George V) spoke to the General Council about the report of the Medical Schools Committee, which had been discussed by the Executive Committee earlier in the month. The report confirmed that of the twelve London teaching hospitals, at least eight had contributed from their general funds for the support of medical education. It did not uncover any mitigating circumstances which might have justified the practice. The Council recognized that its own finances might be threatened, especially the small sums from the many humble subscribers interested solely in patient care. It resolved that with effect from 1906, the whole of the grants from the King's Fund must go solely to the relief of the sick poor. The teaching hospitals were given nine months in which to reconsider their position.[43]

Several hospitals adopted the recommendations, but the controversy smouldered for years. In 1910 the Metropolitan Radical Federation, in a letter to George V, accused the Distribution Committee of flouting the directives of its own constitution in giving money to St George's Hospital, which wound up in the pockets of laboratory staff.[44] The Fund interpreted the Federation's complaint as sour grapes for not being granted representation on the Council. Nevertheless, in 1911, the Fund withdrew its grant from St George's over payments to its medical school, and this triggered a bitter dispute between the two institutions. The machinations resulted in a management crisis at the hospital.[45] For the Fund it resulted in the resignation from the Council of its former Honorary Secretary, Danvers Power, who had worked with the Medical Schools Committee years before. Having called for an independent body to assess St George's grant application, he was outvoted by 18 to 1. The Fund did not take kindly to suggestions that might set a 'dangerous precedent'.[46]

As the letter which launched the Fund suggests, it did not doubt that medical education was important in improving patient care. In this it was rather out of step with hospital governors, who traditionally did not take medical education very seriously.[47] But the decisions resulting from its investigation into medical schools showed that it was not prepared to risk losing contributors over the issue. The unlikely coalition of middle-class anti-vivisectionists, working-class radicals, and Lord Mount Stephen was sufficiently powerful to launch an inquiry and sharpen policy. As long as it remained predominantly a money-raising charity, the Fund had to be sensitive to the views of contributors. This is not to say that pressure from them caused it to depart from first principles, but that it accommodated certain dissenting voices. Before 1948, the continual need to raise money thus mitigated the charge that it was an unrepresentative body insensitive to the views of the public it wished to serve.

The Fund's knowledge of the administrative failings of individual hospitals depended largely on reports from teams of visitors or inspectors. Made up of doctors and laymen, these 'eyes and ears of the Distribution Committee' were first appointed in 1898.[48] (Though the visitors were spoken of as a Committee, their duties were personal rather than corporate.) The Prince of Wales hoped that all of them could be drawn from the Council, but the burden of work made this impossible. Burdett recommended a dozen lay visitors with the qualifications most calculated to make them effective.[49] His list included Crossley, Sandeman, and Wernher, all members of the Council, and these were eventually appointed. John Craggs (Sir John Craggs after 1903), J. Pierpoint Morgan Jun., Lord Duncannon, and Burdett himself were among those who joined them. Lord Lister, after consultation with the Presidents of the Royal Colleges, chose the visitors on the medical side, who were approved by the Prince of Wales.

The affable Sir Trevor Lawrence, Treasurer of St Bartholomew's Hospital, was the first elected Chairman of the Visiting Committee. (In 1902 he was created KCVO.) The son of Sir William Lawrence, Sergeant-Surgeon to the Queen, he was an unassuming man with a passion for orchids. President of the Horticultural Society, formerly a surgeon in Bengal, and Conservative MP for Mid-Surrey, he had a range of experience beyond the narrow confines of the London medical establishment. His St Bartholomew's connection, however, stood him in good stead. In his letter to the Prince of Wales in March 1898, Lord Lister had pointed to Lawrence as a man of 'great ability' who took an 'especial interest in hospital management. At the same time, being the Treasurer of Bartholomew's Hospital, which does not need or desire assistance from the Fund, he is entirely unprejudiced.'[50]

Lord Lister's choice of medical visitors produced a formidable team, mostly surgeons, like himself, who were drawn from the more prestigious teaching hospitals and known to the Prince of Wales. Though guided by a determination to find men experienced in hospital management, he wanted to avoid any suspicion of favouritism towards individual hospitals. Most of the teaching hospitals in the metropolis were not represented on the initial Visiting Committee. When Sydney Holland discovered that the London Hospital was not to provide a visitor, he was indignant, and he accused Burdett of organizing a vendetta against his institution.[51] (Holland, who wanted an appointment to the Fund, had to wait until 1909, when he joined the Executive Committee.) Burdett had a low opinion of the management at the London, for which he held Holland responsible, but he had recommended that the London provide a representative.[52] It was Lister, however, who was responsibile for selecting the visitors. In putting together his team he must have taken into account the particular claims of the London Hospital.

Everyone knew that St Bartholomew's would not be applying for grants. To Lister and others in the Fund, it also had the advantage of being richly endowed with Conservatives. It provided half the original medical visitors: William Selby Church, President of the Royal College of Physicians, who succeeded Lister as Chairman of the Distribution Committee in 1903; Henry Power, FRCS; Sir Thomas Smith, Surgeon Extraordinary to HM the Queen; Alfred Willett, FRCS; and Lawrence. Church, a man of considerable distinction, typified what the Fund was looking for in its representatives. By birth and inclination a country gentleman, he was a firm but popular administrator, 'absolutely devoid of self-seeking or log-rolling'.[53] The remaining five medical visitors in 1898 were A. D. Fripp, FRCS (Guy's), who declined an honorary secretaryship in the Fund when it was offered to him by the Prince of Wales; Edwin Cooper Perry, FRCP (Guy's), a man of rare gifts who was to chair the Distribution Committee in the inter-war years; John Croft, FRCS (St Thomas's); T. Pickering Pick, FRCS (St George's); and N. C. Macnamara, (Westminster), Vice-President of the BMA and the RCS, with a background in India.

The medical visitors were a closely knit group at the top of their profession. Picked for their seniority and knowledge of hospital affairs, most of them were already well known to one another. (Several of them were members of the Athenaeum, where they came into contact with various laymen in the Fund.) Their addresses are very telling of the small, exclusive world inhabited by London's leading medical men at the turn of the century. Whereas the Fund's rich businessmen inhabited Mayfair, they preferred the salubrious climes north of Oxford Street, close to their private patients. Lister's house in Park Crescent served as meeting-place for the Distribution Committee; Church lived in Harley Street; Fripp in Portland Place; Croft in Cavendish Square; Willett in Wimpole Street; Smith in Stratford Place; Pick in Portman Square; Power in Great Cumberland Place; Macnamara, perhaps the wealthiest of them, across Oxford Street in Mayfair. Of those not in retirement, Perry, who lived in the Superintendent's House at Guy's, was the only one not living within a half mile of Cavendish Square.[54]

Hospital-visiting expanded with the years and was one of the principal means by which the Fund recruited new talent. In 1908 the area of operations was extended to 9 miles around Charing Cross, with a consequent increase in the number of grant applications and visitors.[55] By 1914 there were sixty-six visitors inspecting over 100 institutions. The job was so prestigious that there was no shortage of doctors or laymen willing to offer their honorary services; but there were worries in the Fund that many of them did not have a sufficient knowledge of hospital management.[56] The mix between medical men and laymen remained. (There were no women visitors until 1918, when Miss L. B. Aldrich-Blake, MD, and Lady Barrett, MD, were appointed.) The older teaching hospitals, led by St Bartholomew's, continued to figure prominently in the ranks of medical visitors. In time, a few of the specialist hospitals were represented and the balance between surgeons and physicians evened out. Needless to say, general practitioners, low in status and lacking an intimate knowledge of hospital management, were not in evidence.

A full list of the visitors before the First World War would show the extent to which the Fund attracted the doyens of London's medical establishment, leading businessmen, and philanthropic aristocrats. On the medical side, it included Sir William MacCormac, President of the Royal College of Surgeons; Sir Frederick Treves, who operated on Edward VII in 1902 (the first visitor from the London Hospital); Sir Felix Semon, Edward VII's

Physician Extraordinary (a friend of Cassel's); Sir James Reid, the King's physician who attended at his death; and Sir Benjamin Franklin, the Surgeon General. On the lay side, it included William F. D. Smith, head of W. H. Smith and Son and Conservative MP; the publisher Frederick Macmillan, knighted for his hospital work in 1909; and Lord Sandhurst, who had chaired the select committee on metropolitan hospitals in 1892. One can imagine the effect on a hospital staff of a visit by a pair of such men, say Lord Lister or a President of one of the Royal Colleges, accompanied by a Governor of the Bank of England or Sir Henry Burdett.

The Fund invited grant applications through press advertisements. Upon the receipt of an application, the Fund arranged for two visitors, one a doctor and one a layman, to meet representatives of the institution by appointment. Given the size of London, the city was divided initially into four areas, and a group of doctors and laymen assigned to each. Typically a pair of visitors carried out about six to eight visits a year, though as the number of visitors increased, the figure dropped. The rules of conduct were designed to counter any suspicion of corruption. Every two years, the pairing of visitors was altered. The Executive Committee agreed to the policy that no member of the Distribution Committee was allowed to take part in discussion or voting with reference to any institution with which he was affiliated in the past three years. Visitors who also served on the Distribution Committee were asked to leave the room when the reports of their own visits came up for discussion by that body.[57]

Secrecy about the proceedings of the Distribution Committee became rather an obsession, which may seem paradoxical for an institution that saw itself as a clearing-house of information. Some in the Fund took the view that even members of the Council should not have access to the visitors' reports. Eventually, the President ruled that they should be available for inspection by the Council only after the final deliberations of the Distribution Committee. This was quite a departure from Burdett's belief that the publication of the reports would 'be calculated to do immense good', but then he preferred directness and expected others to be grateful for his censure.[58] When the pressure increased from hospital managers to make the remarks of visitors available to them, a compromise was struck, by which extracts from the visitors' reports were sent to the institutions concerned. This reconciled the Fund's keen sense of diplomacy with the demand to release useful information.[59]

The Visiting Committee worked out the details of what its members were to investigate, from the state of the books to the cleanliness of the cupboards.[60] Burdett knew as much about hospital management as any man alive, and he encouraged visitors to combine a critical spirit with sensitivity to the special needs of each institution.[61] He drew up 'suggestions' for visitors which pointed to specific problems. Before an inspection, they should consult building-plans, note the system of returns used for costs per patient, and read the book *Suggestions to Hospital Visitors* by Drs Billing and Hurd.[62] They were not to concern themselves with the size of any potential grant, which might lead hospital managers to expect support. The Distribution Committee, not the visitors, decided on the size of grants and any conditions attached to them.

Armed with printed enquiry forms, which structured the inspections and brought them into conformity, the visitors set off. Ideally, the medical visitors, with their inside knowledge of hospital administration, had an eye for good practice and departures from it; the lay visitors, who typically had hospital connections, were to bring their practical knowledge into play. On the whole the combination worked effectively, but visits did not always go smoothly; sometimes one set of visitors recommended something that another set condemned.[63] In 1905, the visitors doubted the value of St Mark's existence; the next year it was worthy of every support.[64] It was not unknown for the medical visitor to be distracted by an operation or an emergency and forget to look into the matters assigned to him. Such human failings added to the worries of the Fund's staff, who had to reply to the complaints from hospital managers. If a visitor dared to criticize the Fund publicly, he was dismissed. In 1907 Lord Cheylesmore expressed doubts about distribution policy in a newspaper article and was asked to resign.[65]

The earliest of the Fund's visiting-forms asked specifically about a hospital's records and accounts, the fabric of the building, the condition of the wards, nursing accommodation, immediate and long-term special needs, and the admission of doubtful cases, meaning 'undeserving' patients, including abusers of charity and drunks. There was ample room for the visitors' remarks and recommendations. Each report was to comment on whether the institution had complied with the conditions attached to any previous grant. A decade later the forms were more elaborate, with questions about fire precautions, accommodation for resident staff, more on nursing facilities, occupied beds, and costs per bed.[66] Though it recognized that hospitals of different types used their beds in different ways, the cost-per-bed-occupied became a major test of hospital efficiency to the Fund.

The visitors' reports, compiled with few interruptions until 1974, are an invaluable guide to hospital conditions. They confirm that the Fund had taken on board an awesome task in its attempt to improve London's voluntary medical services. A representative sample from the Edwardian years may help to explain why the Fund preferred to keep its enquiries secret. The reports often contain comments such as 'admirably managed' (St Thomas's) and 'first rate' (the Middlesex). Guy's, visited by Sir Frederick Treves and Duncannon in June 1903, was 'worthy of every support'. But the following year other visitors, who concentrated on different things, found fault with the flooring, windows, lifts, and corridors, and recommended that Guy's out-patients department 'should be condemned'. St Thomas's did not require much assistance from the Fund, remarked the visitors in 1904, 'but we think that some donation may with general advantage be given to it, as the connection of the Fund with the hospital is likely to be of mutual benefit'.[67]

Many institutions came in for a grilling, especially the poorer, less-established ones. Frederick Macmillan and Dr Owen Lankester, met only by the Matron, were 'very unfavourably impressed' with the Oxygen Hospital in 1905, and commented, in rather stilted language, 'a hospital for whose existence there seems no reason'.[68] (It never received a grant from the Fund.) The Woolwich and Plumstead Cottage Hospital also failed to impress: 'this hospital hardly seems to be required'.[69] (Despite the reviews, it did receive small donations from the Fund, perhaps because Burdett was enthusiastic about cottage hospitals.) Other hospitals were picked up on matters large and small, from hopeless management (Moorfields) to bottles marked poison found in lavatories (Metropolitan Hospital) to the Matron taking it upon herself to diagnose cases (Passmore Edwards' Hospital).[70]

Visits to the London Hospital were complicated by the sheer size of the place and Sydney Holland's objections to the many forms the Fund required him to fill in. When Sir James Reid and J. S. Wood inspected it in May 1903, they were satisfied with the nursing accommodation and improvements in the wards, for which the Fund could take some credit. But they criticized the financial management, the accounts, the excessive number of beds, and the 'effete and dirty custom of keeping butter, tea, sugar and other foods in the patients' lockers beside the beds'. This last criticism was doubly worrying to the Fund because the practice, which was widespread, made for confusion when comparing figures for expenditure with other hospitals. The report ended with remarks perhaps best kept from Holland's attention: no increase in grant recommended, for the public support to this hospital was so generous that it was 'almost to the detriment of other general hospitals equally deserving'.[71]

Despite such remarks from the visitors, the London Hospital received more money from the Fund than any other institution.[72] By 1917 the Fund had awarded it £194,236, far more than Guy's at £149,113 and King's College Hospital at £101,300. These figures did not stop Holland from grumbling, but they did take the sting out of his complaints. Totting up the annual figures he must have recognized that his hospital's relative lack of representation on the Fund's committees did not damage it financially. Those sensitive parties who placed the Fund's awards in the context of its hospital connections probably found the exercise reassuring. St Bartholomew's, which was very well represented in the Fund, received nothing from it in these years; St Thomas's grants came to only £12,000 by 1917. Both were, of course, medieval creations with greater endowments than the voluntary hospitals founded in the eighteenth and nineteenth centuries.

The total amount of money awarded by the Fund to hospitals in London by 1917 came to over £2,250,000.[73] As early as 1900, its grants made up over 6 per cent of the ordinary income of the London general and special hospitals. There were considerable variations from one institution to another. At the Royal Free the Fund's award in 1900 constituted over 17 per cent of total ordinary income; at Guy's, 12 per cent; at St Thomas's just over 3 per cent.[74] Between 1902, when the sum it distributed doubled, and the First World War, it provided over 10 per cent of the voluntary hospital income of London.[75] The Fund had reason to be pleased with this level of contribution to the capital's medical provision, but it was aware that the demand for services continued to put pressure on available resources.

Of the money awarded by the Fund in its first twenty years, 38 per cent of it, or £865,098, went to the general hospitals with medical schools in operation at the beginning of the century, with the exception of St Bartholomew's, which did not then apply for grants. The twelve London teaching hospitals, however, maintained nearly half of the roughly 10,000 beds in the capital at the time.[76] Seen in this context, it is clear that the smaller institutions, which did not figure so prominently in the earliest distributions, were far from ignored. Well over 100 London hospitals had received awards from the Distribution Committee by the First World War. Among the more prominent beneficiaries were the West London, the Hospital for Sick Children, Great Ormond Street, the Dreadnought (Seamen's) Hospital, the Hampstead General Hospital, and the Hospital for Consumption (Brompton). That 'excellent institution' the Cancer Hospital (Royal Marsden) rarely applied for grants and received less than £3,000 from the Fund between 1897 and 1948.[77]

Compared to the Distribution Committee, the Convalescent Homes Committee, chaired until 1914 by William Latham, Master of the Clothworkers' Company, had only small sums to give away. But after the Act of Incorporation, it was given wider powers and more money. By the First World War it gave £6,500 a year to over fifty homes and consumption sanatoria. The generous definition of what constituted a 'London hospital' allowed its grants to be spread over a wide geographical area. Most of them went to institutions outside the capital which had either close connections with major London hospitals or had a substantial number of London patients in attendance. Thus the Children's Sanatorium in Holt, Norfolk, the Northampton Sanatorium, and the Friendly Societies' Convalescent Homes in Dover and Herne Bay received assistance.

Just as the Convalescent Homes Committee widened the Fund's sphere of influence, so too did the League of Mercy. Most of the money it raised went directly to the Fund, but as early as 1901 it began to make its own grants to hospitals in those areas outside London where it concentrated its energies. By 1924 it had given the Fund £369,422, but it had reserved for itself £64,798 to distribute to cottage hospitals and other charities.[78] Thus through the League of Mercy the Fund extended its tendrils across the country, giving it publicity beyond the capital. In 1924 the League opened a Scottish branch under the presidency of the Duchess of Atholl. From time to time, there was confusion about the respective territory of the parent body and its auxiliary. After the Fund extended its area of operations to 9 miles around Charing Cross, several hospitals applied to both of them for grants. It was an acute embarrassment when the Beckenham Cottage Hospital managed to receive money from both institutions in the same year.[79]

The Fund included the names of all institutions it visited in its annual reports, whether their applications were successful or not, with separate columns for sums awarded and remarks. It did not broadcast it, but it took the view that it was to some extent responsible for the affairs of those institutions it favoured with continuous awards.[80] Those it rejected, on the other hand, were expected to benefit from public censure. But criticism did not invariably appear in the reports, and when it did it was usually toned down. In 1910, for example, the National Hospital for Diseases of the Heart and the Kensington and Fulham General Hospital (Queen's Jubilee Hospital) were among those which applied to the Fund without success. One visitor wrote to Maynard that the former 'ought not to exist'.[81] Brutally frank, Burdett endorsed a proposal 'to wipe out' the latter, on the grounds that it was of no benefit to the public.[82] None of this appeared in the annual report. Both hospitals, in fact, survived and eventually received grants from the Fund.

Despite visitors' criticisms and the forthright language of officials in their cups, the Fund believed that coercion was unlikely to bring about reform. It did not, after all, have the power to close down a hospital. As an internal memorandum put it in 1906, it was 'indisposed to press hospital officials too hard while they are inclined to fall in with the Fund's views voluntarily'.[83] Persuasion, financial inducements, and encouragements to fruitful competition between institutions were thought the most productive lines of approach.[84] Such views were behind the idea of competitions and prizes. In 1908, Edgar Speyer offered an award of £100 and a silver cup for the best essay on 'the economical management of an efficient voluntary hospital'.[85] The image the Fund wished to promote was of a wise and solicitous grandfather, who respected the various personalities of sometimes wayward and misguided offspring, while keeping the extended family uppermost in mind. This endearing image was easier to fix in the public mind when Edward VII was alive.

The conditions attached to many of its grants were one of the chief means by which the Fund implemented its policy of keeping hospital expenditure under control. It was not long before a precondition of application to the Fund was that hospital secretaries submit audited accounts and statistical tables to it by 15 April of each year. The most common conditions imposed on recipients in the early years were that the money be allocated to the opening of beds, the reduction of debts, maintenance, or improvements. Before the First World War, about 20 per cent of its awards were to reduce debts. Many others were for modest rebuilding-schemes, including out-patient facilities, nursing accommodation, and the installation of fire-escapes.

On the wider front, the Fund's strategy was to discourage further unplanned growth of hospitals or major building-programmes which could not be justified on grounds of utility. In 1902, the Executive Committee passed a resolution that any proposals for new hospitals or significant restructuring be submitted to the Fund.[86] Given its growing financial power, the resolution was widely respected, and a spate of proposals resulted. Burdett suggested that the Fund go further and take responsibility for plans and schemes for new buildings and extensions, but the idea was rejected by the Distribution Committee in 1907. He was left with the impression that members of the Committee opposed the proposal because it would make him more powerful and that he would make money out of it. 'This monster calumny' made him furious and he asked Sir Cooper Perry for a full report of the accusations to pass on to the King and the Prince of Wales. It was not forthcoming.[87] The Fund's meetings could be stormy.

Burdett argued in 1903 that the Fund was carrying out all the functions of a central board 'except the enforced removal of hospitals to new sites'.[88] This exception, it should be said, was highly significant given the distribution of medical facilities in the capital. Population trends in and around London, confirmed by the census of 1901, pointed to continuing imbalances. The desired ratio of hospital beds to population was usually put at about 1:1,000 at the time. When Burdett compiled figures for London in 1903, he discovered that the overall ratio was a generous 1:922. But when he broke down the figures into five concentric districts, the picture changed dramatically. In the City of London it was 1:40, in Westminster 1:418, in Bethnal Green and Islington 1:1,054, and in Stoke Newington and Deptford 1:1,877. In the outer ring, which included West Ham, Tottenham, Richmond, and Dartford, the ratio of beds to population was 1:2,482.[89]

Given London's population, which doubled in the fifty years before 1914, and its pattern of internal migration, the pressure to relocate hospitals or build new ones in suburbia was considerable. It was exacerbated by greater patient-demand and to some extent by advances in medical science, which required ever more space and elaborate facilities. Several of the teaching hospitals, King's College Hospital and St George's among them, had little room for expansion. Still, calls for relocation usually fell on deaf ears. Hospital doctors wanted to be near their private patients; hospital governors prided themselves on their local allegiances and traditional subscribers, who could not be guaranteed to support an institution if it moved miles away.[90] The centre of London had other financial advantages. As we have seen, St George's capitalized on royal parades which passed by Hyde Park Corner. Imbued with a spirit of individualism and sentimental, sometimes ancient attachments to particular neighbourhoods, the voluntary hospitals were not easy to shift.

Since the Fund's purpose was the defence of the voluntary system, it was not altogether clear what it should do about the imbalances in hospital treatment. If it pressed for the removal of established institutions, it might undermine the very traditions it was set up to sustain. If it did nothing, it would be seen as not satisfying the expectations it had aroused. How could it best help the hospitals to keep pace with London's medical needs while maintaining their distinguishing marks as charities? Coercion, which it identified with state intervention, was not an option. A distinguishing mark of the Fund itself was its respect for the integrity of hospitals, which was strengthened by the individual patronage given to many of them by the royal family, including its own President. Nothing acted as a greater check on the abuse of its power than its regard for the variety in hospital provision. Institutional rivalry, which it could exploit to spur reforms, was not a particalar worry. The wasteful practices associated with overlapping charities caused it greater alarm, but the duplication of services offered choice, if not always efficiency.

In so far as it supported hospital amalgamations the Fund was following up a recommendation of the House of Lord's report of 1892. As a practical body with finite resources, it dealt with each case of removal, rebuilding, or amalgamation on its own merits. It investigated conditions and options thoroughly before making recommendations or pledging itself to financial support. Despite the potential danger of tying up its money in long-term projects, the Fund set aside considerable sums for relocation schemes. When King's College Hospital considered the possibility of moving from its cramped and antiquated buildings to a new site in Denmark Hill, it invited the views of the Fund and of King Edward himself. Denmark Hill was a part of South London long in need of a general hospital, so they supported the proposal, and the Fund promised a sizeable grant. With 'the greatest satisfaction', it awarded £5,000 to King's for removal in 1903.[91] It was the beginning of a commitment that lasted for eighteen years and cost the Fund nearly £80,000. The magnitude of this project pointed to the vast financial resources needed from the voluntary sector if it was to keep pace with the ever more elaborate needs of medical provision in a city with a shifting and rapidly growing population.

The rebuilding or removal of established hospitals was invariably problematic.[92] In the Fund itself there were often disputes about particular proposals. Amalgamations were no less difficult to achieve and required delicate negotiations between erstwhile rival institutions. In 1902 the Distribution Committee, having more money at its disposal, decided to give support to the amalgamation of some small hospitals.[93] The policy was given enthusiastic support by Sir William Church, who succeeded Lister as Chairman of the Committee in 1903. But hesitant to take the initiative, the Fund typically waited upon events. If proposals satisfied its concern for the integrity of the institutions involved and the needs of the sick poor, it had money set aside to bring negotiations to a conclusion.

The Fund's general attitude was that it would support any reasonable scheme of amalgamation agreed upon by two or more hospitals. The first result was the amalgamation of the National and Royal Orthopaedic Hospitals in 1903, which became the Royal National Orthopaedic Hospital. The Prince of Wales studied the plans and endorsed the proposal, and the knowledge that he would withhold his patronage if either of them rebuilt separately was an inducement to their reaching agreement. The City Orthopaedic had pulled out of the initial scheme, to the dismay of its patron, the Princess of Wales, and of the Fund. But it was persuaded to amalgamate with the Royal National in 1906. As elsewhere, the combination of financial inducements and royal favour proved compelling; in 1909 the King and Queen opened the new hospital in Great Portland Street.[94] (Tellingly, this was not suburbia, but an area close to Harley Street.) The possibility of royal patronage upon acceptance of a scheme supported by the Fund welled up in the mind of more than one hospital governor.

The pressures and enticements were not always sufficient to bring feuding institutions to amicable unifications. After long negotiations, the Fund failed to bring the five ear, nose, and throat hospitals together, though two partial schemes went ahead in 1914. One brought together the London Throat Hospital, Great Portland Street, and the Hospital for Diseases of the Throat, Golden Square; the other saw the amalgamation of University College Hospital and the National Dental Hospital.[95] Having exhausted virtually all the possibilities, the Fund put the best possible face on these events. Without the power to compel mergers, it at least could not be blamed when they fell through. Perhaps the success rate was remarkable enough given that amalgamating institutions were faced with the loss of their separate identities and their faithful subscribers. Few boards of hospital governors were so fierce for reform that they wished to abolish themselves.

The Fund soon became used to the idea that if a project succeeded, it—the Fund—was unlikely to get much of the credit. It was instrumental in facilitating discussions between the British Lying-in Hospital, Endell Street, and the Home for Mothers and Babies at Woolwich in 1912. A third institution, the General Lying-in Hospital, York Road, Lambeth, also took part in the negotiations. The Fund discussed the possibilities of amalgamation with all three charities, and Sir Cooper Perry and Leonard Cohen of the Distribution Committee produced a report. They discovered that the General Lying-in Hospital wanted the British Lying-in Hospital to merge with it in Lambeth. The British Lying-in Hospital preferred to merge with the Home for Mothers and Babies in Woolwich if certain conditions could be met. For its part, the Home for Mothers and Babies favoured amalgamation with the British Lying-in Hospital if it meant additional money was available for a new maternity building.[96]

Caught in the middle, the Fund acted in what it considered to be the best interests of London's sick. Judging that the population was likely to increase in Woolwich and decrease in Lambeth, it opted for the amalgamation of the British Lying-in Hospital and the Home for Mothers and Babies on a new site in Woolwich. But once negotiations reached an advanced stage, the British Lying-in Hospital, which was anxious about keeping its subscribers if it moved so far away, was critical of the Fund's actions. The Chairman of its committee on amalgamation, A. B. Masters, wrote to the Secretary of the Home for Mothers and Babies, Alice Gregory: 'the King's Fund have come down with a pretty heavy hand and threatened to withdraw their support from the hospital if continued, or alternately require it to be rebuilt'.[97] Nevertheless, he accepted the Fund's importance in getting the Charity Commissioners, who had favoured the rival scheme, to approve the proposal, which it did in 1915.

The amalgamated and newly titled British Hospital for Mothers and Babies opened in Woolwich in 1922, with considerable financial support from the Fund, and royal patronage. The General Lying-in Hospital consoled itself with a campaign to enlist the former subscribers of the British Lying-in Hospital and further grants from the Distribution Committee. The episode proved once again that amalgamation was an expensive and largely thankless proposition for the Fund. In this instance the Borough of Holborn's officials wrote to it deploring the closure of the British Lying-in Hospital, which had been closely identified with the community since its foundation in 1749.[98]

Removals and amalgamations invariably left a residual bitterness in the communities left behind. With a view to the wider interests of health provision in London, the Fund contributed, albeit unwillingly, to the alienation of subscribers who identified with a threatened local charity. Though it wished to avoid putting undue pressure on institutions to restructure, its rationalizing spirit had the unhappy effect of exacerbating relations between hospitals and between a hospital and its community. The resentment which surfaced was sometimes directed towards the Fund, for its wealth and power or what was seen as interference in hospital affairs. Such problems were to be seen in a different context after 1948. The National Health Service would be more ruthless than the Fund ever could be, or wished to be, in amalgamating or closing institutions.[99]

Given its character and activities, the Fund had a unique knowledge of the failings of voluntary hospitals in London. There was little suggestion of fraud, but evidence of negligence, overstaffing, and extravagance was widespread. Money spent on new buildings and the latest scientific novelty depleted the cash available for maintenance, the reduction of debts, or the employment of effective managers with an eye to costs. Discovering just how much hospital treatment cost per patient or per bed was very difficult at the end of the nineteenth century, but Burdett's estimates suggested it was too high. In 1900 twenty-two London hospitals, eight of them general hospitals, were expending over £100 per occupied bed a year, nearly double the figure that was thought necessary.[100]

It was generally acknowledged at the end of the nineteenth century that London hospitals were badly managed compared to those in the provinces. In the Fund's view, good management presupposed an economical outlook. Any metropolitan general hospital which spent over 15 per cent of the cost of maintenance on administration was suspect to Burdett. He set the figure at 12 per cent for provincial institutions.[101] Not everyone in the Fund shared his view, but he believed hospitals were like businesses and most effectively run along commercial lines. His own unusual mix of experience reinforced this view, and throughout his career he was at pains to bring forward people who lived up to his ideals.

Taking its cue from Burdett and other like-minded officials, the Fund sought to create a new generation of capable, well-paid professionals who would revamp hospital management. In doing so it reflected the wider changes taking place in government and commerce, where 'professionalization' had already taken hold. Indeed, the survival of the voluntary system required the hospitals to keep pace with the meritocratic public sector, which was increasingly turning its attention to issues of health and welfare. With its enthusiasm for innovative administrative practices, based on the science of accountancy and social statistics, the Fund contributed to the growth of a 'managerial class', which was an increasingly visible feature of British society in the early twentieth century.[102]

It was said that one reason why people were reluctant to contribute to hospitals was that they thought their money might be wasted by reckless managers. Hospital secretaries, some of whom were still unpaid, were known to run off with the funds, a practice which afflicted all types of charities; others spent money on delicacies and drink which did not reach the patients.[103] Even the reputable ones were reluctant to release financial details on the running of their institutions, or presented them in such a way as to leave a misleadingly favourable impression in the minds of subscribers. Such practices came increasingly under attack from critics and supporters of the voluntary hospitals alike. Many of them, influenced by the contemporary enthusiasm for social science, assumed that statistical investigation was a prerequisite of reform.

The Fund did not invent the statistical approach to hospital accounts. Florence Nightingale had written a paper in the 1860s in which she called for a uniform system of patient registration and the publication of annual hospital statistics.[104] Burdett, whose love of facts would have warmed the heart of Jeremy Bentham, claimed to have been the first to introduce a uniform system of accounts, in the Queen's Hospital, Birmingham, in 1868.[105] Anxious to give charities a means of countering the criticism that they were inefficient, he published his *Uniform System of Accounts* the following year. Hospital secretaries were slow to accept the system but in the 1890s it was widely in use in London, helped considerably by the Sunday Fund, which required its adoption as a qualification for a grant.[106]

The King's Fund thus inherited a statistical tradition, which it refined and extended. It believed not only that methods of hospital accountancy needed overhauling but that comparative statistics should be made publicly available. It did not automatically assume that a costing-system appropriate to commercial firms which sold goods and services would apply to a hospital; at least one committee man, Herbert Eason, who succeeded Perry as Superintendent of Guy's, argued that it would not.[107] But there was general agreement that managers should have inducements to haggle over the cost of goods and equipment and to be fastidious in their use. If, for example, they discovered that other hospitals spent less on provisions, they would be encouraged to shop around.

It was accepted in the Fund that keeping beds occupied was critical to improved efficiency, and this too required reliable statistics. Here, conflict with doctors, who looked at the matter from a different perspective, was inevitable; but from the point of view of management, 'the machine of organization', it was essential to treat every suitable patient who could be admitted to a bed.[108] Enabled to make comparisons of the cost of occupied beds between hospitals, the public would be able to judge the economy and efficiency of different institutions and respond accordingly. At least this was the argument.

Building on Burdett's accounting-system, the Fund set up a team of experts in 1901, who revised it. Up to then hospital statements were uniform in style, but different items appeared under similar headings, making it impossible for administrators to make useful comparisons. All hospitals which sought the support of the King's Fund and the Saturday and Sunday Funds had to complete the new forms. Before long there were calls for further revisions. In

1906 J. G. Griffiths, formerly head of the Fund's firm of auditors, revamped the forms. That he managed to do so without alienating Burdett was a personal triumph. The new system came into effect in January 1907. Among its chief features were improved methods of counting in-patients and out-patients and a more uniform plan of separating their respective costs, which increased the reliability as to the cost per occupied bed.[109]

The uniform system of accounts provided the basis of the Fund's annual *Statistical Report*, which first appeared in 1903, as part of its campaign for economic reform. It was initially prepared by Danvers Power, who as Chairman of the National Hospital for the Paralysed and Epileptic had a knowledge of hospital costs. It was eventually taken over by the Fund's Secretary, H. R. Maynard, whose ability, zeal, and sheer doggedness kept it going year after year. It was not unusual for Maynard, who had the mentality of a civil servant, to work half the night on a mountain of papers; and he and his staff scrupulously assessed the facts and figures submitted for the *Statistical Report*. Here, as elsewhere, the Fund relied on the co-operation of hospital managers. It was not always forthcoming. St Bartholomew's refused to use the uniform system and thus was not included in the *Statistical Report*. It was only brought into line in 1921, when it too needed money from the Fund.

The range of information compiled in the *Statistical Report* was impressive and included figures on rent, salaries, and pensions, down to the cost of cod-liver oil and scrubbing-brushes. As the secret of hospital economy lay in sound methods of purchasing and the prevention of waste, discrepancies in the price paid for goods provided crucial information. The Fund discovered that the cost of tea, for example, varied by up to 7*d*. in the pound from one hospital to another. In the first year the report pointed out that the aggregate value of sums paid in excess of average cost of commodities came to nearly £40,000 for the sixteen hospitals tested. According to the Fund, they were soon able to save £20,000 by reference to this evidence.[110] Within ten years the number of hospitals included in the statistical reports rose from sixteen to 109, making wider comparisons possible within types of hospitals. The Fund estimated the consequent savings to be nearly £50,000 annually.[111]

Everyone accepted that the *Statistical Report* and the revised system of hospital accounts, on which it was based, had done excellent work. Among other things, they resulted in the elimination of the practice of in-patients providing their own food and clothing. But they did not enable the public to judge between the economy and efficiency of different hospitals. To discover that one hospital spent £90 per occupied bed and another £60 was no guide to which was giving better value for money. As the Secretary of the London Hospital remarked, the term 'hospital' had a wide application and was used for institutions which did not do the same kind of work 'and so are not fit subjects for comparison'.[112] Moreover, the Fund's demand for hospital statistics was no guarantee of the accuracy of the information; as ever, managers had internal reasons for creative accountancy. Many of them dreaded opening their post for fear of yet more forms to fill in. That the Fund gave them so little time to do so, decreased the likelihood of the information's being wholly accurate.

The Fund's passion for numbers may be seen as a feature of a time of relative statistical deprivation. But as in other co-ordinating organizations, not least government departments, the systematic compilation of statistics was one of the principal means by which it gained power over institutions. For the Fund, information provided a stick to balance the carrot of grants. The fact that the statistics were of uncertain accuracy did not diminish their authority or usefulness. The annual *Statistical Report*, elegantly and formally presented, offered hospital administrators, at whom it was directed, institutional comparisons and a guide to reform. Few administrators wished to be seen to carp about its format or its evidence when grants from the Fund were so considerable.

There were those who complained that the Fund's statistical inquiries were misguided when what was needed was more practical work and more money. One friendly critic, himself a hospital secretary, argued that what was wanted from the Fund was 'less control in matters of detail, more guidance in matters of principle, less statistical inquiry, more practical inspection—above all things, not less financial help, but more influential assistance in putting the methods and the value of the voluntary system before the public'.[113] Burdett, who never lost his faith in numbers, lamented: 'statistics seldom receive the attention the labour of compilation should win for them'.[114] He seemed convinced that the public was as interested in the cost of bandages and cod-liver oil as he was. To the vast majority of hospital subscribers, who of course never looked at the *Statistical Report*, such details must have been pretty meaningless. But to the Fund, as Burdett insisted, they were essential.

The *Statistical Report* and the *Uniform System of Hospital Accounts*, whose formats were updated regularly, should be seen as part of the Fund's information service. Its provision of useful intelligence put it squarely in a charitable tradition that dated back to the late eighteenth century, but which it uniquely applied to medical administration. Using the publishing services of Spottiswoode and other companies, it produced a continuous stream of clearly written, well-presented books and pamphlets of use to the voluntary hospitals.[115] Some of them were the result of needs identified by the visitors and were used, in due course, to sharpen their inspections. Others were dictated from above, by committees looking into particular abuses. Before the First World War there were publications on the finances of medical schools, fire precautions, charity entertainments, co-operative hospital contracts, and the out-patient question.

This last work was the result of an inquiry by a Special Committee set up in 1910, chaired by the judge and skilful cross-examiner Lord Mersey, to look into methods of out-patient admission. (The social investigator Charles Booth had been invited to serve on the Committee but declined on health grounds.)[116] The abuse of hospital charity had been a concern for decades. But Lord Mount Stephen's uneasiness over out-patient practices, which he had complained about to the Palace, invigorated the Fund's interest in the issue.[117] To reach an out-patient department, most voluntary hospitals required a person to come under the scrutiny of an inquiry officer, or lady almoner, who asked for financial details to determine whether free medical treatment was appropriate. Dress was not a very good guide, for poor people, especially women, often hired clothes for the day to arrive at the hospital looking respectable;[118] middle-class women were known to dress down to avoid payment. Mount Stephen had recently donated a large sum to build an out-patient block at Aberdeen Royal Infirmary, and he was disturbed to be told that many patients in London received care who were insured by a Friendly Society or who could afford to pay a general practitioner.[119]

Lord Mersey's report observed that while out-patient departments were not widely abused, they did overlap with other forms of medical treatment. For instance, the complaint of GPs that out-patient departments took away their custom was taken up by hospital governors because they wanted their funds to be used for the deserving poor not for those slightly better-off, who could afford to pay small sums to general practitioners. Out-patient departments also suffered from a lack of co-ordination with other forms of charity. The principal recommendation of the report, which found favour with the Charity Organisation Society, was an extension of the system of specially trained inquiry officers, or almoners, which was already in operation in many hospitals. But the Fund hesitated to press for reform because of the uncertainty as to the effects of the National Insurance Act of 1911 upon out-patient departments and hospital finances.[120]

Lloyd George's National Insurance Act capped the Liberal government's pioneering, albeit piecemeal, social legislation, which included school meals, old age pensions, and selective unemployment insurance. The provisions for health insurance in the Act have been discussed at length elsewhere, but they are usually seen as a response to the problems of national efficiency, which had been alarming politicians and voluntarists alike.[121] The intention of the Act was not primarily to attack the causes of sickness but rather to relieve poverty due to illness. A compulsory contributory scheme, it offered care from a 'panel doctor', that is a doctor selected from a panel organized by local Insurance Commissions, for about 12,000,000 insured workers, though not their dependants. It also provided for tuberculosis sanatoria, but it did not provide for a stay in hospital, partly because hospital care was not thought to be a great advance on what a GP could provide. An uneasy compromise, it soured relations between government and voluntarists and created considerable anxieties for the Fund. It set the pattern of social legislation that followed in the inter-war years.

The Act, which suffered from a lack of consultation with the medical profession, left the health services fragmented. It had little to do directly with the voluntary hospitals. Though it conferred specific powers on friendly societies to make contributions to hospitals, they were not legally obliged to provide the costs of treatment of their members in hospital. The BMA, the British Hospitals Association, and other bodies argued that it added to hospital burdens without adding to their revenues. It was widely believed that an indirect consequence of the Act would be a sharp decline in subscriptions to the voluntary hospitals, which aroused fears of potential state control or municipalization.[122] Lloyd George, no enemy of the voluntary system, recognized the limitations of the Act and called it an 'ambulance wagon' driven through the twists and ruts of Parliament.[123] But to managers of voluntary hospitals it was an ambulance that would create its own emergency.

The Fund followed the passage of the Bill with great interest and set up a subcommittee to inquire into the effects of the Act. Having canvassed over thirty hospitals, it took a relatively calm and cautious line. It expressed worries about a possible decline in hospital subscriptions and an increase in the number of in-patients, but anticipated that a different class of out-patient might have to be treated, which would effectively reduce out-patient numbers.[124] In a most irregular outburst, Burdett publicly criticized the Fund for its timid response and predicted that 5,000 insured people would turn up each week in the voluntary hospitals of London alone. He acidly remarked that politicians were 'the curse of the sick' and that 'Mr Lloyd George's Act would speedily come to an end' without hospital co-operation.[125] Along with others, he called for the government to defray the costs of treating insured workers. 'You cannot hold over the voluntary hospitals the bogey of government interference and control where the government are the debtors.'[126]

Events justified the Fund's unhysterical, wait-and-see attitude to the National Insurance Act. The measure did not, as widely anticipated, result in a marked decline in hospital subscriptions, though the Fund's own receipts fell slightly in 1913, the year in which the Act came into effect.[127] Nor did it result in Burdett's apocalyptic vision of hospitals swamped by insured patients, as he later admitted. While many hospitals put obstacles in the way of treating insured persons, few turned them away for fear of risking further meddling by the State. According to the Fund's statistics, the number of in-patients attending London voluntary hospitals in 1913 was only 100 more than 1912. As anticipated by the Fund, out-patient attendances were down, by 200,000, because many hospitals referred patients with minor ailments back to their panel doctors.[128]

The National Insurance Act precipitated a shift in the role of the voluntary hospitals which would have important repercussions for their finances and propaganda. As a consequence of the Act large numbers of patients became insured. Increasingly, hospitals expected to be paid for treating them, which was not easy to square with charitable traditions. Insured patients, on the other hand, saw themselves 'receiving medical care more as a right and less as charity'.[129] Having brought voluntarists together to defend their position, the Act propelled them into a fresh examination of their role. Advances in Poor Law medical provision and the accelerating pace of social legislation made it clear that they could not operate in isolation; they needed to be attuned to government thinking and party politics in a more dynamic way, a process in which the Fund would take a leading role.

The growing uncertainty in the voluntary hospital movement after the passage of the National Insurance Act increased demands for government money, though not government control. For its part, the Fund rejected the idea of financial assistance from the State, thinking it would set a dangerous precedent.[130] Outright state control, though it had advocates on the medical and political fringes, was certainly not a serious political possibility at the time. Deep down, most people probably took Burdett's view that the government would never spend the enormous sum of money necessary to achieve it. The Royal Commission on the Poor Laws (1909) had not been uncritical of the voluntary hospitals, but neither its minority nor majority reports suggested that they should be nationalized. It had little to say about what the relationship between voluntary and public hospitals should be. The Fabian Socialists Beatrice and Sydney Webb called for a unification of the Public Health and Poor Law services, but insisted that this need not interfere with the voluntary hospitals or private medical practice.[131]

Though Labour Party conferences flirted with the idea of a National Health Service before the First World War, there was little pressure for it from below. The working classes of the Metropolitan Radical Federation, for example, preferred treatment in the voluntary hospitals to their experience of Poor Law infirmaries, which did not arouse pleasant memories. To them, there was a stigma associated with state provision, a humiliating denial of individuality. At the time, the advocates of a full-blown public health service incorporating the voluntary hospitals came largely from outside the working classes. Among them was a minority of the medical profession, whose dislike of charitable paternalism bolstered their faith in state paternalism.[132] They were inclined to see the Fund's work as a stopgap, and its statistical information as further evidence of the need for government intervention.

Before the First World War, hospital provision in Britain was not ineffective. Increasingly, it was its effectiveness that highlighted the need for reforms in administration. To be sure, the separate systems of state and voluntary provision were confusing and socially divisive; *ad hoc* and fitful government legislation exacerbated the muddle. The voluntary hospitals, though admired, remained disorderly; the public hospitals, though enlarged, were not widely respected. But relations between them hardly existed, and no one had a compelling blueprint for co-operative action. Would reforms specific to public or to voluntary provision make co-ordination between them easier or more difficult? Given their divergent histories, patients, and practices, a synthesis of the two was unlikely without a level of coercion heretofore unknown.

In the changing social and political atmosphere, the Fund could be seen as either a catalyst of reform or an agency of reaction. Its undemocratic character told against it as a potential central board for London, even though it fulfilled most of the proposed functions of such a board. By 1914, it had settled into a pattern. Its grants and information were beneficial and its practical work humane. Hospital expenditure was under tighter control, administrative reforms were under way and the level of co-operation between voluntary institutions, as evidenced by amalgamations, was in advance of what had come before. But while it could revive flagging institutions and make them more sensitive to the needs of poor patients, it was ill-equipped to tackle the wider issue of co-ordinating voluntary and public hospitals. Given its aims and ethos, it had no wish to do so. The National Insurance Act was a shock to the charitable system, which pointed out the necessity of improved public relations and joint action to defend the voluntary principle. As the Fund and the hospitals began to adjust to it, the First World War added to their worries.

4

The First World War and its Aftermath

THE First World War offered fresh opportunities to the voluntary movement, but at considerable cost. It allied charity to national purpose to a degree unknown since the Napoleonic wars; but as issues of health and welfare shot upwards on the political agenda, the war exposed the shortcomings of voluntarism and pointed to the need for greater state involvement. It encouraged closer relations between philanthropic bodies and the expanding state bureaucracy, but not always to the advantage of the former. Moreover, the war unsettled charitable institutions and eroded religious faith, which was often at the root of philanthropic activity. As men went to the front, the women who filled their jobs had less time to spare for voluntary work. In the changing social terrain, those who had taken up new employments and seen new possibilities did not always wish to return to the disrupted activities and institutions with which they had been associated. With ever more distractions and rival centres of loyalty, charities had to adapt or decline.[1]

In a conflict of such dimensions, few charities were unaffected, from humble mothers' meetings, which provided clothes for men at the front, to the Charity Organisation Society, which contributed to the general reassessment of voluntary policy taking place at the time. Established charities reflected the patriotic fervour, and their revenues often rose dramatically with the outbreak of hostilities. Those with royal connections and imperial sympathies were prominent in support of the war. They were joined by over 10,000 new societies set up before its close, including the National Federation of Women's Institutes, founded in 1915 to assist in food production, and King George's Fund for Sailors (1917). The government welcomed their activities and gave some of them financial assistance.

Just as the war offered fresh fields for voluntary work, it also brought about measures of centralization and control of the economy, which had repercussions for health provision and the social services. Philanthropists soon recognized the danger that the war and its management posed to the voluntary principle and their view of society. They could be forgiven for believing that the growth of state intervention during the First World War, as after the Boer War, would not have been so urgent without government bungling. They were not invariably hostile to state social action; indeed, they had paved the way for it in such areas as factory reform and children's health; but they would wave away the notion that it stemmed from progressive politicians with unsullied motives. As individualists, suspicious of Whitehall, they were inclined to see government intervention as a means by which politicians sought to make amends for the unhappy conditions which they had exacerbated or brought about. This is not to say that good did not come from state action, however suspect the reasons for it.

Politicians and generals placed an awesome burden on charitable societies in the unprecedented catastrophe of the war, particularly hospitals and funds for their support. Steeped in traditional views about Treasury restraint and the importance of individual accountability, they turned to voluntarists for assistance. Initially, the government did not appreciate the extraordinary costs that would be incurred by war on such a scale. Nor did voluntarists realize that rising prices and heavier operating-expenses would soon deplete their reserves. They were anxious to assist in the national emergency, but with their local traditions and limited resources, they were ill-prepared to cope with the myriad national and international problems thrust upon them. That they were then criticized for a lack of co-ordination added to their consternation.

Within weeks of the outbreak of war the voluntary hospitals began to wonder whether they might join the casualty list themselves. 'Never before or since', remarks Brian Abel-Smith, 'had so many patients been accommodated in the hospitals of Britain.'[2] Only recently reeling from the effects of the National Insurance Act, they were now asked to cope with hundreds of thousands of casualties.[3] Speaking at the Annual Meeting of the League of Mercy at the end of 1916, the Reverend R. J. Campbell remarked that every year the charity hospitals were finding it more difficult to maintain their ground. With their staffs depleted by war service and the continuing demands of the civilian sick, they 'have had to undertake an amount of new work for which they were not designed, more than they ever dreamed they could'. What most alarmed him in the prevailing 'policy of drift and muddle' was the prospect of the hospitals 'becoming mere departments of State, ruled by State officials'.[4]

Burdett shared many of the same concerns. He was more patriotic than the next man and flung himself into the war-effort with characteristic vigour. But, long-disenchanted with the drift of Liberal politics, he denounced the War Office for its 'invasion of our voluntary hospitals' and its failure to 'organize proper facilities of its own'.[5] He had a point, for the treatment of military patients drastically reduced the accommodation available to civilians. In London, about 20 per cent of the beds were taken from the normal establishment to make room for service patients.[6] Initially, the government did not have a fixed policy on the treatment of war-wounded; it was unprepared for a long war and a casualty list numbering men in the millions, more than a few of whom would call on medical facilities for decades afterwards.

The war soon exposed the inadequacies of the military hospitals, and of the workhouse infirmaries and lunatic asylums which the government commandeered. Charitable agencies had the decided advantage of providing high standards at low cost. For their part, the voluntary hospitals responded with spirit to the war effort, but most of them soon accepted War Office grants. There was a note of hypocrisy here, for their appeals to the public, which met with a generous response, were launched on the grounds that they were shouldering the burden of the State. But still smarting from the government's unwillingness to make payments for insured patients, most of them were little-disposed to do the government's bidding for nothing. Early in 1915 the War Office offered London's voluntary hospitals limited capitation grants for war pensioners. The King's Fund studied the matter and corresponded with the authorities on the formulation of these grants.[7] Under pressure of events, it had concluded that government payments could be accepted by the hospitals without injury to the voluntary system as long as they were for services rendered.

A decision to accept government money was decidedly awkward for a voluntary hospital, as for all charities, for it raised the delicate issue of independence. At Guy's, for example, the governors had previously resisted the temptation to accept financial payments from public authorities in return for services. They addressed the question of capitation grants for wounded servicemen in a letter to the King's Fund in 1915. Wishing to remain true to the charitable spirit of Thomas Guy, they argued 'that agreements of the kind carry with them a right of interference in the management of the Hospital which the Governors are unwilling to admit'. Should the public realize that the acceptance of government money was widespread, they concluded, 'the Voluntary Hospitals will inevitably by degrees cease to be so regarded by the Public and will no longer attract the support they now receive as charitable, as distinct from rate-supported, Institutions'.[8] Like other charity-hospitals, however, Guy's swallowed its principles and took the money.

Such compromises would have been less painful to the hospitals had the money been enough to cover their expenditure on war-related casualties. Many hospital administrators suspected that the level of grant, which rose to 5s. 9d. per day, was insufficient. In all, the War Office paid the voluntary hospitals about £880,000 during the war for the care of servicemen.[9] But King's Fund statistics in 1918 confirmed that in London at least the government's payments did not offset the true costs of treatment. The gross ordinary expenditure of London's hospitals was just under £2,000,000 in

1918, an increase of over 70 per cent since 1913. Even when War Office grants were taken into consideration, the figure stood at 41 per cent. The Honorary Secretaries ruefully concluded that the cost of maintaining the 1,800 additional beds provided for naval and military patients in London would 'greatly increase the strain on the Hospital finances already caused by the general rise in prices'.[10] To make matters worse, the influenza epidemic of 1918 put further pressure on hospital beds.

An analysis of the Fund's statistics for 1918, carried out by Burdett, revealed just how much the voluntary hospitals were spending on patients who were assumed to be the government's responsibility. The shortfall in government funding arose because the authorities adopted the view that their pro rata payments needed only to meet the maintenance expenses for the reception of the servicemen, for the expenditure on standing charges would have to be met in any case. Nor did they take into account the abnormal damage unruly soldiers did to furniture and equipment or the more liberal diet provided to servicemen. Taking these factors into account, Burdett calculated that London's voluntary hospitals 'made a present to the government' of £285,310 in 1918 alone. 'What then was the contribution made by the voluntary hospitals of the United Kingdom to the cost of the war during the four years of its duration?'[11] A King's Fund report presented to the Cave Committee, which investigated hospital finances after the war, put the figure at £530,000 for London.[12]

Though the Fund did not deal with casualties directly, it was not immune to the war's immediate effects, nor insensitive to its long-term implications. With its up-to-date information about hospital costs, income, and expenditure, it quickly recognized that London's hospitals were undergoing pressures that might lead to an upheaval in medical provision after the conclusion of hostilities. Lord Iveagh, one of the Fund's Governors, pointed out to his colleagues in the Council in 1916 that servicemen would make extraordinary demands on hospitals for years after their return to civilian life.[13] Invariably, references to the war in the Fund's annual reports dwelt on the problems rather than the opportunities for the voluntary sector; they conveyed a sense that while support for the war was solid, the longer it continued the more difficult it would be to return to normality when it was over. The tone of the Fund's meetings and consequent reports was sombre and less bellicose than in some charities further removed from the effects of the hostilities; this may be explained in part by the number of Germans who supported the institution.

An immediate effect of the war on the Fund, as on virtually all other charities, was the disruption to personnel. It caused serious worries, though not so serious as in the hospitals themselves, where over half the medical profession was called up after the introduction of conscription in 1916.[14] For

six months the Fund's Secretary, Maynard, was seconded to the Ministry of
Food as a result of a request for his services from William Beveridge, a former
colleague from his days at Toynbee Hall.[15] Of the Fund's six office staff,
three served in the forces; one died and another was taken prisoner. While
they were on active duty, the Fund paid their salaries, minus their army pay
and allowances. It paid bonuses to those who stayed behind for taking on extra
work. In the unusual circumstances the Honorary Secretaries appointed their
first female clerk in 1916, Ethel Millns. The following year the Fund took out
insurance against risks to office staff from air raids.[16] Because of the
exigencies of war, particularly salary increases and the greater cost of
stationery and printing, administrative costs rose to about 1.5 per cent of
monies received by 1918.[17]

There were no casualties among the Fund's Councillors or committee men,
but the war marked a watershed in the administration of the Fund none the
less. The Duke of Teck, a Governor, and Sir Savile Crossley were among
those who took on special war-duties. (Crossley was created Baron
Somerleyton in 1916.) With so many members, medical and lay, absent on
war service, the Fund's ordinary activities naturally fell into the background.
An inquiry into pensions for nurses and hospital officers was interrupted, as
was the investigation into out-patient admissions. Because of restrictions on
travel, the visitation of consumption sanatoria was suspended in 1917. Despite
the pressures on visitors, hospitals in London continued to be inspected; in
1918, with the King's consent, the first 'lady' visitors joined their depleted
ranks. As elsewhere in the charitable world, the war opened up possibilities
for women, if only by default.

The war years saw the death or retirement of many of the men associated
with the Fund's foundation. Among the deaths were the Councillor and
benefactor Lord Strathcona and the genial Duke of Norfolk, who had
attended the meeting in Marlborough House which launched the Fund in
1897. Lord Rothschild, whose services to the institution were, in the words of
George V, 'of inestimable value', died in 1915.[18] The Fund immediately
recruited his son the Hon. Nathaniel Charles Rothschild to replace him on
the Finance Committee (Lord Revelstoke succeeded Lord Rothschild as
Chairman of the Finance Committee and as Honorary Treasurer.) When
Nathaniel Charles Rothschild died in 1923, he in turn was replaced by
another member of the family, Lionel de Rothschild. These appointments
were part of a pattern of patrimony that the Fund, like the City Companies,
found congenial and often financially beneficial. A committee man whose
father sat on the committee before him inherited a sense of responsibility to it.
Recourse to family ties and old-boy connections, though undemocratic, also
simplified recruitment to honorary positions.

Retirements from the Council included the banker Albert Sandeman and the renowned Professor Sir William Osler. (Osler, who rarely attended meetings, was perhaps a rather surprising member of the Council given his commitment to medical education.) Sir William Latham, Chairman of the Convalescent Homes Committee since its formation, resigned because of ill health in 1915. Dr Edwin Freshfield, the head of the Fund's honorary solicitors, replaced him. When he died in 1918 Sir William Bennett, a St George's surgeon and Red Cross volunteer during the war, succeeded him as Chairman. In the same year, Sir William Church resigned as Chairman of the Distribution Committee, and was replaced by Sir John Tweedy, a past President of the Royal College of Surgeons. With an unbiased, judicial mind, Tweedy had the ideal temperament for Distribution Committee work.[19]

The most important change in the management of the Fund in these years was the accession to the presidency of Edward, Prince of Wales in May 1919. For nine years the Governors had fulfilled their duties in accord with the Act of Incorporation. Somerleyton, among others, had wanted George V to stay on as President after 1910, until his son was of age.[20] But the Fund's constitution made this impossible. Still, the King, who was by now quite expert on hospital affairs, kept in close touch with the institution as its Patron and continued to advise on matters large and small. It was his wish that the Prince of Wales should become President as soon as possible, but Edward's service overseas delayed the event until the end of the war, by which time the Fund too had reached its majority.

A letter from Lord Stamfordham at the end of 1918 outlined various new offices that the King expected his eldest son to assume, including the presidency of the Fund. The 'dismal catalogue' of duties, as Edward's official biographer puts it, 'must have chilled the Prince's heart'.[21] Whatever his feelings, Edward presided over his first annual meeting of the Council as President on 6 May 1919 at St James's Palace. In a speech provided for him by the Fund, he ritually thanked the Governors for their services during his minority and praised his distinguished colleagues on the Council for their invaluable assistance to London's hospitals. 'It was an honour to carry on the work' of his father and grandfather, he announced, 'and it will be my earnest endeavour . . . to adopt and to develop the principles which they have so well laid down.'[22] Few of those in attendance could have known at the time that it was a promise the vulnerable and easily distracted 24-year-old Prince would find difficult to keep. For his part, Burdett had convinced himself that Edward was a 'strenuous upholder of the voluntary system' on the strength of the Prince's education and his recent acceptance of the presidency of St Bartholomew's Hospital.[23]

In his maiden speech as the Fund's President, Edward announced that the society's distribution in 1918 had reached £200,000 for the first time. This was a symbolic figure and it disguised what were somewhat disappointing receipts during the war. (The Metropolitan Sunday Fund fared little better.)[24] In the emergency the public preferred to give its money directly to hospitals and other agencies more immediately associated with the casualties. The Red Cross, for example, which along with the Order of St John of Jerusalem ran the auxiliary hospitals on behalf of the War Office, raised £21,000,000 in the war years.[25] Among the other charities whose receipts rocketed after 1914 were those dealing with one-parent families and memorials to the war dead.

In the Fund, annual subscriptions remained steady at about £25,000 a year during the war, though exceptional donations of £28,000 from Sir Ernest Cassel in 1915 and another of £35,000 from Viscount Astor in 1917 helped considerably. Legacies continued to come in but were unpredictable; one from Isabella Countess of Wilton, which realized over £163,000, made a significant difference to the amount distributed in 1916. But the level of the annual grant-distribution, which rose from £157,000 in 1913 to £200,000 in 1918, did not keep up with costs, which rose by about 80 per cent during the war.[26] As the Fund's *Statistical Report* showed, the level of ordinary expenditure of London's voluntary hospitals at the end of the war was 70 per cent higher than at the beginning. The shift back to civilian patients in 1919 helped to drive costs up further still, so that in 1920 ordinary expenditure was 135 per cent higher than in 1913.[27]

The war's effect on the Fund's portfolio of investments was considerable. With Rothschild's death, the senior director of Barings, the autocratic and public-spirited Lord Revelstoke, took charge of the Fund's investments as Chairman of the Finance committee.[28] Cassel had resigned from the Committee in 1913 and Mount Stephen, whose presence had loomed so large behind the scenes, was now in his eighties and less involved. Yet his influence over the Fund's investment policy remained pronounced until wartime conditions dictated that transatlantic securities be sold in favour of British government securities.[29]

The patriotic disposal of the Fund's American securities in 1915 and 1916 was not straightforward. Barings, who handled the Fund's business, without charge, reported that because of the danger to shipping brought about by the war, rates of marine insurance were prohibitively high. At the time, shares were still physically transported across the Atlantic. His Majesty's Treasury facilitated matters, for it was willing to exchange American securities held in Britain for war stock and send them to be sold in the United States at its own risk.[30] Barings assisted in these transactions by working with the Bank of England in taking over American shares, 'a measure which would have reduced Revelstoke to apoplexy in other times'.[31]

By the spring of 1917 the Fund's Finance Committee had sold all its American shares in favour of British war bonds, removing the last trace of Mount Stephen's gifts to the Fund.[32] What Mount Stephen thought of all this is unclear, but he may have felt that the shift into British securities in the confused and depressing international climate was the patriotic thing to do. Revelstoke, in addressing the Fund's Council, accepted that the sale of American holdings, many of which were of 'the very highest character', had resulted in a 'small diminution in the income from investments', but he argued that the income, apart from this consideration, was still 'practically unaffected by the war'.[33] He might have added that investment income was not unaffected by the need for an enlarged cash-account, which had grown to meet the ever more unpredictable needs of the hospitals.[34]

Inevitably, the war influenced the Fund's policy towards the institutions it supported. Uncertainty about the future made it wary of speculating on hospital needs. By 1915 caution dictated the policy of postponing building-schemes which had been under way before the war and discouraging fresh schemes that were not exceptionally urgent. Consequently, the percentage of its grants in aid of general maintenance increased. In the emergency it was more anxious than ever to ensure that when capital was expended due regard was given to the wider needs of the metropolis and to 'economy, efficiency, and the prospect of funds for future maintenance'.[35] With its own experience of fickle contributors, the Fund recognized that the charitable purse, opened by war, might well close in peacetime.

Though the amount of money it distributed during the First World War failed to keep up with inflation, the Fund nevertheless tightened its control over London's voluntary hospitals. In the crisis, the hospitals preferred to look to their traditional friends in order to avoid more entangling alliances with the government. Frightened by the prospect of increasing state controls, and short of cash and staff, they naturally turned to the Fund. In general they followed its guide-lines of deferring capital schemes until after the war, perhaps assuming that they would in time receive the grants necessary to complete their building-programmes. When the war ended, however, construction costs were often prohibitive. The Committee of the London Hospital, for example, discovered that the expense of erecting a doctors' hostel, estimated at £60,000 in 1913, was £149,000 in 1919.[36] The Fund reported in 1919 that it had received particulars of fifty-seven hospitals with schemes of extension requiring capital expenditure. The lowest estimate of their capital cost was £3,000,000, with the additional annual upkeep of £500,000.[37]

When the Fund's Council met on 30 April 1920, the Earl of Donoughmore, who presided in the absence of the Prince of Wales, then in Australia, pointed to the gravity of the problems confronted by the hospitals. They 'are passing through difficulties even greater than those with which they were faced when the King's Fund was founded'.[38] He did not refer directly to the phenomenal costs of proposed extension-schemes, but noted that since 1897 hospital expenditure had risen threefold; and while their income had increased at the same rate, he was not optimistic for the future. As he saw it, 'the present difficulties are not the result of any failure on the part of the Hospitals, but arise solely from the general effects of the war'. What was needed, he argued, was 'very great energy . . . and possibly even some new departure requiring powers of imagination and originality equal to those shown by King Edward VII'.[39] Like others in the audience he confidently expected 'great things' from the presidency of the Prince of Wales.

Just minutes before Lord Donoughmore made these remarks to the Council, its members rose in tribute to the man who had provided much of the 'imagination and originality' behind Edward VII's hospital initiatives. Sir Henry Burdett, after a short illness, had died of heart failure at his home only the day before. The measured tributes from his colleagues in the Fund were perhaps less fulsome than might have been expected given his singular importance to the institution.[40] The many obituaries which appeared in the *Hospital* and elsewhere heaped a mountain of praise on the man.[41] Certainly, the voluntary hospitals would never see his like again; his ideas, enthusiasm, and eloquence would be sorely missed, as would his influence at court. Yet the institutions which he had set in train could carry on without him. This was as Burdett, with a strong sense of trusteeship, would have wished.

In the same King's Fund annual report announcing Burdett's death came a brief statement that his old rival and sometime friend Lord Knutsford had resigned from the institution. Knutsford had had to wait for an appointment to the Fund but once inside was less enamoured of it. His first love was the London Hospital, and he could never quite reconcile himself to money going anywhere else. The London, as noted, did very well out of the Fund. As its Secretary, E. W. Morris, confirmed, the rebuilding of the hospital in the early years of the century developed out of a scheme suggested and supported by the Fund.[42] Knutsford, however, fell out with his colleagues in the Fund in late 1919 over its criterion for determining hospital efficiency, i.e. cost per bed. Not only were the figures 'not properly arrived at', he argued, but the cost per bed, which was higher at the London that at comparable hospitals, was the 'wrong basis' for analysis of efficiency. Concluding that the Fund's policy worked to 'fine' his institution, he called for an inquiry.[43] It was refused. Somerleyton, anxious to avoid public rows, especially in the presence of the Prince of Wales, tried to avert Knutsford's resignation but to no avail.[44]

If public confidence in the voluntary principle was to be sustained, the Fund needed to avoid public rows and potentially embarrassing inquiries. What was the point in calling for greater co-ordination of agencies for the support of hospitals if it could not speak with one voice itself? Propaganda and public relations had to show the Fund and its associated institutions moving ahead together. The hospitals could only be rescued by cash given in good faith. By 1920, the reconstruction of hospital finances was of the greatest urgency. But it would have to be achieved against the background of rising costs, changes in the direction of expenditure, and growing public demand for new services.

The war had not only increased hospital costs and put pressure on facilities, it had stimulated medical progress. Consequently, it pointed to the need for further reforms in hospital administration. Most significantly, the war 'forced the new science to organise its material for mass application'.[45] Notable advances in surgery and the treatment of wounds and shock contributed to greater public approval of hospital and convalescent care. Hardly a year passed without a new method of diagnosis or treatment being devised, and this required the expenditure of capital. But capital expenditure in a hospital, unlike in a business, did not increase its earning-power, but simply its spending-capacity.[46] Just when the hospitals were under financial strain, the public expected more from their services. It was the post-war variation on a theme which had helped to bring the King's Fund into existence.

The First World War pointed to health as a national asset, and, like the Boer War before it, created and exposed deficiencies in health provision and its organization. The voluntary hospitals responded with varying degrees of success to wartime problems and opportunities, but the public was less willing or less able to pay for hospital reforms by traditional means at the end of it. One reason for this was that the war resulted in vastly increased levels of taxation on higher incomes, which reduced the amount of disposable wealth available for charitable purposes. Families living on earned income of £10,000 a year, for example, paid over 500 per cent more in tax in 1918–19 than in 1913–14.[47] As the King's Fund suspected, financially hard-hit and weary subscribers would not sustain appeals that had been successful in wartime. The statistics, though fragmentary, suggest that the real income of London's numerous charities began to fall in 1920 and did not recover their pre-war position for several years.[48]

The particular crisis in the hospitals began in 1920, exacerbated by the ending of War Office payments for servicemen. The immediate response of the King's Fund was to make an emergency distribution of £250,000 out of its capital funds. The decision was a difficult one, for as Lord Donoughmore pointed out at a special meeting in June 1920, it would cost the Fund 'a very substantial amount of income' which had hitherto been available for the annual grants.[49] The emergency distribution reduced the Fund's accumulated reserves by about 10 per cent. Deeply imbued with conservative financial views, the Council only reconciled itself to the idea of dipping into its capital on the grounds that it was absolutely necessary to save the hospitals from bankruptcy. But no one at the meeting believed that £250,000, which was earmarked for maintenance work, was sufficient to resolve the problems of the hospitals. In a message to the Council, George V said that the 'continuance of the voluntary system' depended on private individuals, as well as on the concerted efforts of the Fund and kindred institutions.[50]

A month after the meeting to announce the Fund's emergency grants, another special meeting took place to distribute a further £250,000 entrusted to the Fund by the Joint Finance Committee of the British Red Cross Society and the Order of St John of Jerusalem. Here was a prime example of what George V and other voluntarists desired, charitable institutions working together in defence of the voluntary system. The money came from the Joint Finance Committee's surplus funds at the end of the war; the expertise on hospital needs came from the King's Fund, which examined the proposals submitted and visited the hospitals. Unlike the Fund's own emergency grants in 1920, however, the Red Cross money was to assist schemes of extension or improvement and was restricted to London institutions which treated ex-servicemen.[51]

After careful scrutiny of the eighty-one proposals submitted, the Fund's Distribution Committee allocated the money to forty-nine hospitals in respect of fifty-four schemes.[52] The Committee took into account the financial position of each hospital and favoured those schemes which did not unduly encourage the provision of additional beds. At this time, the provision of further beds was not a priority in the Fund, for it was anxious to avoid increases in future expenditure on maintenance. Among the beneficiaries of the Red Cross money were St Bartholomew's, awarded £24,000 for a new nurses' home, and the Royal National Orthopaedic Hospital, which received the same amount to extend its out-patient department and to provide X-ray and other equipment. The Woolwich and District War Memorial Hospital, now the Memorial Hospital, Shooters Hill, received the largest grant, £25,000, to cover construction costs. This building-scheme, which the Fund had been supporting since 1918, is of particular interest, for it was an exception to the Fund's policy of not assisting in the building of new hospitals. The Fund justified its support on the grounds that Woolwich urgently needed a medium-sized general hospital and that it had local backing.[53]

Nineteen-twenty proved to be a most remarkable year for the Fund, particularly for the size of its distribution. The ordinary grants, announced in December, reached £200,000, assisted by contributions from the King George's Fund for Sailors and from S. R. Guggenheim of New York. Including the sums already given away, the total amount of money distributed by the Fund in 1920 came to £700,000. This was the greatest sum ever allocated to grants by the Fund in real terms, and it represented 26 per cent of the total ordinary expenditure of London's voluntary hospitals for the year.[54] But as the Prince of Wales, now back from abroad, pointed out at the December meeting, the Fund could not itself enact a cure for the ailing voluntary hospitals; rather it provided time for remedies to be devised. In a speech prepared for him by the Honorary Sercretaries, the Prince outlined a series of measures which needed further investigation. They included exemptions from tax for donors; more systematic collections from employers and employed; and the possible extension of pay-beds.[55]

The war and the hospital crisis stimulated the voluntary sector to greater exertions, as the Fund's distribution in 1920 confirms; but it also stimulated those who saw a greater role for the State. Health was increasingly seen as a national asset, which easily translated into a national responsibility. Planners thrive in wartime conditions, and the peacetime virtues associated with voluntary medical provision were less obvious in a command economy anxious about national security and efficiency. However useful the charity hospitals had been to the State during the war, when it ended, many of those responsible for reconstruction rather forgot the nation's voluntary traditions, though they were soon reminded of them. Lloyd George, like Beveridge a liberal who undermined voluntarism in practice, said to Labour leaders in 1917: 'The whole state of society is more or less molten and you can stamp upon that molten mass almost anything so long as you do it with firmness and determination.'[56] The euphoria even swept up the medical correspondent of *The Times*, who, soon after the armistice, announced that the voluntary hospitals 'must be brought within the control of the State'.[57]

By the 1920s hospitals and health had become politicized as never before and the stage was set for a propaganda battle between voluntarists and state-interventionists that would last for decades. As long as the medical profession dealt largely with prognosis and therapy of symptoms, the hospitals had been of greater interest to churchmen than to politicians. But the growing faith in scientific cures, enlivened by wartime medical improvements, helped to push the hospitals towards the centre of the political arena. By 1918 the Labour Party, and many in the Liberal camp, emboldened by the extension of state power during the war, were turning their minds toward greater state direction of health. With its long-standing doubts about the viability of voluntary hospitals, the Labour Party was now discussing a national health service under central and local control. Imperceptibly, modes of expression changed, which suggested a growing predisposition to collective action. The phrase 'the Nation's Health' was by now part of the language. 'National Health Service' had been used at least as early as 1910, in Benjamin Moore's *Dawn of the Health Age*.[58]

The formation of the Ministry of Health in 1919 has been seen as symbolic of changing attitudes towards medical provision, and it probably contributed to the perception that government would increasingly meet the costs of hospital care.[59] The new Ministry merged the old Local Government Board and the Insurance Commissions, and in the minds of some reformers it was essentially an agency for unifying the various public and voluntary health services. Its first Minister, Dr Christopher Addison, believed that an extension of state power was essential to advances in health.[60]

The signals sent out by the Ministry of Health were confusing. One of its first acts was to appoint Dr Bertrand Dawson (created Lord Dawson of Penn in 1920) as Chairman of the Ministry's Consultative Council on Medical Services. Soon afterwards it invited the Council to consider a scheme or schemes of 'systematized provision' for medical and allied services. Dawson, Physician in Ordinary to George V, had been a consultant in France during the war. Though far from a socialist, he accepted that a greater degree of state intervention was necessary to improve British medical services. Such ideas were not in favour at Buckingham Palace. In early 1920 the king was becoming agitated about government meddling in the affairs of voluntary hospitals and told the Minister of Health as much.[61] This may help to explain why George V, always discerning where honours and hospitals were concerned, doubted the wisdom of raising Dawson to the peerage, despite his close association with the royal family.[62]

The Dawson Report, published in the middle of 1920, was the product of the peculiar circumstances of the war, the experimental thinking it excited, and the short-lived post-war boom. Its recommendations, resonant of wartime provision, provided for a reorganization of hospital services based on primary health centres staffed by general practitioners. Secondary health centres, equipped for more specialized treatment, were to be based on hospitals. The diagrams of the proposed primary health centres appended to the report suggested that a massive construction programme would have to be undertaken to bring the reforms to fruition. Particular stress was laid on co-ordinating preventive and curative medicine within the sphere of the general practitioner. It also introduced the idea of regional planning, with new health authorities to supervise the local administration of all medical and allied services. Hospital care was to be available to all classes, though it would not necessarily be free.[63] Dawson avoided discussion of how the scheme was to be financed, but it was most unlikely to be realized without funding from government in one form or another.

Dawson's scheme, which in many respects resembled one favoured by the Labour Party, was still-born. (Some weeks before it appeared Lord Stamfordham wrote to Somerleyton that the Palace had assurances that the government was not about to take over the voluntary hospitals.)[64] The usual explanation for the failure to implement the Dawson Report is that by the time the government considered it, the economy had deteriorated and potentially costly programmes were out of favour.[65] Looking at it from the perspective of the Welfare State, historians are inclined to see the Dawson Report as a 'forward looking' and 'revolutionary document' which prefigured the NHS.[66] Thus, with hindsight, it represents 'one of the more important, although tragic, documents in the history of British medicine'.[67] Brian Abel-Smith calls it a 'lost opportunity' to overcome the prevailing 'patchwork' of hospital provision.[68] Such remarks show up the danger of reading a post-1945 mentality into the 1920s, for they leave the impression that the country wanted such a dramatic break with the nation's traditions of hospital care, and that only inter-war 'pessimism' and a parsimonious Exchequer prevented it.

The economic explanation for the failure to implement the Dawson Report, though inviting, is somewhat misleading; it fails to take into consideration the weakness of the Ministry of Health, the resilience of the voluntary movement, and the unrealistic character of the Report itself. The electorate trebled in size in 1918, but there is little evidence to suggest that it wished to see, much less pay for, the extension of state bureaucracy that the implementation of the Report would entail. 'Universalism', that rallying cry of post-1945 social policy, was far less attactive in the 1920s, for most people, still deeply imbued with 'Victorian values', did not wish to make a decisive break with a familiar liberal society in which localism and selectivity were deeply ingrained. Many working-class mothers did want local government support for maternity hospitals.[69] But in general the labour movement was divided on the best way to proceed in regard to the social services or hospital provision in the 1920s.[70] Workers who still feared the stigma associated with Poor Law institutions were reluctant to support further state intervention.

Voluntarists sought to perpetuate Victorian traditions of benevolence and self-help, and many of them delighted in keeping the State at bay, a policy made easier by the support they received from the royal family. Their recruitment of working-class and lower-middle-class subscribers was motivated partly by a desire to safeguard charitable principles in a time of growing political democratization. It was an oblique way of dishing socialism. The Liberal Party expected to dish socialism through social legislation, a policy whose limitations became increasingly apparent. The success of voluntarists in reaching the new electorate was particularly noticeable in regard to hospital provision, as institutions like the King's Fund, the Saturday Fund, and the League of Mercy attest. Along with their many influential allies, including the King and many members of the House of Lords, they probably could have seen off or emasculated any state medical scheme had it reached Parliament. In the social and political context of the 1920s, the Dawson plan was not so much a 'lost opportunity' as utopian.[71]

One of the principal reasons why Dawson's plan was unpopular with voluntarists was that it challenged their traditions and rationale. Dawson admired the charitable hospitals and certainly did not wish to see them nationalized, but he took the view that they had fallen on 'evil days' because of rising costs and the greater complexity of treatment. Many voluntarists would have accepted this diagnosis, but they recoiled from the prescription. They had reconciled themselves to accepting government grants for services rendered, but they did not see their salvation in greater government controls, or, as Dawson put it, 'their readiness to come into coordination with the general plan'.[72] To the King's Fund and its hospital allies, the 'general plan' was anathema. Steeped in a libertarian philosophy and a tradition of care, 'splendid' hospitals, many of them in existence for over a century, were little disposed to become 'secondary health centres', despite their financial worries. The Fund's emergency distribution in the summer of 1920 should be seen against the background of the Dawson Report, which was published only a few weeks before.

Only months after the Ministry of Health received the Dawson Report, it appointed the Cave Committee to look into the finances of voluntary hospitals. Set up in January 1921, it was the result of a Commons debate over a bill which included a clause, thrown out by the House of Lords, to empower county councils to subscribe to voluntray hospitals.[73] Though it has received far less attention than the Dawson Report, the report of the Cave Committee, which sought the reconstruction of hospital care along traditional lines, was more in tune with economic realities and opinion in the 1920s.[74] Viscount Cave, later Lord Chancellor, and his colleagues were little known in the medical world; none of them were doctors or connected with hospital administration. One of the Committee was Vernon Hartshorn, the miners' leader and Labour MP. But predisposed to support the voluntary hospitals, appointed precisely to recommend 'any action which should be taken to assist them', they were soon highly regarded by the King's Fund and the hospitals, which were invited to give evidence to the Committee.

The day after the Cave Committee was appointed, the Fund held a special meeting of the Council to formulate the policy it wished to recommend to the government 'for the preservation of the voluntary system of hospital management'.[75] Dedicated to the proposition that the voluntary system was 'the most efficient method of providing at the least cost the best medical and surgical treatment combined with advance in medical knowledge and practice', the Fund's officials assumed that charitable contributions must continue to meet a substantial portion of hospital costs. But they now accepted the need for additional income from other sources, including payments from patients under treatment, regular insurance contributions from prospective patients, and increased government payments for the treatment of patients for whom the authorities accepted responsibility, such as those suffering from tuberculosis and venereal disease. Finally, they proposed that while direct grants from the State might endanger voluntary management, some form of government assistance based on the amount received from voluntary sources might prove practicable.[76]

The Cave Committee took evidence from various public bodies, hospitals, and other voluntary institutions in the early months of 1921. The King's Fund was prominent. It provided more witnesses than any other single institution and compiled the background information and statistics for London. Among the Fund's representatives were Maynard, Sir Cooper Perry, Lord Somerleyton, and Sir Alan Anderson. They were not disappointed when the interim report appeared in March. Doubtless reacting to the Dawson Report, it concluded that 'the evidence already received has convinced us that it is desirable, in the public interest, to maintain the voluntary system of management'.[77]

The final report, published in June 1921, vigorously defended the charitable system, which, it argued, was going through a temporary crisis due to the war. Cave and his colleagues were unanimous in their view that the independent governance of the hospitals was worth saving because it preserved medical freedom, fostered progress in medical research, and served the patient in a way that would be difficult to imagine under a state regime: 'The Voluntary hospital system, which is peculiar to the English-speaking people, is part of the heritage of our generation; and it would be lamentable if by our apathy or folly it were suffered to fall into ruin.'[78]

The Cave Committee's recommendations were so in tune with the Fund's views that they could have been written by Maynard or Somerleyton. A year later the Fund appointed Cave to its General Council. Upon his death in 1928, the Management Committee noted that the Cave Committee 'did more than anything else to preserve the [voluntary] system'.[79] The chief recommendations of the Committee's final report were that Parliament should make a temporary grant of £1,000,000 to help the voluntary hospitals get through the crisis; that a central Hospitals Commission should be established to administer the grant; and that local voluntary hospital committees should be formed to advise the Commission on the amount of aid required in their areas and to improve co-ordination between hospitals. In London, the necessary institution existed in the King's Fund, 'which has already performed admirable work in the organisation of the London hospital system'.[80]

The government's response to the Cave Report was not altogether satisfactory to the Fund or to the hospitals. They warmed to the appointment of Lord Onslow as Chairman of the Hospitals Commission (he joined the Fund in 1932). But Parliament, now fierce for cuts in public expenditure, only sanctioned a temporary grant of £500,000, not the £1,000,000 recommended. Wishing to throw the hospitals back on their own resources as quickly as possible, the Treasury also attached the condition that fresh money from voluntary sources must be raised pound for pound with the government grants. This was an idea vaguely mooted by the Fund earlier in the year, but as the Cave Committee had not recommended it the Fund now felt that it would lead to 'great injustices' and passed a resolution opposing it.[81]

The sum offered by the government was clearly inadequate to overcome hospital deficits in London, let alone in the country at large. The Cave Committee had taken the view that the wartime capitation grants for wounded soldiers 'in no way covered the full cost of maintenance'; and accepted the figure, provided by the Fund, of a £530,000 shortfall for London.[82] The government's offer, therefore, struck many voluntarists as niggardly and the strings attached insensitive. But it was said in defence of the government that the hospitals would not have raised so much from charitable donations during the war had the government's capitation grants been larger'.[83] However one interpreted that particular issue, it was clear that the government had no intention of bailing out the hospitals. Indeed, the means of financing them in 1921 were very much as they had been in 1913, only they cost almost three times as much.

In the post-war world, the voluntary hospitals felt threatened politically. The Labour Party, becoming a viable potential government, wanted more state control of medical provision. The Liberal Party, though ostensibly pro-voluntarist, expected the hospitals to pull themselves out of the crisis without much help from the State. So too did the Conservatives. That the crisis had been created by a breakdown in politics, not by a breakdown in the hospitals, carried little weight. To add to the dilemma, there was, as the Cave Committee reported, 'a crying need in many parts of the country for further hospital accommodation'.[84]

In this inauspicious environment, in which much was asked of the hospitals and little given, the Fund became more political and began to follow the machinations of parliamentary and extra-parliamentary politics with greater vigilance. In 1924, for example, Maynard and Somerleyton attended a Labour Party conference on the role of the State in hospital provision.[85] By then, the Fund had stepped up its own efforts to find permanent solutions to the problems of hospital provision compatible with the voluntary principle. But as ever, the issue was about money. How were the hospitals to pay off the debts of the past and how were they 'to pay their way in the future'?[86]

As the Fund constituted the Voluntary Hospitals Committee for London under the newly appointed Hospitals Commission, its responsibilities increased. The new work, along with much enlarged older work, resulted in a reconstitution of the committees in 1921, which came into force the following year. The Finance and Distribution Committees carried on much as before. The latter, however, now took over the work of the Convalescent Homes Committee, which, with relatively small sums to distribute, was disbanded. The Executive Committee became the Management Committee. Its Chairman, Lord Stuart of Wortley and its Vice-Chairman, Lord Somerleyton, were joined by the Chairman of the four other standing committees. Bringing together more often the heads of departments gave the Fund greater capacity to respond quickly to emergencies. Two new committees were added, both of which related to proposals coming out of Lord Cave's report. The Hospital Economy Committee, chaired by Leonard Cohen, was to deal with accounts, statistics, and schemes for hospital co-ordination.. The Revenue Committee, chaired by Sir Alan Anderson, was to oversee fund-raising and propaganda.[87]

The committee changes saw a reshuffling of officials and the appearance of several new faces. Most of the fresh recruits were already known to the Fund; those less familiar were carefully vetted for their commitment to the voluntary principle. When the Secretary of the London Labour Party asked for Labour Party representation in early 1922, the request was refused on the grounds that it was 'inadvisable' to have members who represented a political party; in any case, as Lord Somerleyton pointed out, the Fund already had Labour MPs on its Council.[88] Deaths or retirements necessitated several new appointments. Among the more significant losses were Lord Bessborough, the long-serving Chairman of the Executive Committee, who died in 1920; and Sir John Tweedy, Chairman of the Distribution Committee, who retired in 1921.

Tweedy's replacement was the formidable Sir Cooper Perry, who also sat on Lord Onslow's Voluntary Hospitals Commission. With a background of Eton, Cambridge, and Guy's Hospital, he had a swift intellect which he turned to his many passions, which included morbid anatomy, knitting, and motor cars. For a man who might have been 'a second Porson,* an Archbishop of Canterbury or a Lord Chancellor', it is perhaps surprising that he chose to be a hospital superintendent.[89] (He was Vice-Chancellor (1917–19) and later Principal of London University.) As an administrator, he was 'weighty and wise', though inclined to impatience. His colleagues in the Fund, as elsewhere, found him demanding, but easier to deal with when they expressed themselves in Horatian witticisms.

Arguably more important than any of the changes in the committees was Lord Mount Stephen's death, formally announced to the Council in December 1921. A letter from HM George V was read by Viscount Finlay, in the chair in the absence of the Prince of Wales. 'His Majesty desires to record his most grateful appreciation of the noble generosity ever displayed towards the Fund and to the Hospital World generally by his old and valued friend'.[90] At the same meeting, Lord Revelstoke read a communication from Lady Mount Stephen, which simply stated: 'I have been allowed to tell you by the executors that my husband has left the residue of his fortune to King Edward's Hospital Fund.'[91]

The news of Mount Stephen's legacy could not have come at a more

* Richard Porson (1759–1808) was Regius Professor of Greek at Cambridge and the most eminent Greek scholar of his day.

opportune moment, for as Revelstoke remarked, the Fund's finances, which Mount Stephen had done so much to build, had been depleted eighteen months earlier by the emergency distribution. Predictably, the bequest came in the form of Mount Stephen's beloved American securities, just the type of investments the Fund had jettisoned during the war.[92] Within a year, £581,354 was put on account from Mount Stephen's estate, a figure which rose to £815,000 upon the death of his wife in 1933 (even her diamond tiara was auctioned for the Fund's benefit). Thus Lord and Lady Mount Stephen's total contribution to the Fund, by gifts and legacy, came to £1,315,000.[93] This sum was about one-third of the Fund's total invested capital by 1933.[94] It would have met the costs of the twelve London teaching hospitals for about a year in the 1930s.

Nineteen twenty-two was a memorable year in the Fund's history for reasons apart from its financial success. The government made its temporary grants conditional on the adoption of the Uniform System of Accounts, which was an early example of government-led hospital co-ordination. As a result, the Fund published a simplified system of accounting for cottage hospitals.[95] The Fund's growing authority was also recognized by the London Regional Committee of the British Hospitals Association, on which more than 100 London hospitals were represented. It asked the Fund to draw up a scheme for a Combined Public Appeal, the object of which was to pay off hospital deficits by voluntary contributions. If sufficient, they would earn the government grants, which were set at £500,000 for the country at large and £250,000 for London. By January 1922 the constituent hospitals had been circulated and the London Regional Committee invited the Fund to press ahead with the scheme.

The omens were unfavourable. The Hospitals of London Combined Appeal was launched against the background of trade depression and high taxation. Moreover, the Prince of Wales was decidedly unenthusiastic about it. To date he had shown himself to be far less committed to the Fund than either his father or his grandfather. His attendance at meetings was sporadic, and, unsure of himself, he referred business submitted to him by the Fund back to his father.[96] His speeches to the Council were invariably written for him, and according to an eyewitness his handling of meetings was ineffectual.[97] He was in India when the decision was made to go ahead with the Combined Appeal. Given the advantages of bringing its royal President into its fund-raising campaigns, Lord Somerleyton cabled Edward to ask his permission to give his name to the appeal. The Fund wished to call it 'the Prince of Wales's Appeal' and to enlist Edward's participation in a grand dinner at the Mansion House upon his return to England.[98]

The Prince's response to Lord Somerleyton, cabled from India, was dispiriting, for he refused most of the Fund's requests with the excuse that he would be out of the country at the launch of the appeal.[99] This 'somewhat blunt refusal' was explained further in a telegram from Godfrey Thomas, who was on tour with the Prince, to Lord Stamfordham in April 1922. The Fund's officials probably never saw this cable; if they had, they would have been most disturbed. The Prince's reluctance to involve himself in the appeal, apart from allowing his name to appear in the literature as President of the Fund, was not due simply to the fact that he would be absent during part of the campaign. He also had grave doubts about its success. 'He is of opinion', wrote Thomas, 'that all who can afford to give money and are disposed to do so would have already contributed as far as their means permit to the touching appeals which every individual London Hospital has for so long been making, and cannot help thinking that this general appeal which is presumably last effort to save voluntary system is therefore foredoomed to failure.'[100]

At a crucial juncture, the Fund had a President who not only thought its appeal would fail but who had no confidence in the continuation of the voluntary system. This was an extraordinary departure for a member of the royal family, which had for so long been devoted to the voluntary hospitals. It is intriguing to speculate on how the Prince came by his views. He may have come under the influence of Lord Dawson, who was well-known to him and who became one of his physicians in 1923.[101] But it may have been simply another example of his cavalier rejection of the values of the older generation. In any case, the opinions expressed in the cable would have shocked his father, who followed the Combined Appeal with interest.

George V's active patronage of the Appeal helped considerably to make up for the Prince's lack of enthusiasm for it. His support reflected not only his own personal interest in the hospital cause, but also the advice of his courtiers. Lord Esher, who had superintended the Diamond Jubilee in 1897, was still an influential figure behind the scenes at the Palace. As he put it in a letter to Lord Stamfordham at the end of the war: 'the monarchy and its cost will have to be justified in the future eyes of a war-torn and hungry proletariat, endowed with a preponderance of voting power.'[102] Here was a rationale, reminiscent of Burdett's views in the 1890s, for increased royal participation in charity. The Combined Appeal may be seen as a further stage in the development of what in recent years has been called the 'welfare monarchy'.

In June 1922, just before his son's return, George V excused Edward in an open letter in support of the Appeal: 'I know that my son, the President, would have taken an active, personal part in this great effort had circumstances so permitted.'[103] It would appear that when Edward returned from India, his father had a word with him in regard to his duties, for he turned up at more than one fund-raising event. The success of the appeal obviously surprised the Prince.[104] It moderated any misgivings in the Fund about Edward's detachment from the campaign. Still, when the Combined

Appeal was over, there was a hint of hypocrisy in the remarks of Sir Alan Anderson, who said that the Prince had given it 'great personal assistance'.[105] By this time, some of the Fund's officials may have regretted the enormous powers and responsibilities granted to the President by the Act of Incorporation. As the critics had warned, it might not always be possible to have a President as competent and supportive as Edward VII or George V.

Under the direction of the King's Fund, the Combined Appeal brought together the Joint Council of the Order of St John and the British Red Cross, the Saturday and Sunday Funds, and the League of Mercy. Alexandra Rose Day, which the Fund previously had avoided on the grounds that it was given to 'self-advertisement', refused an invitation to co-operate.[106] Given the sensitivity of the King's Fund to the wishes of the hospitals, it agreed to mount the Appeal only on the condition that it receive a high level of support from the London hospitals themselves.[107] In the end, 120 out of the 127 of them rallied to the idea. Of the major hospitals, only the Charing Cross refused to join in, because it disagreed with the methods proposed and fully expected them to fail.[108] Under the direction of the Organising Committee, who appointed the experienced money-raiser E. S. Shrapnell-Smith as Director-General, the Fund launched the Combined Appeal in April 1922. It was to be the greatest mass campaign on behalf of hospitals in London's history.

The Fund drew on its vast money-making experience and, as ever, exploited its royal connections, even reluctant ones, with determination. Among its first acts was to write to the forty-seven members of the General Council to remind them of their responsibilities.[109] Special letters signed by Lord Revelstoke and Montagu Norman, the Governor of the Bank of England, were dispatched to the chairmen of banks, financial houses, insurance companies, brewers, and millers. As ever, it found a faithful ally in its Patron, George V. His letter in support (see Plate 5) had been solicited by Lord Somerleyton to give a boost to the appeal at a critical time, as well as to forestall criticism of the Prince of Wales's absence. It was published in facsimile in the newspapers and displayed on posters. Other letters were published from Queen Alexandra, the Chancellor of the Exchequer, and the Chief Rabbi. In June, Sir Alan Anderson solicited a letter from Lloyd George, which was used to 'put us up "several pegs" in the press and with the public'.[110]

Lloyd George's letter provided the Fund with telling propaganda. It was the voice of a politician whose traditional liberalism, with its inducements to self-help, had been revived by the slump in the economy. After paying tribute to the hospitals of London as 'great healing institutions' and 'pioneers of medical science' he added: 'This appeal is to the head as well as to the heart. If the voluntary system were to collapse, the State would necessarily have to step in. The flow of voluntary contributions would be checked. Endowments would be lost. The full cost would fall upon the heavily burdened taxpayer or ratepayer. But I feel confident that the voluntary system will be saved. We have inherited it. It has been our peculiar pride. It is our duty to hand it on unimpaired.'[111]

The Combined Appeal displayed the same entrepreneurial flair as the campaigns carried out by the Fund in 1897 and 1902.[112] The object was to reach all classes of the community, to impress on local residents that the hospitals were 'their' hospitals and that they relied on neighbourhood support. The devices used to extract contributions were as ingenious as ever, with new twists suited to the 1920s. That perennial ally and victim of royal charity, the gamebird, played its part; pheasants shot by the King sold for over £3 a brace. Smaller contributions came from the sale of eggs, organized on 'egg days', which had become popular during the war. But the notice seen in a country church, 'ladies are requested to lay their eggs reverently in the font' was not reported in London.[113] Prize-winning posters praising the hospitals bedecked railings and buildings all over the metropolis. Collecting-boxes adorned shops, hotels, and pubs. Fifty thousand women rattled tins on the streets. Cinemas, theatres, and music-halls hosted events, which included a 'Review of Revues' at the Hippodrome, attended by the King and Queen, and a film, *When Knighthood was in Flower*, attended by the Prince of Wales.

With greater originality, the Fund produced its own film, *When George was King*.[114] It celebrated the advances in hospital care by contrasting the smooth and efficient modern methods of treatment with the unscientific and haphazard methods available 100 years earlier. (The film betrays the Fund's indifference to GPs at the time.) In it we have one of the first examples of a film made for charitable purposes, a link between the Victorian lantern-lectures and today's promotional videos. It was made available to hospitals free of charge and shown in selected cinemas as a way of raising money, perhaps the earliest example of that particular fund-raising ploy. A later version included an appearance by Queen Alexandra; it was said to have brought in 100,000 new contributors to the hospitals.[115]

Another ingenious idea was the appearance of 'give to-day' in the skies over London, which may have been the first time sky-writing was used for charitable purposes. The Sports Branch of the Appeal sent 1,500 medical students down to Epsom on Derby Day to fleece the punters and organized competitions in tennis-, golf-, and wrestling-clubs. Here was the merging of philanthropy and sport, which has been used profitably by charities ever since. The Fund drew the line at baseball, however. In 1924, it refused to have its name associated with exhibition games between the New York Giants and the Chicago White Sox, despite an offer of 10 per cent of the gate receipts.[116]

Perhaps the most striking feature of the Combined Appeal was the success of its Educational Branch. Under the chairmanship of Lord Burnham, this auxiliary secured the co-operation of the Education Committee of the London County Council, the independent schools, and the universities. Principal events included an inter-schools cricket match at Lord's, two school flag-days, a display of physical fitness by children at the Albert Hall, and a display of intellectual fitness by lecturers at the London School of Economics. Virtually every school in London participated in one way or another. More than three million stamps bearing the arms and badges of the hospitals were sold to schoolchildren. In March 1923 the Prince of Wales, reinvigorated as the Fund's President, received a cheque for over £50,000 from the schools at County Hall.

The Combined Appeal eventually raised over £481,000, just under its target of £500,000, most of it made up of small contributions collected locally.[117] This was well in excess of the sum required to earn the government grant available for London's hospitals, and it was a clear sign of buoyancy in the voluntary sector. For its part, the Fund deemed the result 'satisfactory' given the prevailing economic circumstances. But it was just as interested in the propaganda value of reaching such 'a multitude of new potential subscribers'.[118] Not only had the general question of the voluntary hospitals been raised, but by circulating information and pictures of hospitals in each district the Fund impressed on residents the value of their local institutions. By means of raising money, the Fund also kept its own name before the public.

With its rich brew of commerce and entertainment, sport and education, the Combined Appeal was in step with social change. Where it was most effective it made the act of charity natural and diverting, a part of everyday life. The presence of members of the royal family at many of the events brough distinction, fashion, and enlarged receipts. At the same time it democratized the monarchy, for it brought members of the royal family into a wider social circle, which was just what advisers like Burdett and Lord Esher had always encouraged. All in all, the Appeal made no small contribution to that weaving of charitable traditions, visibly led by the royal family, into the life of the community. No other contemporary institution did more to perpetuate or to enliven these distinctive traditions than the Fund. By astute campaigning it perennially reminded the public of the need for personal service and the leading role of the monarchy, which it saw as the vanguard of the proletariat. In later years the Combined Appeal would be seen as a model charitable campaign.[119] Looking back, the Fund's officials saw it as the high point in the institution's inter-war activities.

The bulk of the money raised by the Combined Appeal was distributed to the co-operating hospitals, based on the number of occupied beds and out-patient attendances and on the evidence of their efficiency and financial need.

Along with the grants made by the government, the money proved a life-line to many institutions. So too did the ordinary distribution of the Fund, which reached £233,000 in 1923 and 1924. In 1924 the King congratulated the Fund on its financial success, which, as he put it, had brought 'a general improvement in the position of the hospitals'. A letter signed by the Prince of Wales said that the gap between hospital income and expenditure was 'closing year by year', though he reminded the Council that 'this does not mean that the hospitals and the public can go to sleep in the belief that everything will come right of itself'.[120]

By the mid-1920s voluntary contributions in London appear to have been picking up in the charitable sector.[121] This was the case in the hospital world, where controls on expenditure also reduced deficits. Voluntary gifts, combined with interest on investments, hovered around 66 per cent of the total ordinary income of all London's voluntary hospitals in the early 1920s. But these figures did not include legacies or the proceeds of the special distributions such as the Combined Appeal, which counted as extraordinary income. In 1924, for example, voluntary gifts accounted for precisely 66 per cent of total ordinary income of 118 London hospitals, which came to £2,412,840. Payments from patients, which were increasingly significant, contributed 23.8 per cent, public authorities under 9.5 per cent. But looking at total general fund income, which included legacies and special grants, the voluntary contribution rose to 72 per cent in 1924.[122]

Of course, the sources of the different hospitals' income varied widely. At St Bartholomew's, Guy's and St Thomas's investment income predominated. Subscriptions and donations were higher in the children's hospitals. The consumption and lying-in hospitals, with their particular medical responsibilities, received more from the public authorities. However they made up their income, 64 of the 118 institutions surveyed by the king's Fund in 1924 had a surplus. Total deficits were only one-quarter of the figures for 1920, while the number of beds available in London had risen from 12,587 in 1920 to 13,460 four years later. The Fund summarized the statistics by saying that 'rapid progress towards financial stability is being made by the Hospitals taken in the aggregate, while taken individually the numbers making progress show a steady improvement'.[123]

The Fund's statistics showed that the post-war hospital crisis was over, and with industrial production back to pre-war levels and trade improving, the future looked brighter. So much brighter that the Prince of Wales could say at a special meeting of the Fund's Council in July 1924, 'I wonder if there is any one who still thinks the Voluntary Hospital system is dead, or dying.'[124] Presumably he no longer did. Indeed, in his speech he looked forward to hospital expansion. A few institutions continued to have financial worries, he admitted, but income was increasing from various quarters. The Fund, which had had to act as a restraining force in the past, was now in favour of extension schemes and additional accommodation. This, he remarked, 'is life—and very vigorous life. More than that, it is growth.'[125]

The Onslow Commission, which reported on voluntary hospital accommodation in 1925, also detected 'a distinct improvement' in hospital affairs: 'the amount of money which has been raised for hospital extensions is a gratifying proof—if proof were needed—of the vitality of the voluntary system and of its hold upon the people in this country'.[126] Despite these sentiments, the Commission called for further government grants toward capital expenditure on hospital extensions, which it felt could be given without prejudicing the voluntary principle. It warned that failure to meet the nation's hospital needs entailed the risk of ultimate liability falling upon public funds.[127] The government preferred to be told about the vitality of the voluntary system and did not accept any further responsibility to prop it up with additional grants. The Onslow Commission was disbanded in 1928.

The mid-1920s thus saw the reorganized Fund in expansive mood. Fortuitously, legacies worth £255,000 from John Wells, a British-born silver-trader based in New York, and his wife Florence, made it possible for the Fund to extend its area of operations in 1924 to 11 miles around St Paul's. As a consequence, the number of hospitals applying for grants rose from 118 in 1924 to 133 the following year.[128] The Fund had recommended the provision of 2,000 additional beds in London to the Onslow Commission.[129] As part of its own contribution to this aim, it allocated the Wells bequests to extension schemes and the provision of additional accommodation, including accommodation for accident cases. Among the beneficiaries of this special distribution were the Miller Hospital, which received £16,000 for additional beds and a nurses' home, and the Middlesex Hospital, which received £20,000 for a reconstruction scheme. In 1927 alone, the Fund supported the building of three new hospitals and the rebuilding of four others on new sites.[130]

Increasingly, the Fund turned its attentions to producing what it called 'permanent remedies' for the preservation of the voluntary hospitals. The Cave Committee recommendations, which the Fund had helped to shape, gave it a reforming agenda and various new functions. One recommendation was the adoption of further measures to reduce hospital expenditure, which the Fund pursued through its new Hospital Economy Committee. As part of its policy it added an analysis of the sources of individual hospital income to its annual statistics. Increasingly attuned to and in touch with government thinking, the Fund also pursued Lord Cave's recommendations to seek relief in respect of income tax on employers' contributions, death duties on legacies, and income tax on income from residuary bequests not paid within a year. It received a concession from the Chancellor of the Exchequer on the latter in

1922.[131] Not forgetting the contribution of personnel to efficient hospital management, it launched a contributory Federated Superannuation Scheme for Nurses and Hospital Officers in 1928.[132]

Lord Cave's committee had laid particular stress on the development of mass contributions as a way forward for the voluntary hospitals. The Fund enthusiastically endorsed this recommendation. After all, it gave a government seal of approval to the Fund's established practices. By its success in reaching into working-class homes and neighbourhoods, the Combined Appeal stimulated further schemes. Some of them were more notable than others. A campaign to extract subscriptions from domestic servants, which was connected with the growing influence of women in the Fund, disappointed. More productive was the idea of collecting regular contributions from prospective patients as a kind of insurance or partial patient's payment in advance.

The war and the consequent hospital crisis concentrated the mind of the Fund on contributory schemes which could be reconciled with the continuation of voluntary hospital management. It found particular scope for increasing hospital income from weekly contributions out of wages, supplemented by the co-operation of employers. The Cave Committee, which looked at several schemes already in operation in various parts of the country, endorsed the idea.[133] Invited to develop a scheme by the London Regional Committee of the British Hospitals Association, the Fund devised the Hospital Saving Association in 1922. A notable example of the voluntary sector's ability to identify and to satisfy a market in health provision, it was to become the largest scheme of its type in the country.[134]

As a charity whose first responsibility lay with the poorest patients, the Fund decided against operating the Hospital Saving Association itself. Instead it supported an independent institution, which was headed by one of the Fund's Honorary Secretaries, Sir Alan Anderson, and composed of representatives of hospitals, contributors, and the general community. The plan was designed to create a new kind of personal tie between the hospitals and wage-earners who valued a combination of personal independence and mutual aid.[135] It was anticipated that people would subscribe without the intention of taking up the benefits, thereby giving emphasis to the charitable element in the scheme. The object was for contributors to give freely while in health 'bearing in mind that if they do not suffer themselves what they are giving will go to help those who do suffer'.[136] Anyone earning less than £6 a week could join. In exchange for a subscription of 3d. a week, the scheme offered free hospital treatment *as a privilege, not as a right*.

The Hospital Saving Association was not universally admired. The BMA thought the scheme antagonistic to the interests of general practitioners, for it did not require a subscriber to visit his doctor before turning up at a hospital. The Labour Party argued that the scheme would favour 'queue-barging' paying patients at the expense of poorer people who could not afford insurance.[137] There were also reservations in the charitable establishment, because it was thought that successful provident-schemes might result in a reduction in ordinary voluntary subscriptions. By 1924, however, there were 62,000 contributors to the HSA, a figure which rose to 650,000 in 1929.[138]

Although there were 300 contributory schemes operating in the country by 1930, we should not exaggerate their financial importance to the hospitals. According to the King's Fund's statistics for 1929, receipts from patients and societies came to just over 26 per cent of the total general fund income of the 140 London voluntary hospitals. In the twelve general hospitals with medical schools the figure was 21.3 per cent.[139] These figures included payments from uninsured better-off patients in pay-beds as well as the insured in ordinary beds. Payments from public authorities contributed under 7 per cent, which was less than in 1924. Despite a decline in interest on investments, voluntary sources provided 67 per cent of the general fund income of the London hospitals in 1929.[140] Though down from 72 per cent in 1924, this figure was impressive given that the total general fund income of London's voluntary hospitals had risen by a quarter in those five years, to stand at over £3,600,000.[141] It was all the more impressive when seen against the background of the 1929 crash, which affected disposable income and hospital endowments alike.

These figures are further evidence of the resilience of voluntary traditions in the aftermath of the First World War. Contrary to received opinion, the voluntary hospitals were not in perpetual crisis, let alone terminal decline, in the inter-war years, or only salvaged by patients' payments. It is facile to say that in the 1920s the finances of the voluntary hospitals were rescued largely by patients, or that 'by 1924 no distinguishing characteristic of a voluntary hospital could be found'.[142] The hospitals were undergoing changes in the way they were financed, and they were taking on a new role in dealing with larger numbers of paying patients. Charity could not pay for the whole work of the hospitals (it rarely had), but as the Fund was at pains to point out, it continued to pay for millions of poor patients who could not afford the cost of hospital care. In addition, charitable contributions continued to pay for the treatment of thousands of insured patients without any financial support from approved societies.[143]

Just what constituted a voluntary hospital was less certain after the First World War, as pressures from within and without took their toll. But clearly, it was not thought necessary than an institution receive *all* its income from charitable sources. The Cave Committee had studiously avoided a definition. The Voluntary Hospital Commission vouchsafed a rather nebulous one. A King's Fund memorandum of 1921 took a more rigorous, traditional view, which not all hospital managers would have fully endorsed. Specifically, it stipulated that to qualify as a voluntary hospital an institution must be *mainly* supported by charitable subscriptions or endowments; that its staff must consist of honorary physicians and surgeons who render gratuitous service to patients; that it must admit destitute patients without charge; and that it must be managed by a board of unpaid governors who were independent of state or municipal control.[144]

The Fund had never taken the view that the charitable status of hospitals was incompatible with patients' payments, as long as they were kept within bounds. In response to the growing demand from the middle classes, it began to encourage a limited expansion of pay-beds for better-off patients and further recommended the organization of a mutual insurance scheme to meet their medical costs. (National Insurance and Hospital Saving Association patients, whose incomes were usually below £300 a year, were in ordinary beds.) An investigation published in 1928 by the Fund's special Pay Beds Committee, chaired by Viscount Hambledon, found that eighty of London's 136 voluntary hospitals had pay-beds. Their total number came to 1,005, which constituted about 7 per cent of the nearly 16,000 beds available in London.[145] The Fund proposed raising the number of pay-beds by another 900, but wished to be satisfied that they did not take accommodation away from ordinary patients and that the charges for them were sufficient to yield a profit that could be used to benefit the sick poor.[146]

The report of the Pay Beds Committee provided further evidence of the elasticity and business acumen in the voluntary sector. These features were particularly marked in the Fund. Richly endowed with successful business-men, it applied their mentality to welfare provision. Nor was it slow to find a rationale for shifts in policy which it thought necessary to keep pace with London's changing health-needs. The Fund justified pay-beds on the grounds that a mix of patients from different classes increased the usefulness and prestige of the hospitals. Furthermore, it saw great advantage in people of various backgrounds having personal experience of the part they played in the advancement of medical science and treatment. 'This experience', the report of the Pay Beds Committee concluded, 'would be a further stage in the movement by which the Voluntary Hospital system is already becoming largely a co-operative effort in which all classes of the community, including the Hospital patients themselves, combine, as their means permit, to provide Hospital services which produce benefits for all classes'.[147]

Looking back on hospital provision between the wars commentators have tended to see the increased power of paying patients as incompatible with the voluntary system of hospital management. Preoccupied with the view that control of the hospitals was passing to patients, they have rather overlooked the degree to which it was passing into the hands of the central agencies. This was especially apparent in London, where the King's Fund was in the ascendancy. Its reputation extended well beyond the capital, where attempts were made to set up institutions modelled on it.[148] (The Emperor of Japan instigated a scheme of 'charitable organisation' for the sick poor in 1911, which appears to have been based on the King's Fund.)[149] Increasingly, British provincial hospitals regretted that they had no equivalent organization to look to for sympathy and assistance.[150] (The Nuffield Provincial Hospitals Trust was not set up until 1939.) They were well aware that revenues from charitable gifts and investments in the provinces had fallen below London levels in the early decades of the century.[151]

Paradoxically, the Fund's own financial contribution to the London hospitals was less in percentage terms in 1930 than in 1910.[152] Yet its influence was greater, largely because the hospitals it served perceived, rightly or wrongly, that the threat to the voluntary system was more menacing. Its financial assistance and guidance were, as always, welcome; but increasingly it was seen as the premier voice in the propaganda war to save the hospitals from state control. As Guy's superintendent Herbert Eason put it in 1925, every hospital admired the Fund because 'they still treat us as self-governing units, with idiosyncracies of our own, peculiar constitutions and varying administrations, and that is the great contrast between the King's Fund and a government department, which treats one and all as stereotyped organisms, who are judged by figures and figures alone'.[153]

5

Embattled in the 1930s

RELATIONS between philanthropic institutions and the State remained fitful in the 1930s. The timidity of successive governments in tackling problems of health and unemployment gave impetus to voluntary initiatives, which were often in advance of government thinking. Calls for a more professional relationship between voluntary and public bodies, advocated by the 'organizing' charities themselves, grew stronger. But as the decade progressed, there was growing disquiet among philanthropists at the mounting pressures for charities to sacrifice their independence in favour of a more intimate partnership with the State. In areas such as infant welfare and family planning, this partnership, sometimes called the 'new philanthropy', advanced. The voluntary hospitals, for their part, were much more sensitive about their independence. With ancient traditions and valuable properties, the hospitals had more to lose from government controls than most charities. They also served a powerful and vocal medical profession.

The King's Fund presented the case of the London hospitals to the government and the public. As a result of the depression and the associated political uncertainty, it decided to expand its activities and propaganda. The aggregate income of London's voluntary hospitals actually showed a slight improvement after 1929, yet many individual hospitals were hard hit.[1] The Fund was well placed to offer them assistance, and both hospital doctors and administrators broadly welcomed its initiatives. Its self-electing character limited its power in a democratic age but gave it the capacity to react quickly and coherently to events. Its cautiously invested capital protected it from the ravages of the depression and the whims of subscribers. Given the occasional royal fillip, its fund-raising also flourished, and made possible an increase in grants, which rose to over £300,000 a year in 1932.

The Fund also benefited from the post-war charitable trend towards large-scale, secular institutions. Perhaps the growth of government bureaucracy encouraged largeness of scale in those charities which had contacts with the State or saw the State as a rival. But the larger an institution the more likely it was to distance individual philanthropists from beneficiaries and thus undermine those much-heralded traditions of personal service. Still, a criticism of charitable societies was that they were often too small and too isolated to be effective. Larger institutions, which played down doctrinal differences, were better able to call on broad public support and to work with other agencies. In these respects, as in its financial stability, the Fund was in a stronger position than most of the hospitals it aided.

As an 'organizing' charity, the Fund was itself an expression of that fashion for rational planning in the voluntary sector that dated back to the nineteenth century. In practice this meant it sought greater hospital co-ordination as a means of encouraging self-help. But rational planning led others to different solutions, particularly state intervention and control. In the Labour movement, collectivist ideals were gaining an ascendancy over co-operative traditions. This trend was invigorated by the crisis in capitalism after 1929 and by the growing power of middle-class intellectuals within the Labour Party. Though few noticed it, state collectivists and voluntarists of the co-ordinating school had much in common. Both groups disliked waste and shared the technocratic mentality, with its faith in statistics and accountancy. Yet institutional allegiances and ideological differences kept them well apart.

Collectivists, who distrusted private enterprise, sought unity in social life, and were thus inclined to favour coercive forms of organization. They looked at charitable hospitals in the aggregate, and they saw little beyond inefficiency and chaos. Voluntarists, who may be seen as the welfare equivalents of Victorian entrepreneurs, distrusted regulation and flourished in diversity. Attuned to the particular, they delighted in the efficiency of individual institutions, which they saw as 'living societies' each with their own histories and practices. At bottom, it was the voluntary sector's respect for tradition that was its most distinguishing characteristic. Collectivists, on the other hand, were steeped in a philosophy that assumed the inevitable triumph of their programme. There was, in fact, nothing inevitable about the future shape of the nation's hospital provision, but the belief that history was moving in their direction encouraged collectivists to disregard traditional practices in favour of root-and-branch reform.

The two camps held out such different solutions to welfare provision because they viewed social problems from radically different perspectives. Voluntarists, even those conscious of the needs of national efficiency, continued to see issues of health and welfare in individual, familial, or local terms, or in terms of an urban crisis best resolved by personal discretion and good neighbourliness. The King's Fund, for example, focused on London and saw its health needs best remedied by locally run hospitals supported by those who used their services. But charities, fragmented and often pulling in different directions, were not well-placed to investigate the interrelationship of social ills. Just as they were reforming themselves along the lines approved by societies like the Fund, social scientists were changing peoples' assumptions about sickness, poverty, and old age. This put voluntarists on the defensive in the intellectual debate on health and welfare. So too did the trend towards government absorption of erstwhile individual responsibility brought about by social legislation. In a society in which expectations were becoming more egalitarian, philanthropists found their position increasingly ambiguous.

Philanthropy's socialist critics had a more rarefied and politically dynamic understanding of health and welfare. They not only spoke of the abolition of distress but identified a class, the bourgeoisie, who were responsible for exacerbating social tensions. This message was especially seductive to middle-class intellectuals, alienated by the persistence of social divisions in a political democracy, who were disillusioned with liberalism after the First World War. In socialist analyses, poverty and disease were invariably bound up with complex social and economic factors. The causes of poverty, which had marked implications for health, were to be found in the capitalist social structure, not simply in individual or familial circumstances. The remedy thus required was something much more comprehensive than was on offer from parochial charities with their inducements to self-help. The argument that only the State could conquer poverty and enlarge human freedom would prove useful to politicians and civil servants of any political persuasion who wished to expand their authority in the fields of health and welfare.

Believing as they did in the efficacy of legislation and centralized bureaucracy, collectivists dismissed charity, with its addiction to local, individualist measures, as irrelevant, the residue of a discredited Victorian liberalism which would be swept aside by state action. Richard Crossman, Labour Secretary of State for Health and the Social Services in the 1960s, remembered the left-wing Labour view of inter-war philanthropy as an 'odious expression of social oligarchy and churchy bourgeois attitudes. We detested voluntary hospitals maintained by flag days.'[2] That charities worked within the existing social structure made them anathema to their more hostile critics, who assumed that because philanthropists accepted social divisions, they necessarily approved of them. When voluntarists initiated a variety of self-help schemes to combat unemployment in 1932, socialists denounced them for deviously buying off the unemployed.[3]

Socialist propagandists preached a gospel of human perfectability. Unencumbered by the Christian belief that poverty was ineradicable, they assumed that their economic explanations of the causes of social distress would lead to its elimination. All that was needed was the will of government and the right financial arrangements. In their writings they helped to create the view that the State, and only the State, could transform society. Crossman's early essays, later brought together under the title *Planning for*

Freedom (1965), were an example of the genre. With a strong paternalistic
streak, which exceeded that of the philanthropists whose views they
disavowed, Labour's collectivist wing took it for granted that the poor
themselves wished for an extension of statutory provision and that taxpayers
would happily pay for it. Given a weak and divided Labour Party, they made
little political headway in the 1930s, but the expectations they aroused would
place an enormous burden on later governments, not least in the management
of the health services, and would form an ineradicable part of the prevailing
climate of British opinion in the second half of the twentieth century.

Voluntarists in the 1920s and 1930s saw proposals for an extension of state
power against a particular, and to them sinister, background. For a generation,
memories of the First World War and its consequences coloured their
perceptions of the State and deepened their anxiety about its pretensions.
While collectivists saw the nation's emergency mobilization of resources in
1914–18 as rational and progressive, voluntarists were inclined to see it as a
muddle with dangerous implications. To some of them, especially those of a
religious disposition, it aroused the bogey of godless Russian communism.
There was also the bogey of the German state. Germany, declared one of the
League of Mercy's wartime propagandists, the Reverend R. J. Campbell, was
a 'moral monster . . . intent only upon its own aggrandisement'. In Britain, he
exclaimed, the State 'must never be allowed to supersede or absorb into itself
individual responsibility and voluntary effort'.[4]

During the inter-war years the Fund and the voluntary hospitals
campaigned in the specific context of a worrying international climate and the
emergence of socialism at home as a political force. For propaganda reasons
they tended to overstate the threat from Labour. If anything, they were more
agitated by the drift of *ad hoc* liberal social legislation, which, without
intending to do so, undermined their interests and traditions. The Fund's
long-standing Councillor Sir William Collins, who was inclined to see a red
under every hospital bed, lamented that voluntary hospital provision had come
to harm 'half unconsciously, as the result of a series of legislative enactments,
nearly all making in one direction, but as is our wont in this country without
any very clear preconception of the end in view, and often accompanied by
ingenuous disavowals of any socialistic trend on the part of the authors of the
legislation in question.'[5]

In the long term, perhaps the most damaging result of piecemeal social
legislation to the voluntary cause was that it enlarged the public sector
bureaucracy. The number of established civil servants grew from 168,000 in
1914 to 387,000 in 1939.[6] By the outbreak of the Second World War nearly
10 per cent of the working population was employed in the public sector, most
of them men.[7] The expansion in the number of public employees was to a

large extent accounted for by the growth in the welfare services, activities traditionally monopolized by the charitable sector. State welfare workers had many of the same ends in mind as voluntarists, and they often worked in partnership with them. But as their strength and numbers grew, their disregard for the voluntary sector increased, a trend not unconnected with their attitudes toward the ever growing number of women in charity.[8] The tendency of health and welfare departments in local and central goverment to dismiss perceptions of social need that differed from their own was to become deeply ingrained.

In the inter-war years, the Local Government Act (1929) did more to unsettle relations between the voluntary and public hospital sectors than any other single piece of legislation. Its aim was to dismantle the administrative structure of the old Poor Law system and bring Poor Law infirmaries and fever hospitals into line with municipal provision under the control of elected local authorities. It did not question the efficiency of the voluntary hospitals, but it created an entirely different set of circumstances from those which obtained previously in regard to hospital provision. Given the political will, it had the potential to alter dramatically the nation's hospital services. The details of the legislation have been discussed elsewhere.[9] But to the King's Fund and its allies, it was seen as yet another disturbing piece of legislation.

As with the National Insurance Act, the Local Government Bill was drawn up by another professed friend of the charitable hospitals, in this case the Conservative Minister of Health, Neville Chamberlain. The Fund had been monitoring Chamberlain's speeches on health provision since 1925 and had sent a deputation to see him in 1928.[10] It took him at his word when he said he had no desire to undermine the voluntary hospitals. But as Lord Hailsham (1872–1950), the Lord Chancellor and a member of the Fund's Council, said at the Distribution Committee meeting in December 1928, the transfer of the infirmaries to county council control was the 'biggest of all the problems with which the King's Fund and the Voluntary Hospitals are faced at the present moment'.[11] These worries increased soon after the passage of the Act, for a Labour government came to power charged with implementing the legislation.

Voluntarists feared that if the local authorities were given the wherewithal to create competitive institutions, complete with well-paid physicians and surgeons, the outcome could be disastrous for charitable provision.[12] The voluntary hospitals had a vested interest in state institutions continuing to suffer from the stigma of the Poor Law. An erosion of the stigma and an injection of cash into the municipal system would remove differences between the two sectors and increase the pressures for merger. The Fund's officials discovered at their meeting with Chamberlain that he was in favour of greater co-ordination, to which they were themselves committed, at least theoretically.

But with a minority of the hospital beds in Britain, the voluntary hospital might be at a grave disadvantage, should co-ordination lead to homogenization.[13]

The Cave Committee had recommended greater co-ordination between the municipal and voluntary hospital sectors. Section 13 of the Local Government Act, which was moved in the House of Lords by Lord Dawson, required local authorities to consult with representatives of the voluntary hospitals in planning their services. It did not, however, oblige the voluntary hospitals to consult the local authorities when they, in their turn, proposed to expand their services. The reason for this discrepancy was that the framers of the Act wished to safeguard the rate-payers while giving the voluntary hospitals some assurance 'that they would not be wiped out by an arbitrary use of the power of the purse'.[14] The essence of the charitable system resided in the independence of its constituent parts. Central control would mean their demise. On the other hand, it was widely believed that a failure to act in co-ordination with the municipal sector would bring about the same result. It was now more imperative for the voluntary hospitals to agree a strategy and to strengthen their machinery for consultation.[15]

As the leading central agency representing London's voluntary hospitals, the Fund stood to benefit from concerted action. But it preferred to work behind the scenes. In 1928 it had set up a special Local Government Bill Committee to lobby the Ministry of Health.[16] It had a distinguished membership, which included Viscount Knutsford, now attached to the Fund again, Sir John Rose Bradford, President of the Royal College of Physicians, Sir Cooper Perry, and later Lord Dawson. It was chaired by J. H. Whitley, a Liberal MP who had formerly chaired the committee on relations between employers and employed which recommended joint consultative machinery known by his name. Along with the teaching hospitals and the London Regional Committee of the British Hospitals Association, the Committee worked out a scheme of hospital representation for the purposes of consultation with the London County Council. The result was the setting-up of the London Voluntary Hospitals Committee, which was elected to consult with the LCC. The Fund thus ceased to have any direct responsibility in connection with the Local Government Act, but it provided staff assistance and information to the London Voluntary Hospitals Committee.[17]

In the meantime, the Fund produced a memorandum, signed by Whitley, on the future relations between the voluntary and municipal hospitals under the new legislation.[18] It opened with a comprehensive defence of the voluntary system as the standard-bearer of good practice and advanced research. It paid especial tribute to the distinctive voluntary hospital spirit, whose origins it saw in the spontaneous desire of individuals to give personal service to the sick poor. But it did not forget to mention examples of co-ordination already in practice between the voluntary and public hospitals, which included the sharing of facilites and local authority grants to voluntary hospitals for the accommodation of special classes of patients. Tellingly, the examples cited turned on the different functions of the respective systems. In the Fund's view, if the two systems treated similar patients with comparable facilities they would soon be seen to be in competition.

For the history of philanthropy the Fund's memorandum was a revealing document. Developing the arguments put forward earlier in the Pay Beds Committee report, it depicted the voluntary hospital as having evolved from the 'merely personal charity' of rich benefactors into 'a great community service', a co-operative effort by all classes to supply a service of benefit to everyone. Here we can detect the usefulness of the Fund's long-standing policy of raising funds from the poorer classes, which it saw as essential to combat state socialism and to keep charity up to date with changes in social life. Intriguingly, such a policy was in tune with the co-operative traditions in the Labour movement. Be that as it may, the voluntary community element was described as particularly favourable to hospital service. It gave the freest possible scope for the work of doctors, nurses, and administrators, on which the well-being of patients depended; and it encouraged elasticity in the development of new methods at each separate hospital, which was difficult to reproduce in any centrally organized service controlled by an official hierarchy.

With its distinctive traditions, the voluntary hospital had set 'the highest standard of medical and surgical work', stated the Fund's memorandum.[19] Without such standards before them, the Poor Law infirmaries would not have made the recent improvements in their own sphere. 'An efficient and adequate hospital service can be created', the document concluded, 'not by converting the voluntary hospitals into official institutions, but by developing municipal hospitals in cooperation with, and under the influence of, a vigorous voluntary hospital system.'[20] Such opinions delighted pro-voluntarists, though not advocates of municipalization. Apart from the closer links in the training of nurses and in medical education, the Fund did not see much immediate scope for co-ordination with rate-aided services. On the contrary, it gave the impression that working out effective guidelines for co-operation and differentiation would be difficult enough. Clearly, the Fund and the hospitals it represented did not wish to go down the path of co-ordinating services if it threatened their independence.

Perhaps negotiations to co-ordinate London's hospital services would have been more productive had the London County Council dealt directly with the King's Fund rather than with the more cumbersome London Voluntary Hospitals Committee.[21] This was the view of Sir Frederick Menzies, the County Council's Medical Officer of Health, who led the LCC's delegation.

Informally, he met officials of the Fund, who had a high regard for his abilities. In turn, he understood the worries of the voluntary hospitals, though he could not be said to sympathize with them. But whoever sat across the table, negotiations between the two sides were never likely to get very far given the interests at stake. The Fund, for its part, sought precision on what co-operation entailed and was highly sensitive to detail. When it saw LCC documents in which the phrase 'homogeneous services' appeared, it scratched this out and replaced it with the words 'co-ordinated services'.[22]

Maynard and the Fund's Assistant Secretary, Ives, took a friendly but wary line in their dealings with the London County Council. Maynard in particular was unhappy with what he saw as government pressure being put on the voluntary hospitals. But preferring the statistical side of his work, he let Ives deal with the LCC. Ives discovered for himself what Eason had said in a letter to the Fund, that Menzies was 'extremely touchy' and that the LCC was ready to stand on its dignity 'at the slightest provocation'.[23] As Secretary to the London Voluntary Hospitals Committee, chaired by the President of the Royal Free Hospital, Lord Riddell, Ives found Menzies 'dictatorial' and his committee obsessed with upholding its own position.[24] For their part, the LCC delegates disliked Riddell and resented the requirement that they had to consult privileged and obstructive voluntary hospitals in the first place. It struck Ives as unpromising that when the two sides first met, the LCC officials sat themselves on a dais from which they could look down on the members of the London Voluntary Hospitals Committee.[25]

The two bodies kept up a display of cordiality in public while fighting their respective corners. Relations between representatives of the two systems were less fraught in the provinces, for those responsible for the voluntary hospitals more often had links with the local authorities. In a few cities, including Liverpool and Manchester, there was extensive co-operation.[26] In London, reform was arguably most notable in medical education, where the sharing of facilities became more common; but the sheer scale of co-ordinating over 100 independent institutions with the LCC, a single centralized body, created enormous obstacles. There was also the issue of co-ordination within the two systems. If anything, the public system was more complex and disorganized than the voluntary system. By 1932 in London, the LCC had to co-opt 12,500 voluntary workers to assist in the management of its hospitals and mental homes, a practice which brought wry amusement to voluntarists. Lord Riddell asked whether it was not desirable for the local authorities to make greater use of the voluntary hospital services.[27]

The King's Fund had a particular interest in the negotiations when they dealt with issues such as LCC grants to voluntary hospitals. It preferred that they be given for specific purposes and not for general maintenance.[28] On the wider issues, it wished to be seen as a peacemaker mediating between the two sectors. But it was far from unbiased. To the voluntary hospitals it recommended a sacrifice of a little of their independence for the sake of presenting a common front. But its first impulse was to take every opportunity to remind the LCC of the many virtues of the voluntary system and to restrain it from rushing ahead without regard to the indirect consequences which its actions might have on the voluntary hospitals.[29] That the LCC's style of management was centralist did not endear it to the Fund.

In common with the propagandists for municipalization, the Fund rather exaggerated the potential of the local authorities to challenge the charitable hospitals.[30] (Without royal patronage municipal institutions were at a significant disadvantage in attracting loyal support.) Yet it found the spectre of municipalization useful in extracting money from its traditional subscribers.[31] Against the background of trade depression and the haphazard system of local government, the rationalization of municipal hospital services was unlikely to advance very quickly. The power of local health authorities was on the rise, but ten years after the passage of the Local Government Act, the results were disappointing. Between 1930 and 1939, the LCC planned only one new hospital.[32] Moreover, the stigma of the Poor Law, though diminished, persisted.

The Fund and its allies, for all their apparent willingness to co-operate with the local authorities, had an interest in the continuation of the ethos of the Poor Law. They remained the willing captives of a Victorian mentality in regard to medical provision, with its division of responsibilities between the two hospital sectors. In particular, the public provision of beds for fever patients and the chronically ill had long taken the pressure off voluntary institutions. For their part, the London County Council and its allies benefited from voluntary provision, particularly its teaching and research. Like partners in a less-than-happy marriage, by turns tolerant and censorious, municipalists and voluntarists depended on each other for their own survival more than they liked to admit.

At the time the Local Government Act was causing the Fund alarm, it was preoccupied elsewhere. The King's near-fatal blood-poisoning, contracted in November 1928, overshadowed activities in 1929. For an institution so long associated with George V, and so dependent on his patronage, his recovery was a cause of especial celebration. And any celebration to do with royalty meant an opportunity to raise money. Across the country spontaneous appeals sprang up in the spring of 1929, which altogether raised about £700,000 for charity.[33] The Fund was the first in the field with its Thank-Offering for the King's Recovery. Organized by Somerleyton and his fellow Honorary Secretary, Harold Wernher, it was initiated by George Roberts, a wealthy resident of Wimbledon who served on the Fund's Council and Revenue Committee.

Roberts had for some time wanted to make an anonymous contribution to the Fund, but on the condition that it should trigger donations from others.[34] The announcement of the King's convalescence offered just the occasion which could be exploited on the Fund's behalf, and Roberts, using the name 'Audax', promised £105,000 to start it off.[35] (He received a knighthood in the New Year's Honours List in 1931 for his contribution.) The Fund raised an additional £152,000 by a variety of devices, which included the sale of post-card photographs of the King. By 1930, it was able to award £155,000 over and above the normal distribution, in respect of seventy-one hospital applications, most of them for extensions or improvements. The larger grants included £14,000 for the reconstruction of the Middlesex Hospital, £12,000 to reduce the deficit on an extension to the Miller General Hospital, and £10,000 for the first stage of the new King George Hospital in Ilford.[36]

When the Fund was putting together its thank-offering campaign, it discovered that *The Times* was organizing an appeal on behalf of the National Radium Trust. As it was undesirable to have so many appeals in competition, the Radium Trust and the Fund joined forces under the umbrella of the thank-offering campaign. The King's Fund had a long-standing interest in radium. Edward VII had believed it to be *the* cure for cancer after he underwent radium treatment for an ulcer on his nose in 1906. Aware of the work of the Radium Institute in Paris, he had pressed Sir Ernest Cassel and Lord Iveagh to found a similar centre in London.[37] Thanks to their generosity the Radium Institute in Portland Place opened in 1911.[38] True to the enthusiasms of its founder, the Fund kept an eye on the Radium Institute, and paid particular attention to radium supply, an issue in which, it noted in 1914, the government had little interest.[39]

Hospital appeals for radium were commonplace before 1914, but the First World War stimulated radium therapy and thus heightened interest in radium supply. The Medical Research Committee, which had been set up by the government in 1913, contributed radium used in the war to hospitals. Having changed its name to the Medical Research Council (MRC), it contributed funds for cancer research and radiology in the early 1920s. The British Empire Cancer Campaign, founded in 1923, also contributed money for the purchase of radium, but it was dogged by the desire of the MRC to control all medical research and by competition from the Imperial Cancer Research Fund. No single agency, whether government or voluntary, was ever likely to defeat cancer on its own. In regard to radium, the government promised £100,000 for further purchases in 1929, if a matching sum could be raised by charity.[40]

It was about this time that the Fund became directly involved, largely because of a gift from Sir Otto Beit, the brother of the Jewish mining-financier Alfred Beit. Sir Otto was convinced of the curative value of radium and the inadequacy of supplies in London. He gave the Fund £50,000 for the purchase of radium on the condition that it be used as efficiently as possible for the relief of suffering and the advancement of medical science. The Fund seized the opportunity. Initially the Management and Distribution Committees undertook the additional work, until the formation of the Radium Committee in 1937. Following Beit's instructions, 4 g. of radium were purchased and 20 suitable hospitals given the material on loan.[41]

Beit's gift resulted in further benefactions for the Fund's radium supplies. The thank-offering campaign, which easily secured the government grant of £100,000, provided it with £37,000 for further purchases. The Fund thus found itself the principal distributor of radium stock in London. Its holdings reached 17 g. in 1936 and were second only to the National Radium Commission, which, acting for the National Radium Trust, administered supplies in the provinces. The uncertain dangers associated with radium created a need for professional assistance. Here the Fund took advice from a leading expert in the field, Professor Sidney Rus, and followed the guidelines provided by the Radium Commission.[42]

The transport of the material was of immediate concern. The Fund answered the problem with a 'radium car' fitted out with a safe in the back seat surrounded by 200 lbs. of lead to protect the driver. It carried not more than 1 g. at a time, which was worth over £5,000 in the 1930s. Another problem was that such small amounts of the material were easy to lose or to mislay. In America a pig once swallowed £6,000 worth of it. The fate of the pig is known, but not that of the drivers of the radium car.[43]

The 1930s saw a continuous flow of fresh faces in the Fund, as many of the older staff and committee men died or retired and new activities, such as radium distribution, required additional personnel. The Earl of Donoughmore, who became Chairman of the National Radium Commission in 1933, remained Chairman of the Fund throughout the period. A man noted for great courtesy, he was masterful at handling committees, as he had shown as Tory Chairman of Committees in the House of Lords. He had to cope with important losses among the Fund's honorary officials. Among the most notable was the Treasurer, Lord Revelstoke, who died in 1929, leaving £100,000 to the Fund. Lord Stamfordham, who had for thirty years provided a formal channel of communication with George V, died in 1931, as did that sometime ally, Viscount Knutsford. Lord Somerleyton, Honorary Secretary since 1897, died in 1935. Leonard Cohen, an Honorary Secretary who also served on the Distribution Committee for many years, died in 1938, only a few months before the Chairman of the Committee, Sir Cooper Perry.

Such men were not easy to replace, but the Fund's reputation and its connections with the teaching hospitals, the financial world, and the royal family ensured that people of stature came forward. As in the past, some came up through the visiting-ranks to sit on committees. Others, whose fathers served before them, went straight into senior positions. On the medical side there were eminent men like Ernest Rock Carling, Henry Letheby Tidy, and Lord Dawson. With his own report in cold storage, Dawson pursued the line that the municipal and voluntary systems should work together more effectively. As he was the King's principal doctor, he was offered a seat on the Council in 1929. But while he played a prominent part in the Fund until his death in 1945, he was not much loved by his colleagues.[44] Among the Fund's leading laymen were Sir Harold Wernher, Vice-Chairman of the Management Committee, Sir Ernest Pooley, Chairman of the Distribution Committee after Cooper Perry, and Sir Edward Peacock, who after Revelstoke's death became Treasurer and Chairman of the Finance Committee. These men made up what Ives called the 'big three' by the late 1930s.[45]

Sir Edward Peacock (1871–1962), who stayed on as Treasurer until 1954, was arguably the most distinguished of the Fund's lay officials.[46] He began his financial career in his native Canada, but his abilities attracted the attention of Lord Revelstoke, who made him a director of Barings in 1924. He was soon involved in British financial affairs at the highest level. After Revelstoke's death, he became Receiver-General of the Duchy of Cornwall, which gave him responsibilities over the royal family's finances. In the 1930s he was probably the most powerful man in the City after the Governor of the Bank of England, Montagu Norman, who was also a member of the Fund's Finance Committee. Ives described Peacock as old-fashioned and effective, a man of such presence and clarity of mind that he made a case look irresistible.[47]

Under Peacock's guidance the Fund weathered the Depression financially. In 1930 it had assets worth nearly £4,000,000, the bulk of it invested in securities. By 1939, with prices just recovered to their 1930 levels, its assets had risen by a further £600,000, helped considerably by legacies.[48] Despite a penchant for the world's railways, which was the legacy of Mount Stephen, the Fund's investments ranged widely, from shares in Malayan rubber plantations, to American Telephone and Telegraph stock, to Belgian bonds. During the Depression, as during the First World War, the Finance Committee purchased additional British government securities; and with the gift of various properties, including several houses in Holland Park from Edwin Radford in 1933, it became increasingly involved in property investment.[49] Peacock handled the annual meetings of the Committee with great authority; on one occasion, so the story goes, he read out the wrong year's accounts without comment and with congratulations.[50]

The Fund's financial power underlay its greater responsibilities in the hospital world, which, in turn, required the recruitment of additional paid staff. By 1930 their numbers reached twenty-two, most of them male.[51] Three years later, the need for space resulted in a move to 10 Old Jewry, in the City.

As a consequence expenses rose to between 4 and 5 per cent of total income. Salaries made up the bulk of the administrative costs and were competitive with comparable jobs elsewhere; bonuses, royal visits, and a judicious paternalism on the part of the management encouraged institutional loyalty. Employees commonly stayed, and they counted their blessings in a time of high unemployment.

The administrative staff came largely from the meritocratic middle class. Ives, like Maynard, was an Oxford-trained historian. He came to the Fund from the London Chamber of Commerce. So did Roger Peers, the son of the Surveyor of the Fabric of Westminster Abbey, who was appointed as a Secretarial Assistant in 1936. More and more people of this description, Beatrice Webb called them an 'élite of unassuming experts', were moving into the expanding central and local government offices at the time. But the voluntary sector continued to attract talented personnel, and it reflected the general trend towards professional management. Just as it encouraged better management practice in the hospitals, the Fund was itself becoming more managerial in outlook.

As the Fund's senior paid manager, Harry Maynard kept a firm grip on the Fund's affairs. But he had been Secretary for thirty years and was increasingly prone to bouts of irritability. It was said that when someone asked him for two hours' leave to attend a funeral, he was told 'won't one hour do'.[52] Ives remarked that Maynard communicated only by notes brought in by an office-boy.[53] In 1938, it was decided to make a change, but it took a firm hand to remove Maynard from office, a task carried out by Sir Harold Wernher. Maynard stayed on as Clerk to the General Council until his retirement in 1941, when the Management Committee paid formal tribute to him with the statement that the 'present position and prestige of the Fund is largely due to Mr Maynard's disinterested service'.[54] Years later it helped to pay the costs of his nursing-home care.

Arthur Ives, who replaced Maynard, promoted a more relaxed and congenial atmosphere in the office. 'The public school type', he was quiet in address and academic in style.[55] When he joined the Fund in 1929 he found it 'a very grand body'. Surrounded by titled men of ability be confessed that he felt that he would have 'to pull his socks up'.[56] Other empolyees felt the same. Their world of clerks and bureaucrats, after all, had little in common with the lives of the Fund's honorary officials, many of whom were of great prominence. Yet the mix of office-boys, clerks, doctors, businessmen, landed gentlemen, and royals was not unhappy or ineffective. The Fund's distinctive flavour in the 1930s is best captured in details: the excitement generated by the visit of the Prince of Wales to the new offices, or Ives's remark that he and Lord Somerleyton sometimes dropped into Brooks's for lunch before a hospital visit.[57]

Of all the changes inside the Fund in the 1930s none was so important, nor so ominous, as the death of George V in January 1936. The patron of over fifty hospitals in London alone, he was arguably the best friend the voluntary hospitals ever had. For thirty-five years, first as Prince of Wales and then as King, he was the Fund's foremost asset. In his last year he brought it into his Silver Jubilee celebrations, and as he lay dying gave it a £20,000 capital gift. In turn, the Fund honoured him with a Silver Jubilee Distribution, which added £120,000 to its annual distribution in 1935. (About 10 per cent of it was raised from the sale of seats at Jubilee processions.)[58] The Jubilee, it transpired, was the last time the Fund was to mount a major appeal tied to royal commemoration. The running-down of this tradition was indicative of its altered relations with the royal family after the death of George V, as well as of the changing character of its operations after the Second World War.

Edward, Prince of Wales, presided over the Fund as President for the last time at a meeting of the Distribution Committee in December 1935. The Fund's first official historian, Frank Long, writing in 1942, encapsulated the events associated with the presidency after the death of George V in a sentence: 'In the following May the Duke of York became the President, an office which he held to December 10th, 1936, when he was succeeded by his brother, the late Duke of Kent'.[59] He makes no further mention of Edward VIII, who was briefly Patron of the Fund until his abdication.

The abdication was a blow to the Fund, for anything which brought royalty into disrepute had implications for royal charities. Sir Edward Peacock, who advised Edward on financial and other matters in the weeks leading up to the crisis, must also have advised his colleagues in the Fund as to how to proceed in the awkward circumstances.[60] They drew a veil over Edward VIII. Among his last contacts with them was a letter dated 4 February 1936, in which he pledged to watch the Fund's progress and welfare 'with feelings of genuine and unabated interest'. Such a letter, signed by a king, would normally be a prized document to an institution, but this one was only recently redeemed from a pile of unimportant papers in an attic in Palace Court.[61]

Unlike his father, Edward VIII never took the initiative in defending the voluntary hospitals. He nevertheless carried out many of the duties asked of him, though at times ungraciously, as when, in a temper, he kicked the superintendent's dog on visit to the Cardiff Royal Infirmary.[62] The Fund received more support from him than most of the 200 charities with which he was associated. He turned up at meetings, read long prepared speeches, entertained the Fund's officials, wrote thank-you letters to large benefactors, and made appearances at special events. He also succeeded to the Grand Presidency of the League of Mercy, whose social duties he disliked and frequently refused to undertake.[63] Given the distractions of his private life, his dislike of ceremony, and his ambivalence towards hospital causes, he can rarely have looked forward to the demands that voluntarism made on his time.

George V's death and Edward VIII's departure from the scene unsettled relations between the monarchy and the Fund. Reviving the link with the royal family was of paramount concern to the institution's officials. Not only was it desirable on constitutional grounds, but royal attachments guaranteed favourable publicity even in the smallest details. Over twenty newspapers carried the report when King George VI signified his intention to raise his subscription to the Fund in 1936 to £1,000.[64] With an ingrained sense of public service, George VI became a dutiful Patron of the Fund, as well as of twenty-two London hospitals, but his interest in hospital affairs did not compare with his father's. His voluntary interests lay primarily in industrial relations and in the youth camps which he established in the 1920s.[65]

Running out of royals is always a concern to the philanthropic establishment, and with the accession of George VI the charitable pressures on his brothers, the Dukes of Kent and Gloucester, rose considerably. Despite a busy schedule, the Duke of Kent took a lively interest in the Fund's activities as its President, and his appearances on its behalf guaranteed wide press-coverage and a useful increase in donations. He was soon a popular figure in the Fund. For his part, the Duke of Gloucester accepted the presidency of the League of Mercy in 1936. But however much the royal dukes may have wished to promote voluntary hospital affairs, they were no substitute for a Prince of Wales, even a distracted one.

A nagging worry in the Fund after the mid-1930s was that its influence at the Palace was waning. The deaths of Stamfordham and Somerleyton had severed important links with the royal family. Attempts to recreate the level of co-operation with the monarchy that it had enjoyed earlier in the century were not very successful. As the years passed, members of the royal household turned up less often at meetings of the Fund.[66] Eventually, this became a worry to Wernher and Pooley, who dealt with the Palace. Two things flowed from a lower level of support from the royal household. Honours of the Victorian Order, which the Fund's officials had so often been awarded in the past, became more difficult to come by. More importantly, waning royal connections meant that the opposition the Fund could mount to schemes which threatened the voluntary hospitals was less effective. It would miss George V when it had to deal with Aneurin Bevan.

Making the most of the Fund's royal associations was one of the jobs of the Propaganda Committee, which was set up after the Combined Appeal of 1922 to bring the voluntary hospital cause before the public. It was initially under the chairmanship of Lord Burnham, the well-connected proprietor of the *Daily Telegraph*, who chaired the joint committee of teachers and local authorities which formulated the 'Burnham scales'. When he died in 1933, the Propaganda Committee was taken over by Lord Luke, another long-serving Fund man, who chaired the Revenue Committee. Assisted by E. A. Jay and Professor Winifred Cullis, they brought together a team of enthusiasts from the fields of educaton, science, art, literature, and law, among them the actor Sir Nigel Playfair, the historian Philip Guedalla, and William Beveridge, whose support for voluntarism has been obscured by his associations with state welfare.[67]

The use of the word 'propaganda' was a sign of the voluntary sector's nervousness in the inter-war years. It was not unusual to find it used by the hospitals themselves. The Kent and Canterbury Hospital set up a Propaganda Committee to raise money in 1921.[68] Lord Burnham argued that there was no other word which would cover the ground; Lord Luke defined it as 'a kind of special method of putting our case so that it may be understood by the people we want to influence'.[69] Raising money was an aim, but this was secondary to the desire to make the public aware of the importance of the voluntary hospitals in the nation's social organization. In short, the Fund's Propaganda Committee carried the voluntary hospital flag in the battle against state control.

Although serious in purpose, the propaganda campaign was rarely heavy-handed. A pioneer of charitable radio-broadcasts, the Fund received permission from the BBC to make an appeal in the 'Week's Good Cause' series in 1928. Delivered by Lord Hailsham it raised £700.[70] Happy with the results of its film in the 1920s, the Fund produced a second, made possible by a gift of £1,000 from Lord Wakefield. *War without End*, which celebrated the glories of scientific medicine, opened at Leicester Square Theatre in 1937, attended by the Duke of Kent.[71] Volunteers delivered lectures to schoolchildren on their hospital services and, with a view to contributions, guided rich Americans around places of historic interest. Drawing-room meetings, at which a collection was taken for the Fund, boasted speakers as diverse as Walter de la Mare, Harold Nicholson, and Megan Lloyd George. A series on foreign views of the English enticed André Maurois to give a lighthearted address at the French Embassy. Virtually anyone of prominence was likely to be approached for support, though Lord Burnham drew the line at Lord Beaverbrook.

Among the most enjoyable occasions arranged by the Propaganda Committee were the 'mock trials' at the Great Hall of the London School of Economics. Organized by Beveridge, the LSE's Director, they ran for twelve years, with the object of raising money for the Fund through frivolous disputes by celebrated men and women. The first debate, between Rebecca West and Alfred Duff Cooper on the question 'Is Woman's Place in the Home?', which was simultaneously broadcast by the BBC, caused a furore.[72] More successful was the debate between Bernard Shaw and Hilaire Belloc, who took for their subject 'What is Coming?'[73] Beveridge himself wrote several of the scripts. In one of them, he charged politicians with keeping their ears too close to the ground. Acting as prosecutor, he declared that 'what the ordinary citizen wants is to choose his politician as he would choose his doctor—with liberty to change from time to time'.[74]

This brief description of the work of the Propaganda Committee's activities would be incomplete without some reference to the King's Fund Miniature Hospital. Based on the idea of the Queen's doll's house, it was a replica of a 1930s hospital, with wards, operating-theatres, X-ray apparatus, and an electric lift which was worked by pressing a button. (It can be seen today at the Science Museum). It was an ingenious idea that received royal favour. Queen Mary presented the lace handkerchiefs which were used as bedspreads. In 1933, the Prince of Wales opened the model at the Building Centre in London (see Plate 7), and it was then loaned to exhibitions around the country. Seen by hundreds of thousands of people, it had an educational value and raised considerable sums of money for local hospitals. Queen Mary liked it very much, though she believed her doll's house 'was higher'. When Queen Elizabeth, formerly the Duchess of York, saw it at an exhibition in Glasgow, she exclaimed, in a friendly tone, 'Where are the bedspreads?'[75]

Most of the Fund's activities in the 1930s were decidedly less entertaining than the work of the Propaganda Committee. Given the background of national economic decline, pusillanimous politics, and the growth of a left-wing intellectual movement in the Labour Party, anxieties mounted in the charitable sector. The Fund, more attuned to politics than most philanthropic bodies, kept an ever more watchful eye on government legislation for opportunities to represent the voluntary hospital interest. It stepped up its lobbying of Parliament after the Local Government Act of 1929. Its Local Government Bill Committee, led by Whitley and Lord Macmillan, transformed into a Parliamentary Committee in 1930 and extended its powers to cover any Bill or Act.

The Parliamentary Committee claimed an early success when an amendment, moved in the Lords by Luke, resulted in a clause being added to the Road Traffic Act (1930). It provided that up to £25 should be paid by insurers to hospitals treating persons injured in road accidents. With 6,000 road-deaths a year by 1930 in Britain and 150,000 cases of injury, the demands made on the hospitals were awesome, the equivalent of war.[76] Casualty departments expanded and in hospitals near busy roads new wards had to be built to care for the victims. Across the country local residents complained that beds provided for their needs were being taken over by outsiders. As Luke pointed out in the Lords, the provincial hospitals alone treated 65,000 accident victims in 1927. They cost the hospitals £230,000, only £26,000 of which was recovered from patients or insurance. Luke's amendment, and later legislation, provided much-needed relief, but the voluntary hospitals were never fully reimbursed for their work. Few social changes proved such a drain on hospital resources in the inter-war years.[77]

With the years, the Parliamentary Committee took an active interest in a variety of bills, from the Charitable Collections (Regulation) Bill to the Voluntary Hospitals (Relief from Rating) Bill. One of the most important concessions it extracted from government came in 1936 when the Voluntary Hospitals (Paying Patients) Bill received the royal assent. The Act enabled the Charity Commissioners to give hospitals whose trusts dated from a time before the need had arisen the same power to provide pay-beds that was enjoyed by other hospitals.[78] But there was an important condition attached: that the beds provided should not diminish the accommodation available for the sick poor. St Bartholomew's came up against this clause in 1938, when it wished to erect a paying-patients block but could not prove that the new addition could be opened without disadvantage to the sick poor.[79]

Back on the hospital front, the Fund continued its involvement in various schemes to stimulate fund-raising. It studied the work of individual hospital appeal-offices in minute detail and was not always happy with what it found. Notably, the number of hospital flag-days had grown out of control, to reach seventy-seven a year. In consultation with the Commissioner of Police and hospital representatives, the Fund was able to reduce this number in 1936 to two. With the establishment of a central flag-day organization, the annual receipts rose from £25,000 to nearly £74,000.[80] It was an excellent example of the Fund's power of persuasion, which produced greater co-ordination, and results.

It was said that 'no amount of enthusiasm' on the part of an individual hospital could get far without the Fund's approval, for it held the purse-strings and had an unrivalled technical knowledge.[81] But as the Fund did not wish to be coercive, it tiptoed through the minefield of often conflicting hospital proposals. Redevelopment was a particularly sensitive area. As ever, the Fund wished to encourage the relocation of hospitals to sites in the expanding suburbs. But it rarely pressed the point, especially with the teaching hospitals, which it saw as serving national as well as local interests. When St George's decided to remain at Hyde Park Corner in 1935, the Fund reluctantly approved the scheme. The Westminster Hospital flirted with sites in Wandsworth and Clapham, but its new buildings opened in 1939 back in the heart of Westminster, assisted by a special grant from the Fund to offset debts.[82] By propping up so many institutions in central London, the Fund helped to perpetuate the very imbalances it was set up to relieve.

Inside the hospitals, the Fund's inspections and technical expertise had visible effects and made a notable contribution to the dramatic changes taking place in the London hospitals in the 1930s. It advised on matters large and small, from overall hospital design to the shape of signposts to the wards. In a trend not unconnected with the growth in the number of pay-beds, the lives of patients were becoming more comfortable in these years. The Fund played a part in this process. In 1931, for example, it set up a subcommittee to look into the issue of patients' waking hours. Asked specifically to take note of the issue, the Fund's visitors discovered wide variations in the practice at different London hospitals. At about two-thirds of them the hour of awakening was before 6 a.m. The Fund thought this unreasonable and over the next few years it persuaded an increasing number of institutions to set the hour of waking at no earlier than six o'clock.[83]

In a major campaign, the Fund took another look at the out-patient problem, which it had first investigated in 1910. By 1930 there were nine million out-patient attendances a year in London's 140 voluntary hospitals, a figure which rose by another million in less than a decade.[84] The sheer numbers placed an enormous burden on space and staff and resulted in congestion and long delays for patients. By this time the Fund perceived the central problem to be out-patient waiting-times, whereas before the First World War it had paid greater attention to the abuse of hospitals by the out-patients. This suggests that its support for hospital almoners, which was central to its report on out-patients in 1912, was not without some effect. It is further evidence that the Fund was becoming more patient-centred.

There was little agreement on the best way to deal with waiting-times. A feature of out-patient departments was the variation in their procedures. To the Fund, the variety of procedures was not so much a worry as an expression of those qualities of independence and choice that made the voluntary services special.[85] In the 1930s it published a stream of publications on out-patient care, which flowed from the work of a special committee, set up in 1932, under the chairmanship of Lord Onslow. The committee accepted that out-patient attendances were too numerous for the facilities available; something had to be done to deal with patients' complaints about waiting. It recommended that hospitals should develop the consultative side of out-patient work, that non-urgent minor cases should be referred to suitable agencies which provided GP treatment, and that various time-saving methods should be studied with a view to reducing delays.[86]

An Outpatient Arrangements Committee, led by Sir John Rose Bradford and later by Dr Morley Fletcher, took on the onerous task of carrying out the recommendations. Its work was typical of the Fund's approach to hospital administration, for it assumed that the problems could only be solved by attention to detail. Once it had identified the best practices, the Fund encouraged their adoption elsewhere. In time it provided standard out-patient forms, timetables, and more effective seating-arrangements.[87] Such small changes, when added together, probably did reduce waiting-times. But Roger Peers, who worked on the project, found the work 'unimaginative'. He recalled a visit to Guy's led by Sir Cooper Perry, who argued that waiting did not matter anyway. To prove his point he went 'to a long queue of miserable people waiting for dispensary and ... seized a little man by the shoulder, swung him round and said "You like waiting, don't you?" To which the terrified man replied, "Oh, yessir, yessir, yessir!" and Sir Cooper turned to the King's Fund party and said, "You see—they like waiting!" '[88]

A more imaginative project set up by the Fund was the Emergency Bed Service (EBS). In 1937 the Voluntary Hospitals Committee approached it with a scheme suggested by the University College Hospital surgeon A. J. Gardham. The proposal was that a central clearing-office should be set up to overcome the delays and dangers inherent in admission of urgent cases to voluntary hospitals. Harold Wernher knew of a similar project under way in Stockholm, and he dispatched members of the staff to Sweden to investigate. The tendency to seek out contemporary foreign experiments while forgetting domestic precedents is endemic in British charities, and the Fund was no exception. It appears to have been unaware of the much earlier British scheme, set up by Burdett and the Hospitals Association in the 1880s, in which a central bureau of information found places for both acute and chronic patients in suitable hospitals.[89] Nor did it refer to its own Ambulance Cases Disposal Committee, which inquired into methods used to find out about bed accommodation in the early 1920s.[90]

What appealed to the Fund about the scheme suggested by the Voluntary Hospitals Committee, apart from its obvious benefits to patients, was that it had the advantages of central co-ordination while retaining hospital independence. If it could be made to work, it would show the voluntary hospitals co-operating in the cause of patients and put them one up on the municipal hospitals. It would also guarantee that the voluntary hospitals had a steady supply of emergency patients for the purposes of medical education.[91] After receiving assurances that about 100 institutions in London would participate, the Fund set up a joint committee with the Voluntary Hospitals Committee, chaired by Wernher, to oversee the service. To ensure its success, the Fund provided a grant of £3,000, and hired a dozen staff, all women, who were paid £3.10s. a week. The office opened in Old Jewry on 21 June 1938 and the Duke of Kent inspected it at work a few days later.[92]

The EBS began with a fourteen-hour service, soon extended to twenty-four hours, within the Fund's area of operations. Each day the staff telephoned participating hospitals to discover the number and type of their vacant beds. The beds were then represented on a large board by tickets of different colours, according to sex and medical classification. Thus when a doctor rang to make arrangements, suitable accommodation, preferably nearby, could be found at a glance. Within a few minutes the bed could be booked, an ambulance laid on, and the doctor called back to confirm arrangements.

Seeing the merits in the scheme, the London County Council soon joined it, and it was not unusual to see an LCC ambulance taking a patient to a voluntary hospital. The EBS proved to be one of the more successful examples of hospital co-ordination in London pioneered by the voluntary sector. Within a year 2,500 doctors used the scheme. The number of patients assisted rose to over 8,000 in 1939, which was about 3 per cent of all new in-patients admitted to the voluntary hospitals for the year.[93] Despite occasional 'incidents', including abortion cases which the voluntary hospitals wished to avoid, the EBS soon reached, in the words of the *Lancet*, a 'high pitch of efficiency'.[94] It would be severely tested during the war.

The Emergency Bed Service should be seen against the background of the report of the Sankey Commission published in 1937. Set up by an initiative of the British Hospitals Association, the Commission investigated the management and finances of the voluntary hospitals. The King's Fund had little to do with it on a formal level but paid close attention to its recommendations, which in many respects resembled those of the Cave Committee. Indeed, had the recommendations of the Cave Committee been fulfilled, it is unlikely that the Sankey Report would have been written. Sankey, a former Labour Lord Chancellor, had called for the nationalization of coal as Chairman of the Coal Industry Commission in 1919, but he had no enthusiasm for a nationalization of hospitals. An ardent hospital voluntarist, he saw the strength of the charitable tradition in its freedom, spirit, and elasticity. Further still, he believed a 'dislike of over-control and bureaucracy' was 'inherent in the genius of our race'.[95]

Like so many others before him, Sankey saw the principal disadvantage of the voluntary hospitals flowing from their unsatisfactory finances. He pointed out that if hospital revenues were taken as a whole, the resources looked satisfactory. Yet individually, too many hospitals were in deficit. The problem, in his view, was created by the rising costs of new treatments and the increasing burden of taxation, which prevented people of all classes from giving as much as they might wish to. A further disadvantage was the lack of co-operation between hospitals, which led to congestion here and empty beds there and the provision of new hospitals without regard to needs. This, of course, was just the sort of criticism that had been laid at the door of the voluntary hospitals for over fifty years and which the King's Fund had been set up to dispel. The Sankey Report may be seen as evidence that the Fund, despite its many achievements, had failed to overcome the problem of imbalances in London's hospital provision.

Most of the Sankey Commission's recommendations were, like its criticisms, familiar: improved methods of fund-raising, provision of more accommodation for paying-patients, the further development of contributory schemes, greater co-ordination with the local authorities, and the establishment of machinery to make the best use of available beds. (The last encouraged the development of the Emergency Bed Service.) More intriguing were the recommendations to divide the country into voluntary hospital regions with regional councils to correlate their work. A central council would also be established to co-ordinate the work of the regions.[96]

On the financial side, the Commission wanted money redistributed to deserving institutions by means of a pool into which hospitals would contribute a percentage of their income; but, like the Fund, it doubted whether the hospitals were prepared for it. As a first step it recommended the creation of regional funds modelled on the King's Fund, which, it believed, would create new sources of revenue and educate the public to value its hospitals. In a speech to the British Hospitals Association in Torquay in May 1937, Sankey advocated a system of government grants in aid, which would do for the hospitals what the University Grants Committee, set up in 1919, did for the universities. What he particularly liked about this idea was that it would provide long-term government funding with a minimum of administrative overheads and a maximum of hospital autonomy.[97]

The idea that hospitals might be treated financially like the universities also appealed to the King's Fund as a long-term solution to the national problem. Professor Ernest Barker, a former member of the Propaganda Committee, spoke up for it in 1938. In his view a hospital grants committee might receive an annual parliamentary grant which it then distributed to individual hospitals through regional hospital councils.[98] The wit and MP for Oxford A. P. Herbert wrote that it was degrading that such great hospitals should be 'like hens scratching in the dust for sustenance'. He believed that a hospital grants committee, based on the University Grants Committee, would have the happy effect of providing 'state assistance without state control' and not diminish private support.[99] The currency of such ideas led the Duke of Gloucester to advocate a national fund, like the King's Fund, for all the nation's voluntary hospitals. The *North Shields Daily News* called it a 'stupendous idea not lightly made'.[100] The King's Fund did not comment.

The Sankey Commission's report and the ideas it aroused were the results of a hospital crisis in the late 1930s which brought to mind the early 1920s. With its detailed knowledge of the financial worries of individual London hospitals the Fund was in a privileged position to know the depths of the crisis. It was, after all, the first stop for London hospital managers whose institutions were in distress. As in the early part of the century, a higher proportion of the Fund's grants went for the reduction of debt. There were awkward moments, as when the Treasurer of St George's, Lord Greville, came bearing the news that the hospital's medical staff thought the voluntary system bankrupt and wanted the institution given to the LCC.[101] Ives remembered the House Governor of St Thomas's 'literally on his knees' begging for £10,000 to avoid the bank foreclosing. 'The cheque was made out and taken over by messenger there and then,' he recalled.[102] Small wonder that the Fund, which distributed nearly £10,000,000 between its foundation and the Second World War, was called the 'fairy Godmother to London Hospitals'.[103]

Long familiar with hospital crises and having a wider perspective than individual hospitals, the Fund played down the dramatics, preferring to take a dispassionate look at the facts. Its statistics for 1938 showed that London's 146 voluntary hospitals had a total of just under 19,000 beds, up by 3,000 in the decade. The aggregate deficit in 1938 was £146,608, only the third aggregate deficit since 1921; and on a turnover of nearly £5,000,000 it did not seem unduly large.[104] To put the figures in perspective, the overall deficit in 1938 of the London hospitals was no greater than it had been in 1897, when the Fund came into existence, despite the vast increase in provision.[105] Many institutions were in real financial difficulty, including several of the teaching hospitals, but to the Fund, hospital finances in the 1930s suggested not 'bankruptcy' but 'stability' in the voluntary system.

What worried the Fund was the growth in expenditure, not because of bad management or extravagance, but because of scientific demands and the expenses arising from social betterment. Advances in medicine and surgery after the First World War resulted in new departments, more operations, and increases in staff, which put hospital finances under enormous pressure. But as patient-demand accelerated, not least among the middle classes, the Fund noted, with alarm, that hospital revenue was being seriously affected by political and economic tensions, which resulted in higher taxes and decreased personal income.[106] These last points were of no small significance, for tax levels in 1937–8 were higher than at any time since 1918–19 and interest rates on securities were down.

The Fund argued that charitable contributions had held up remarkably well given the less-than-buoyant economy. With its interest in making the best possible case for the voluntary hospitals, it pointed to the increased number of patients being treated. On the financial side, it preferred to look at aggregate figures for income and expenditure, which put the overall picture for London's hospitals in a relatively favourable light. Critics of the voluntary sector, on the other hand, tended to emphasize the financial worries of individual institutions and to turn the smallest deficit into a crisis. Their criticisms were often fuelled by the hospitals themselves, which often spoke in terms of crisis because it was an effective way of extracting contributions.

More recent commentators have taken up the case of the contemporary critics, and they see little but bankruptcy and confusion in inter-war hospital provision. There is a tendency for each generation to traduce the achievements of the recent past, and this seems to have especially infected post-war hospital reformers. The celebratory articles surrounding the fortieth anniversary of the NHS illustrated a near total disregard for the achievements of inter-war provision.[107] Reading them one can hardly credit the fact that in the 1930s the British voluntary hospitals were widely accepted to be, in that phrase that rings with every hospital crisis, 'the best in the world'.[108] Care in London was often singled out for praise. The *Lancet* declared that 'nowhere can better treatment be found than in one of the large general teaching hospitals of London'.[109]

Historians have contributed their share to the misunderstanding of 1930s hospital provision. Typically they conjure up an ideal form of hospital administration and distribution against which inter-war medical provision looks chaotic.[110] Treating the rise of state provision as inexorable, they fail to give the voluntary sector its due. One influential scholar studying the statistics of hospital income for 1938, concludes that 'charity . . . had long ceased to be the main financial mainstay of the voluntary movement. Payments, either in cash or from "insurance contributions", were the principal source of revenue'.[111] But his statistical analysis is deceptive, for it excludes legacies, and he does not count hospital investments as voluntary income. Nor does he consider that contributory schemes might have a charitable dimension. According to the British Hospitals Contributory Schemes Association, this was what made them so worthwhile.[112]

The Fund's statistics for 1938 show that 55 per cent of the total maintenance income for London's 146 voluntary hospitals came from charitable sources, including legacies and investments. Though it shared the view that payments from contributory schemes were partly philanthropic, for statistical purposes it included them under insurance contributions. Thirty-four per cent came from patients and their insurance societies in 1938. Fees and payments by public authorities made up less than 10 per cent. In the twelve teaching hospitals the figures were more heavily weighted to voluntary gifts: over 62 per cent came from charitable sources, including legacies and investments, 30 per cent from patients and their societies, and just over 5 per cent from fees and the public authorities.[113] Thus in the Fund's analysis the charitable element in the financing of London's voluntary hospital provision, though less prominent than in the past, remained the most significant.

Clearly, the financial picture presented by the voluntary hospitals in the 1930s defies easy analysis and is open to interpretation. Individually, they revealed extremes, from solvency to penury. Voluntary contributions were unable, in themselves, to keep the hospitals in step with the demands of patients and science. This was particularly so in the provinces, where charitable receipts lagged behind those in London. The problem was exacerbated by the pressure for improved services from better-off patients, who frequently complained to the Fund about the failings of hospital provision. Increasingly, they felt that the institutionalized division of the population into paupers and non-paupers was arbitrary and against their interests.

A poignant letter to the Fund in 1932 from a gentleman 'ruined in health and in pocket' captured the feelings of many others of his background. He lamented that 'butchers, bakers, candlestick makers . . . come in [to hospital], helped by charity in many cases, but for such as I, who have helped to keep the flag flying in storms and stresses of weather overseas there are no such aids'.[114] The Fund noted with growing concern the dissatisfaction among the middle classes, whose servants often had better chances of hospital treatment than they had themselves.[115] The prospect of universal and, for themselves, less expensive health care would put egalitarianism in a more favourable light to the better-off.

The Fund argued, with some justice, that hospitals had become 'co-operative' institutions providing a service for the entire community. But as the British Medical Association pointed out, the principal beneficiaries of hospital care in the 1930s were workers and their dependants.[116] The challenge was to satisfy middle-class demand. With the years, the Fund found itself under growing pressure to assist those above the wage-earning class, which was already served by institutions like the Hospital Saving Association. It lobbied for the extension of pay-beds, a few of which were set aside for patients in straitened circumstances. And to enable more professional people to make provision towards the cost of treatment in a pay-bed, it gave financial assistance to the British Provident Association. (It merged with other schemes to form the British United Provident Association, BUPA, in 1947.)[117]

But pay-beds were expensive and still in short supply. In the late 1930s, they cost, on average, about 7 or 8 guineas a week in London, excluding medical or surgical fees.[118] (This was more than the weekly income of the Fund's senior clerks.) To complicate matters further, the Ministry of Health was unconvinced that paying-patients were reconcilable with the original trusts of hospitals.[119] As noted, the Paying Patients Act (1936) laid down conditions that restricted moves to accommodate better-off patients which might disadvantage the sick poor. At the end of 1938, there were only 2,260 pay-beds available in London. Thirty-five hospitals, including the Charing Cross, St Bartholomew's, and St George's, had none at all (see Plate 8).[120] They would have to wait until they were part of the National Health Service before they were free to open pay-beds.

The failure to satisfy middle-class demand for hospital treatment led some to predict the dissolution of the voluntary system. Unable to take advantage of ordinary hospital beds, and without sufficient pay-beds at their disposal, the better-off had no choice but to enter expensive nursing-homes. This was bound to hurt hospital appeals in a society in which the divisions between rich and poor were less marked than in the past. The Mayfair physician, Sir Bruce Bruce-Porter, spoke directly on the issue to the new Health Club in 1937. He accepted that the very rich could afford treatment but lamented that what he called the 'black-coated workers', not rich but above the insurance level, were left out. Along with unconscionably high tax-levels affecting traditional hospital supporters, it spelled doom for the voluntary system. He forecast that the State would have to nationalize the hospitals in order to deal with a problem that it had largely created.[121]

Such predictions were heresy to the Fund's old guard. To them the nationalization of hospitals would be an act of vandalism comparable to the dissolution of the monasteries. (If capitalized, the assets of the nation's voluntary hospitals were worth about £300,000,000 before the war.)[122] Still, there was no shortage of soothsayers in the late 1930s, friends and foes alike, who believed the voluntary system doomed. Precisely what they expected to replace it was rather less clear, though schemes for reorganization were in plentiful supply. What most of them had in common was a call for government money and a regional approach. On the Left the Socialist Medical Association wanted a new system of hospital care in which the country would be divided into regions in which all hospitals and personnel would be pooled for the common good.[123] The Labour Party, despite reservations from some in the leadership, had committed itself in 1934 to a broadly similar hospital service: comprehensive, free, and salaried, administered by a reformed regional government.[124]

The King's Fund was open to the idea of government payments to hospitals run along the lines of the University Grants Committee, but it was primarily concerned with defending London's voluntary institutions. It must also have realized the unlikelihood of any government deferring to a panel of experts when health issues were moving up the political agenda. Its proposals for London were familiar, and by 1939 looked rather tired: closer co-ordination between voluntary bodies and public authorities and an immediate cash transfusion from the State, especially for the larger hospitals which were under the greatest financial strain. Unable to guarantee the security of the hospitals itself, the Fund was not too particular whether the additional money came from the LCC or the Ministry of Health. To some critics, fishing around for money to prop up an inefficient system was a 'national scandal'.[125] 'If there is likely to be a national scandal', noted E. A. Jay of the Propaganda Committee, 'it will be the failure of government to realize the necessity for taking some action. The voluntary Hospitals have done all they can.'[126]

In 1938 and early 1939, the Fund joined in a flurry of formal and informal meetings with the teaching hospitals, the LCC, and the Ministry of Health.[127] All agreed that greater co-operation between the municipal and voluntary hospitals was necessary and worthy, but with so much at stake there was no unanimity about how it was to be achieved. In any case, by 1939 such discussions were being overtaken by political events. As the images of aerial bombardment, drawn from the Spanish Civil War, welled up in the minds of government planners, voluntary institutions were brought into negotiations to prepare for the worst. Few doubted the gravity of the situation. The Fund and its allies recognized that the hospitals might soon come under fire from something more threatening than the London County Council. They had survived the First World War, the Depression, and the vicissitudes of politics, but only the more sanguine among them expected their cherished institutions to survive intact should another war break out.

6

The Second World War and the Creation of the National Health Service

THE impact of the Second World War on state social policy has attracted such attention that its impact on the voluntary movement has been obscured. As in 1914, the crisis both threatened and challenged voluntarists, and it accelerated the process of co-operation with state officials. While the number of civil servants rose dramatically, a problem for charities was how to cope with the continual calling-up of their personnel for the forces. At the local level the picture is very confusing, for while all communities and their institutions were affected, some were more affected than others, depending on the degree of bomb damage and whether there was an influx of evacuees, troops, or war workers. Where the fear of aerial bombing was most acute, mass evacuation also had important repercussions for philanthropic activity. In short, the war disrupted the work of most charities, killed off some, and promoted a host of new ones.

All the nation's hospitals were vulnerable to aerial attack, but those in London were particularly so. They adapted themselves to wartime conditions under the direction of the Emergency Medical Service, a centralized state agency empowered by the Ministry of Health to provide treatment for air-raid victims.[1] The complex scheme had to meet the danger to civilians as well as military casualties, and it drew on the goodwill of local-authority hospitals, voluntary hospitals, and ancillary organizations. As in the First World War, the British Red Cross and the Order of St John of Jerusalem ran the auxiliary hospitals. Other charities, especially female societies like the Women's Voluntary Service (1938), offered government departments a range of emergency services, from evacuating children to entertaining the troops.

On government orders the London hospitals prepared for enormous numbers of casualties. The impact of the war on individual institutions varied, depending on their grouping by the Emergency Medical Service. A common pattern was to close some beds, to use others for ordinary patients, and to prepare the rest for air-raid victims. University College Hospital, for example, evacuated both charity and private patients, and set up emergency facilities, including operating-theatres. Meanwhile, its medical students and porters filled over 70,000 sandbags, which they placed in strategic positions.[2] Such labour not only dislocated the normal running of the hospitals but proved expensive. At a time when their costs were rising, the hospitals felt that they had a rightful claim on the State for expenditure incurred on its behalf.

To the regret of hospital officials, the government did not pay for many of the necessary air-raid precautions.[3] Conscious of costs, the Ministry of Health did not question the autonomy of the voluntary hospitals; and it accepted that it had to pay them, at least for their services. But as the King's Fund pointed out, it only paid for the casualty service not the civil work.[4] In the event, it was agreed that the grants provided by the Ministry of Health to individual hospitals would be determined by the proportion of beds, whether occupied or not, reserved for casualties. But the payments did not include charges for administration, and in the case of unoccupied beds did not provide money for provisions, surgery, or medicines.[5]

It is said that the voluntary hospitals took advantage of wartime circumstances by keeping so many subsidized beds in reserve for casualties. When the casualties did not turn up in the expected numbers, they nevertheless took the money to jack up their reserves. During the war, the London voluntary hospitals had an aggregate surplus, created by the rise in payments from public authorities. The payments peaked in 1944 at £1,800,000, which constituted just under 32 per cent of overall London voluntary hospital income for the year.[6] Looking back, one historian remarked acidly, 'the hospitals had hesitated to touch public money when they desperately needed it; they showed no hesitation when they did not'.[7] The Socialist Medical Association was even more damning at the time. In its view, the Emergency Medical Service seemed to be designed 'primarily for the benefit ... of the voluntary hospitals'.[8]

This was not the way the voluntarists saw it. Sir Bernard Docker, Chairman of the Westminster Hospital and the British Hospitals Association, argued that when the history of wartime hospital arrangements came to be written 'the highest praise will inevitably be given to the contribution made by voluntary hospitals'.[9] As he reminds us, the hospitals remained independent institutions throughout the war despite massive state intervention. The government obtained the use of thousands of their beds, without the outlay of capital sums, and it made arrangements with them based on its own projection of the number of casualties, just as it dealt with private firms for the supply of provisions. The hospitals could hardly be blamed if the government projections were mistaken.

It was understandable that the voluntary hospitals were in no hurry to comply with requests from the Ministry of Health to return beds to civilian use when the anticipated number of casualties did not appear. To do so would require yet another upheaval of staff and procedures. And who was to say that the original estimates of casualties would not one day be realized? In fact, the London hospitals did return many casualty-beds to civilian use.[10] But they argued that civilian waiting-lists were much reduced in any case, not least because of the marked decline in the capital's population due to mass evacuation.[11] Given the degree of dislocation which the government imposed on them, the voluntary hospitals did not wish officialdom to bankrupt them into the bargain. They had not forgotten the financial aftershocks of the First World War.

To hospital voluntarists, the issue was not their patriotism but the survival of their institutions. Predictions of vast casualty-lists suggested more than a little destruction to property as well. Financial arrangements to treat casualties were important, but they would not put flattened hospital buildings back together again. And there was no guarantee that the government would ever pick up the bill to do so, despite a scheme whereby hospitals could lodge claims for compensation. If the government did pay for rebuilding-schemes, would it not want greater control? If it did not, could voluntary contributions cover the cost? From early on in the war, the King's Fund took the view that the responsibility for repairing bomb damage belonged to the government.[12]

The anxieties of hospital voluntarists increased in the summer of 1940, in a hail of bombs and incendiary devices. The first great attack on London took place on 7 September 1940, followed by over 200 raids in the next nine months.[13] The Ministry of Information said the hospitals had been singled out for attack, though statistical analysis suggested that they did not receive much more than their share of random bombs.[14] As a consequence of evacuation and preparedness, the number of casualties sent to the voluntary and municipal hospitals in the London region during the raids of September 1940 to May 1941 was only 10,113.[15] As R. M. Titmuss put it, the capital's hospital services 'were more seriously affected by losses of beds through damage than by the influx of casualties'.[16]

Damage to both voluntary and municipal hospitals in the London region was severe and rendered several institutions uninhabitable, including the Dreadnought Hospital and the King Edward VII's Hospital for Officers. As the information came in, the Fund compiled statistics on the number of blitzed institutions. By the end of 1940, thirty-five voluntary hospitals in London reported that they had been severely damaged, twenty-two less seriously. By July 1941, the numbers increased to forty-three and thirty respectively.[17] Among the larger institutions, only St Mary's, Paddington was able to keep open all its beds by the end of 1941. At St Thomas's, which was hit particularly hard, 508 beds out of a total complement of 682 were lost by bombing (see Plate 9).[18]

As a repository of voluntary hospital information, the Fund saw the picture in the round, in stark detail. The graphic reports of bomb damage which it received brought the raids to life as statistics never could. On 7 September 1940, Queen Mary's Hospital for the East End was among the first London hospitals to receive a direct hit, which demolished two large wards and residential quarters. 'In a moment', reported an eyewitness, 'the bomb tore through the three floors and finally burst leaving a hugh crater which was immediately filled by large masses of masonry and steel girders twisted into all manner of fantastic shapes, broken equipment and unfortunately the bodies of six patients and two of the nurses.'[19]

The recently opened block of the National Hospital, Queen Square, built of steel and concrete, stood up rather better but still sustained serious damage. In the raid of 9 September it had a 'miraculous escape'. According to its Secretary, 'the noise was terrific, and at 11.50 pm there was an ear-splitting crash, the building rocked, and, accompanied by the noise of splintering glass and wood, the building was plunged into darkness. Nurses and maids appeared, some crawling out from under the debris, many lightly clad. A roll call was taken on the first floor—all present, a few bruises and scratches, but luckily no casualties.'[20]

Suddenly, in the midst of the confusion a voice exclaimed ' "the children's hospital [Great Ormond Street] is on fire!" Immediately the doctors went over with offers of help and shelter. Extra mattresses were fetched and placed in a long line in the sheltered corridor on the first floor and nurses, clad only in dressing gowns, armed with torches, went to meet and guide the children and their nurses to safety. It was a moving spectacle to see these little ones, who had so narrowly escaped death, once more dropping off to sleep, while overhead the Nazis still seemed to be endeavouring to destroy them.' On a lighter note, when daylight appeared, 'strange articles were to be seen hanging from the lamp-posts and tree tops and murmurs were heard that the blast had removed some of the nurses' underwear!'[21]

Over on Lambeth Road, near the War Museum, the Hospital of our Lady of Consolation was less fortunate. Having narrowly escaped destruction in late 1940, it took a direct hit on 11 January 1941. The sisters, huddled in the basement, heard the explosive coming. 'We heard water pouring, or rather rushing down the stairs. . . . The Hospital was full of smoke like a fog, and smelled terribly of blast. . . . About 10 minutes after we were hit Mother Lucy and Sisters Gertrude and Helen were found dead at the east end of the corridor on the first floor, having been blown by the blast from the main stairway. . . . Their bodies were intact. Mother Lucy and Sister Gertrude had terrible injuries but Sister Helen appeared to be asleep.'[22] Over the next few months the hospital itself came under further attack, and its new building, with fifty beds, was half demolished.

As these accounts and the statistics suggest, hospital finances would be severely crippled by the blitz. At St Bartholomew's the cost of the damage to the College alone was put at over £100,000.[23] After the raids of 1940–1, St Thomas's calculated its losses to be over £1,000,000, which turned out to be an underestimate.[24] At Guy's, the cost of repairs ran to £288,000 in 1946, a sum paid by the hospital not by the government.[25] Some of London's voluntary hospitals escaped unscathed, but the overall bill for reconstruction and the replacement of equipment massively outweighed the surpluses built up from government payments. The eventual cost of rebuilding St Thomas's was greater than the aggregate surpluses of all the 169 London hospitals during the entire war.[26] To the Fund, the criticism that the voluntary hospitals had somehow taken advantage of the government's good offices was ludicrous, and mischievous.

As a consequence of the destruction to hospital property, the Ministry of Health had difficult decisions to face. As early as 31 October 1940, a departmental minute suggested the ominous implications for the hospitals: 'As a result of the dislocation of hospital services in London, the partial closing of voluntary hospitals, and their damage by air raids, questions are arising that threaten the continuance of certain of these hospitals as independent institutions. Action by the Ministry may determine their continued existence as independent units, or make such existence impossible.'[27] Clearly, the blitz was softening up the voluntary hospitals, and the municipal hospitals as well, for post-war reorganization. As A. J. P. Taylor put it: 'the *Luftwaffe* was a powerful missionary for the welfare state.'[28]

Historians have long recognized that the Second World War triggered change in hospital affairs.[29] In their analyses of the making of the National Health Service, they have emphasized the deficiencies of hospital provision in the 1930s and the extension of government controls under the Emergency Medical Service. Disregarding the contradictory evidence, they have tended to exaggerate the growth in public support for state intervention during the war.[30] Nor have they fully explored the implications in the sheer physical devastation to the hospitals by aerial bombardment. Principally, they have ignored the compromises it necessitated in the charitable sector. The mountains of rubble were a terrible blow to the morale of voluntarists, not least those in the King's Fund, who had such an intimate knowledge of war-torn hospitals.

The war interrupted many of the Fund's own operations, including its normal propaganda and fund-raising activities. (It also drastically reduced the activities of hospital appeal offices, many of which were bombed.) Voluntarists worried particularly about the tendency of people to assume that the State was now solely responsible for all hospitals. In the circumstances, the Fund reorganized its publicity. On the suggestion of the Honorary Secretaries, Pooley and Luke, it set up a Public Relations Committee to replace the former Propaganda Committee. Early in 1914 it established a Voluntary Hospital News Service in Kingsway Hall. A big hospital fund-raising drive, along the lines of the Combined Appeal of 1922, was also contemplated. In the meantime, publicity was to be geared to eliminating the notion that the State was responsible for the sick, and to remind people of their long-standing affection for voluntary institutions and of the heroism of hospital workers.[31]

The Fund's public relations work ranged widely but had limited success. Among the most notable events was a broadcast by Gracie Fields on Christmas Eve 1939 from France. It was the first national wireless appeal on behalf of all voluntary hospitals and raised £18,000.[32] Later broadcasts, given by less popular figures, were unsuccessful, which proved yet again that it was not so much the cause but the backer that mattered. Meanwhile, the Fund had stickers put on broken hospital windows saying 'help your voluntary hospital'. It placed stories and pictures of bombed hospitals in the papers, appealed directly to America for aid, wrote speeches delivered by the Dukes of Kent and Gloucester, and arranged a broadcast with Ed Murrow. Not all of its work was applauded. The Secretary of the Middlesex Hospital, S. R. C. Plimsoll, himself a former member of the Fund's Propaganda Committee, complained that the story of a tea-kettle found in the stomach of a patient by X-rays lowered the tone of the voluntary system.[33]

In 1941, eight people worked for the Voluntary Hospital News Service, including Frank Long, a journalist who, on Lord Luke's initiative, was asked to write a history of the Fund as part of the propaganda campaign. Long became disillusioned with his work at the News Service. Though he wrote the history in a year, he felt that it was not properly appreciated. (A thousand copies were printed and the Fund made him a gift of £100 for his labours.) He complained that public relations work generally was not properly supported by his employers. This was clearly so, for in February 1942 the Fund 'damped down' the News Service and cut the number of its staff to one.[34] Long was among the casualties. The running-down of the institution's public relations work was indicative of its changing attitudes to the future financing of the voluntary hospitals.

One of the Fund's propaganda ideas which never reached fruition is worth special mention. At the end of 1941, Sir Hugh Lett, an Honorary Secretary, wrote to John Masefield, the Poet Laureate, asking him to write a book on the London voluntary hospitals and the blitz. Masefield, who was a friend of the voluntary system, agreed in January 1942 to write the book, which he saw as a record of the healing services under fire. His plan was to treat the hospitals not as individual institutions, 'but as a Troy, all by themselves united and walled against death and disease'.[35] In his reply to Lett, he asked to have sent to him any available hospital war-diaries, complete with recommendations for gallantry awards.

About thirty hospitals in all sent diaries to the Fund for the Poet Laureate's use. But Masefield never completed his book, which he found to be a most difficult project. (His correspondence with the Fund deals largely with his applications for petrol-coupons needed to visit the hospitals.)[36] The diaries, some of which have been cited above, have thus remained unpublished. They are a unique, often moving, record of wartime conditions and the ingenuity of staff in keeping the hospitals open in adverse conditions.[37] To Lett and his colleagues they were a poignant reminder that many hospitals would not survive the war's effects without government money. Masefield's choice of Troy as a metaphor was perhaps more apt than he imagined.

Voluntary contributions to the London hospitals remained fairly stable during the war, as did the Fund's own income; but the widespread destruction of property, coupled with the extension of government wartime controls, eroded confidence that the charitable hospitals could recover their former glory from the proceeds of flag-days, subscriptions, and contributory schemes. The loss of confidence was gradual and not universal in the Fund, but it was to play a significant part in the institution's diminished enthusiasm for raising money (the idea of another big appeal was dropped), and its eventual acceptance of a health service financed primarily by government.

The war seriously affected the Fund's personnel. Staff numbers increased due to the development of new projects, but there was a large turnover, for, as with other charities, many employees joined the services. Roger Peers obtained a commission as a sub-lieutenant in the Royal Naval Volunteer Reserve. Ives continued to oversee office affairs, but took on additional work as Secretary of the War Emergency Committee, which gave him a national responsibility. As part of his duties, he helped to organize the 'Bundles for Britain' campaign, which provided American money and supplies for the voluntary hospitals during the blitz.[38] Of the honorary officers, Sir Edward Peacock was absent briefly on national service and Major-General Sir Harold Wernher joined Lord Mountbatten in Combined Operations Headquarters, which meant he had little time to spare for the Fund.[39]

Death took a heavy toll of the Fund's honorary officials during the war. The institution lost two of its oldest friends in 1943: Sir Frederick Fry, who had attended the first Distribution Committee meeting in Lord Lister's house, and Lord Luke, who had joined the Fund in 1910. His death was a particular blow to the Fund's political and public relations work. The most notable loss came in August 1942, when the President of the Fund, the Duke of Kent, was killed in a plane crash on his way to Iceland. In October, the King appointed

the Duke of Gloucester President, the appointment having been recommended by the Lord Chancellor, the Prime Minister, and the Governor of the
Bank of England in accordance with the Fund's Act of Parliament. By the
terms of the Act, which excluded females, the Duke of Gloucester was
the only candidate available.

The Fund continued its day-to-day-activities during the war. In the
summer and autumn of 1944 its offices in Old Jewry suffered blast damage,
and all committee meetings removed to the Drapers' Hall. Much time was
spent simply in keeping the office open and getting the staff to and from work
safely. The work of the Emergency Bed Service suffered particular disruption,
for the air raids prevented patients from coming into London and knocked out
telephone lines, which suspended activities on more than one occasion. Still,
the development of a more efficiently co-ordinated service across the capital
continued to be an object, and it was heartening to the EBS to find that LCC
ambulances sometimes took patients to voluntary hospitals. By the end of the
war, despite an acute shortage of beds in London, the EBS dealt with nearly
500 cases a month. It was work which the Ministry of Health was grateful to
have undertaken by the voluntary sector.[40]

In 1940 the Fund responded to the regional boundaries adopted by the
Emergency Medical Service by extending its own area of operations to include
the whole of the Metropolitan Police District. The result was that twenty-two
more hospitals came within the Fund's purview and qualified for grants. Few
of them were visited, for a shortage of staff and the problems of transport
made the routine inspection of hospitals impossible. But visits to bombed
hospitals became common, and they provided useful information to the
Distribution Committee on the specific needs of affected institutions. The
Duke of Kent and Sir Hugh Lett were among those whose appearance a day
or two after an air raid also made a difference to the morale of patients and
staff alike.

The needs of London's hospitals varied, depending particularly on whether
they suffered bomb damage or liabilities on building-work which had been
under way in 1939. The Fund thus had a ticklish problem of how to divide up
its awards. Most of them went for maintenance, though some went to reduce
building-deficits and others to support recovery or convalescent homes in the
country. As ever, grants to schemes for capital expenditure turned on the
quality of the proposals submitted. The level of awards and special
distributions remained in excess of £300,000 a year for the duration of the
war, though it meant drawing on reserves.[41] In 1940, the total amount
distributed by the Fund since its foundation surpassed £10,000,000.

The Radium Committee found its work more complicated as a
consequence of the war, despite the restricted amount of radiotherapy carried
out in London. The risk of radium exposed to air raids was a constant worry;

some was lost. The Fund kept in close contact with the Radium Commission and the Ministry of Health on safety and related matters. Meanwhile, safe boreholes and steel receptacles were devised. By 1941, twenty-one hospitals stopped using radium in London and the Fund allowed some of the material to be used outside its area of operations. The Women's Voluntary Service took over responsibility for transport.[42]

The war interrupted or halted the Fund's work in many ways, but there were new projects to engage the staff. They ranged from the preparation of a provident scheme for the middle classes to publications on the supervision of nurses' health. Nursing was coming increasingly to the fore. The Fund had been awarding grants of £2,000 a year for the promotion of district nursing since 1936, and over the years it had spent large sums of money on the provision of nursing accommodation.[43] In June 1939, the Management Committee decided, at the request of the Voluntary Hospitals Committee for London, to set up a central bureau to encourage the recruitment of nurses for voluntary hospitals. The country needed 20,000 women a year to join the nursing profession, but wastage rates were high and during the war many women joined simply to avoid munitions work. In co-operation with the Royal College of Nursing, the Fund set up a committee, chaired by Lord Luke and after his death by Dr H. Morley Fletcher, to manage the Nursing Recruitment Centre. Miss Muriel Edwards, formerly Assistant Matron at St Thomas's, acted as the Centre's Secretary.

As Ives remarked, Muriel Edwards was the first nurse to be appointed by the Fund. Indeed she was one of the few members of the paid staff to be recruited with any experience of hospital work. Ives and Peers opposed her appointment because of her connection with the Royal College of Nursing, which they wanted to keep out of the Fund's affairs. Sir Ernest Pooley disregarded their views and she was hired, at a salary of £500 a year.[44] She soon settled in, despite some initial difficulties over the appointment of her deputy at the Centre. Full of ideas, she brought fresh life into the Fund at a time when it was most in need of it.

The Nursing Recruitment Centre opened on 1 April 1940 at 21 Cavendish Square. Its general aim was to act as a public relations department for nursing in the voluntary hospitals. Among its functions was the forging of links with schools, government departments, and other charitable agencies. It answered thousands of enquiries from prospective nurses and recruited about 2,000 women to the profession in the first two years of its existence. Relations with the London County Council and the Ministry of Health were sometimes strained due to the general shortage of candidates during the war and the rivalries between voluntary and municipal hospital services. The Fund was not pleased when the Ministry put out nursing-recruitment posters which directed applicants to County Hall and not to the Centre.[45] But relations with other voluntary bodies prospered. A grant from the Nuffield Trust in 1941 helped to finance an extension of the service to training-schools outside London.[46]

In June 1939, the Fund employed Captain J. E. Stone as a full-time consultant on hospital finance. Two years later he became head of the Economy Department, now under the management of the Distribution Committee, at a salary of £1,500 a year. Stone was a formidable figure in the history of hospital administration, a man in the tradition of Sir Henry Burdett. A dapper character, he had a lightness of touch which found expression in conjuring and tap-dancing.[47] He had been Chief Accountant at St Thomas's in the 1920s and then Secretary to the Birmingham Hospitals Centre. There were some in the Fund who hesitated over his appointment, but Ives and Wernher felt that the opportunity to employ him could not be missed, despite the dangers of bringing such a powerful man on to the scene.

Ives confessed to being intimidated by Stone at first. Stone had an encyclopaedic knowledge of hospital administration, which was evident from his books.[48] More to the point, he disapproved of the unified system of accounts, which, since Maynard's day as Secretary, the Fund had imposed upon hospitals. He favoured a departmental system, which he believed was a more flexible and effective instrument of administrative control. As Ives ruefully concluded, 'Stone was right and we were wrong. We'd been imposing the wrong system for a generation.'[49] It was a coincidence that the Management Committee accepted Maynard's resignation on the same day that it appointed Stone to be head of the Economy Department.[50]

Stone brooked no interference with his own department, but proved a loyal member of staff. He was just the man to steer the Fund's statistical work in a time of growing complexity in hospital services. What was needed, in his view, was a more elaborate advisory service to supplement the provision of statistics. It would further co-ordinate hospital experience and counter the charge that the voluntary hospitals were inefficient and pulling in different directions. Thus under Stone's guidance, the Fund became increasingly interested in the numerous day-to-day problems of hospital administration, including those associated with catering, equipment and supplies, stores control, domestic staff, and medical records.[51] Such practical considerations would become more prominent in the Fund as its fund-raising and propaganda waned.

Stone's interest in catering and stores illustrated the growing importance of hospital diet in the Fund's thinking. The visitors' reports had suggested to the Distribution Committee that changes were needed to bring hospital food into line with new knowledge of nutrition. As the *Lancet* pointed out, wartime rationing 'had the odd effect of showing where catering in some hospitals had been parsimonious'.[52] Food was traditionally the responsibility of the Hospital Secretary or Matron, whose interest in keeping costs under control dissipated even the best intentions.[53] One critic thought anything to do with food in a hospital was 'a beastly nuisance', for 'however good the service somebody grumbles'. He discovered one sweet child who idled away her convalescence inventing a culinary lexicon, in which jam roly-poly was 'putty and red paint' and rice pudding 'frog skin and maggots'.[54]

In its first *Memorandum on Hospital Diet* (1943), the Fund argued that the catering department in each hospital should be upgraded and that the officer in charge should be an experienced dietician. (There were under 300 dieticians in the country at the time.) Furthermore, a permanent Food Service Committee should be set up in every institution. The Memorandum was well received by the voluntary hospitals and by the Ministry of Health, which forwarded copies to the local authorities. Consequently, at the end of 1943 the Fund set up a Committee on Hospital Diet with Sir Jack Drummond, Scientific Adviser to the Ministry of Food, as Chairman. He was joined on the Committee by General Sir Kenneth Wigram, who had recently served as an Honorary Secretary of the Fund, and Sir Wilson Jameson, Chief Medical Officer of the Ministry of Health.[55]

By the end of the war over 100 hospitals had contacts with the Fund's Dietetic Advisory Service. Many of them sent catering staff, who were then in short supply, to refresher courses offered at the London Hospital. The Ministry of Food provided a demonstration of the use of dried egg. Impressed by the Fund's knowledge of catering, the Ministry of Health asked it to comment on its own circulars on diet and issued the second edition of the *Memorandum on Hospital Diet* (1945) to 900 hospitals.[56] The *Lancet* called the handbook 'a treasury; but it is more—it is a new approach to hospital feeding, based on the honourable doctrine of responsibility'.[57] As this remark suggests, hospital administration had come a long way since the days when patients provided their own food. Catering was a prime example of the institutional controls increasingly imposed on patients.

The work of the Fund's Dietetic Advisory Service may also be seen as an example of useful, though uncelebrated, charitable activity on behalf of patients in both the municipal and voluntary hospitals. It was probably the most notable practical project which brought the Fund into co-operation with the Ministry of Health before the foundation of the National Health Service. (The Fund's Committee on Hospital Diet was the first committee which included a representative from the Ministry.) The Dietetic Advisory Service was a model for the pioneering activities which the Fund and other voluntary bodies provided for the National Health Service after 1948.

While the Fund's staff occupied itself with practical work during the hostilities, its senior officials were growing increasingly concerned about proposals for the restructuring of the health services after the war. The mobilization of medical resources under 'war socialism' was much more efficient in the Second World War than it had been in the First. The

Emergency Medical Service, as Charles Webster reminds us, 'marked a secular shift towards a nationally planned and rationalised hospital service'.[58] A regional approach, which had been under discussion for many years, became a reality under the EMS. London had been divided into ten sectors, each centred on a teaching hospital. (This pattern proved a forerunner of the metropolitan hospital regions under the NHS.) The co-operation imposed on the municipal and voluntary systems resulted in the disappearance of many of the distinctions between them. But it did not obliterate essential differences and long-standing rivalries.

At no time during the war did the Fund assume that the voluntary hospitals would be 'nationalized'. But the war's effects convinced it that the Emergency Medical Service would be followed by some 'permanent system of co-operation between all institutional health services'.[59] It took the view that the EMS showed that an effective hospital service could be run on the basis of two different systems. Soon after the outbreak of war, Lord Dawson said to the Fund's General Council: 'The voluntary and municipal hospitals, though both of them are necessary for the needs of modern life, must maintain their individual life to develop along their own lines with complete freedom, but with an ever increasing co-operation so that they may produce between them a united and ordered policy.'[60] This was the general, and familiar, line the Fund wished to pursue in its negotiations with its allies and with government.

Alarm bells began to ring in the Fund in 1941, after a statement made in the House of Commons on 9 October by the Minister of Health, Ernest Brown. Brown declared, for the first time, that it was government's objective to create 'a comprehensive hospital service' at the end of the war. He did not envisage a free service and anticipated a continuation of payments through contributory schemes. And while he ritually endorsed the idea of 'partnership' between the voluntary and municipal hospitals, he proposed that the new service be organized by local government. He also said that it would be necessary to design such a service by reference to areas substantially larger than those of the individual local authorities. Consequently he announced his intention of initiating a survey of hospital services in London. (The Nuffield Provincial Hospitals Trust had already started compiling material for the provinces.) The object was to gather information about the availability of hospital facilities, which was essential as a basis for any future planning.[61] Ives later called the decision to carry out the survey 'a momentous step'.[62]

In response to the government statement the King's Fund and the Voluntary Hospitals Committee for London established a Joint Committee to consider post-war hospital problems in the capital. As in its other committees, the Fund put together a team of City businessmen and doctors connected to the teaching hospitals and the royal family. Its representatives included Lord

Donoughmore (Chairman), Sir Ernest Rock Carling, and Sir Ernest Pooley. Lord Dawson and Sir Bernard Docker were co-opted at a later stage. The Joint Committee invited the voluntary hospitals to comment on proposals for the future hospital service and appointed a Medical Sub-Committee under the chairmanship of Sir Hugh Lett, a retired London Hospital surgeon. (Lett was the only medical man in the Fund's history to serve as an Honorary Secretary.) The Fund's first reaction to the government's ideas was to try to limit the power of the local authorities. It accepted that a regional or 'sector' scheme was inevitable, but insisted that within it the influence of the teaching hospitals must be as extensive as possible.[63]

Meanwhile, the Fund decided to collaborate with the proposed London survey. It was undertaken by Dr Archibald Gray, President of the Royal Society of Medicine and a member of the Fund's Distribution Committee, and Dr Graham Topping, the London County Council's Deputy Medical Officer of Health. The statistical work fell to Captain Stone, who provided the information on the voluntary hospitals in the Metropolitan Police District. There were fears at the time among voluntarists, especially those attached to the specialist hospitals, that such surveys might lead to the destruction of their institutions.[64] They believed that planners with a regional perspective were not disposed to notice the value of smaller institutions, however popular in their neighbourhoods, which did not have friends in high places.

While Captain Stone and his colleagues compiled statistics for the planners in the Ministry of Health, the Fund's management prepared its defence of the voluntary sector in anticipation of further government initiatives. (It is not clear whether anyone in the Fund suspected that these two endeavours might be at cross purposes.) Government thinking on the shape of post-war hospital provision was in flux and to voluntarists it was crucial to keep informed. But in the atmosphere of 'total war', with the government making inroads on every front, they were running to stand in place. Even where the voluntary movement thrived, it was bound to look diminished. For in creating and exposing scarcity and deprivation, the Second World War made traditional philanthropic remedies look inadequate. In contrast to what had happened in the First World War, the British public was turning its mind to post-war reconstruction before victory was certain. This had a propaganda value for the government, but it raised expectations of a better world that would be difficult to meet.

The Beveridge Report, published in December 1942, was on social security, but it assumed that its proposals for comprehensive social insurance would be complemented by a national health service free at point of need. On crucial matters affecting the voluntary hospitals, including how they were to be administered, Beveridge did not go into detail, for it was not part of his brief. Against the background of evacuation, ration cards, and the state direction of labour, which 'nationalized' daily life as never before, the Report became a bestseller. The popularity of Beveridge's proposals worried government officials, including those at the Ministry of Health, who had to deal with the expectations it aroused.[65] Comprehensive social services and medical provision excited widespread enthusiasm, but there were dissenting voices both inside and outside government, including members of the Friendly Society movement, who wanted local control of social insurance and less red tape.[66]

Given the prospect of 'universal' state provision offered by Beveridge, could the charitable emphases on 'selectivity' and local initiative be sustained? Would the public respond with its traditional enthusiasm to future appeals to self-help after all the sacrifice the war itself demanded? Beveridge did not intend that the State should monopolize the welfare services, for he saw a continuing role for voluntarism in the drive for social progress. But to the more dedicated voluntarists, he was just another in a long line of liberals doing the dirty work of collectivism by the back door. His respect for voluntary traditions might easily be forgotten by others without his knowledge of the charitable sector, not least by the army of non-industrial civil servants in central government, whose numbers rose dramatically during the war, to over 700,000.[67]

In sombre mood, the Fund's officials received advance details of the Beveridge Report in the summer of 1942 through Lord Dawson. They knew Beveridge to be a supporter of charitable agencies. He had, after all, served on the Fund's Propaganda Committee. But his proposals threw doubt on the continuation of contributory schemes, thought to be essential to the survival of the charitable hospitals. They also left unresolved the crucial issue of the future relationship of the hospitals with the local authorities and Whitehall. Chary of anything which threatened the independence of the voluntary hospitals, the Fund was inclined to see Beveridge's scheme as potentially dangerous. The Medical Sub-Committee dismissed it as 'a mechanistic solution', which 'in the long run would be a mistake'.[68]

The publication of the Beveridge Report animated the coalition government, which now felt obliged to come up with positive proposals for a comprehensive health service, including reorganization of hospital provision. Following the lines of the Ministry of Health's statement of October 1941, it was decided that the hospital services in each area should be organized by the local authorities in 'collaboration' with voluntary agencies. Just what was meant by 'collaboration' was unclear, nor was it obvious how the traditions of the voluntary hospitals were to be 'safeguarded' in a unified hospital service. As Brian Abel-Smith put it, 'the delicate issues could be sidestepped in statements of broad principle but if there were to be a plan, eventually they would have to be faced'.[69]

The Ministry canvassed opinion from the local authorities, voluntary bodies, and the medical profession, and each group jockeyed for position as the ground began to shift beneath them. In March 1943, Sir John Maude, the Permanent Secretary to the Ministry, invited representatives from the Fund, the Nuffield Provincial Hospitals Trust, and the British Hospitals Association to a series of preliminary discussions about the future health services. The Joint Committee of the Fund and the Voluntary Hospitals Committee for London had just completed a 'Statement' on the 'Co-ordination of Hospital Services'. Partly drafted by Lord Dawson, it provided a basis for the Fund's case in its discussions with the Ministry. It did not refer to the Beveridge Report.

In its Statement, the Fund argued that it was premature to examine in detail the form which the hospital service should take until the outline had been agreed. It did not question the need for increased institutional provision, and it accepted that the 'haphazard distribution' of hospitals throughout the country must be reordered in the interests of the entire population. Unlike the state planners, however, it did not use the word 'haphazard' in a derogatory sense. As in previous statements, the Fund pointed to the need for a pattern of hospital services organized along regional lines with local authority hospitals and voluntary hospitals working in 'partnership'. Such a 'partnership' should find expression in a joint council for the area. Wherever possible, the 'key hospital' at the top of each region was to be a teaching hospital attached to a university.[70]

The Fund's views betrayed a deep suspicion of local-authority control of charitable institutions, which its own relationship with the London County Council exacerbated. The centralizing tendencies of local authorities and the differences in management between municipal and voluntary institutions were fundamental obstacles to the Fund's acceptance of a national health service run by local government. In a voluntary hospital, a medical committee, working side by side with the administrative committee, had the power to initiate and to advise on medical policy. But in most local authority hospitals, the doctors had no such status. On professional matters, as well as administrative ones, they were under the authority of a Medical Superintendent, an office which doctors held in low regard. The Superintendent reported through the Medical Officer of Health to the local authority, whose Health Committee, though often made up of amateurs, made important decisions on medical matters.

In the light of these administrative problems, the Fund recommended that the government establish a Central Hospital Board, which would secure the vocational principle at the centre and lay the foundation for an effective partnership between the local authorities and the voluntary hospitals. The proposed Board was not itself to take over the administrative responsibilities

OUR NEW KNIGHT-HOSPITALLER.

1. The launch of the Fund as seen by *Punch*, 20 February 1897

2. *Daily Mail,* 27 November 1902

3. Advertisement, *The Lady*, April 1902

4. A collector for the Coronation Appeal, 1902

BUCKINGHAM PALACE.

I am following with the closest interest the progress made by King Edward's Hospital Fund in organising this combined appeal on behalf of the Voluntary Hospitals of London & I congratulate the Organising Committee on the results already achieved.

My family have been intimately associated with the Fund from its inception: & I know that my son, the President, would have taken an active, personal part in this great effort had circumstances so permitted.

His happiness in returning home will be increased by the knowledge that the people of London have generously resolved to save their Hospitals. It is impossible to contemplate the closing of any of them, for in character & organisation our Hospitals are unique among the charitable Institutions of the world.

June 12th 1922.

George R.I.

5. An open letter from King George V in support of
the Fund's Combined Appeal, 1922

6. King George V and Queen Mary visiting Queen Mary's Hospital, Stratford, 9 June 1923

7. HRH the Prince of Wales opening the King's Fund
Miniature Hospital, 1933

HOSPITAL.	Bed Complement at 31 Dec.	Pay Beds included in Col. 2 (See App. I).	AVERAGE DAILY NUMBER OF					Percentage of average Bed Complement Closed.	Percentage of Open Beds Vacant.
			Bed Complement during the year	Beds CLOSED on account of Cleaning, Repairs and Other Causes.	Beds OPEN (i.e., Col. 4 minus Col. 5).	Beds VACANT (i.e., Beds in Col. 6 unoccupied).			
(1)	(2)	(3)	(4)	(5)	(6)	(7)		(8)	(9)
								%	%
SECTION A— (Over 500 Beds).									
Guy's	691	77 at 5 to 12 gns.	690·3	3·5	686·8	104·2		0·5	15·2
London	891	52 at 5 to 10 gns.	894·0	9·0	885·0	140·4		1·0	15·9
Middlesex ..	614	75 at 4 to 12 gns.	603·8	3·1	600·7	29·6		0·5	4·9
St. Bartholomew's ..	763	—	756·4	30·5	725·9	76·7		4·0	10·6
St. Thomas's ..	682	40 at 6 & 9 gns.	682·0	22·8	659·2	65·3		3·3	9·9
University College ..	617	77 at 6 to 12 gns.	617·0	25·3	591·7	50·1		4·1	8·5
Totals and Averages of A—6 Hospitals	4,258	321	4,243·5	94·2	4,149·3	466·3		2·2	11·2
SECTION B— (Under 500 Beds).									
Charing Cross	293	—	293·0	3·0	290·0	34·1		1·0	11·8
King's College ..	420	96 at 5 to 10 gns.	420·0	38·0	382·0	51·8		9·0	13·6
Royal Free	327	24 at 5 & 7 gns.	327·0	15·0	312·0	29·2		4·6	9·4
St. George's	334	—	334·0	3·6	330·4	49·8		1·1	15·1
St. Mary's	476	66 at 7 to 15 gns.	476·0	15·6	460·4	70·5		3·3	15·3
Westminster	258	41 at 5 to 10 gns.	258·0	0·8	257·2	28·5		0·3	11·1
Totals and Averages of B—6 Hospitals	2,108	227	2,108·0	76·0	2,032·0	263·9		3·6	13·0
Totals and Group Averages, 1938	6,366	548	6,351·5	170·2	6,181·3	730·2		2·7	11·8
Do. do. 1937	6,295	547	6,165·7	232·5	5,933·2	661·2		3·8	11·1

8. Some King's Fund statistics on hospital beds in London for 1938

9. The view from St Thomas's, 1940

10. The Emergency Bed Service in the 1950s

11. HRH Princess Alexandra opening the King's Fund College Library, 1988

12. HRH the Prince of Wales and the Fund's Treasurer, Robin Dent, on a visit to the South Western Hospital, 1989

13. 'London Think Tank Launched', *Health Service Journal*, 13 December 1990

of the hospitals, but its relationship to them should resemble that of the University Grants Committee to the Universities. Composed of medical men and lay hospital managers, it would have a financial responsibility for the service. According to the Fund, direct government grants to the voluntary hospitals would guarantee them a measure of independence. On the other hand, if the government made block grants to the local authorities to redistribute, it would spell disaster for the voluntary hospitals. Moreover, it would introduce an intolerable level of political interference in the system. 'The long-term importance of this consideration cannot be over-emphasized,' the Fund concluded.[71]

Such were the arguments put forward by the Fund in its dealings with the Ministry of Health in the spring and summer of 1943. In a meeting with Maude in March, Pooley compared the voluntary hospitals to independent secondary schools threatened by local-authority takeover after the Education Act of 1902; Dawson argued that Section 13 of the Local Government Act of 1929, which required local authorities to consult the voluntary hospitals in planning their services, had not worked, but had simply soured relations between municipalists and voluntarists. Maude kept his counsel, but repeated the government's position that the new service would be based on local government.[72] The battlefield was most clearly apparent in London, where the Fund and the London County Council stood in the front line. Bounced into the fray by the Beveridge Report, the Ministry of Health was caught in the crossfire of the voluntarists, who wished to parry the local authorities, and the municipalists, many of whom wished to wound, if not finish off, the voluntarists. Everyone spoke warmly of 'partnership'.

The latent rivalries between municipalists and voluntarists came to a head when the new Minister of Health, the Conservative lawyer Henry Willink, presented the long-awaited White Paper on health provision in February 1944. In it he announced the government's intention of establishing a 'free' comprehensive health service for everybody in the country based on local responsibility, coupled with central control vested in the Minister. As Charles Webster has noted, the key words 'free' and 'comprehensive' were hedged in with reservations. On the adminstrative side, little was said about the adoption of regional organization; and, for convenience, 'joint authorities' made up of county councils and county boroughs were to manage the local-authority hospitals. Though the White Paper guaranteed the voluntary hospitals full independence and a role in joint planning, the Ministry accepted that a universal public hospital service might have the effect of undermining voluntary traditions. But it was not the wish of the government, in the words of the White Paper, 'to destroy or to diminish a system which is so well rooted in the good will of its supporters'.[73]

The lay public and the daily newspapers generally approved of the White

Paper. The Trades Union Congress and the Labour Party, noting its limitations, thought it an acceptable 'interim solution'.[74] Doctors and voluntarists went over it with a magnifying glass and found faults. The latter discovered that their request for direct central government grants to the voluntary hospitals had been rejected in favour of payments through the local authorities. The White Paper anticipated the dying-away of contributory schemes, which would throw the voluntary hospitals on to the rates. At the same time, it argued that the survival of voluntary institutions depended on their ability to continue to raise subscriptions. But could they survive if their former subscribers understood that payments for treatment came from the rates? Moreover, would subscribers continue to support a health system described by the Ministry as 'free'? The White Paper was not only a blow to self-help. Its switch from the idea of 'minimum' public provision to the provision of the 'best' medical services for everyone threatened to undermine 'the use of the price system for encouraging economy'.[75]

The local authorities generally welcomed the proposals. The London County Council asked to be in on any discussions between the Ministry of Health and the voluntary hospitals. The voluntary hospitals themselves, fearing that they would become vassals of local government, looked on the White Paper with 'the greatest apprehension'. As the Secretary of the Charing Cross Hospital wrote to Willink, it threatened 'to destroy these free institutions.'[76] The medical charities and widely popular contributory-scheme associations feared that the government's proposals would also sweep them away. As the Manchester and Salford Medical Charities Fund wrote to Willink, 'this Fund would cease to exist'.[77] Apart from the principles at stake, the government's scheme threatened thousands of jobs in the voluntary sector, in medical missions, contributory schemes, and hospital funds. The paid personnel in the King's Fund and the League of Mercy must have wondered about their tenure.

The Fund's officials read the White Paper with an eye to saving the hospitals from, in Lord Dawson's words, 'the stranglehold of local authorities'.[78] It was also worried by the government's cavalier use of the word 'free' in regard to future health provision. And it wished to disabuse people of the view that any government, of whatever political persuasion, would ever deliver more than a basic service. From the days of Burdett, the Fund had assumed that the Treasury would only pay for the nation's health with the greatest reluctance. Thus for financial reasons alone, it believed voluntary traditions would continue to be vital. On the issue of control, it argued that autonomous voluntary hospitals were needed to keep at bay the dead hand of bureaucracy and to provide a way of assessing the progress and efficiency of the system generally.[79] In this respect, it was desirable to maintain the rivalry between the municipal and voluntary hospitals, however unproductive it might appear to government planners.

In the White Paper, the Ministry of Health spoke of its hospital proposals, with their mix of central government control and local-government responsibility, as embodying democracy.[80] But the voluntary mind did not limit democratic action to conventional politics. Indeed, it saw the continuation of voluntary institutions as a way of protecting the public from the wasteful factionalism of party politics. With their traditional emphases on local decision-making, innovation, and self-help, the voluntary hospitals saw themselves promoting democratic pluralism in health. Would a national health service preserve it? Would the loyalty, enthusiasm, and generosity of the voluntary hospital system, which many saw as its essential spirit, continue to provide a check on the standardizing tendencies of the State? 'This spirit must not be allowed to die,' exclaimed the Fund in the summer of 1944.[81]

At the time, the voluntary hospital spirit was under strain not only from government proposals but from a renewal of German aerial attacks. By the end of October 1944, seventy-six more hospitals in the London sector alone, both municipal and voluntary, had been damaged by flying bombs, with a loss of 8,600 beds. The Royal Free Hospital in Gray's Inn Road suffered a direct hit with the loss of five lives.[82] The renewal of bombing added urgency, and gravity, to the deliberations over the White Paper. The Fund had been preparing its case to be presented to the Ministry of Health over the spring and summer months and in the autumn felt a meeting would be beneficial. It noted that representatives from the London County Council had already been to see the Minister.[83]

In its discussions on the White Paper, the Fund maintained close contact with the hospitals and the British Hospitals Association. But it decided to make independent representations to the Ministry of Health. This allowed for the voluntary hospital view to be pressed on the Ministry from different quarters. It is also likely that the Fund did not wish to be too closely identified with the British Hospitals Association, whose style differed from its own. The BHA under Sir Bernard Docker was obdurate, the Fund under Peacock amenable to compromise. Ministry officials preferred the latter. In the preliminary notes to one of their meetings with the Fund they accorded it 'special value' for its experience and independence.[84] It is unclear whether this had anything to do with the fact that among the Fund's delegation was Sir George Aylwen, Treasurer of St Bartholomew's, who was Henry Willink's father-in-law.

On 17 October 1944, Peacock, Wernher, Lett, and Aylwen had a meeting with Willink, Maude, Sir Wilson Jameson, and Sir Arthur Rucker at the Ministry of Health. (The British Hospitals Association had a meeting at the Ministry the following day.) They discussed various points raised in the Fund's Memorandum on the White Paper, which had called for greater participation of the voluntary hospitals in planning the service, the spreading of the influence of the teaching institutions, self-government of the individual voluntary hospitals, and that well-worn idea, a central hospitals board. The Minister displayed open-mindedness about his proposals, but he rejected the idea of a central hospitals board because it departed from the normal system of ministerial responsibility.[85]

The Fund's officials urged the case for equal representation of voluntary hospitals in local planning in view of the financial and other resources they would bring into the service. The Minister appreciated the point, but said that there had been some misunderstanding of the implications of partnership, which to him did not necessarily imply 'equality in control'. He did not share the Fund's worry that the voluntary hospitals would be undermined by receiving payments from local authorities, for they would, after all, be partly responsible for the formulation of the service. Peacock demurred and said it was a 'large request to make to the voluntary hospitals that they should look to rate monies to replace contributory schemes and subscriptions'. Maude, however, remarked that it was essential for service payments to come from the local authorities in view of their statutory obligation to provide the service. Direct payments from the Exchequer, which the Fund supported, would 'mean a continuation—and indeed an accentuation—of the present division into two systems'.[86]

The meeting between the Fund and the Ministry was preliminary and dealt with first principles. Both sides accepted the need to flesh out proposals with greater detail. London posed particular problems because of the complexity and level of hospital provision. As Sir Arthur Rucker conceded to the Fund's officials, the local planning-machinery for London would eventually need 'special consideration'.[87] He added that the London Hospital Survey, which the Fund and the LCC had provided with statistics, would soon be available. In fact, the Survey had been completed in early 1944, just before the publication of the White Paper. (It was not published until April 1945.) It did not include information on the extensive damage sustained by the hospitals in the aerial attacks of 1944.[88]

The London Survey, like the companion volumes for the other areas, was a product of the opportunities provided by the war for a radical rethinking of hospital administration.[89] It was brutal in its judgements on individual hospitals, especially the smaller ones. It recommended the closure of many institutions which the Fund had long supported, including the London Fever Hospital, the Mildmay Mission Hospital, and that charmingly named hospital in Highgate, the Santa Claus Home for sick children, which had only twenty-six beds. Unsympathetic to the local allegiances of the hospitals, the London

Survey was a preview of post-war hospital planning. It represented a dramatic break with the traditions of Victorian hospitals and 'homes', in which a domestic, neighbourhood character was highly valued. With hindsight, it may seem ironic that the King's Fund expended so much labour on helping a project that recommended the demise of hospitals it had for so long protected.

In favouring big institutions, the London Survey typified collectivist planning. It was rather better at pointing out deficiencies in the existing system than in providing a workable blueprint for administrative reform. Its detail suggested that the reorganization of hospital services was bound to be expensive, an impression which its conclusions on staffing and accommodation reinforced.[90] The call for a massive rebuilding-programme for the South-east would have given fiscal conservatives in the Treasury the shivers. The bomb damage sustained by so many hospitals after its completion could only make the situation worse. The Ministry of Health under Willink adopted the view that the London Survey represented the personal views of those who drew it up.[91]

The Fund was acutely aware of the financial burdens likely to be incurred in rebuilding and reorganization and, as suggested, this put it in a mood to compromise with the government in exchange for direct financial support for voluntary institutions. Following its discussions in October with the Fund and the British Hospitals Association, the Ministry asked itself again whether hospital reorganization as outlined in the White Paper might result, as the voluntarists insisted, in the drying-up of charitable income. If it did, the government would have to pick up a much bigger bill or provide an impoverished service.

To iron out this issue, Willink had lunch with the Fund's officials, Peacock, Donoughmore, and Wernher, on 5 December 1944. His staff described the meeting as 'encouraging' and 'thoroughly friendly'.[92] By now Willink was himself more amenable to persuasion. Peacock and his colleagues pressed yet again for direct Exchequer grants to the voluntary hospitals, which they believed necessary to sustain charitable contributions. To overcome their objection to local authority payments, Willink suggested a 'clearing-house' system of payments, which would avoid the appearance of rate subsidies. Everyone agreed on the need to provide 'a gap' for voluntary contributions.[93]

As Willink was by now reminded, there were over a thousand voluntary hospitals in the country, along with thousands of ancillary charities providing medically related services. He was also aware of the scale of voluntary contributions and of patients' payments through contributory schemes, which voluntarists insisted were threatened by the White Paper. He had to consider the possible loss of this revenue in the light of his estimate of the cost of the services he proposed.[94] The White Paper had argued that if 'the situation were to arise in which the whole cost of the voluntary hospitals' part in the public service was repaid from public money … the end of the voluntary movement would be near at hand'.[95] Willink now noted that the White Paper might 'sink some voluntary hospitals, but "the total cost" policy would sink us'.[96]

By giving such great responsibility to the local authorities, the White Paper had antagonized not only the voluntary hospitals, the managers of contributory schemes, and charities like the King's Fund, but also the doctors.[97] The BMA conducted a survey which showed a majority of doctors opposed to its proposals.[98] Most hostile were the consultants. They had long had uncharitable feelings towards local authority officials, whose social status was lower than civil servants in central government and whose hospitals compared unfavourably with voluntary institutions. Nor did they warm to the prospect of local-authority interference in clinical work. But had the White Paper given more control to the doctors, or had it brought governors of voluntary hospitals into an equal planning-role, it would have alienated the local authorities, who continued to press their case. Besieged on all sides, Willink and his colleagues went back to the drawing-board.

By the summer of 1945, after further consultation, Willink had cobbled together a revised and highly elaborate scheme.[99] Among its many proposals, it offered voluntarists a greater say in planning the service and adopted a standard service-payment from a 'clearing-house' for each region, which avoided any direct financial relationship between the local authorities and the voluntary hospitals.[100] These concessions were partly due to the state of the British economy and the Ministry's fear of a financial crisis in the new system if voluntary revenues collapsed. Though widely criticized as producing 'a planning and administrative system of almost unworkable complexity', the revised Willink scheme bowed to economic realities as well as to the powerful voluntary lobby.[101]

While Willink was revising his White Paper proposals, the Joint Committee of the Fund and the Voluntary Hospitals Committee for London prepared a report on post-war hospital problems.[102] Appearing in July 1945, the month of the general election, it was a cogent statement of the voluntary hospital case, one of the last ever made. In some respects it was in agreement with the recently published London Hospital Survey, particularly in its criticisms of the maldistribution of hospitals. But the report put a premium on preserving choice and institutional diversity in the system, and it did not have a fixation with large-scale economies. This stemmed partly from the Fund's desire to maintain friendly, informal relations between staff and patients within institutions, which were more notable in smaller, neighbourhood hospitals. But it also had to do with defending the patients' freedom to attend hospitals of different types and sizes. Freedom of choice was necessary in order to make it possible to distinguish between a popular and an unpopular hospital;

it was an essential guide to the standard of hospital services and an index of their relative efficiency.

The report of the Joint Committee rejected a 'single hospital system', in which all institutions were at a uniform level under local authority control. Returning to its central theme, it argued that in such a system the public would never know whether the service it was receiving was good or bad. Unlike a business, where the annual profit or loss showed whether it has been successful or not, there was no absolute standard by which to determine the success of a hospital. The public must judge, and it could only do so when there was variety within the system. Thus the 'true justification' for the continuation of the voluntary hospitals was that they offered 'an independent standard against which hospitals provided by the public authority can be judged'.[103] The report also castigated the public hospital system for distancing the patient from the makers of policy: 'Take away the voluntary hospital and its direct impact of patient upon management without intermediary, and there is no telling to what lengths remote control may go nor how deadening that handicap may become.'[104]

Judging from the report, the Fund still felt there was mileage left in the voluntary hospitals. It took hope from the changes being made to the White Paper and a statement of policy from the Prime Minister published in *The Times* on 11 June 1945, a month after the defeat of Germany. As head of a 'caretaker government', Churchill declared that 'the voluntary hospitals which have led the way in the development of hospital technique will remain free. They will play their part in the new service in friendly partnership with local authority hospitals.'[105] The question of what Churchill and his colleagues meant precisely by 'free' was never resolved, for in July the Labour Party won a resounding election victory. With it, Willink's revised proposals disappeared into the archives. The Fund and its allies looked on the election results with foreboding. Labour Party policy on hospital provision, enunciated in 1943, assumed that an overhauled local government would take over the voluntary hospitals and make them conform to a 'plan'.[106]

Aneurin Bevan, the new Minister of Health, was in an enviable position. His party had a large political majority and his department a backlog of proposals. Bevan was a Welshman with a reputation for pugnacity and Marxism; his appointment caused widespread alarm among doctors and voluntarists, and even a few of his civil servants. Churchill called him a 'squalid nuisance'.[107] Clear-headed and persuasive, he had a gift for spotting and exploiting the divisions among his adversaries. In preliminary meetings with them, he let his natural charm come to the surface, which disguised a firmness of purpose. In a draft Cabinet Paper written soon after coming into office, he noted the need to move quickly if the gains made by the Emergency Medical Service were not to be lost, and he added: 'We shall have to be ruthless in any further negotiations with the various interests, particularly the local authorities and the voluntary hospitals.'[108] Such remarks suggest that in Bevan's mind it was not inevitable that his health proposals would come to fruition, rather that he must act quickly and decisively in order to prevent pre-war voluntary traditions from reasserting themselves.

Bevan had little use for voluntary traditions, which to his Welsh mind were an expression of the English class system. In Parliament, he diplomatically accepted that the Labour government should make full use of voluntary bodies, but he had no intention of doing so as Minister of Health. He equated them with nurses organizing flag days on their weekends off, which struck him as an indignity in a modern society. Fairness in health provision was one of his chief aims, and he did not believe that spontaneous charity could achieve it. In this he personified the collectivist, 'planning' wing in the Labour movement, which had been doing battle with voluntarists for decades. Parochial traditions of personal service and self-help were repugnant, remnants of a tribal past. In Bevan's words, they were 'a patch-quilt of local paternalisms' and thus the 'enemy of intelligent planning'.[109]

Bevan also disregarded the co-operative societies in the Labour movement. In his view they lacked centralizing power and had integrated into the mixed economy. Moreover, like all voluntary bodies, they were too self-contained and apolitical to challenge social injustice and the corruption of British political life. As Richard Crossman, one of Bevan's disciples, wrote in 1955, the co-operative movement did not have the capacity to move 'to the next stage of socialism'.[110] With an unwavering faith in the triumph of his creed, Bevan was transfixed by the idea that the State was the embodiment of good, the ultimate source of welfare. Deeply paternalistic, he and his followers believed that it was 'only through state action' that a transformation of society could be achieved.[111] They did not encourage popular participation in their reforms, as Crossman later conceded. 'Instead the impression was given that socialism was an affair for the Cabinet, acting through the existing Civil Service.'[112]

Bevan was determined to bring the voluntary hospitals, which to him were a prime example of hierarchical charity, into a unified system. The various reports and hospital surveys at his disposal, which described the deficiencies in the existing services, confirmed his faith in large institutions and central planning. The fact that independent local hospitals were often run highly efficiently made no impression on him. Soon after taking office, he wrote to his Cabinet colleagues that 'the notion of the self-contained, separate, independent "local hospital," is nowadays a complete anachronism. I think the system has outlived its usefulness and the time has come to leave it behind.'[113] Bevan's proposals, which he put to the Cabinet in October 1945, did just that. In the health service that he envisaged, there was to be no room for individualistic voluntary hospitals, with their arcane practices, private patrons, and idiosyncratic governing bodies. But he disguised his disregard for voluntary traditions with the simple argument that, if publicly financed, the hospitals must come into public ownership.

Having dismissed the voluntarists, Bevan turned to the municipalists. It was assumed by most observers that the new service would be based on the local authorities. But propelled by his centralist views and the need to appease the leading consultants, who were so hostile to local-government control, Bevan concluded that the option of nationalization, which had been mooted in 1939, offered 'a more rational geographical framework, and a chance to create a system of administration that would be more palatable to the profession and the voluntary lobby'.[114] He used much the same argument against the local authorities, whose hospitals he criticized, that he used against the voluntarists: since most of the money would be coming from central funds, it would be unwise to put the new service in municipal hands.

Bevan antagonized his Cabinet colleague Herbert Morrison, the former leader of the London County Council and a proponent of local democracy. But Morrison too was affected by the much-heralded promise of central planning. Himself persuaded that nationalized services were more efficient than municipal ones, he failed to come up with an alternative to Bevan's scheme.[115] In the battle over the National Health Service Bill, the municipalists put up less of a struggle than the voluntarists. Ultimately, the decision to place the NHS under ministerial control may have been a greater blow to local government, to its morale and recruitment, than to the voluntary movement, which by its very nature was more resilient.

The King's Fund heard of Bevan's intentions early in November 1945, at about the time when the press leaked the news of 'hospital nationalization'.[116] For nearly fifty years nationalization had been a recurring nightmare to the Fund's officials. Lord Dawson, now dead, had argued after the publication of the White Paper that such an 'abrupt change' in hospital affairs would result in 'chaos'.[117] It was perhaps just as well that he and other members of the Fund's old guard, such as Lord Luke, were no longer on the scene. Be that as it may, the Fund's management showed remarkable sang-froid and resilience in the face of Bevan's proposal to bring the voluntary hospitals under government control.

Bevan's advisers noted that 'the King Edward's Fund people were wise and sensible men'.[118] They were certainly realistic enough to recognize that times had changed, not least politically. The information which they were receiving from visitors and other sources convinced them that rising medical costs and the war's effects meant that the hospitals could no longer support their activities as they had done in the past.[119] And in light of high levels of personal taxation, the omens were not good that great benefactors or mass appeals could bail the hospitals out. The Fund's committee men were thus willing to cut their losses and to shift their policies. Looking at Bevan's proposals they still felt there was much to play for. If they could no longer prevent the hospitals from falling into the hands of the State, they would promote the continuation of voluntary traditions within the new health service.

To the Fund's officials, Bevan's preference for nationalization had at least saved the voluntary hospitals from the prospect of something they believed to be even more sinister: local-authority control. The Minister intended that the voluntary lobby should see the exclusion of the local authorities from the new service as a concession. The Fund, which was lining up with the consultants, did see it in this light. And it took further comfort from the possibility of a 'special provision' being granted to the teaching hospitals. Ives wrote immediately to Peacock when he heard of the Minister's plan: 'to oust the local authorities in favour of a national service . . . would be so beneficial—if linked with independence for the teaching hospitals—as to outweigh almost all other considerations'.[120]

If the Fund's initial response was to find a *modus vivendi* with Bevan, this could not be said of many other voluntary institutions, including many of the hospitals themselves. A storm of protest blew up when the Ministry revealed its plans, and not only in the Tory strongholds. Many complained about the loss of jobs, the uncertain future of 'life' governors, and the status of endowment funds. The Perth Royal Infirmary argued that the NHS would create 'an elaborate and complicated machinery . . . of a bureaucratic department and the financial limitations of the Treasury'.[121] The President of the Royal Halifax Infirmary explained that working-class Labour supporters wanted the continuation of the hospital's voluntary status because they preferred local control.[122] Consumers were not unanimously in support of Bevan's proposals, as the many petitions to the Ministry of Health attest. Traditions of self-help remained strong in working-class communities. There was still such 'general dislike of state officialdom' that the assumption that ordinary citizens were in favour of further state intervention in civilian life must be questioned.[123]

Whatever the public wanted, the war offered opportunities to social reformers and state planners. In January 1946, the government circulated its hospital proposals to interested parties and arranged a series of confidential meetings with them. Representatives of the voluntary hospitals, with some exceptions, divided between those from the teaching hospitals, who saw some merit in Bevan's scheme, and those from the smaller, non-teaching hospitals, 'who were horrified and outraged' by it.[124] Docker and the BHA took the 'horrified' line with Bevan, arguing that state ownership was unnecessary and the confiscation of trusts undesirable. Though the BHA stood rather in isolation from the hospitals it served, Docker spoke for all voluntarists when he told the Minister that a 'personal interest in the hospitals by those using them was essential to progress'. Bevan agreed that the system would collapse if state control could not be reconciled with personal interest and local participation, and he sought to reassure Docker that he did not object to the 'spirit of voluntary service'.[125] Docker, who later described Bevan's Bill as the 'mass murder of the hospitals', did not believe him.[126]

Compared to those of the BHA, the Fund's links with the teaching hospitals were intimate, and the more Bevan offered them the more it moderated its criticism of his proposals. In their meeting with the Minister on 5 February 1946, the Fund's representatives stressed that they wished to support his efforts to produce a first-class hospital service. But they had two reservations, which to them were crucial. First, they were worried that the hospitals would not have sufficient independence to maintain their own personalities. Bevan agreed and said that one reason he had rejected a hospital service run by the local authorities was because of their inability to delegate powers. Secondly, as Peacock observed, the proposal to take over hospital endowments cut at the root of charitable trusts. The money involved, estimated at £50,000,000 for the nation at large, should be retained by the hospitals to provide for special purposes. Bevan thought that the Chancellor of the Exchequer might object to taking over liabilities without assets, but agreed to look at the issue. He accepted that the endowments of teaching hospitals might present a special case.[127]

Before the meeting adjourned, Donoughmore asked Bevan if the County of London would be a region. The Fund opposed the idea, which the London County Council had supported, because it thought such a boundary would be artificial and over-concentrated. It preferred a larger region which would spread the influence of the London teaching hospitals more widely. Bevan replied that he did not intend to designate the County of London as a region and agreed that Regional Hospital Boards should include representatives of university teaching-centres. Finally, Aylwen asked about the Minister's views on the King's Fund itself, with reference to its own endowment. Bevan had not given this any thought but remarked that it might well be proper to leave the institution in possession of its monies, which should be devoted to general hospital purposes.[128] Several weeks later he told Peacock that the Fund would not be adversely affected by the Bill and asked whether it might consider the possibility of extending its area to coincide with the different regions likely to be based upon the London teaching hospitals.[129]

In March 1946, just a few days before the publication of the National Health Service Bill, the Fund printed an elaboration of the views that it had put to Bevan. Drafted by Ives, it was an emphatic restatement of the need to promote the voluntary hospitals as the nucleus of the new service. The need to maintain and to extend local interest and initiative, always paramount in the

Fund's thinking, was behind its preoccupation with independence of local management and the need to respect the trust character of voluntary hospital endowments. As to local management, it was anxious that every hospital, not simply the teaching hospitals, should have a governing body with control of appointments to the medical and administrative staff and some discretion in expenditure. It wanted a definite place in the scheme for the medical committee. As to endowments, it argued that if the State assumed ownership of investments without provision to protect the trusts attached to them, it would 'compromise gravely' future local initiative and future voluntary support for the new service.[130]

As the Bill progressed through Parliament, the Fund pressed its case. Peacock corresponded with Bevan.[131] Donoughmore spoke in the House of Lords.[132] Ives put amendments to the Ministry of Health.[133] Lett and Pooley wrote to *The Times*.[134] Well-orchestrated, these voices all expressed general support for the Bill, but insisted on the dangers inherent in management by 'remote control' and the need to protect endowments. Individual hospitals which did not have their own financial resources from outside the State would have no 'corporate personality', would suffer problems of recruitment, and would lose local allegiance. It was essential, in the Fund's view, that hospital managers be jealous for the reputation of their institutions, but this could only happen if they had a degree of self-government, with controls over finance and appointments.

Peacock wrote to Bevan along these lines in April, emphasizing that the Bill did not provide adequate powers and status for the Hospital Management Committees. Bevan's reply was equivocal. He spoke in general terms of the need to balance 'rational planning' with decentralization. He was willing to make a few technical changes to the Bill but insisted that the Minister must ultimately be in charge.[135] Further correspondence between them dealt with the issue of whether institutions in the National Health Service would be able to accept future gifts of property. In the Fund's view the confusion over this issue was deflecting legacies from hospitals to other charitable causes. Bevan replied that modifications to the Bill would enable hospitals to accept and hold property.[136]

Unlike Willink before him, Bevan did not see the necessity of encouraging voluntary support for the new service. He thought it an irrelevance, but as a clever tactician he kept this opinion to himself and threw a few bones to the philanthropists. The estimated total cost of the new service, put at £152,000,000 was considerably higher than that of the White Paper scheme.[137] Still, few people appeared to see cost as a problem, including officials in the Ministry of Health. Bevan himself assumed that by improving the nation's health, a comprehensive service would reduce demand for medical treatment. As his biographer John Campbell says, Bevan and his colleagues 'expected the cost of the Service would grow *less* as the population got healthier'.[138] The Fund's officials, hardened by decades of raising money for ever expanding medical services, were less inclined to a belief in man's perfectability. They assumed that voluntary income would be needed to buttress the system, which is why they kept arguing the case for a charitable 'gap' in the Bill

The details of Bevan's Bill, which received the Royal Assent on 6 November 1946, have been discussed at length elsewhere.[139] From the Fund's point of view, the Act contained important concessions, particularly for the teaching hospitals. The endowments of former voluntary institutions designated as teaching hospitals, which were in some cases considerable, were to remain under the control of their new governing bodies. This ensured that the former charitable teaching-hospitals would have financial advantages denied to the former municipal hospitals. The endowments of the other hospitals entering the service were to be taken into a central pool and used for purposes outside the official budget. Though a central pool was not ideal in the Fund's view, its lobbying over endowments had not been in vain. (Ives thought Peacock's role in their protection was crucial.)[140] Another concession granted to voluntarists was that Regional Hospital Boards, Boards of Governors, and Hospital Management Committees were empowered to accept gifts, thus making possible the continuation of private charity to hospitals in the National Health Service.[141]

On the issue of independence, Bevan felt obliged to devise a scheme in which the large teaching hospitals received a measure of autonomy. Such a compromise undermined regional planning, but Bevan thought it necessary to divide the voluntary hospital movement, to minimize the resistance to his Bill from the teaching hospitals and their medical and political allies.[142] Undoubtedly, the concessions to the teaching hospitals placated the Fund and may be seen as a major reason why it reconciled itself to 'socialism'.[143] Offered their own Boards of Governors, the teaching hospitals remained outside the framework of the Regional Boards. As Ives remarked, with obvious pleasure, they were 'accorded a privileged status. Though technically transferred to the Minister, they retain much of their former freedom.'[144] But he and his colleagues were not enthusiastic about the implications of the Act for the autonomy of the Hospital Management Committees.[145]

A feature of the new service which also pleased the Fund was that the whole of the Metropolitan area, together with the Home Counties, was to be treated as one unit and organized as four regions centred upon the twelve London teaching hospitals.[146] The Fund had always wanted a better disposition of hospitals to satisfy the needs of the outlying industrial and suburban areas, and the new arrangements were consistent with its recommendations to the Ministry of Health. What was now needed was sufficient financial backing to reconstruct hospital services in the capital. Whether such restructuring could have been achieved by means which would have preserved the voluntary system was now an 'academic question' in the Fund's view. 'What is important is that the initiative and humanity of which the voluntary hospitals have been justly proud should be carried over into the new system.'[147]

It was a tribute to Bevan's persuasive powers as much as to his carefully judged concessions that the nationalization of the voluntary hospitals could be so easily rationalized by the Fund. (About 200 'disclaimed' voluntary homes and hospitals throughout the country, many connected with religious denominations, remained outside the National Health Service.)[148] Only eighteen months before the passing of Bevan's legislation, the Fund had wanted Exchequer grants to save the voluntary hospitals. Now, it put its faith in the survival of their traditions within the framework of ministerial control. But the municipal hospitals, which had helped to define those traditions, were no longer available for comparisons about standards and efficiency.

For better or for worse, the former voluntary and municipal hospitals were now in it together. Consequently, the Fund no longer dwelled on the dangers of a unified hospital service. Nor did it wish to be reminded of those features of state provision that were antithetical to voluntary traditions: a new officialdom heavily armed with bureaucratic regulations, the politicization of hospital care, and Treasury restraint. Few outside the voluntary world had considered seriously just how dismissive of tradition a state system, given to social engineering, might become. The war had pointed out the failings of inter-war politics and social provision. And ordinary people were less nostalgic about the past than had been the case after the First World War. But post-war politicians and planners, in the hospital service and elsewhere, would show a wilful disrespect for past practice or inherited tradition. In their world, the past was not something upon which to build; it was something to overcome.

Unlike the hospitals, the Fund was not directly affected by the National Health Service Act. Still, the reorganization of hospital provision was bound to unsettle its view of itself. Like other charities, it had to question whether the public would continue to support it in the changed circumstances. And like other charities, how was it to adjust to the new context without abandoning its abiding principles? In 1947, the Fund celebrated its fiftieth anniversary. Turning to its past, it sought continuity and reassurance. With capital assets of between £5,000,000 and £6,000,000 it found reassurance. But what was to be done with the money now that the State had accepted the responsibility for financing the nation's hospitals? The Fund would have difficult decisions to make in regard to its grants and projects, as well as to its fund-raising. There was some consolation in the thought that it would no longer have to scratch around trying to find money for hospital building or maintenance.

Whatever was to be the Fund's future role, it could not be a straightforward continuation of the old. A clue to its future could be found in the remarks of Prime Minister Clement Attlee, a former member of the King's Fund Council (1937–45). Speaking as President of Toynbee Hall, he remarked, 'we shall always have alongside the great range of public services, the voluntary services which humanize our national life and bring it down from the general to the particular'.[149] This was an agreeable message to all voluntarists, many of whom concluded that the Welfare State might be a blessing in disguise. The Fund was among the first to recognize that in freeing them from former thankless tasks it offered fresh opportunities. Shedding its traditional role as a central fund for London's hospitals, it might now concentrate on the particular, on patient care and the promotion of experimental projects.

By 1947, the Fund was already talking in a different language, of 'state partnership', of acting 'as a bridge between the official services on the one hand and informed public opinion on the other'.[150] Peacock said in a letter to the Palace in early 1947 that the changed conditions of the Health Act enabled the Fund 'to do even more useful work for hospitals than in the past'.[151] He was thinking of the many new hospitals, ex-local authority, which now came within the Fund's purview. 'No better way could have been found of marking its fiftieth anniversary', intoned the annual report, 'than by the widening of its scope to embrace the whole of the hospital and allied services within its area.'[152] Such hopes belied the awkward reappraisal taking place behind the scenes. When an institution turns its mind to its history, as the Fund did in the 1940s, it does so because it has something to celebrate or something to lose.[153] The 1950s would see a spate of histories published by the former voluntary hospitals. They were deeply imbued with a sense of loss.

7

A Fragile Partnership, 1948–1960

THE vast expansion of state-directed health and welfare services after the war threw voluntarists into disarray. The creation of the National Health Service pushed them to the periphery of the debate on health. Associated legislation on welfare pushed them to the periphery of the debate on social security. Politicians of all parties, transfixed by the role of the Welfare State in their election prospects, narrowed discussions of social policy down to government action. So did civil servants in the welfare departments, who jealously guarded their new authority. Under the sway of collectivist ideals, post-war historians and social commentators began to revise the past in such a way as to make social reform coterminous with government provision.[1] Charities were only of interest if they were seen to have prepared the ground for the State. But the more philanthropy was studied simply in relation to government, the more marginal it came to be seen by those predisposed to state solutions.

In the extraordinary post-war atmosphere of social experimentation, central government seemingly was sweeping all before it. The damaging propaganda-war between the public and voluntary sectors gradually subsided, though a residual hostility persisted, which was especially noticeable in the health services. Philanthropists, for their part, took the idea of partnership down from the shelf, brushed off its unhappy associations with local government, and looked forward to a more positive relationship with the central State. But no one was in any doubt about which partner had seniority. In the light of social legislation, voluntarists no longer made exaggerated claims about their pre-eminence in British life. State spending on the social services dwarfed the funds available to charities. But would further government action make their work unnecessary or endanger their flow of funds? Would their growing co-operation with government departments, accentuated by the war, eventually undermine their cherished independence?

The impact of broadened government services on charities proved more erratic than the foregoing analysis might suggest.[2] Many institutions, from parish societies to the National Trust, were little affected. Some, like the

Women's Institutes, gave greater emphasis to the social side of their activities. Others changed their names and shifted their priorities. The Charity Organisation Society became the Family Welfare Association and concentrated on social casework. Many with a long-standing welfare role, such as the Salvation Army and the city missions, must have wondered about the efficacy of legislation, since so many people continued to fall through the welfare net. The fact that lighthouses were run by civil servants and lifeboats by philanthropists suggested the muddle that prevailed.

The nationalization of the majority of voluntary hospitals by the State killed off a number of their associated societies, including the League of Mercy and the British Hospitals Association. Others, including the Saturday Fund, the Sunday Fund, and the Nuffield Provincial Hospitals Trust shifted their priorities as necessary. The question of survival sometimes turned on a charity's capital reserves rather than on the services it provided. The League of Mercy and the British Hospitals Association might have carried on had they had more money of their own. As the management of the King's Fund appreciated, it was much easier to find a new role in the Welfare State with financial assets in the millions. The Fund, in fact, never contemplated folding up, for it had something invaluable to offer the hospitals—whoever ran them: an unrivalled technical knowledge.

Though few noticed it at the time, voluntarists showed great resilience in the post-war years, often pioneering terrain which the government would not or could not enter. Many new societies in the health and welfare fields started up, among them MIND (1946) and the Samaritans (1953). In the hospital sector, a number of the contributory schemes decided to carry on, and in 1948 they formed the British Hospitals Contributory Schemes Association. The societies not only provided benefits for members but, in keeping with their charitable leanings, made substantial grants to NHS hospitals to provide amenities not offered from public funds.[3] Other local groups, who had formerly supported their voluntary hospitals, reorganized themselves into Leagues of Hospital Friends, which sought to improve conditions for patients. In 1949, the National League of Hospital Friends was set up to facilitate their work. (Lord Beveridge became its President in 1953.) By 1956, 2,100 out of a total of 2,600 state hospitals had Leagues of Friends or benefited from the services of the British Red Cross, the St John Ambulance Brigade, or the Women's Voluntary Services.[4]

Despite the ritual nod from select committees and politicians towards the idea of partnership, civil servants in the early years of the NHS gave little support to voluntarists in and around the hospitals. They tended to dismiss the Leagues of Friends as a nuisance, especially those run by women. (They would later take them for granted.) Nor did they wish to encourage charitable donations. Section 59 of the National Health Service Act permitted hospitals to receive gifts, yet obstacles were put in their way. Many benefactors who had made out seven-year covenants to non-teaching hospitals before their transfer to the NHS were offended to discover that they were legally required to fulfil their financial obligations after 1948 by redirecting their payments to the Ministry of Health. Legacies left to former voluntary hospitals also created legal complications, which discouraged individuals from considering hospital causes in their wills.[5] Nor would benefactors have been happy with the questionable use of their money by the Regional Health Boards, which often applied endowment funds to staff purposes, not least entertainments.[6]

The Ministry took the view, which was mistaken, that people would not wish to be asked for charitable donations to hospitals that were paid for by the Exchequer. (The Fund itself had argued a similar line during its propaganda campaign against the White Paper in 1944.) Bevan went so far as to notify NHS staff that patients should not be asked to contribute money to their hospitals.[7] When a number of hospitals initiated fund-raising drives in their neighbourhoods in 1948, the Ministry directed that such practices should stop. (Even collection boxes were removed from post offices.) Furthermore, it issued a circular which required that Leagues of Hospital Friends must work independently of the hospital boards and committees and officially forbade members or officers of the committees from taking part in their activities.[8] This edict, which many believed to have been drawn up without consultation with hospital people, caused a stir in the Fund. Lord Wigram, a Councillor and former Honorary Secretary, denounced it as 'sheer bullying'.[9]

The Fund decried what it saw as the politicization of the incipient service: 'The Labour Party', it declared, 'was fiercely anti-voluntary and endeavoured to prevent hospitals from having any voluntary support.'[10] Ives, who had been persuaded by Bevan that the NHS would welcome voluntary initiatives, felt that he had been duped.[11] The apparent concessions made to the charitable sector in the Act had cleverly disguised the depth of Bevan's statist philosophy. An insensitivity to voluntary initiatives became ingrained in the fledgling NHS bureaucracy. As the voluntarists had foreseen, an elaborate administrative machine given to remote control proved inelastic in dealing with initiatives on its periphery. Matters were not helped by the residual bitterness between ex-voluntary and ex-local authority elements in the Regional Boards and Hospital Management Committees. The bitterness was perhaps understandable given the former level of antagonism between the voluntary and public sectors. It was so deep, according to the Fund, that 'the very use of the word voluntary' was anathema to large sections of hospital management.[12]

In the circumstances, it was not obvious to the Fund how best to proceed. Towards the end of 1948, Ives advised that publicity should be avoided. As long as the hospitals enjoyed the freedom to spend Exchequer money at will, the need for voluntary contributions was unproven. 'This situation cannot last,' Ives concluded, 'the bill for the Hospital services is soaring daily and the Ministry will certainly have to curb it when the budgets come in.... One's guess is that in twelve months' time the picture will be very different and that the power to seek and use voluntary gifts will come into its own and prove the salvation of the hospitals.'[13]

Before the transfer of the hospitals took place, the Fund, fearing that its money might be squandered, took the precaution of cutting the size of its annual grants by two-thirds, to £100,000. A portion of the money went to those voluntary hospitals remaining outside the NHS, which the Fund wished to encourage as models of administrative efficiency for the new service. The bulk of it, distributed before the appointed day in July, was awarded to hospitals inside the new service, largely for improved facilities and comforts for patients. The grants for 1948 brought the Fund's total distribution between 1897 and the transfer of the hospitals to the NHS to over £12,400,000. Thirty-six per cent of it had gone to the twelve London general hospitals with medical schools which were in existence at the time of the Fund's foundation.[14]

The Fund's initial caution in dealing with the NHS was due partly to its reservations about the service, which the restrictions on charitable support increased, and partly to its feeling that it might be swamped by applications for money from the relatively poor ex-local authority hospitals.[15] Its reservations deepened still further as the predicted financial uncertainty in the new service undermined efforts to improve the more backward institutions. There was little sense of 'we told you so' in the Fund's attitude, just a nagging worry that the patients it served and the hospitals it nurtured were to have inflicted upon them another cash crisis and more administrative muddle. There was never any doubt about its sympathies. As it wrote to a Select Committee on Estimates in 1957: 'In so far as there must always be some degree of tension between the hospitals and the guardians of the public purse, the Fund is by virtue of its constitution on the side of the hospitals!'[16]

The Treasury, of course, not the voluntary sector, had to find the money to run the hospitals after 1948. At least that was the theory. But as the Fund, among other charities, had assumed, the Treasury would not wish to get a reputation for compassion. To voluntarists, an endemic problem with a health service under Treasury control was that medical provision would not always be seen as 'rational' in economic terms. With the next budget-round impending, civil servants would ask themselves how much money should be spent on, among others, the elderly and the disabled, people who were unlikely to return to productive life. It was partly this understanding that kept voluntarists committed to medical causes, often specializing in those categories of patients neglected by the statutory services. The Fund further expected that a uniform state service would simply become stagnant and mediocre without the stimulus of informed opinion and experimentation which the voluntary sector offered.[17]

The problem for hospital voluntarists was to find a role in the new service consistent with their traditions. However unfavourable the climate, these traditions were unlikely to disappear, for, as Ives put it, they had at their heart an acceptance, moulded by Christian thought, of permanent responsibility, of personal service 'stretching out towards infinity'. The idea that the Minister, working within the framework of a quantitative conception of health, could ever be 'responsible' for the sick was a 'fiction'. 'We smile at the refinements of mediaeval scholasticism,' Ives remarked, 'but our own notions about the Minister's ultimate responsibility are just about as far fetched.' What he hoped to see develop was a truly 'national' health service, which combined the spirit of the old voluntary system with the universality of the new. The solution was for the government to devise financial arrangements which provided a sound basic service, while encouraging voluntarists with an 'unlimited' sense of responsibility to extend its humanity.[18]

As Ives and his colleagues had anticipated, the NHS had hardly opened its doors before it was engulfed in a financial crisis.[19] Government discussions about the level of NHS provision were complicated by the estimates of the cost of a comprehensive service, which, as one Labour spokesman put it, were 'fantastically underestimated'.[20] But unlike the crises in the inter-war voluntary hospitals, the initial threat to the NHS was created by a failure of financial control, especially in regard to increases in staff costs. (Sixty per cent of NHS expenditure was spent on salaries by 1950.)[21] In the Fund's view, the failure to control costs was 'inevitable' without a mechanism for objectively assessing the amount of money to be given to each Hospital Management Committee. 'The whole future welfare of the hospitals', it lamented in its report on the first year of the NHS, 'has despite much good will been placed in jeopardy.'[22]

The Fund was in the unusual position of being able to stand back from a hospital crisis for the first time in its history. Indeed, it was the judicious thing to do with voluntary activity so out of fashion. It decided to concentrate on putting its own house in order, until the Ministry, having exhausted the alternatives, came around to seeing the necessity of enlarged voluntary support. Among the most pressing demands was an alteration to its organization. With this in mind Pooley and Ives, financed by the Commonwealth Fund of New York, visited North America to investigate the methods being used there by charities with an interest in hospitals. Impressed by the divisional approach to administration adopted by the Rockefeller and Kellogg Foundations, Ives prepared a memorandum recommending that the Fund change to a modified form of divisional organization suited to its distinctive constitution.[23]

In November 1948, the Management Committee approved the recommendations, and these were agreed by the Council the following month. The object of the reorganization was to allow the Management Committee greater initiative in determining the allocation of money between newly created divisions and the Fund's other activities. Two divisions were established straight away: a Division of Hospital Facilities, under the direction of Captain Stone, and a Division of Nursing, under the direction of Muriel Edwards. The establishment of a further Division to deal with hospital catering was expected to follow. The Emergency Bed Service was to continue along existing lines under the direction of Roger Peers. In future, meetings of the Management Committee would begin with an executive session followed by an open session in which the business affecting the respective Divisions would be transacted with their Directors in attendance.[24]

One result of the changes was greater parity between the Divisions and the formerly unrivalled Distribution Committee. An assumption behind the reorganization was that in dealing with hospitals financed by government, innovative projects might be more appropriate than grants. It was a view that Stone and Edwards, backed up by their committees, encouraged. In so far as the new arrangements gave greater autonomy to the constituent parts of the Fund, it increased the rivalries between them for allocations of money. The centrifugal forces inherent in a divisional system encouraged a proliferation of staff, activities, and views. A future challenge for the Fund, long-experienced in co-ordinating hospitals, would be to co-ordinate itself. Administrative expenses, which in 1947 accounted for 7 per cent of expenditure, began to rise.[25]

The reorganization did not affect the Fund's constitutional arrangements under its Act of Parliament, but it did bring about the disappearance of the office of Honorary Secretary. (It also resulted in the appointment of the first woman, the Hon. Mrs A. Murray, to the Management Committee.) The Honorary Secretaries Wernher, Pooley, and Lett decided that they were redundant under the new arrangements and resigned in December 1948. The change in the nature of the Fund's work was said to be the reason for their departure, but perhaps they also felt that as volunteers identified with inter-war hospital affairs, they would be out of place dealing with NHS officials. The services of the resigning men were not entirely lost, however, for with the death of Lord Donoughmore in 1948, Pooley became Chairman of the Management Committee. Lett and Wernher, who was made a GCVO in the New Year's Honours list in 1949, continued to sit on the Council. But they would no longer be seen so often in the Fund as in the past.

The elimination of the office of Honorary Secretary marked a watershed in the Fund's administrative history. Since Lord Somerleyton's day, the men who had served in the office had contributed mightily to the institution's character and distinction. Most of them had been honoured by the Crown for their unpaid services. The change meant that the paid staff had to take on additional responsibilities. This eroded voluntary traditions of administration in the Fund and encouraged the trend towards professional management. Another, largely unforeseen, consequence of the reorganization was that the paid officers, despite their representation at committee meetings, found themselves rather more isolated from the Management Committee. For a central role of the Honorary Secretaries, who sat on all the committees, had been to keep the management and the staff informed of one another's views.

The Fund's adjustment to the dramatic changes in hospital provision had distinctive practical features, but it should be seen in the context of the general reassessment of voluntarism taking place at the time. The publication of William Beveridge's *Voluntary Action* in 1948, and an illuminating debate in the House of Lords the following year, gave the charitable sector some initial guidelines.[26] The Fund had supplied Beveridge with information for his researches but did not think much of his book. Peacock thought that he had failed to give sufficient attention to the role of the voluntary worker in the health services and advised the Fund to sponsor a further inquiry, in collaboration with the National Council of Social Service. In early 1949, the Fund allocated £6,000 to cover the cost of a two-year study into hospitals and voluntary social service, to be undertaken by John Trevelyan, a former Director of Education for Westmorland.[27]

Trevelyan's brief was to assess the significance of voluntary service in the hospital field and to make suggestions for the future. The result was *Voluntary Service and the State* (1952), a study of the relationship of charity to NHS administration. It was an elaboration of the Fund's abiding principles in the new context of the Welfare State. Invoking Bunyan, Mill, and Beveridge, Trevelyan celebrated the familiar philanthropic themes of freedom, enterprise, and humanity. If the State 'guaranteed a full measure of "welfare" to all its citizens' and asked for nothing in return save a compulsory tax, 'it would create a division between the State on the one hand and the people on the other, and between them there would be a "great gulf fixed"'. The worth of the State, he concluded, quoting Mill, was 'the worth of the individuals composing it . . . a State which dwarfs its men in order that they may be more docile instruments in its hands even for beneficial purposes—will find that with small men no great thing can be accomplished'.[28]

Coming down to earth, Trevelyan detected worrying signs of greater central control in hospital administration, which threatened the voluntary interest. In a section influenced by Ives, he argued that charities, the Hospital Management Committees, and the Boards of Governors should be offered a full measure of administrative responsibility and be 'trusted to exercise "enlightened economy"'. In turn, the Boards and Committees must delegate real responsibility 'so that the hospitals themselves are not excluded from the administration which affects them so vitally. . . . Above all we believe that voluntary service has something vital to give to the administration of the hospital service, something that administration by the professional, however efficient, can never give.' Far from anticipating a reduction in charitable services in hospitals, Trevelyan expected its expansion. Quoting Beveridge, 'there is a perpetually moving frontier for voluntary action'.[29]

Despite the rhetoric of voluntary expansion, the Fund's 'perpetually moving frontier' initially moved in reverse. Some of its responsibilities were incompatible with the new hospital service, and consequently they were taken over by the State or abandoned altogether. On the advice of the Radiotherapy Committee, formerly the Radium Committee, the Fund decided to dispose of its holding of radium, which amounted to 17 g. The Ministry of Health purchased the bulk of the stock in 1950, which it delegated to the Middlesex Hospital, and the remaining supply, representing Sir Otto Beit's gift initiating the radium appeal, was retained in the ownership of the Fund and loaned to the Royal Cancer Hospital. The Radiotherapy Committee disbanded.[30]

After forty-five years of continuous publication, the Fund's Annual *Statistical Summary* also came to an end. As hospitals were now required to submit their accounts to the Minister of Health, it was not thought appropriate to expect them to submit them to the Fund as well. The former local-authority hospitals, of course, had never provided statistics to the Fund, and would have objected to doing so after 1948. Unfortunately, no definite arrangements were made by the Ministry to provide an equivalent statistical service. As the Fund remarked in its annual report for 1949: 'for the first time for nearly fifty years there are no published data available by which a hospital administrator may compare his costs with those of a neighbouring hospital of a similar category'. The lack of such data was particularly sad, it added, 'at a time when the need for true "economy" was never more insistent'.[31]

The last issue of the *Statistical Summary*, published in 1948, threw up some fascinating detail. Subscriptions and donations to the London voluntary hospitals in 1947 were up 10 per cent on the figures for 1938, and despite the disincentives, legacies continued to hold up. The income of London's voluntary hospitals had more than doubled since 1938, in part because of emergency payments from public authorities to repair bomb damage; yet the charitable contribution to total income remained quite high, over 30 per cent. This, in the Fund's view, was 'striking evidence' of continued voluntary support.[32] Given the prevailing conditions and the imminent transfer of the hospitals to the State, it was convincing proof that the Ministry would be unwise to disregard the potential in voluntary contributions to the new service. The point was brought home by the Fund's statistics on London voluntary hospital expenditure. In 1938 the average total cost per occupied bed was £233 per annum; by 1947 it was £639, and rising.[33]

The Fund's own finances had held up reasonably well during the war, though many of its securities had to be written off as valueless after 1945.[34] Its subscription income was in decline, in part because many of its industrial sponsors ceased to contribute with the introduction of the NHS. The days of the great bequests were apparently over, but legacies remained important to the Fund; and though it did not canvass solicitors or scour obituaries as in the past, it hoped to reap benefits from those who hesitated to leave money to an individual hospital as a result of the Health Act. Contributions from other charities also showed promise, and they became an increasingly important source of income to the Fund with the years.

In 1948, the Fund received a windfall of £425,000 from the Nuffield Trust for the Special Areas.[35] Lord Nuffield had set up the charity in the 1930s to assist those parts of the country affected by industrial depression, and the Trust Deed provided that any money unspent should be passed to the King's Fund. In the 1950s, the Fund received further monies from the Nuffield Trust, and by 1962, when the last instalment arrived, the total came to £1,912,000. It made Lord Nuffield the Fund's largest single contributor, surpassing Lord Mount Stephen, at least in terms of stated sterling values, without adjusting for inflation.[36]

The Fund's considerable endowment and the apparent ease with which large sums could be found from other institutions disguised the fact that it lost its enthusiasm for public appeals after the war. Of course, there was far less incentive for it to expend energy on fund-raising when the government had taken on the burden of hospital finance. Since the State had been so determined to nationalize the hospitals, it was widely assumed that it would pay for their essential services. Still, the Fund's own evidence suggested that the public wished to continue to support the hospitals. Given its vast experience in raising money, it may seem odd that the Fund did not more actively tap this reservoir of goodwill for its own purposes. Uncharacteristically, it let the coronation of Queen Elizabeth II pass without a commemorative appeal. When Muriel Edwards suggested a fund-raising drive in 1958, Lord McCorquodale, then Chairman, remarked 'that the Fund ought not to enter the field of general appeals because in fact we have got all the money we know what to do with'.[37]

The coming of the NHS, and the uncertainties in its early development, created divisions of opinion in the Fund. By the end of 1950, several members of the Management Committee wanted to take a more positive line towards giving grants to NHS hospitals. Others, including Peacock, remained sceptical.[38] The difference of opinion caused particular problems for the Distribution Committee, which in 1948 had a new Chairman, Sir Archibald

Gray, who replaced Sir Ernest Pooley. Gray, co-author of the London Hospital Survey for the Ministry of Health, was a distinguished dermatologist with a wide knowledge of hospital affairs. He and his colleagues had to reshape the Fund's grants to fit the new conditions. The Committee followed the cautious line argued by Peacock; it kept its distance from the new service, in part because it expected that an avalanche of begging-letters would appear once the Exchequer cut hospital budgets. Consequently, it did not advertise its grants as in the past, but applications were welcome from institutions within the Metropolitan Police District and those outside it which took London patients.

Though at first guarded, the Distribution Committee's general outlook was upbeat, for potentially the NHS offered it opportunities to widen its scope. It identified three main targets for support: NHS hospitals, voluntary bodies outside the NHS, and institutions providing ancillary services for the relief of the aged sick, who were often discriminated against. The voluntary bodies, which included 'disclaimed' hospitals, were high on the Fund's agenda because, in its view, they would profoundly influence the progress of NHS hospitals. The interest in the aged sick was a most interesting development, for elderly patients were commonly part of a medical underclass which had been the preserve of the Poor Law. With their primary interest in acute cases, the voluntary hospitals, and consequently the Fund, had traditionally neglected them.

As anticipated, the cash crisis in the NHS awakened the hospitals to the availability of ready money from the voluntary community. For its part, the Ministry of Health respected the Fund because it was both informed and entrenched, and it specifically advised the hospitals that they might apply to it for support.[39] The Regional Boards, having been approached through Sir Wilson Jameson, 'cordially welcomed' grants from the Fund.[40] As the applications poured in, the Distribution Committee decided that it would be wrong to reject them where convincing need could be shown. But it did not wish to pay for items that might be met out of the official budget. But what distinguished an 'amenity' that charity might provide from an essential service that was the responsibility of the State? Feeling its way, the Fund concluded that 'there is not, and perhaps never will be, a clear line laid down, category by category, of what items can be met out of the official budget'.[41]

Grants to NHS hospitals were further complicated by the question of visits. In the past all hospitals receiving awards had been visited, but in 1948 the practice was in suspense, restricted to institutions outside the NHS and to the London teaching hospitals, with which the Fund continued to have a special relationship. Without the information provided by inspections, the Fund was chary of making sizeable grants. Necessitous hospital-managers appreciated this and invitations to the Fund to visit soon became customary. In the early

1950s, the familiar pattern of inspections reasserted itself, though on a three-year rather than an annual cycle. Visits proved useful in forging links with the new Hospital Management Committees. But assessing the needs of an institution was not made any easier when hospitals polished their wards for the visitors and told them what they wanted to hear. As Roger Peers put it: 'no one is rude to his rich uncle'.[42]

As in the past, the visitors included an equal number of laymen and doctors, mostly well-established men, with a sprinkling of younger ones with an eye to making their way in the world. As in Lord Lister's day, the medical visitors were drawn largely from the London teaching hospitals. In 1950, they included A. J. McNair, a leading obstetrician from Guy's and A. E. Gow, an Emeritus Physician from St Bartholomew's. They served with a team of businessmen and country gentlemen, several of whom, like Lord Somerleyton and Lord Luke, were following a family tradition of service to the Fund.

The Fund published an updated *Hospital Visitors' Manual* in 1950, which illustrated the growing emphasis on the chronic sick, physiotherapy, catering, and medical records. The visitors' reports themselves are even more revealing for post-war hospital conditions. By far the most frequent complaint in the reports in the early 1950s concerned washing and toilet facilities.[43] In 1953, at St Stephen's Hospital, a former Poor Law infirmary in the Chelsea Group of Hospitals, the visitors discovered an acute shortage of accommodation and such an urgent need for basic equipment that 'patients from the better class areas of Chelsea and Kensington are deterred by the conditions'. Enid Blyton, who had been a patient, was recruiting a friend to paint murals in the children's ward to relieve the gloom. The visitors, who were asked to look for signs of voluntary activity, reported that a League of Friends had recently started up and had plenty to do.[44]

Guy's Hospital, visited by Sir Archibald Gray and Lord Ashburton in 1954, was a different world altogether. A teaching hospital with over £2,000,000 in its endowment fund, it was relatively rich and well-equipped. Dorcas Ward, which had been bombed, was now back in excellent order. A medical-records office had just been installed and the highly efficient X-ray department had the latest automatic developer. Nursing accommodation, however, was unsatisfactory. But the chief problem for the institution was over its rebuilding-scheme. Having been frustrated by both the London County Council and the Ministry of Health, 'the hospital seemed desperate at the ever widening circle of officials with which it had to deal without ever achieving anything'. As the visitors concluded, Guy's 'is not the only teaching hospital which is having difficulty with large capital projects'.[45]

Given the confusion in the new service and the uncertainties over the level and nature of the voluntary activity permitted in it, the Fund remained reluctant to spend heavily on NHS hospitals. It was also conscious that however heavily it spent, the sum would seem small by comparison with the amount of money being pumped into the system by the State. Of the £1,225,859 allocated to grants in the five years 1949–53, the Fund gave only £322,232 to NHS institutions.[46] The teaching hospitals received only £33,380 over this period, or roughly 10 per cent of the Fund's awards to NHS institutions. Guy's, St Bartholomew's, St Thomas', and the Charing Cross were among those which received nothing at all. The bulk of the money given to the NHS went to the ex-local-authority hospitals, in an attempt to improve patient comforts and bring their standards up to those of the former voluntary hospitals.[47]

The Fund's grants to NHS institutions concentrated on adding to the comfort and well-being of patients and staff. Typical of the 'amenities' provided in the early years of the service were improved wireless equipment, refrigerators, tennis courts, recreational centres, pictures, and picture-frames. Given the restrictions on hospital expenditure imposed by the government, a more elastic policy of distribution came into being. The notion that an 'amenity' was a frill or non-essential item was unworkable in practice. Was a garden, for example, an amenity? Presumably not at a hospital for chronic patients who had nowhere else to go. As Ives wrote in 1953 'an amenity is anything the hospital needs but cannot afford: excepting, of course, structural alterations or expansions, which it is not the Fund's duty to finance'.[48] Although the Fund's grants were relatively small, they could have disproportionate effects, especially during periods of financial strain. One Hospital Management Committee, acknowledging grants worth £7,250, wrote: 'the Fund's gift has really been the best tonic and encouragement that any of us have had since the Health Service came into being'.[49]

The simple provision of amenities, however described, was soon overtaken by the financial crisis in the NHS. By the mid-1950s some Boards of Governors were already applying their non-Exchequer money to the provision of new hospital buildings.[50] The Middlesex Hospital, for example, established an institute for clinical research and experimental medicine in 1953 from its endowment money. As early as 1951, the King's Fund set aside £50,000 to be allocated to Hospital Management Committees for purposes other than amenities. It classified these grants under the headings of wards, nurses, kitchens, domestic, and miscellaneous. Many of the awards reflected the Fund's growing interest in nursing and catering. Even the policy of avoiding spending on structural alterations was breached in 1951, for £2,000 was given to the Woolwich Hospital Management Committee for the enclosure of ward balconies to relieve pressure on beds at the Memorial Hospital.[51]

The Fund's departure from the expected pattern of support for the NHS was in tune with what was happening across the spectrum of medical philanthropy. Soon after the creation of the NHS, research funds from such institutions as the Nuffield Foundation and the Wellcome Foundation began to provide money to fill gaps in medical research created by government cash-shortages.[52] The Cancer Research Campaign and the Imperial Cancer Research Fund soon overtook the contribution from the Medical Research Council for cancer research. Between them, they provided 29 per cent of all money expended on cancer research in 1952; twenty years later it was 62 per cent.[53] The Sunday Fund, in addition to helping 'disclaimed' institutions, contributed grants for the use of NHS almoners, to meet the needs of patients not provided for by the State.[54] The numerous charities working in the fields of disability, mental health, and the aged sick, found that the public authorities depended on them increasingly.[55]

The King's Fund remarked as early as 1951 that 'although the hospital service has been nationalised there are indications that the amount of voluntary service to-day is greater than ever before'.[56] A survey of voluntary contributions in Manchester and Salford in the early 1950s confirmed the vitality of hospital charity. Despite nationalization, the hospitals in the region continued to receive more in philanthropic donations than any other single cause.[57] Though few commented upon it, the State's post-war intervention in welfare had the paradoxical effect of reinvigorating voluntary traditions. This was not simply because the government could not afford the ever widening number of services now deemed essential, but also because it had effectively raised the public's expectations of welfare provision.

As in the past, the Fund awarded its grants with the patients foremost in mind, whether they were found in NHS hospitals or attended by independent institutions. A considerable portion of its distribution in the early 1950s went to hospitals and charities outside the NHS. As they were largely dependent on the goodwill of the public, the Fund did not hesitate to consider applications from them for capital projects. The French Hospital, the Italian hospital, the King Edward VII Sanatorium in Midhurst, were among the independent institutions which received awards for purposes large and small, from rebuilding to television sets. Other awards went to a wide range of charities, including the Family Welfare Association, the National League of Hospital Friends, and the Council for Music in Hospitals.[58] The Fund's allocation of grants to other non-hospital charities was to become a feature of its distribution after 1948. It was a natural result of hospital nationalization, which had widened the scope of the Fund and other charities. But it was also a form of insurance against an overbearing State.

In the 1950s, the Fund sought to complement the NHS in those areas where assistance would be most beneficial. Consequently, it revitalized its long-standing interest in voluntary homes for convalescent patients and the aged sick. Convalescent homes typically treated physically ill patients past the acute stage of treatment who needed a short period of recuperation. They have not aroused much research, but arguably the National Health Service Act was a greater landmark in their history than in the history of hospitals. Prior to the NHS, convalescent homes were not widely available. Many of them closed during the war, some destroyed by bombing, and never reopened. At the end of the war, even many large voluntary hospitals did not have an auxiliary home to which patients could be transferred, and they depended on the haphazard supply of convalescent beds available through charities. In the rushed transfer of hospitals in 1948, under 40 per cent of convalescent homes were nationalized and attached to Boards of Governors or Management Committees. But as the Fund put it, convalescence was suddenly 'a medical necessity . . . a right to which everybody is entitled'.[59]

A particular problem for hospital almoners was that they could not find beds in homes for those patients, typically elderly, who needed long periods of recuperation. Some of them had no homes to return to; many were in that no man's land between 'health' and 'welfare'. Geared to specialized treatment, the hospitals did not wish to admit patients who were likely to become permanent residents. They took the view that 'chronic' cases should be the responsibility of the local authorities. But the beleaguered welfare homes and hostels run by the local authorities did not wish to be burdened with such cases either. There was an obvious shortage of intermediate institutions, the equivalent of nursing homes, in the public sector.[60]

Anticipating the needs of the new health service, the Fund had reappointed a Convalescent Homes Committee in 1946 under Sir Henry Tidy and Oliver Chadwyck-Healey. The Committee published an annual *Directory of Convalescent Homes* and printed a confidential *Statistical Summary* of their income, expenditure, and work. It also introduced visits and grants to institutions around the Home Counties and the south coast to help in the modernization of their facilities. But it recognized the urgency of increasing the number of beds available, particularly for patients who needed longer periods of recuperation than was usually provided by convalescent homes. In 1949, the Fund allocated £250,000 to launch an experimental scheme of 'half-way houses', which would provide something between a hospital and a home, for long-stay patients but with nursing provision. The object was not simply to empty hospital beds of chronic patients, but to provide specialized facilities and comfortable living-conditions for patients who had reached a certain stage in their recovery.[61]

With Bevan's approval, the Fund discussed its proposals for 'half-way houses' with the Metropolitan Regional Boards and the Hospital Management Committees, which were happy to participate in schemes of such benefit to their geriatric units. They struck an agreement, by which the Fund would pay for the properties and their adaptation, the NHS would pay the running-costs, and voluntarists, mostly from the British Red Cross, would provide the management. Co-ordinating the voluntarists and the HMCs proved complicated, but in 1950 the first two homes, Whittington in Highgate and Westmoor in Roehampton, opened for patients from the Archway Group of Hospitals and the Battersea and Putney Group respectively. A few years later twelve homes were in operation, at a total cost to the Fund of £350,000. By 1956, when the Queen Mother visited Holmhurst, a small house in the Dulwich College Estate, over 6,600 patients had had a spell in one or other of the homes.[62]

The voluntary and public sectors worked reasonably well together in experimental convalescent care as long as the aged sick were a priority in the new hospital service. The Fund's intervention in the field was appreciated by the hospitals whose beds were lightened and by other institutions, whose representatives came to study its procedures. But having proved the value of the experiment, the Fund decided to disengage itself from the homes. In a most generous gift to the NHS, especially in the light of enhanced property values, it gave almost all the homes to their respective Hospital Management Committees in 1966, on the understanding that they would be kept in operation for at least ten years. None of them have survived, though a few remained open until the early 1980s, when it was decided that their property values outweighed their usefulness to the aged sick.[63]

The Fund's 'half-way house' scheme was in many ways typical of its projects after 1948. In the altered circumstances of hospital provision, it did not want to tie up its resources in long-term commitments, but preferred to initiate pioneering work which, if successful, might be carried forward by the NHS or other institutions. This rationale made sense given the size of its budget compared to the State's, but it had drawbacks, which the chronic underfunding of the NHS made apparent. More than a few of its schemes over the years started with an excellent idea and high hopes, but were dashed by the inability of the NHS to develop them. In the highly fluid medical world, in which new treatments and management techniques were being introduced, the Fund's experiments could turn a frill into what was arguably an essential service. But given rising costs and the shortage of government money, the less glamourous end of health provision with which the Fund was associated did not always compel support.

One of the Fund's projects, which complemented its half-way houses, might have produced far greater benefits had there been more money available. This was the Personal Aid Service for the Elderly, set up in 1955, the brainchild of Walter Graham. When working for the Emergency Bed Service, Graham noted that large numbers of elderly patients no longer needed hospital treatment but having nowhere else to go continued to occupy beds desperately needed by others. He persuaded the Fund to support a domiciliary assessment of patients' waiting-lists. The cost to the Fund was

£9,000 a year, but it was supplemented by the four Metropolitan Regional Hospital Boards, which each contributed £500 per annum toward the project.[64]

The chief objects of the household visits were to keep waiting-lists 'live' by removing names of those who had died, moved, or recovered, to consider alternatives to in-patient treatment, and to suggest the degree of priority in individual cases for admission to the hospital concerned. The effect on a hospital waiting-list could be dramatic, for it was not uncommon for it to be reduced by as much as 90 per cent after household screening.[65] As it transpired, 15 per cent of patients on the lists in south-east London were either dead or already in hospital.[66] Graham, who acted as Secretary to the Fund's Personal Aid Service Committee, and his assistant Joceline Owen, whom he later married, had visited over 20,000 patients in London and had hopes of extending the survey to certain provincial areas when the project was wrapped up.

The Fund anticipated that the work of the Personal Aid Service would be expanded and eventually become 'a necessary part of the Health Service'.[67] Indeed, as soon as it passed out of the 'experimental zone' the Fund was anxious that it be taken over by the NHS. The timing of its closure of the service in June 1962 turned on a speech by the Minister of Health, Enoch Powell.[68] At a meeting of hospital administrators in May, Powell had spoken warmly of the project and added: 'the pioneer phase of this operation is now over . . . and the hospital service ought now to be able itself to produce similar results and then to maintain its waiting lists efficiently, intelligently and currently'.[69] The NHS did not, however, match Powell's enthusiasm with hard cash and the project died just when it was beginning to show results. There was little the Fund could do about it, short of restarting the service, which it did not. Frustrated, Graham moved on, to become Secretary of the Elderly Invalids' Fund, now known as the Counsel and Care for the Elderly.[70]

The Fund's aversion to tying up its money in long-term projects was moderated in cases where the government was willing to pick up much of the bill. A prime example of this was the Emergency Bed Service. Popular with doctors, it had proved its worth over the years. In the Ministry's words, it was of 'obvious great value'.[71] Expecting the Service to grow, the Fund was unwilling to finance it on its own. Thus it struck an agreement with the Metropolitan Boards by which it provided the administration and the first £6,500, which was the cost of the service in 1947; the Boards agreed to provide anything in excess of that amount. It was a form of partnership with the NHS which was unusual for a charity, for the Fund undertook executive responsibility for the EBS, hiring its employees and providing accommodation.

Adapted to the four Metropolitan Boards, the EBS expanded rapidly.

Though now more formal in its practices, it retained its nautical flavour, which Peers, as a former Naval officer, had encouraged.[72] Under the new arrangements, in which a team of two Medical Officers appointed by the Boards refereed problem cases, the definition of an acute emergency became more elastic. The number of applications for admission to hospital rose from 10,000 a year in 1946 to over 50,000 in 1949. Shortage of space led to the opening of branch offices in the London suburbs.[73] The great smog pushed the service to the limits in the winter of 1951–2. Jack Langworthy, a retired naval commander who had recently joined the EBS as Assistant Secretary, remembered as many as 600 patients applying for beds in a single day.[74] In 1954 things were again on an even keel, and the Fund closed the branches and centralized the service in purpose-built offices by London Bridge Station. The following January, the EBS received its five-hundred-thousandth application, an occasion honoured by a visit from the Duke of Gloucester.[75]

Relations between the Fund and the NHS showed signs of improvement because of joint projects like the Emergency Bed Service. As with the revival of hospital visiting, such partnerships encouraged voluntarists and hospital administrators to get to know one another rather better. Still, in the early 1950s, the Fund's officials remained chary of the NHS. They recoiled from the public sector's general disregard for voluntary activity, which was particularly marked under the Labour government. Furthermore, they disliked the centralizing tendencies and the proliferation of committees in the NHS. Perhaps most of all, they disapproved of its lack of financial control, which undermined the very efficiency and economy that had always been central to the Fund's philosophy. Comparisons with the former voluntary system sprang to mind, and not often to the advantage of the NHS.

An illuminating memorandum by Ives, entitled 'A Coiled Spring', set out the Fund's anxieties about the financing of the new service. It was intended to provide the Management Committee with background material for its submission to the Guillebaud Committee, which was set up in 1953 by Iain Macleod, the Minister of Health, to review NHS costs.[76] The 'Coiled Spring' referred to the pent-up demand for hospital care, which had bedevilled the voluntary system and which was now threatening to overwhelm national resources. The case was unanswerable—'that human life and welfare is at stake, and that better theatres and diagnostic departments will mean so much more good medical work done... You cannot say no, you cannot retrench without the gravest consequences.'[77] According to Ives, the widespread criticism of the organizational deficiencies of the voluntary hospitals had distracted attention from an appreciation of how they had kept the costs of acute medicine within bounds by a system of checks and balances. Without those checks and balances, the effects of the coiled spring were becoming more apparent.

The root of the problem, as Ives saw it, lay in the desire of every Hospital Management Committee to offer the widest range of surgical techniques and other acute treatments. This meant upgrading nursing and other services, which inevitably led to a steep rise in costs. The problems were aggravated by a system of payment that encouraged GPs to take as many patients as possible and to unload them on to hospitals. Formerly, GPs did not often find themselves in close touch with hospital services. 'From every quarter the pressure is gathered in and multiplied and directed upon the Minister and the Chancellor of the Exchequer.' So great was the pressure that, if unchecked, it would 'throw the national finances out of balance'.[78]

There was obviously no quick fix to the dilemma of rising hospital costs, but the Fund believed that the experience of the voluntary hospitals should be recalled, for in their limited way they did manage to achieve local solutions to the problem. As Ives argued in 'A Coiled Spring', their system of checks and balances flowed from two principles. First, decisions about priorities rested with the lay body, acting on medical and nursing advice. Secondly, demands for medical facilities were tested by being placed in competition with one another. In the process, many projects for the expansion of facilities never got anywhere because they came into collision with other projects which enjoyed greater support.[79]

Such principles, Ives argued, were not widely observed in the NHS. (They were, however, retained by 'disclaimed' hospitals and widely adopted by new private hospitals.) After making allowances for differences of scale between the local and the national and for the inadequacy of hospital accounts, he lamented the low level of competition and exposure to criticism in the service. It could not be said 'that the handling of vast sums of Exchequer money now flowing into the health and hospital service is thoroughly subjected to a degree of criticism comparable to that which pervaded the old voluntary hospitals'. Without a greater degree of competition and criticism, Ives concluded, the public could not determine the necessity of the monies voted for medical provision.[80] The Fund's annual reports in the early 1950s drummed in the point: 'Can the arbitrary sums set aside by the Chancellor be justified by any rational process of thought? Can the public be satisfied that this money is not being wasted right and left?'[81]

The Management Committee invited Captain Stone, the Director of its Divison of Hospital Facilities, to present a more detailed report on the state of the NHS for possible submission to the Guillebaud Committee itself. He produced an outspoken, devastating critique of the service, rather in the style of Sir Henry Burdett. In his opinion, the causes which had led to the 'unsatisfactory position' of the NHS were 'its rushed introduction; impersonal character; emphasis on control; uncertainty; division of responsibility; lack of any systematic provision for cooperation; apparent lack of funds; and lack of an informative accounting system'.[82] Given these many failings, the patient, though now more intolerant of ill health, was 'being lost in the intricate working of a vast administrative machine.' Nor, according to Stone, could the NHS claim any credit for recent advances in medical treatment: 'They were just as likely to have happened, as did so many others before the appointed day, under the old arrangements as the new.'[83]

On the cost of the service, which was of primary interest to the Guillebaud Committee, Stone pointed to a new conception of budgeting for health under the NHS, which he compared unfavourably with that of the former voluntary system. Economic circumstances had forced successive governments 'to limit the Service to a sum determined *not by needs but by what can be spared from national income*, that is to say, productivity, and in competition with the rival claims of education, defence and so forth'. Thus the amount that could be spent on health could only be raised by greater productivity. If productivity fell, then the amount spent on health inevitably fell. But the government, by offering free treatment, had made the public increasingly health-conscious and desirous of taking advantage of hospital provision. 'As time goes on the gap between what the country can afford and what the people think they ought to have, free of cost, will get bigger and bigger.' Stone believed the government had already abandoned the task of providing 'the full measure of treatment demanded by the new health-consciousness'.[84]

One of the most damning sections of Stone's report was on the lack of co-operation and co-ordination in the NHS. These were matters which the Fund's officials viewed with the utmost gravity, and they well remembered the attacks on the voluntary system for its institutional rivalries and overlapping services. In Stone's view, the NHS, with its functionally distinct corporate bodies, had created a phenomenal level of waste and duplication. 'Due to the almost complete division of responsibility for the welfare of the patient, thinking is parochial; manpower is wasted in providing a continuity of service to the same patient; vision is foreshortened to one's own immediate problems; and each body follows a natural human tendency towards sovereignty, and the avoidance of any responsibilities which do not lie clearly and unmistakably within the letter of its statutory powers.'[85]

Nor was Stone impressed by those who recognized the problem but could only recommend the setting-up of additional committees. (The Guillebaud Report took the same view.) Such committees, he argued, would only make matters worse. 'So many authorities dealing with what might easily be the same group of patients, makes cooperation very difficult if not almost impossible.' In the present arrangements the existing unification of the service was 'achieved only at the level furthest removed from the patient, i.e. Ministry level'. In Stone's view, *'the best cure for a lack of co-operation is to avoid the need for it by a concentration of functions and the elimination of cross sectional interests'*.[86]

The Fund's management was far too diplomatic to present such a trenchant critique to the Guillebaud Committee undiluted. But the difference between what it did submit and the views of Stone and Ives was remarkable. In the spring of 1954, Sir Ernest Pooley, on behalf of the Management Committee, took Stone aside and explained to him that such a critical report was 'inappropriate'.[87] Instead, the Fund presented a brief, anodyne submission, with an appendix on hospital toilets, in which it declined to remark on the costs of the NHS.[88] Wishing to be positive about the service, it noted improvements in the relationships between Regional Hospital Boards and Hospital Management Committees, but suggested that the process of transferring authority to the local units needed to be carried further. Greater hospital independence would not only lead to greater efficiency but would increase neighbourhood interest and voluntary commitment.

The letter to the Committee expressed the hope that the NHS would recognize the important part which voluntary effort continued to play in the health services. In hospital affairs, it argued, it is 'a sound principle that the greater part of the burden should be borne by the state and the minor part by voluntary gifts; the latter can ensure a degree of elasticity in response to public demand out of all proportion to their monetary value and be an important factor in avoiding any sense of final frustration such as may develop in a service wholly financed by public monies'.[89] Such remarks were further evidence of the Fund's continuing struggle to see its traditions enshrined in the Welfare State, but they were a far cry from what might have been submitted to a government inquiry on hospital costs.

Why the disparity between the Fund's internal line and its public pronouncements? It had partly to do with the Fund's perception of itself after 1948 as a less influential body than in the past. And it had partly to do with its perception of the NHS: for all its faults, it was unlikely to go away; better to reform it from below than to attack its commanding heights. It also had to do with the Fund's reluctance to rock the boat when it was beginning to forge partnerships with the Ministry and the Metropolitan Boards. Would the money coming from the Ministry and the Boards to assist in joint projects continue to flow if the Fund spoke out too critically?

But the Fund's discretion had chiefly to do with the concessions offered to voluntarists from the Ministry of Health under Iain Macleod. The Fund had always felt more comfortable with the Conservative Party than with Labour, and Macleod's 'one nation' philosophy, with its commitment to social welfare, was in tune with the views prevailing among senior members of the Fund. So was his determination to contain costs and to bring stability to the NHS. The financial pressures on the Exchequer from the hospital sector reawakened Conservative enthusiasm for charity. Macleod, unlike Bevan, cultivated voluntarists. Like Willink before him, he believed their efforts were not only desirable but necessary. In a party-political broadcast in October 1952, he reported, with regret, that 'local pride' in the hospitals had diminished since the State had taken them over.[90]

The following January, at the annual general meeting of the National League of Hospital Friends, Macleod had endeared himself to the Fund, among other bodies, by encouraging hospital charity in the strongest terms. He did not go so far as to allow Management Committees and Boards of Governors to authorize charitable appeals, but he assured voluntarists that the restrictions on Management Committees to form or to work with local Leagues of Friends, rescinded in 1952, would not be reimposed; and he added that he regarded those employed in voluntary service to patients 'as providing the most suitable of all fields for recruitment of members to serve on hospital management committees'.[91]

The result of such encouragement from the Minister, the Fund observed, was a 'notable resurgence of voluntary effort in hospital work'.[92] Its own visitors' reports started to show a noticeable growth in local leagues, especially in the former municipal hospitals, which had little tradition of voluntary service. As a consequence, the Fund stepped up its grants towards projects in which the leagues were interested. The Guillebaud Committee also pointed to the vast amount of 'invaluable work' carried out by hospital voluntarists, and was at pains to encourage charitable effort in renewing the links between local communities and their hospitals.[93]

Macleod also encouraged the voluntary sector by his decision to end the uncertainty regarding the extent to which items of a capital nature paid for by charity counted against the total Exchequer payments to hospitals. In some cases the allocation of Exchequer money was so rigid that charitable grants to hospitals could be an embarrassment. In early 1954, Macleod announced that it was no longer necessary for him to require capital expenditure from non-Exchequer monies to count against capital allocations to hospital boards. The Fund welcomed the decision and saw it as a 'fresh phase in the partnership between voluntary service and the state in hospital work'.[94] As expected, a wave of new grant applications to the Fund resulted, and its awards to NHS hospitals began to rise in the mid-1950s, a fact which aggrieved the independent hospitals. In 1955, the Fund contributed £250,000 to state mental hospitals, an area which had formerly been outside the scope of its activities.[95]

Concessions to voluntarists from the Ministry under Macleod were the crucial factor in bringing the Fund round to the NHS. Because of them it swallowed its fundamental criticisms of the financial and administrative problems of the service. How else can we explain the Fund's public pronouncement that 'the years 1953 and 1954 will perhaps go down in history as marking a turning point in the life of the nationalised hospitals in this country'.[96] There was greater stability in health-service expenditure in 1953–4, but it was certainly insufficient to trigger the Fund's about-face. For public consumption at least, the Fund's assessment of the NHS was not at odds with the findings of the Guillebaud Report itself, published in January 1956, which vindicated the achievements of the hospital service.[97] It is unlikely that the Report, which Macleod found 'almost embarrassingly favourable', would have looked any different had the Fund submitted Stone's evidence.[98] But there was something rather disingenuous in the Fund's declaration that the Guillebaud Report had given 'the *coup de grace* to much discussion of controversial issues'.[99]

The Guillebaud Report, though not rich in useful proposals, encouraged projects with which the Fund was long-associated. One of these was hospital accounting. It was widely accepted that there was far too little statistical information available in the NHS. As early as 1950, Bevan invited the King's Fund and the Nuffield Provincial Hospitals Trust to undertake a costing-investigation in a number of selected hospitals. Two years later, they recommended that a departmental system of accounting be substituted for the prevailing subjective analyses.[100] Captain Stone believed that if accounting were made an integral part of hospital administration, it would prove a dynamic instrument in the hands of managers with reponsibility for the control of expenditure. But as he argued, 'it is the return obtained for expenditure and not the expenditure itself that is of vital importance'.[101]

Given the Ministry's anxieties over hospital expenditure, it followed up the preliminary investigation by appointing a working party on hospital costing in 1953. It was charged with devising a system of accounting likely to be of permanent value to hospital administration. Stone, who joined the working party, had the pleasure of seeing the departmental system of accounts, which he had promoted since the 1920s, preferred to the unified system of accounts, which the NHS had inherited. The unified system, based on the unit of cost per occupied bed, was no longer believed to be a reliable measure when so many services unrelated to occupied beds had to be taken into account. Nor did it allow for useful comparisons between hospitals. In contrast, the departmental system related the cost of each department to the volume of work performed. If properly implemented, it should enable comparisons to be made on a departmental unit basis rather than the existing all-in total expenditure basis.[102]

In 1956, the Minister of Health, Richard Turton, following the recommendations of the working party and the Guillebaud Report, announced the decision to introduce departmental costing into the NHS. The Fund continued to assist by providing advice on the installation of modern accounting-methods. But Stone was not altogether happy about the pace of reform. It was decided that the new approach would be introduced gradually into the larger, acute hospitals. The cost of implementing the scheme proved, in itself, a strain on resources. But the Fund was also frustrated by the complexities in the NHS, which could undermine the best-laid plans. In 1959, a year after Stone's retirement, its Division of Hospital Facilities complained that the needs of the various tiers of responsibility in the service resulted in distinct forms of accounting for the same expenditure. Failing a simplification of responsibilities, the development of the main departmental scheme would be impeded and its extension to other hospitals deferred.[103] In the 1960s much less was heard in the Fund about departmental accountancy.

Accountancy was but one interest of the Division of Hospital Facilities after 1948. The NHS had the effect of expanding the Fund's long-standing role in providing useful advice and information on matters from catering and construction to equipment and medical records; and the Division under Stone's leadership responded by setting up an advisory service and a library of hospital books, journals, and plans. These facilities were not restricted to hospital authorities but were open to government departments and other organizations, both at home and abroad. The library was an excellent example of continuity with voluntary traditions, for Sir Henry Burdett and the Hospitals Association had set up a similar scheme in 1901.[104] Through a link with the International Hospital Federation, of which the Fund was a member, the Division obtained information from around the world and forged closer ties with experts and students alike. The International Hospital Federation set up offices in the Fund, and Stone served as its Honorary Secretary and Treasurer. It was a sign of the Fund's growing internationalism, which the nationalization of Britain's hospitals stimulated.

One of the more intractable problems for the NHS, which the speed of hospital nationalization exacerbated, was that of recruiting and training administrative staff. The service needed people of the right calibre at all administrative levels, but bright young graduates and former servicemen and servicewomen tended to find the Civil Service and private industry a more attractive proposition than NHS management. With no national plan for recruitment and training and no proper career structure, the NHS, to prospective administrators, looked decidedly makeshift. Good people were hard to find and difficult to keep. Many senior posts were taken up by the second-rate, ignorant of hospital affairs. As the Guillebaud Committee noted, it was possible for a person with no practical administrative experience at hospital level to become a Secretary of a Regional Board. By the time the Committee reported, the problems for the NHS were acute. One of its conclusions was that 'a suitable training scheme covering administrative staff throughout the hospital service is very badly needed'.[105]

The King's Fund, as the Guillebaud Committee pointed out, had anticipated the problem. In 1945, on the suggestion of Sir John Mann, the

Chairman of the London Hospital, it had initiated a scheme of bursaries for training administrators.[106] It awarded most of them to men and women whose careers had been interrupted by the war. In 1948 it expanded into the field of social medicine with the offer of six bursaries to hospital almoners. At the same time it began to support that downtrodden breed, the Medical Records Officer, by helping to set up a School for Medical Records at the Middlesex Hospital.[107] (The Fund initiated a further medical-records project in the mid-1970s, but this foundered because doctors were reluctant to change their behaviour.) With the encouragement of the Ministry of Health, the Fund also established a Staff College for Ward Sisters. It bought a suitable building in Cromwell Road and ran its first course in March 1949 for twenty-five students.[108] Methods of staff management and ward administration took up much of the timetable.[109]

'With foresight and public spirit', as one NHS historian put it, the Fund decided on a new departure in 1949.[110] Speaking to the Council, the Duke of Gloucester announced a proposal to initiate a Hospital Administrative Staff College, in concert with the Institute of Hospital Administrators. Sir Wilson Jameson, who provided a strong personal link between the Ministry and the Fund, spoke enthusiastically about the scheme. It was to be 'in part residential for students, in part a centre for the exchange of ideas between existing administrators, members of Boards and Management Committees, doctors, nurses and others connected with hospital work'. The object of the institution was 'to raise the standard of hospital administration in this country'.[111]

Setting up the Staff College took a considerable amount of money and forward planning. A new committee, chaired by Lord McCorquodale, oversaw the project. Two properties were acquired—2 and 14 Palace Court, Bayswater; the former, which cost £14,000 in 1949, suffered from dry rot and had to be adapted. Philip Constable, House Governor of St George's Hospital, having been dispatched to survey American practices, accepted the post of Principal. He was joined by an enthusiastic Director of Studies and Senior Tutor, R. A. Mickelwright, formerly Secretary of South-West Middlesex HMC, who became Principal in 1955.[112] The eminent former Chief Medical Officer of Health, Sir Wilson Jameson, joined them as a part-time Medical Adviser.[113] The atmosphere at the College in the 1950s resembled that of an officer's mess, a trend which the Warden, a former Brigadier, encouraged. The hospitality, for which the College would become a byword, was enhanced by the provision of meals and drinks at the Fund's expense. One of the students on the first course, Frank Reeves, recalled that McCorquodale launched the College with sherry at ten o'clock in the morning.[114]

The ethos of the Staff College ran counter to the centralizing and bureaucratic tendencies in state hospital provision. Indeed, the Fund expected the college to produce managers who would promote flexibility, initiative, and decentralization in the NHS. As Ives wrote in the annual report for 1948, 'we need to determine the form of administration calculated to preserve under the new conditions the best elements in the older tradition built up in this country since the days of Sir Henry Burdett'.[115] In the 1950s, the Staff College had a strong historical sense, which found expression in lectures which surveyed past practices. These lectures were an important element in its attempt to perpetuate a particular tradition of hospital administration, which was part of the Fund's overall campaign to recreate voluntary practices in the new service.

Writing in the *Lancet*, Ives gave some hints of what the Staff College sought to encourage. Unhappy with the muddle created by the Ministry's merging of voluntary and municipal administrative practices, he cited Florence Nightingale. The primary administrative function was 'the enlightened pursuit of economy so far as it is consistent with the requirements of the sick'. Efficiency and harmony in a hospital, as he saw it, depended 'on a recognition by all parties of the extent and limits of their respective responsibilities'.[116] Such goals were not achieved by ignorant, albeit well-meaning, Whitehall officials, issuing directives which did not relate to the problems of individual hospitals. Nor were they achieved by members of Management Committees who represented the sectional interests of hospital workers rather than those of patients.

What Ives and his colleagues would not accept in the 1950s was that the administrative practices associated with former voluntary hospitals were inappropriate in the NHS.[117] They had some official support from the Bradbeer Report into the internal administration of hospitals, which was published in 1954. It recommended the continuation of tripartite administration and argued that the conception of partnership between medical, nursing, and lay staff should determine the future lines of hospital development. But it recognized that the existence of hospital 'groups' complicated decision-making. At group level, it was impossible to imagine distinct divisions of function in terms of individual officers.[118]

The first course held at the Staff College, attended by Secretaries of some of the larger Hospital Management Committees, took place in April 1951. The Fund deliberately set out to put hospital work in a wide perspective and to encourage the students to think of the fundamental principles governing the relationship of the medical and nursing staff to hospital administration.[119] But the course quickly got bogged down in detail. As Ives reported, the participants had responsibility for vast budgets, and many of their needs required specific approval from the appropriate committee while having to satisfy the policies of the ministries and the Regional Boards.[120] The complex network of procedure in the NHS, already well-entrenched, made the administrative principles of Nightingale, Burdett, and Ives look rather simplistic. If the initial course was any guide it was the Fund's officers, not those from the NHS, who would have to adapt and to diversify.

In the 1950s, the Staff College, while not forgetting voluntary traditions of management, adjusted itself to the mundane needs of the NHS. Its first study-group, set up in 1952, considered how hospital beds could be better used. It concluded that the less satisfactory institutions had to be upgraded.[121] The results of Health Service enquiries further widened its scope. On the recommendation of the Guillebaud Report, the College, along with Manchester University, played a prominent part in the National Selective Recruitment and Training Scheme in Hospital Administration. In 1956, eight trainees on the scheme, known colloquially as 'the anomalies', entered the College on a two-year course supervised by the Fund and the Ministry of Health. To relieve the pressure on the Fund's facilities, another property—10 Palace Court—had to be purchased.

By 1960, eighty-two courses of sixteen different kinds had been offered to nearly 700 hospital officers. Practical work came to the fore, in subjects ranging from engineering to catering. Management theory, as one witness remarked, did not so easily relate to the realities of hospital life.[122] Still, the College proved an exhilarating experience, especially for those tired souls coming from dilapidated hospitals. Guest-nights and distinguished visitors added to the atmosphere of experimentation and *bonhomie*. Most students remembered their courses with affection, as much for the contacts made and the hospitality received as for the advantages of learning.[123]

Against the backdrop of the NHS, innovation became the watchword in the Fund. Hardly a year passed in the 1950s without a major new initiative being devised. Given the circumstances, many of them were courageous ventures. In the Division of Nursing, the Recruitment Service continued to operate and the College for Ward Sisters soon passed beyond the experimental stage. On the back of these successes, Muriel Edwards proposed to set up a Staff College for Matrons. She visited America, where she was impressed by courses at Harvard which trained women for managerial posts. (One of her worries was that the training of nurses in Britain was falling behind that in America.) The Royal College of Nursing already offered courses in administration, but she was convinced that the Fund could experiment along somewhat different lines. In 1953, the Staff College for Matrons, under the direction of Irene Warren, opened at 22 Holland Park, W11. Her Royal Highness the Duchess of Gloucester honoured it with a visit.[124]

Inside and outside the Fund, people thought the College for Matrons especially successful. Combining theory and practice, its main object was 'to develop the student's administrative ability by helping her to gain a fuller understanding of human beings at work'.[125] Consequently, much attention was given to the problems of what by then was called 'personnel management'. Lectures, followed by discussion groups, dealt with subjects ranging from how to praise a colleague's work to dealing with complaints. More generally, Sir Wilson Jameson opened courses with lectures on the development of the hospital system since 1820, and other experts dealt with the management of special groups, including unions. As the syllabus put it, the trade-union movement was studied, so that some who have perhaps thought of it 'with impatience and dislike are able to understand the strong necessity from which the movement was born, and the solid worth of its achievements'.[126]

The Fund's colleges partook of a doctrine that in modern social life 'management' could not be left to 'born leaders' but demanded knowledge and skills that could be taught.[127] They were institutional expressions of the desire in the post-war years to develop a body of theory and best practice without which, it was argued, a modern hospital could not be run effectively. As such, they were in tune with the NHS, which was seeking to create a bureaucratic hierarchy, complete with professional career-structures, for its workforce. But as in other bureaucracies seeking to establish themselves, a certain discrete jargon crept into the NHS, which eventually insinuated itself into the Fund's colleges. One result was a rather tortuous analysis of what distinguished 'management' from 'administration' and what constituted the role of a manager.

The professionalization of hospital administration, of course, went back to the days of Burdett, but the growing complexities of the state welfare services invigorated it tremendously. In administration and nursing, there was a growing demand for professional status, which was both cause and effect of the erosion of the vocational spirit in the NHS. One insider argued that in nursing the NHS drove out the altruistic ethic 'and replaced it with the search for status'.[128] The administrative skills taught in the Fund's colleges and elsewhere became the ladder to promotion in nursing. The call to upgrade the status of nurses and administrators, and to keep pace with American experiments, lay behind the Fund's use of the title 'colleges' for what were essentially training schools for adults.[129] The usage was also a means of upgrading the status of the Fund itself, which needed to build a modern image after the war.

The early 1950s saw the establishment of one further educational centre by the Fund, the School of Hospital Catering. The Dietetic Advisory Service, founded during the war, had pointed out the deficiencies of British hospital catering. Dieticians were few and far between; untrained kitchen-staff worked in unhygienic surroundings; pilfering was rife. As the Fund's hospital visitors all too often noted, ingredients were indifferent and so badly prepared that dishes were both unpalatable and unhealthy. As everyone recognized, however, improving hospital food would be an uphill task, for the problem was a cultural one. The Fund cited the Italian miners in Britain who were well-satisfied with everything in the country save the cooking.[130]

In 1948, the Fund's Catering and Diet Committee, chaired by Sir Jack Drummond, decided to launch a training centre for caterers at St Pancras Hospital, which was now part of University College Hospital. J. Chadwick Brooks, who was a pillar of the Fund until his death in 1964, took responsibility for building and equipping the school. At the same time the former Dietetic Advisory Service was to transform into the Hospital Catering Advisory Service. It had an expanded brief, in keeping with the needs of the NHS and the advances in catering taking place elsewhere in the hospital world, especially in America. Under the guidance of D. G. Harington Hawes, Secretary to the Catering and Diet Committee, and George Stormont, Catering Adviser, it carried out surveys of catering departments around the country, advised on reorganizing and refitting kitchens, and published numerous pamphlets on hospital diets. In the 1950s, its essential purpose, as Stormont put it, consisted of setting 'standards of catering'.[131]

After some delay, the training centre, called the King's Fund School of Hospital Catering, opened in September 1951 in a former laundry building at St Pancras Hospital. By the end of the year, under the direction of its Principal, C. C. A. Gibbs, it had offered short refresher courses to eighty-nine catering officers, head chefs, and cooks. (By 1960, 1,600 students had passed through the School.)[132] Bringing new recruits into hospital catering was essential, and consequently the Fund organized a bursary scheme. Part of the trainees' time was to be spent in the School, part in selected London hospitals. An essential ingredient in the School's coursework was the costing of provisions and meals and their relationship to hospital finance generally. One of the project's aims was to define the general principles which might serve as guides to catering and finance officers. This was in keeping with the Fund's overall policy of rationalizing hospital practices and resources. Another object of the School was to improve the status of caterers, which was what the Fund was doing elsewhere for nurses and administrators.

The history of the Fund's work in catering and diet would be incomplete without reference to Dr Francis Avery Jones (knighted 1970), a gastro-enterologist who joined the Committee on Hospital Diet in 1947 and became the Chairman of the Catering and Diet Committee in 1956. He was unusual among the medical men attached to the Fund in that he came from a former municipal hospital, the Central Middlesex. Working unostentatiously behind the scenes, he had a talent for sensing a need and getting on with the job, just the sort of man the Fund admired and promoted to chair its committees. As another of the medical men in the Fund, Ian McColl (now Lord McColl) remarked, no doctor ever visited more kitchens than Sir Francis and 'countless thousands of patients had much better food as a result of his enthusiastic activity'.[133]

Sir Francis Avery Jones was prominent among the new generation of men and women who joined the Fund's committees in the post-war years. Fresh talent was much-needed because of deaths, retirements, and the changing character of hospital provision. Sir Edward Peacock, who had steered the Fund through a troubled period in its history, retired in 1954, the year he retired from Barings. His colleague at the bank, Alexander Francis Baring, Lord Ashburton, replaced him as Treasurer and Chairman of the Finance Committee. In 1956, after twenty-seven years in the Fund, Sir Ernest Pooley retired as Chairman of the Management Committee. The President appointed Lord McCorquodale to replace him. As President, the Duke of Gloucester continued to take an active interest in the operations of the institution, chairing meetings, launching new projects, and entertaining the staff at garden parties. But it could not be said that the royal influence in the Fund was as strong as it had been before the war, though the Queen became Patron in 1952.

Nineteen-sixty was a turning point in the Fund, if only because of the departure of the Secretary, Arthur Ives (CVO, 1954). Seriously injured in the Lewisham train disaster of 1957, he never fully recovered and had little choice but to retire. He was replaced by Roger Peers, the Assistant Secretary, who had been with the Fund since 1936. Without Ives—and Stone, who left in 1958—the Fund's office atmosphere, its internal debate and memoranda, became less academic, despite the proliferation of colleges. Ives's career had overlapped with the most radical changes in twentieth-century hospital affairs. He regretted that there was not more scope in the NHS for greater hospital independence and voluntary traditions of management, but he came to realize that these could not be achieved without a drastic reform of the service. On a more positive note, he applauded the fairness of the NHS and its transmission of medical care to a wider population.

Despite the many continuities in the Fund, the NHS had transformed its character. Physically, it was on several sites by 1960 and staff numbers had doubled since 1948. The Emergency Bed Service and the Hospital Personal Aid Service for the Elderly were in London Bridge Street, the Administrative Staff College in Palace Court, the Division of Nursing in Cavendish Square, the College for Ward Sisters in Cromwell Road, the College for Matrons in Holland Park, the School of Hospital Catering in St Pancras Way. The headquarters itself, which also housed the Division of Hospital Facilities, moved in 1957 from Old Jewry to new, purpose-built offices in King Street, EC2.

The physical separation of the Fund's many functions was a result of the centrifugal forces unleashed in the institution by hospital nationalization. The NHS swept away the Fund's former, overriding purpose—the defence of the voluntary hospitals against the State. In its place it encouraged a host of innovations, some of which it then frustrated. One danger for the Fund was that innovation might become an end in itself. Another was that the more enduring projects might go their own way, each with a different angle on the NHS, leaving the wider aims of the institution unclear. Arguably, its ballast was on the grants side. Direct financial payments to hospitals and charities not only carried on the Fund's oldest traditions; on careful judgement they may be seen to have been less susceptible to the whims of civil servants and cuts in services.

The creation of the National Health Service had, as expected, a liberating effect on the Fund. It brought the former municipal hospitals of London within its sphere of influence and encouraged it to take a greater interest in the national, indeed, the international scene. Furthermore, the Fund no longer felt the need to attend so exclusively to the 'sick poor'. As its annual report for 1960 stated, 'as the concept of the welfare state becomes more fully realised, "charity" to the "poor" in its old form is needed less urgently'.[134] Egalitarianism in health provision had the effect of reducing the Fund's embarrassment at helping the wider community. Tellingly, those awkward letters from middle-class claimants demanding cheaper hospital care no longer landed on the Secretary's desk. The NHS was generally popular with the middle classes. As in other charities which formerly had concentrated on the poor, a growing number of the Fund's own officers and staff used public hospitals for the first time.

Paradoxically, voluntary activity was being broadened, sharpened, and enlivened by the very nationalization of welfare that voluntarists had so long opposed. State social reform precipitated changes within charitable bodies themselves, bringing many of them into tune with modern conditions. Moreover, state provision was egalitarian and materialistic; it tended to erode those hierarchical values and religious pieties that had brought charity into disrepute in the past. For those of a philanthropic disposition who were losing faith, allegiances often shifted from religious charities to other causes thought to be more relevant to social need. Given the proven and ever expanding rewards of scientific medicine, hospitals were among the chief beneficiaries of the changing charitable outlook. The first post-NHS voluntary hospital, the New Victoria, opened in Kingston in 1958, having collected £35,000 from local subscribers.[135]

Despite the reliance of the NHS on charitable funds and activity, most commentators on social policy kept their eyes fixed on the State in the 1950s. In the social services, 'do gooding', as one witness put it, was 'a word as dirty as philanthropy'.[136] Voluntarists put up with the slurs, kept their heads down, and got on with the work at hand. Even before Bevan's departure as Minister of Health they were making their distinctive mark on hospital life. After his departure, things became rather easier for them, at least at ministerial level. But the Labour Left, Health Service trade-unionists, and many civil servants continued to see them as irrelevant, at best peripheral figures dealing with frills, typified by the Red Cross lady running a trolley shop.

Those at the sharp end of hospital life did not see things so quaintly. Dr Francis Avery Jones, an avid reader of charitable directories, wrote to *The Times* in 1958: 'in the past 10 years the few growing points in my hospital have come almost entirely from outside sources—the Nuffield Foundation, King Edward's Hospital Fund for London, and the Guinness Trust'.[137] To many others at the time, the future of the NHS looked bleak without an expansion of voluntary support. As the Secretary to the Board of the Royal Bristol Infirmary said: 'I am sure that most of the money needed to expand and improve the Service will increasingly come, to the limited extent that is possible, from independent organisations such as the Fund.'[138] Iain Macleod, who also knew something of the realities of running a hospital, declared that 'without voluntary service the National Health Service would wither and die'. And he added, 'without voluntary effort I would not want to be at the head of the Health Service'.[139] The voluntarists were listening, if the trade-unionists and civil servants were not.

8

A Decent Anonymity, 1960–1980

THE years 1960 to 1980 were the heyday of state-directed health and social services in Britain. Few people doubted that central government had a primary responsibility for welfare provision, and most commentators assumed that it was well-equipped to administer the system devised by Parliament. The consensus did little to enhance the status of voluntarists, whose impulses were to decentralize, to break a problem down into pieces. Increasingly, charities in the health and welfare fields received money from government sources, which brought the issue of their independence into question. With few exceptions, they accepted whatever money was available, and the more they accepted, the more they cherished their independence. They were now, in the parlance of the 1960s, very much the 'junior partner in the welfare firm'.[1] As they settled into a decent anonymity, they had the consolation that charity was its own reward.

The central State dominated the hospital world, yet trade-unionists and civil servants remained jealous of contributions to the NHS from other patrons, especially those local societies whose volunteers were active inside hospitals. Ministerial endorsements of hospital charity from Macleod, Powell, and others, though much appreciated by voluntary bodies, were not much acted on by their subordinates. When he became Secretary of State for Health and Social Security in 1968, Richard Crossman was 'staggered' by the extent of voluntary activity in the Health Service, but 'astonished by the strength of the resistance' among his civil servants to his proposal that it should be encouraged.[2] He detected a particular tendency of the NHS to treat volunteers 'as cheap, auxiliary labour', while noting that the idealism in the service had drained away. Chastened by his experience as a Minister, he lamented that the Labour Party had done 'grievous harm' to philanthropy.[3] As he was aware, the post-war Labour Party's predilection for welfare provision based on centralized bureaucracy had also done 'grievous harm' to its own co-operative traditions, which, merging into philanthropy, gave socialism its democratic infrastructure and moral centre.

Although the legacy of political bitterness between ex-voluntary and ex-municipal elements in the Hospital Management Committees had largely disappeared by the mid-1960s, the prejudice against voluntary activity persisted. In a world of ever increasing specialization and centralization, the 9,000 or so unpaid members of hospital boards and committees, who were believed to be safeguarders of democracy, began to ask 'Why am I here?'[4] More often than not, the Leagues of Friends and other hospital charities also felt unappreciated. Attempts to break the 'unfruitful deadlock' between public servants and volunteers had only limited success, in part because the trade unions were jealous of losing employment to hospital volunteers.

The very disparity in the scale of their respective operations made an effective partnership between the NHS and charities difficult. Diverse and fragmented, philanthropists were at a disadvantage in a climate disposed to monolithic state programmes. Small movements in government departments required disproportionate activity on their part. This was particularly noticeable in the Health Service. Like mice scurrying around a proud and fabled lion, hospital voluntarists had to keep an eye on every shift in the NHS for fear of being smothered. Politicians and the press, with their eyes fixed on the lion, took little notice of the proliferation of mice.

Cushioned by its wealth and reputation, the King's Fund suffered little of the disregard shown to Leagues of Friends and other local charities. It provided money, with few strings attached, unaccompanied by a swarm of hospital volunteers. Still, there was no disguising its diminished status. On a visit to the Fund, one Secretary of State for Health and Social Security, ignorant of the institution's activities, asked what his department could do for it.[5] Its financial contribution to the London hospitals, once crucial to their survival, had fallen dramatically after 1948 and stood at under 0.5 per cent in 1960. Moreover, the difficulties it had had in the 1950s in adjusting to the NHS persisted. In order to deal with hospitals subject to political interference, organizational upheavals, and cost-cutting exercises, the Fund had little choice but to take risks. It fell into line with the view that money from the Exchequer was at a premium and must be applied only to essentials.

The Fund might have opted to concentrate its resources on the independent, 'disclaimed' hospitals. Such a policy would have avoided the risks inherent in working with the NHS. But while it continued to make grants to the independents, they were not thought sufficiently numerous or important enough for the Fund to favour them exclusively. The notion put forward in the early 1950s that they would have an influence on the administrative practices of the NHS proved to be a chimera. Tellingly, no one representing the independent hospitals sat on the Fund's Management Committee. On the other hand, NHS hospitals, especially the London teaching hospitals, were well-represented. By the 1960s, institutions in the NHS received the lion's share of the Fund's grants and were the principal target of its projects and its colleges. Clearly, the NHS was a great experiment in hospital administration and the Fund wanted to be part of it, despite the risks.

Having committed itself to the NHS, the Fund concentrated its attention on matters relating to patients and staff. The patients needed all the support available to them. If in the 1930s many of them suffered from cheese-paring and the stigma of poverty, they now suffered from cheese-paring and standardization. The Fund saw the failings of the hospital service in a somewhat different light from civil servants with a collective responsibility. In its view, 'inefficiency and indifference are seen as injustice done to individuals'.[6] The hospital-building programme in the 1960s and 1970s, which sometimes created institutions resembling high-rise council blocks, did not allay its fears for the individual. Even so, against the background of central planning and a 'bigger is better' mentality, the patients did not always get their due from their charitable supporters, though one critic exclaimed in 1962: 'Heaven and Mr Powell preserve us from these gigantic, mechanised medical factories.'[7]

By the 1960s, British hospitals, whether NHS or independent, had witnessed a transformation in the way in which individuals were treated and 'administered'. Since the nineteenth century, economic and social changes had been combining with medical advances to encourage more and more patients to enter institutions. Despite the improvements in hospital care, they often felt frustrated once inside, for they were enveloped by institutional controls affecting everything from the salt in their food to the standard of behaviour expected of their visitors.[8] And while doctors could diagnose an illness with ever greater scientific precision, once the course of the disease was known, the mystery of an individual case was lost. The very administration and care in institutions could turn a patient into a passive recipient of medical treatment and isolate him or her from family and friends, who followed the predicted course of the illness, rather than the sick person's response to it. At home, patients at least had a greater say in shaping their own illness or death.

Charities had a crucial role to play in humanizing hospital life. Indeed, an important effect of the NHS on their services was to heighten their interest in the patient. Lord Shawcross, a member of the 1945 Labour government, said in 1962 that the NHS could not provide luxuries or 'the personal touch'. But he was delighted to report that there were charities that could, not least the Leagues of Hospital Friends with their 800,000 members.[9] In the early 1960s, some hospitals remained without the support of Leagues or other local charities, but where they were established, volunteers provided a wide range of services, from outings to routine clerical work. Charitable trusts complemented their activities. The Central Middlesex Hospital, for one, received sufficient awards from charities, including the King's Fund, to provide a lounge, a rest-room, a shop, a diet kitchen, annual travelling-grants for nurses, a rose garden, a lecture theatre, and two research departments. None of these improvements had any priority from the Regional Board, which had commitments elsewhere.[10]

In this hive of charitable activity the King's Fund had a distinctive place. It had committed itself to the NHS in the 1950s, and its links with the service matured in the following decade. Though its influence had diminished, its relationship to NHS hospitals came to resemble its sympathetic, though not uncritical, relationship to the former charitable hospitals. The propaganda element in its work was now much reduced, although it continued to speak out on behalf of voluntary principles. Diplomacy remained at a premium, and never more so than when dealing with hospitals undergoing reorganization in the 1970s. Allied to a state hospital service subject to political wrangling, the Fund wished to be seen as neutral. Thus when it submitted evidence to government inquiries it sought to avoid taking sides and confined itself to matters on which it felt able to speak with authority.

As the Fund's political lobbying diminished, its practical knowledge and skills came to the fore. In the collective context, innovation became its ideal. The emphasis on useful experimentation was a natural response to its diminished responsibility and its association with a state service which was expected to pay for essentials. Still, priority went to projects which met the day-to-day needs of patients and staff. In general, innovations were approved which were compatible with, and contributed to, the development of the NHS. But a feature of its work was that it concentrated on areas which were poorly served, if served at all, by both the NHS and other charitable institutions. As ever, it esteemed hospital efficiency, but 'as the servant of human happiness and not pursued as an end in itself'.[11]

The rise in the number of hospital patients in the 1950s and the prospect of a programme of hospital expansion brought the plight of the individual patient to the fore. (The number of patients leaving the hospitals of England and Wales exceeded four million for the first time in 1959, which was 1,100,000 more than in 1948.)[12] With the object of improving its own efficiency in regard to patients and absorbing new projects more effectively, the Fund reorganized its committee structure in 1959–60. The Distribution Committee, which had been in existence since Lord Lister's day, ceased to exist; the Management Committee took over its function of allocating monies. By 1960, applications for grants went to three newly formed committees: the Hospitals Committee (Hospital Grants Committee after 1963), the Mental Hospitals Committee, and the Auxiliary Hospitals Committee, which replaced the Convalescent Homes Committee.

Changing conditions and opportunities in the hospital world resulted in further alterations to the Fund's committees. In 1960, a Hospital Development Committee, under the chairmanship of Lord Cunliffe, was appointed to guide the work of the Division of Hospital Facilities and the Hospital Catering Advisory Service. Its object was to assess projects coming forward from inside and outside the Fund and to advise the Management Committee of schemes worth promoting. In the same year, a Colleges Committee, under the chairmanship of Lord McCorquodale, was set up to rationalize and to steer the policy of the various colleges, the School of Hospital Catering, and the Nursing Recruitment Service. Thus the individual committees of the colleges and the School of Catering disappeared.[13]

The restructuring of the Fund's committees coincided with the loss of various long-serving committee men and staff. In 1960 alone there were three notable deaths: Oliver Chadwyck-Healey, Sir Henry Tidy, and Sir Ernest Rock Carling. Sir Ernest Pooley, who had served the Fund since 1928 as an Honorary Secretary and then as Chairman of the Management Committee, retired in 1961.[14] Sir Wilson Jameson had departed the year before. (He left behind the gift of a Burmese gong, which is still used to announce meals in Palace Court.) Highly respected in the Fund, Jameson was also unique for having moved from a seat on the Management Committee to a position on the staff. On the staff side, Muriel Edwards retired in 1961, as did V. H. Rushton, cashier at the central office, who had joined the Fund fifty years earlier. Ever generous towards faithful staff, the Fund topped up his pension by the purchase of an annuity.[15]

With voluntarism out of fashion, finding replacements for such people was more difficult than in the past. Derek Harington Hawes, who joined the Fund from the Indian Civil Service in 1949 and rose to be Deputy Secretary, recalled that he had put the Fund last on his long list of job possibilities.[16] For many years, potential recruits to charitable societies were being swept up in the tide of enthusiasm for expanding state services. Not only did the State seem the wave of the future, but government service looked likely to provide better careers. Voluntary societies adjusted as best they could. To encourage greater mobility between state and voluntary sectors, the Fund made its staff pension scheme interchangeable with the NHS superannuation scheme in 1966.[17]

By the early 1970s, the Fund had linked its salaries and bonuses to NHS scales and was appointing more people formerly employed in the NHS or other government agencies.[18] But finding first-class applicants remained a problem for the Fund, and for charities generally. So did inculcating institutional allegiance. In a time of flexible pension-schemes, expanding services, and job mobility, no one was likely to work for fifty years in one institution again. The professionalization of philanthropic administration, combined with the appointment of staff from the public sector, would also undermine the culture of voluntarism; by the 1980s some employees in the Fund were only dimly aware that they worked for a charity.

The 1960s saw the emergence of many new honorary officials in the Fund, some of whom are still familiar figures around Palace Court. Max Rayne (later Lord Rayne) joined the increasingly important Estates Committee in 1961 and the Finance Committee three years later. Commander R. W. Peers, RN, the brother of the Secretary, Roger Peers, served on the Auxiliary Hospitals Committee and became its Chairman in 1965. Andrew Carnwath (later Sir), a leading partner at Barings, joined the Finance Committee in 1963 and two years later succeeded Lord Ashburton, a much-respected figure in the Fund, as Treasurer. The Hon. George Charles Hayter Chubb (later Lord Hayter), Chairman of Chubb and Sons Lock and Safe Co., first served as a visitor, but he soon showed a willingness to take on further duties. A vigorous advocate of voluntarism, with a strong sense of its traditions, he joined the Hospitals Committee in 1962. Appointed to the Management Committee the following year, he became its Chairman in 1965 (he received a KCVO in 1977).

For some time, the ill health of the Duke of Gloucester had prevented him from carrying out his duties as the Fund's President, and he resigned in 1970. Having begun in 1942, his tenure of office had been longer than that of any of his predecessors. Her Majesty Queen Elizabeth II followed the precedent set in 1910 and appointed three Governors: HRH Princess Alexandra, Lord Ashburton, and Lord Rosenheim, President of the Royal College of Physicians. Princess Alexandra was already familiar with some of Fund's activities, for she had visited the Emergency Bed Service in 1958. Nor was she a stranger to hospital work, as she had once taken a student training-course at the Hospital for Sick Children, Great Ormond Street.[19]

There were many new appointments to the staff in the 1960s, which reflected the reorganization of the Fund's activities and the promptings of the NHS. Among the more important was that of Miles Hardie, who had a particular interest in international hospital affairs. He joined the Division of Hospital Facilities in 1958 and succeeded W. E. Hall as Director of the Hospital Centre in 1966. He later succeeded Derek Harington Hawes as Director of the International Hospital Federation. Janet Craig joined the nursing section of the Division of Hospital Facilities from the Nuffield Foundation in 1960. In the same year R. T. Whatley, Catering Adviser to the South East Metropolitan Regional Hospital Board, became Principal of the School of Hospital Catering. Frank Reeves, Group Secretary of the Winchester Group HMC, succeeded Mickelwright as head of the Administrative Staff College in 1963.

Overseeing appointments and steering the Fund's affairs more generally was Roger Peers, who succeeded Ives as Secretary in 1960. If Ives was of an academic temperament, Peers was impulsive and convivial. Described by a colleague as the 'last of the amateurs' in the Fund, he was equally at home with junior staff, royalty, or his friends at the Athenaeum, whose wine committee he chaired.[20] His appointment was suggestive of the Fund's residual uncertainties about the NHS. A contemporary of Ives, he was steeped in pre-NHS voluntary traditions. In 1960, it would seem, the Fund was not ready to appoint a Secretary steeped in NHS culture. But when Peers died suddenly in 1968, he was replaced by a man who was, Geoffrey Phalp. The Secretary of the United Birmingham Hospitals, Phalp was invited to apply because he had such excellent NHS connections. Called the 'doyen of NHS administrators', he had the intelligence and receptiveness to maximize the Fund's contribution to the hospitals in a period when they were subject to considerable disruption and uncertainty.[21]

The recruitment of personnel and the purchase of new buildings and facilities to accommodate them were signs of expansion in the Fund's project work. (In 1965 it moved its headquarters from King Street to 14 Palace Court.) But money spent on additional personnel and new premises increased administrative costs, which reached 10 per cent in 1970; and without the receipt of fresh capital the money available for grants was bound to diminish. Small legacies continued to come in, but there were no further gifts to match Lord Nuffield's munificence. Annual subscriptions and donations provided, on average, only about £10,000 a year in the 1960s and 1970s.[22]

Sensitive to the chasm between what patients expected and what government provided, the Fund, like some other medical charities, was in two minds about raising money. Some thought that the institution's purposes were not sufficiently alluring to attract fresh capital; others felt that it had enough money to fulfil its aims. Still, the Fund invited donations and sought outside money for special projects. But it no longer contemplated public appeals, and by the 1960s few were left in the Fund who had any experience of them. In 1965, the Treasurer, Andrew Carnwath, said in private to the Management Committee that 'the Fund must be regarded as a closed Fund, in that although the income might continue to rise as a reflection of inflation, there appeared to be no grounds for expecting a substantial influx of new capital'.[23]

Like their predecessors, the Fund's Treasurers in the 1960s and 1970s, Lord Ashburton, Andrew Carnwath, and Robin Dent—who still holds the office—advocated a policy of financial prudence and institutional flexibility. Recognizing that it was easier to launch a project than to shut one down, they sought to avoid committing assets on a long-term basis and to strike 'a desirable balance' between grants and services. What constituted 'a desirable balance' was subject to internal debate, which cash crises in the hospitals brought into the open. In 1966, for instance, the shortage of money in the NHS led the Chairman, George Chubb, to call for more grants to be made available to the hospitals.[24] But without new sources of finance this could only be achieved by budget cuts in the Fund's educational and project work. Under financial pressure, the rivalries between the Fund's divisions, which tended to work in isolation from one another, came to the surface. The Assistant Secretary, David Halton, regretted the amount of money allocated to the colleges and the Hospital Centre, whose activities he described as 'harmless' and 'over expensive'.[25]

Although cash crises in the NHS, coupled with inflation, put pressure on its resources, the Fund prospered. It did so by the successful investment of its capital and a measure of luck. Most of the Fund's capital was invested in quoted stocks and shares, though the acquisition of property became increasingly important during the 1960s. In 1964 a Statutory Instrument formally gave the Fund the power to invest in land.[26] By 1972, £4,000,000 of the Fund's total assets of over £16,000,000 were invested in property. As to Stock Exchange securities, about 27 per cent were in fixed interest, 64 per cent in United Kingdom and Australian equities, and 9 per cent in US equities.[27] The Fund's investments, handled by Barings, had long moved on from the world's railways, though in its well-rounded portfolio, distilleries and tobacco companies continued to feature.[28] Apparently the Fund saw no particular reason to restrict the investment manager to what would now be called 'ethical investments'.

One particular windfall, which continues to pay handsome dividends, came from the purchase of the Basing estate. Recommended to the Fund by its property agent, Cluttons, the land was seen as an exceptional opportunity. The Fund moved quickly to purchase it. In 1973, largely as a result of the sale of part of the estate to Hampshire County Council in connection with the development of Basingstoke, the Fund's assets rose from £18,677,000 to £25,522,000.[29] Andrew Carnwath's retirement as Treasurer in 1974 thus coincided with a considerable success. (He received a KCVO in 1975.) In the decade under his financial management the Fund's assets had risen by 134 per cent, over twice the rate of inflation. When he passed on the Treasurer's baton to Robin Dent, another senior Barings man, he said he felt some sympathy for him, 'as it was always easier to start at the bottom'.[30] Dent would have his chance. The Fund's financial performance reflected wider economic trends, and when the 1974 oil crisis devastated share values its assets fell back sharply.

In the expansionary climate of the early 1960s, the Ministry of Health proposed a large-scale increase in hospital construction. The publication of *A Hospital Plan for England and Wales* in 1962, which harked back to the hospital surveys at the end of the war, was indicative of the Ministry's planning-mentality.[31] It promised integrated services and improved facilities in large new district hospitals. The emphasis on economy of scale threatened many small, outlying institutions, which were often very popular in their communities. As in the past, local groups fought to keep open hospitals with which they identified. But in the 1960s and early 1970s, the idea of community hospitals, though discussed, was not in vogue.[32]

The Ministry's problem was not unlike that faced by the King's Fund before the war, when it sought to remove or to amalgamate hospitals in the interests of efficiency. But the government had the power of coercion, and many a hospital built by patronage was destroyed by planning. The eventual list of hospital closures in London proved to be a roll-call of institutions that the Fund had supported for decades. (Many smaller NHS hospitals survived, but their survival rate generally was lower than that of the voluntary hospitals which retained their independent status in 1948.)[33] No longer able to save a threatened hospital, the Fund adopted a philosophical view. It accepted that 'many old ties and traditions will be broken as the new scheme emerges but, sad though this may be, such things are inevitable in a fast changing world'.[34]

The Fund shared the prevailing optimism regarding planning. Despite its respect for the individuality of small institutions, it endorsed the need to create a 'unified Health Service' as outlined in the *Hospital Plan for England and Wales*.[35] Indeed, it took the Whiggish view that the document was 'the latest step forward' in the long history of hospital provision.[36] It moved quickly to make its own internal adjustments. In early 1962, the Management Committee circulated the *Hospital Plan* to all its grant-making committees, with the advice that they should be cautions in making awards to hospitals which were liable to be closed.[37] Following a suggestion by the Ministry of Health, the Fund set up a working party, chaired by Captain A. Lade, RN, (retd.), to look into the problems of establishing new hospitals. Its report, *Commissioning New Hospital Buildings*, appeared in 1965.

In co-operation with the Institute of Hospital Administrators, the Fund set up a working party to suggest a management pattern suited to the emergence of large district hospitals. The result was *The Shape of Hospital Management in 1980?*, published in 1967. Written by Leslie Paine, the House Governor and Secretary of the Bethlem Royal and Maudsley Hospitals, the report pointed to the morass of committees in the NHS and the inadequacies of the existing tripartite administration, with its separate medical, nursing, and business functions. To remedy these 'evils', it called for clear leadership in administration at the local level, in the form of a General Manager who would be responsible for the efficient operation of the whole hospital. The report's recommendations represented a notable departure from a long line of experts, from Burdett and Nightingale to Bradbeer and Ives, who admired the tripartite system for its checks and balances. But in a district hospital of the future, Paine and his colleagues insisted, 'someone must be in charge'.[38] This sentiment would find a strong echo in almost identical words in Sir Roy Griffith's influential 1983 report on NHS management to the Prime Minister, Margaret Thatcher.

The Fund's grants in the 1960s and 1970s also turned on ministerial initiatives and economic vicissitudes. High marks went to officials in the charity who could spot a trend or anticipate a hospital closure. Keeping in touch with changes in NHS policy was all the more urgent when the Fund could do relatively little to influence the direction of government decisions. Other welfare charities had the same, seemingly perennial, problem: a potential for throwing away money in a climate of political uncertainty and stop-go state policy. The Fund's awards covered such a variety of schemes that it is impossible to sum them up, except to say that they were typically patient-centred and practical. If applying for a grant from the Fund resembled queuing for a bus, those projects which contained elements of experimentation and self-help were more likely to reach their destinations.

The creation of the Mental Hospitals Committee (1959–63) was an example of the Fund's watchfulness and experimentation. It was set up in anticipation of the passage of the Mental Health Act (1959), whose purpose was 'to make fresh provision with respect to the treatment and care of mentally disordered persons'.[39] In the 1950s, the Fund's grants to mental hospitals had been made by the Management Committee, which gave priority to social and sports facilities, on the grounds that mental hospitals were often isolated from recreational centres. After the 1959 Act, the Fund expected to play a part in co-ordinating services for mental patients, and it stepped up its allocations for their benefit.[40] It also noted Enoch Powell's decision to provide additional money to the mentally ill.

The effect of the Mental Health Act, combined with new drug-treatments, was to reduce the numbers admitted to mental hospital. The *Hospital Plan* anticipated further reductions in beds allocated to mental illness and, rather optimistically, predicted the closure of many Victorian asylums.[41] The Fund quickly shifted its emphasis to day hospitals and to projects designed to get patients back to work.[42] A £25,000 grant to St Bernard's Hospital to set up an industrial-therapy factory was an example of its desire to ease patients back into the community.[43] But not wishing to waste money on institutions that might be shut at any time, the Fund rethought its priorities and the Mental Hospitals Committee ceased operations. After 1963 the Fund's grants to mental institutions passed into the care of the Hospital Grants Committee, which reduced them.

In compensation for the lack of a 'personal touch' in NHS institutions, the Hospital Grants Committee funded libraries, gardens, pictures, music, and other recreational and social facilities. Having relaxed its London rule, it was able to support more institutions outside the capital. In 1965, for example, it gave a grant for a hostel for patients' relatives at Broadmoor Hospital, Crowthorne, and another for a museum at Royal Earlswood Hospital. It complemented such awards with its more traditional line in grants for fire precautions and central-heating boilers. Nor were clinical needs ignored. It provided Brook Hospital with a medical centre and Hackney and Queen Elizabeth HMC with a physiotherapy department. Even God received a grant, albeit indirectly, for Guy's was awarded £5,000 for a chapel.[44] In the five years 1970–5, the Hospital Grants Committee gave £480,000 to NHS institutions.[45]

One particular award from the Hospital Grants Committee is worth special mention. Prompted by government policy, the Fund began to favour projects which linked up hospitals and extra-hospital services. Thus in the early 1960s, it provided £42,700 for building and furnishing the Kingston Medical Centre, a meeting-place for GPs and hospital doctors and a forum for postgraduate medical education. Supporting medical education was at variance with King's Fund policy, which since 1905 had prohibited grants to medical schools. In 1905, of course, the 'sick poor' took precedence in the Fund's thinking. But as the question of means no longer arose in regard to hospital admission, it decided that it could accept proposals to support medical training.[46]

The Kingston Medical Centre, which Lord McCorquodale formally presented to the Minister of Health, Enoch Powell, in December 1962, was the result of a joint initiative between the King's Fund and the Kingston Group HMC. It was just the type of innovative project that the Fund wished to promote, for it strengthened the links of the hospital service with family doctors at a time when unity and co-ordination were in vogue in the NHS. As Powell remarked in his speech of acceptance, no modern hospital would be able to do without some such instrument as the Kingston Centre 'for expressing the integral unity of the work of the hospital service with that of the family doctor'.[47] The Kingston Centre proved to be the forerunner of other such experiments in postgraduate medical education, which the Fund and the Nuffield Provincial Hospitals Trust generously supported.[48]

The Fund's Auxiliary Hospitals Committee dealt with applications from smaller independent hospitals, convalescent homes, and charities. In the five years 1970–75, it distributed £330,000.[49] If grants to convalescent homes had been essentially a salvage operation after the war, in later years the object was to upgrade their facilities. With the trend towards asking homes to receive patients at an earlier stage of their recovery, there was also support for increased nursing supervision. As the demand for children's homes declined because of adoption and improvements in child health, the Fund helped to adapt some of them for alternative use.[50] In the 1960s and early 1970s support for other charities was as much moral as financial, but among those which received modest sums from the Auxiliary Hospitals Committee were Toynbee Hall and MIND. As the Secretary of the National League of Hospital Friends remarked, 'It must be very comforting to be able to play Father Xmas as you at the Fund do!'[51]

Until the mid-1970s, the Fund continued its tradition of hospital visiting. As Sir Francis Avery Jones remarked, visitors often triggered applications for support by pointing out a problem, say the wash-basins in the nurses' hostel, to a hospital official.[52] But visiting was running down. In the five years 1970–5, only forty-five NHS hospitals were officially inspected.[53] Finding appropriate people with the time to spare was more difficult than in the past. Moreover, the reorganization of the NHS in the mid-1970s created complications. Not only would such visits have to be arranged with the District Management Team, but it was believed that the Area Health Authority and the Regional Health Authority would have to be consulted as well. In 1975, the Fund decided to suspend visits in view of the changes in the management structure of the service.[54] Despite occasional murmurings asserting their former usefulness, they have not been re-established.

A further reason for the demise of visiting was that the balance of the Fund's work had moved away from grants towards projects and services, which might provide benefits throughout the NHS. (In 1947 grants took up 90 per cent of the Fund's total expenditure, in 1969, 34 per cent.)[55] The growing emphasis on projects and services was in keeping with changes in the NHS itself, where expansion and central planning excited schemes of integration and co-ordination. The Fund's Division of Hospital Facilities had proved its worth in providing an information bureau and an advisory service, and in the 1960s the number of inquiries increased. About 10 per cent of them were from abroad, but most were from NHS hospitals. Increasingly, inquiries led to special investigations into problems which affected hospitals throughout the NHS.[56]

The projects taken on board by the Division of Hospital Facilities, though often highly technical, tell us a great deal about hospital conditions and are an oblique record of the changing character of hospital life for both patients and staff. They included studies of hospital blankets, cubicle curtain-tracks, noise, and wireless systems. To find the ideal ward-flooring, the Fund paid for ten different surfaces to be laid in strips along a corridor at Ashford Hospital, Middlesex. Many such inquiries resulted in booklets being distributed to relevant hospital personnel. In 1961, for example, the Division published *Films for Hospitals*, a report based upon replies to questionnaires sent to 341 hospitals in London and the provinces.[57]

The Division's projects sometimes dealt with more contentious issues than hospital floors and films. Its interest in 'dirty walls' sparked off a lively debate in *The Times*, which raised wider questions about morale and working-practices in the NHS. In response to complaints, the Division had launched an inquiry into the question of general hospital cleanliness in the late 1950s.[58] Francis Avery Jones, who supported the project, raised the issue in a letter to the *Lancet*. He pointed to 'a curious discrepancy between the constant cleaning and polishing of floors and the almost complete absence of effort to clean the walls'.[59] The situation was so bad that he had had to close his own wards for a fortnight because of the increasing amount of operation-wound infection as bacteria fell on to patients. The problem was a national one, which arose because the Ministry had directed that only 'skilled' workers were qualified to wash paint in general hospitals.[60] The safety of patients was being jeopardized, in Dr Avery Jones's view, by 'restrictive trade union policy'.[61]

The 'dirty walls' episode, in which the Hospital Management Committees were powerless to introduce changes, may be seen as typical of the problems which afflict bureaucracies. In its small way, it was indicative of the decline in the voluntary spirit in the NHS. Nurses, trade unionists, and MPs leapt into the fray to defend their sectional interests. Florence Nightingale was invoked by all sides. Monica Baly, the nurse and historian, pointed out that Miss Nightingale had said that 'wet dirt is dangerous' and argued that nurses had better things to do than wash walls.[62] Another writer had no doubt at all as to what Miss Nightingale would have said. She would have ordered the first available person, whether a student nurse or a skilled painter, to get on with it, 'and there would have been no nonsense about stopping half-way up'.[63] Wishing to avoid the controversy, the Fund concentrated on practical investigations. In its view, the cure for dirty walls lay in the modification of vacuum cleaners.[64]

Looked at from the patient's point of view, the issue of 'dirty walls' was disheartening, a sign that in the NHS overregulation impeded necessary procedures and that staffing-arrangements could take precedence over the interests of the sick. Dirty walls were not unique to NHS institutions, but the contrast with routine procedure in the former voluntary hospitals was not lost on some of the contributors to the controversy. As they recalled, not without a trace of nostalgic distortion, voluntary hospital staff had had a greater sense of vocation, a disposition to pitch in and to carry on beyond the call of duty. The first principle of the voluntary system was simply that 'the welfare of the patient took precedence over everything else and, however great the burden on its staff, the hospital must carry out its work'.[65] But in the 1960s, the voluntary spirit and goodwill which had helped to sustain the NHS was running out.

The decline in the NHS's idealism, which Crossman and others deplored, has been explained in various ways. Some have found fault with conservative consultants who would not change with the times; others have pointed to the scale of the NHS bureaucracy and the lack of hospital independence. Some have blamed trade-union agitation; others political interference. Richard Crossman censured overpowerful doctors and the Regional Hospital Boards, which he called 'a set of self perpetuating oligarchies or satrapies'.[66] Arguably, as Ives of the King's Fund believed, the loss of idealism was a natural result of the shift to a quantitative conception of health brought into being by state intervention and Treasury control. Whatever its causes, the Fund's officials watched the changes with some regret and took what measures they could to compensate for them in their practical work and the promotion of hospital voluntary services.

At a time when so much attention was being given to building and to expansion in the NHS, the Fund decided to reconsider the status of its Division of Hospital Facilities. A working party, chaired by Francis Avery Jones, lobbied in 1961 for the expansion of the Division into a 'Hospital Centre', on the grounds that there was a shortage of reliable information and advice available to the NHS.[67] It argued that a place was needed where volunteers and paid employees could meet to discuss their problems and to prepare for the future. The Regional Boards expressed an interest in such a project, as long as they did not have to pay for it. Sir George Godber, the visionary Chief Medical Officer at the Ministry of Health, was more enthusiastic (he was appointed to the Fund's General Council in 1961).[68] The London independent hospitals were less keen, because they felt that it would simply expand the Fund's national dimension at their expense.[69]

The Management Committee met to discuss the proposal to set up a Hospital Centre in November 1961. Francis Avery Jones and Lord Cottesloe spoke persuasively on its behalf. Avery Jones considered the information service, including a library, to be the essential element in the scheme. Only Lord Ashburton, the Treasurer, had reservations. He did not object to the project in general terms, but worried that the costs and the tying-up of capital in a long-term commitment might reduce the money available for grants.[70] A subcommittee, led by Dr Avery Jones and Philip Constable, was set up to oversee the project (it became the Hospital Centre Committee in 1963). It saw the proposed Centre as having three main functions: the provision of information concerning hospital organization and practice; the conduct of experiments and inquiries; and a forum for the interchange of experience and new ideas. Anticipating just how widely the Centre would be used posed planning problems, but a suitable new building was found at Nutford Place, Edgware Road, which had the advantage of being central and within easy reach of the Fund's colleges.[71]

After some delay, and cost overruns, Enoch Powell formally opened the new Centre on 21 June 1963. In a speech which endeared him to his hosts, he called the Centre 'a major new extension of the university of the hospital service—which is how I like to think of King Edward's Fund'. The essential quality of a university, he added, was independence, and by virtue of its past and wealth, the Fund had it. 'There is a unique relationship ... between this Fund, this Centre, on the one hand and the Ministry of Health and the Hospital service on the other hand, because in this country the application of the results of this Centre, the application of all that the Fund achieves, rests on responsibilities which have been placed upon the Ministry of Health.' He concluded, recalling Voltaire's view of God: 'If the King's Fund had not existed it would have been necessary to invent it.'[72]

Among the articles on the opening of the Centre, one in the *Manchester Guardian* was particularly revealing, if only for its assumptions. Taking up Powell's point about charitable independence, it noted that the King's Fund and other philanthropic societies could initiate experiments beyond the scope of the Minister. And then, in an intriguing sentence: 'What is even more important is that they can write off unprofitable lines of investigation without guilt.'[73] This attitude was widely held. On the one hand, it simply assumed that independent institutions could do what they believed to be right without worrying about their popularity. On the other hand, it suggested that if Exchequer money was wasted the 'State' would somehow be 'guilty', but no one need feel guilty about the waste of charitable legacies or donations, that is 'individual' sources of finance.

Such logic, which was commonly applied in the use of endowment funds by Regional Health Boards, would have appalled Edward VII or Sir Henry Burdett. It might even have raised the eyebrow of a language philosopher, for 'guilt' is a personal noun of doubtful usefulness when applied to the actions of a corporate entity. The assumption that government money must be more carefully husbanded than private money represented a transformation of values typical of collectivist thinking. But this mentality had even taken hold in the voluntary sector. Allied to the NHS, the Fund had little option but to take chances with its capital. But one wonders whether it would have taken financial gambles on experimental projects had it been making public appeals as in the past. In the circumstances, the Fund's willingness to take risks may be seen as a sign of good management; it undoubtedly benefitted the NHS, which required external innovation. In any case, it was made easier by its view of itself as a 'closed fund'. A large endowment not only permitted a degree of risk-taking, but freed the Fund from accountability to living subscribers.

Widely used and respected, the Hospital Centre proved a successful gamble. In 1965, for example, over 13,000 people visited the facilities, many of them from abroad.[74] Conferences took place on the evaluation of new hospital buildings and occupational health; linked to conferences were exhibitions on such subjects as maternity units and hydrotherapy departments. The Catering Advisory Service, which was struggling for an independent status at the Centre in the mid-1960s, presented an exhibition of labour-saving and cost-efficient foods. In the Fund's view, hospital catering was likely to move in the direction 'of a "food factory" ... using automatic continuous cooking apparatus and deep-freezing'.[75] With hindsight, the Fund's support for convenience foods and 'automation' in the health service may be seen as a concession to hospital accountants rather than to patients.

The most notable research-project undertaken at the Hospital Centre in 1965 was to design, under realistic conditions, a hospital bedstead which conformed to a functional specification.[76] The object was to improve the comfort of patients without putting out a nurse's back. A team led by Irfon Roberts, Assistant Director at the Centre, supported by the School of Industrial Design at the Royal College of Art, came up with a successful prototype after field trials at Chase Farm Hospital. Armed with a specification based on extensive tests, manufacturers were able to produce beds which met rational standards. 'King's Fund Beds', as they came to be called, were soon in evidence in hospital wards across the country. So much so that many patients thought the Fund was essentially a manufacturer of beds.[77]

Among the myriad research projects suggested to the Centre in the 1960s was one on hospital charitable work. First mooted by Francis Avery Jones, the idea was given impetus by a conference on 'The Use of Volunteers' at the Centre in 1966. The Minister of Health, Kenneth Robinson, noted the attention given to the conference; and in a speech to the National Association of Leagues of Hospital Friends, he gave his encouragement to any schemes which improved the co-ordination of voluntary services.[78] After informal discussions with other charities, the Fund decided to undertake a study into the use of paid organizers of volunteers, who were just beginning to appear in NHS hospitals. In 1967, it appointed a social worker, Jan Terdre (Mrs Jan Rocha), to carry out the survey and to write a report.

Organisers of Voluntary Services in Hospitals appeared in 1968. It brought together information on the activities of volunteers and made abundantly clear just how important they were to the hospital service. In each of the London hospitals surveyed, volunteers contributed up to fourteen thousand hours' work a year; at psychiatric hospitals the figure rose to forty thousand hours a year, or the equivalent of over twenty additional full-time paid workers. Given the growing tendency of society to put volunteers, like patients, in tidy categories, the report was at pains to point out that hospital voluntary work was not monopolized by any one section of the community, but appealed to a wide range of men, women, and children of varying backgrounds and social expectations. There were so many of them and their tasks varied so considerably that 'it was difficult to see how a hospital could absorb so much help without a paid employee to coordinate and deploy it'.[79]

The trade unions, however, were suspicious of paid organizers, who they felt would open up spheres of employment to volunteers at the expense of their members. The King's Fund received a letter from the National and Local Government Officers Association (NALGO), which was anxious about the impact of Rocha's research itself.[80] When pressed, trade unionists accepted that volunteers provided a valuable service, but they did not warm to the prospect of hordes of them being recruited by paid organizers for the price of an annual sherry-party. Demarcation disputes were inevitable. At one hospital, the staff threatened a walk-out when a volunteer took a patient in a wheelchair to the X-ray department.[81] Hospital administrators were caught in the middle. Many of them agreed with the unions in principle, but they were forced into pragmatic solutions because of underfunding. As Rocha noted, 'without volunteers to fill the gaps many things would simply not be done, or not be done as efficiently'.[82]

The King's Fund Bed and the report on voluntary services were but two examples of the way in which the Hospital Centre contributed, directly and indirectly, to improvements in patient care. The Fund's enthusiasm for innovation bordered on obsession. As Miles Hardie put it, 'the Fund, and the Centre, can never stand still. As new ideas we pioneered become established practice (or fail), so we have to move on to pastures new. If we are to be of value to the health service and maintain our reputation, we have got to keep constantly on the move and to keep at least one step ahead of everyone else.'[83] Keeping 'one step ahead of everyone else' proved expensive, however, especially as the Ministry and the Regional Boards often acted as though the Fund had a bottomless purse. In the 1960s they refused to pay for mounting their own exhibitions at the Centre, saying they had no funds available to meet the cost of such exhibitions.[84] By 1970, the Centre was taking up about 22 per cent of the Fund's total expenditure.[85]

Expansion and innovation at the Centre resulted in a continual reassessment of its facilities and finances. From the late 1960s there were attempts to find it new premises and to get the government to contribute to its costs. By 1970, it was felt that the original aims of the Centre had been achieved and that it could no longer be considered experimental. As the Fund did not wish to tie up its resources in permanent enterprises, the question of the Centre's future arose. Discussions with the Department of Health and Social Security and health service authorities confirmed the view that its work was valued and should continue.[86] By 1970, the DHSS had more money available for research and in that year it gave the Centre £25,000 as a contribution toward its running-costs.[87] Ten years later, the DHSS and the Thames Regional Health Authorities were covering nearly half of the Centre's annual expenditure.[88]

Government financial aid to the Fund brings to mind the remark of Roger Peers, 'no one is rude to his rich uncle'. It raised the issue of the Centre's independence, and its claim to be a neutral forum for the discussion of hospital affairs. Following negotiations in 1972, it was decided that up to one half of the membership of the Centre's Management Committee should be nominated by the DHSS. (The Fund retained the power of appointment.) It was a sign of just how intimate the relationship between the Fund and the NHS had become that no one on the Fund's Management Committee objected to this concession. On the contrary, the committee members welcomed contributions from the DHSS to the Centre as a way of releasing money for innovation.

For its part, the DHSS had no objection to the Centre's being renamed the King's Fund Centre in 1972 and agreed to the appointment of Sir Francis Avery Jones as the Chairman of its Management Committee.[89] Despite its dependence on government finance, the Centre remained an integral part of the Fund, which retained executive responsibility for its operations. Like the Emergency Bed Service, it was an example of the integration of statutory and charitable services taking shape at the time, an admission by government that voluntary bodies were cost-effective and that pluralism in the health field was worth fostering.

In August 1976, the King's Fund Centre moved to purpose-built offices in Albert Street, Camden Town, which were officially opened in October by HRH Princess Alexandra.[90] The Chairman of its Committee was by this time Professor Ian McColl, and its Director W. G. Cannon. In keeping with the Centre's role as a forum for ideas, the new premises included a library with an expanded information-service. Conferences in 1976 included several on long-term care and mental handicap, issues which were coming into greater prominence in the Fund. The building itself was ingeniously designed to facilitate the Centre's increasingly functional purposes. Its utilitarian ambience was in contrast with the offices in Palace Court, which are redolent of a gentleman's club.

In the 1960s, the Administrative Staff College in Palace Court, renamed the King's Fund College of Hospital Management in 1968, constantly re-appraised its work in the light of NHS requirements. Like the Hospital Centre, it gradually took on a national role, opening up wider contacts with other institutions and universities at home and abroad. In 1960, acting upon a request from the Ministry of Health, it organized training-courses for work-study officers, and hired Pat Torrie from ICI to lead the project. (Torrie would replace Frank Reeves as Director of the College in 1977.) The Lycett Green Report (1963) into hospital recruitment and training stimulated the development of fresh courses in the principles of management.[91]

With a small permanent staff, the College invited visiting lecturers of widely differing interests and persuasions, but it concentrated increasingly on multidisciplinary courses for senior managers. Prompted by George Godber, Reeves initiated the first course for doctors in 1964.[92] This was a notable departure, for it brought together consultants and senior administrators in a neutral setting. One wonders whether it served one of the purposes of the College, as Mickelwright saw it, which was to turn managers into gentlemen, so that they could meet consultants on equal terms.[93] In the 1960s, some people found the College rather too gentlemanly. In the 1970s, others thought it not gentlemanly enough; one member of the General Council complained that it had been infiltrated by 'extreme left-wing' lecturers. The Fund's management took the view that the senior officers in the Health Service who attended lectures at the College were mature enough to form their own judgements.[94]

In the late 1960s, the Fund began to press the DHSS to pay fees for routine College courses. The first payments arrived in 1970, and ten years later they provided about 30 per cent of the College's costs.[95] Selling services to government was becoming more common in the voluntary sector—the King's Fund Centre was a further example—and it had the advantage of releasing charitable income for experimentation elsewhere. Although government support was a matter of survival to some societies, this was not true of the Fund, and it was not unduly worried about the potential dangers in relying upon state assistance. Still, other established charities, from the Royal National Lifeboat Institution to the National Federation of Women's Institutes, could testify that government funding was not always a blessing.[96] Moreover, the move from providing services to selling them brought charities into the market-place, which had implications for their status and character.

Changes in the NHS triggered the College's absorption of its sister colleges in 1968. The Fund justified the running-down of the College for Hospital Caterers on the grounds that it had done an effective job of training catering managers in the regions.[97] The running-down of the nursing colleges was in keeping with the recommendations of the Salmon Report on Senior Nursing Staff Structure (1966), which proposed a new administrative framework for nurses in line with their greater role in management. The Fund was in general agreement with the findings of the Salmon Report, for which it had submitted evidence, and accepted that the training of nurses needed to be more closely integrated with the training of administrators.[98] Consequently the College of Hospital Management provided places for nurses on its courses for senior and middle management. None the less, many of the Fund's officers, and many nurses, regretted the demise of the College for Matrons and the College for Ward Sisters, which between them had provided nearly 200 courses and trained 3,000 nurses.[99]

The Nursing Recruitment Service was also allowed to run down. An approach was made to the Ministry to see if it would pay for the service in the same way that it paid for the Emergency Bed Service, but the suggestion was rejected. The Secretary of the NRS, Miss L. N. Darnell, asked the Fund to consider setting up a Careers Advisory Centre, which would inform members of the public on the whole range of careers in the NHS; but this too was rejected on the grounds of cost and the lack of interest from the Metropolitan Regional Hospital Boards.[100] Supporters of the NRS rallied on its behalf, but its expense and the view that it did not fit in with the Fund's general policy of fostering experimentation were reasons for the decision to close it down. As Peers wrote to the Matron of St James' Hospital, 'the King's Fund, by its nature, has to keep changing and to my Management Committee's regret this time has come as regards the N. R. S.'.[101]

The Fund's 'Permanent Policy of Change',[102] by which it meant organizational flexibility, precipitated so much chopping and changing of activities that it created anxieties for management and staff alike. In the past, employees had been more inclined to accept that their own interests were secondary to the institution's charitable objects. But recruitment from the public sector and the linking of pay and pensions to NHS scales encouraged a less altruistic ethos. The acceptance of fees and contributions for services from the DHSS carried the process further. As the voluntary spirit had drained away in the NHS, it was also declining in the Fund, as one member of the staff admitted.[103]

The Fund was fortunate in having such a tactful Secretary in Geoffrey Phalp, who skilfully handled the effects of the numerous reorganizations and reshuffles. As far as possible, he and his colleagues geared them to the retirement dates of affected employees, or upgraded pensions to ease people into early retirement, or shifted individuals to jobs elsewhere in the institution. The latter course of action was not invariably wise, for people could find themselves in posts for which they were not well-qualified or in which they were frustrated.[104]

The decision to run down the Catering Advisory Service turned partly on George Stormont's wish to retire early and partly on the view that its work was becoming repetitious.[105] The service, like the College for Hospital Caterers, finally closed in 1973. Its various innovations, surveys and publications, with one or two exceptions, had been very useful to the NHS. Despite improvements in kitchen facilities and the appointment of qualified catering managers within the Regional Health Authorities, the Fund might have been expected to have made a stronger case to continue its role in hospital catering. Underpaid and unregarded, catering staff remained highly subject to changing fashions and NHS economies. One wonders what Sir Francis Avery Jones, who was so closely associated with the Fund's catering services, makes of the arrangements in hospital kitchens today?

The longest-surviving branch of the Fund was the Emergency Bed Service, which had been largely financed by the four Metropolitan Regional Hospital Boards since 1949. By the mid-1970s, it had organized over one and a half million admissions to London hospitals and dealt with about 10 per cent of all emergency cases.[106] George Godber, who became Chairman of the EBS Committee in 1972, called it 'a barometer of the health of London'.[107] With a staff of forty, it operated round the clock, every day of the year. Though its functions had broadened to include monitoring epidemics and assessing the availability of specialist services in the capital, its first priority was to speed up the admission to hospital of acute cases at the request of GPs. Despite the system of referees, the definition of acute could be imprecise, and EBS staff were frequently caught in cross-fire between GPs and hospitals, who disagreed about individual patients. Sometimes complications arose because hospital receptionists were unavailable or fast asleep; on one occasion the police had to be sent around to bang on a hospital door and tell them to answer the phone.[108]

In the mid-1970s, the Fund's relations with the Health Service over the Emergency Bed Service deteriorated. At the time of NHS reorganization, a decline in the number of cases created anxieties among the EBS staff about their jobs. The setting-up of a COHSE Branch in the EBS in 1976 and infiltration by the Socialist Workers' Party added to the uncertainties in the office.[109] After much deliberation, The Fund decided to disengage itself. Geoffrey Phalp wrote a dry letter to the South East Thames Regional Health Authority in 1977: 'the increasing need to take account of current health service practice in the management of the EBS presents difficulties in respect of which the agency role of the Fund, and its status otherwise as a charity, can no longer provide an effective means of solution'.[110] Jack Langworthy, a former Director of the EBS, put the reason for the break more directly: The King's Fund 'would never wear' trade union interference.[111] The Fund thus passed on the entire responsibility of managing the EBS to the South East Thames Regional Health Authority in 1978, thus ending an association which had lasted for forty years.

The Fund's views on NHS reorganization, which were influenced by the disruption to the Emergency Bed Service, are worth recording. As early as 1968, it published *Working Together: A study of coordination and cooperation between general practitioner, public health and hospital services*. The report appeared just before the Ministry's Green Paper on the administrative structure of the NHS, which proposed that the regions should be abolished and replaced by a single-tier structure. Francis Avery Jones and his colleagues who produced *Working Together* accepted that the existing organization of the NHS had grave disadvantages and that there was an 'urgent need for both cooperation and coordination between the various departments'.[112] But they did not recommend sweeping reforms. Rather, they stressed that much had already been done to co-ordinate the health services and provided examples of useful local schemes that could be developed without administrative change on a national level, which was 'bound to be a lengthy and possibly a painful process'.[113]

The Fund's annual report in 1968 stated that whatever the outcome of the promised government Green and White Papers, 'the first object of any administrative structure of medical and related services must be the attainment of integrated planning and execution of the whole range of those services'.[114] The question was whether a new administrative structure would make co-operation and co-ordination any easier. 'Would it improve the service to the patient'?[115] The Fund shared the planning-mentality of the day; its colleges were technocratic and managerial in outlook. But with its long-standing reservations about the limits of collective action and the dangers of bureaucratic, centralized control, it did not assume that *dirigiste* legislation would make things better.

Having published *Working Together*, the Fund awaited government proposals on integration and made internal adjustments to meet anticipated changes. The College of Hospital Management, for its part, offered courses on management within an integrated service. The Fund declined to comment formally on the Green Papers of 1968 and 1970 or the consequent White Paper of 1972, which set out the Conservative government's thinking on the reforms necessary to unify the health services. Despite differences of detail, notably over public participation, the Labour and Conservative parties both favoured a unified and centralized service. The Conservative plan, which was embodied in the 1973 Act, was unashamedly hierarchical and managerial. Public involvement was restricted to community health councils, which had a purely consultative role. As Keith Joseph remarked, the key to reform of the health service lay in 'effective management'.[116] 'Patients', as the team who prepared the plan let slip, 'are not part of the organisation.'[117]

As both the Conservative and Labour parties agreed about the need to create a unified service, the Fund had no difficulty in remaining politically neutral. In any case, there was little point in rejecting or endorsing government proposals whose outcome it had little power to influence. As Leslie Paine recalls, the Fund was very quiet about the proposals to reorganize the NHS in the early 1970s, preferring to concentrate on its own demanding domestic alterations.[118] Although the Fund was happy to assist the DHSS in meeting the 'great challenge' of reorganization, these alterations, as Lord Hayter admitted, were causing it 'no lack of problems'.[119] By July 1973, a few days after the National Health Service Reorganization Act received the Royal Assent, Hayter was also anxious on behalf of senior hospital staff, whose future was unclear, and hospital voluntarists, who looked likely to be pushed out from Management Committees and other activities.[120]

The 1974 reorganization of the NHS has been widely discussed elsewhere.[121] Its object was to create a comprehensive, integrated service suited to the nation's future health-requirements. Its supporters saw it as a means of delivering more effective and equitable health-care to a larger population, thereby fulfilling the goals articulated by Aneurin Bevan in the 1940s. Enoch Powell, who opposed the Act, saw it as 'the formal perfecting of the state monolith', whose hidden cause was the collapse of local government finance.[122] The planning-mentality that informed the 1973 Act was in many respects in tune with the 1946 Act, not least in its assumption that tradition and past practice were an embarrassment, something to be eradicated. Its harmful effects on hospital voluntarists were wholly out of keeping with the views submitted to the committee of inquiry into charitable provision, chaired by Lord Wolfenden, by the Home Office Voluntary Services Unit. Just as volunteers were finding life more difficult in the NHS, they were being praised for their humane services and being asked for greater participation elsewhere in government.[123]

The unification of the hospital, general practitioner, and local-authority health services into a single structure under the 1973 Act was designed to promote operational effectiveness by eliminating anomalies. In place of the former tripartite organization, which had failed to eliminate ineqalities in the system, 'a national pyramid of heroic proportions' was constructed. District management teams formed the base and over them Area Health Authorities. The Secretary of State was the point of the pyramid.[124] The Hospital Management Committees and the Boards of Governors of the teaching hospitals, with the exception of the postgraduates, were abolished. 'Accountability upwards' was accepted wisdom, and the DHSS took charge of planning and the allocation of resources.[125]

Reorganization did not live up to expectations. Its proponents had rather taken it for granted that the Welfare State would rise indefinitely, when in fact it had already reached its high-water mark. They could not foresee that national and international economic problems in the mid-1970s would lead to hospital economies, which would delay restructuring and contribute to staff indiscipline. Nor did they fully appreciate that a 'managerial' solution to problems in the NHS presupposed that a large cast of capable managers was waiting in the wings, eager to carry through reform on such a scale.

Many people had falsely assumed that 'unification' would result in a 'simplified' organizational framework. But critics, of varying political persuasions, pointed the finger at a labyrinthine, overcentralized bureaucracy, which failed to deliver better patient-services or effective management. As some of them ruefully noted, it did deliver more managers.[126] (Staff costs rose to 70 per cent of total NHS expenditure by 1980, up from 60 per cent in 1950.)[127] One health-service analyst argued that 'after all the restructuring of 1974, we are left with a national health service which, although dauntingly complex, still seems unable to cope with some of its basic problems'.[128] Less generous was the socialist GP David Widgery, who railed against further central control: 'The platitudes of American management theory, plastered over the informal and rather lethargic amateurism of British hospital administration, have produced the worst of both, a still inefficient but now faceless bureaucracy.'[129]

From a different perspective, Leslie Paine, who served on the Fund's Management Committee in the 1980s, argued 'that reorganisation in practice, as opposed to reorganisation in theory, seems to me to be a prime example of a bad example of a good idea. Its aims are admirable; its attempt to implement them regrettable. Administratively speaking, we have produced an intricately woven magic carpet that just won't fly.' In his opinion, those who designed the new administrative structure had forgotten the first principle of medical provision: 'patients come to health services to be treated and not administered'.[130] Taking up Paine's argument, Sir Francis Avery Jones believed that reorganization had 'weighted the scales against' patients. The combination of 'top-heavy administrative structure' and 'political dogma' had 'wrecked the communication between doctors and administrators' and put the NHS 'off course'.[131]

The Fund's management accepted the diagnosis of Sir Francis Avery Jones.[132] It believed the effects of reorganization to be profoundly disruptive, especially to the London teaching hospitals. The teaching hospitals had managed to retain their endowments, but they resented the loss of their independent status and complained of their remoteness from decision-making. (Opting-out in the 1990s may be seen as their revenge.) In all hospitals, senior administrative staff, medical, nursing, and lay, were compelled to seek fresh employment with the new authorities. Morale in the service plummeted. Many able people took early retirement. Channels of communication, information, and reassurance closed. The Fund itself lost many former allies, which made collaboration with individual hospitals more difficult. Another disturbing feature to the Fund was the disruption of work by 'industrial action'. Its particular anxieties about labour relations should be seen in the light of its own troubles in the Emergency Bed Service.[133]

Invited by the Royal Commission on the Health Service to submit evidence in 1976, the Fund's management appointed a subcommittee made up of Sir Francis Avery Jones, Sir George Godber, and Professor Ian McColl. Assisted by Phalp, they prepared a preliminary submission, which was followed by a more detailed report. Though it did not dwell on the past, the report was a confirmation that many of the worst fears of the Fund's officials in the 1940s about the administration of a health service run by the State had been realized.

The report pointed in particular to the administrative complexities, arbitrary funding, industrial action, and 'infusion of party political dogma' that bedevilled the hospitals. And it argued that the efforts needed to operate such a complex service might 'negate the original objective, which was integration'.[134] In keeping with its traditions, the Fund favoured procedures that maximized the freedom of the operational areas of the service. Morale was a central issue, and it emphasized that the DHSS had the responsibility for improving it in the hospital service. In particular, there was an urgent need to adopt a fresh approach to problems concerning the training of senior management. Finally, the Fund stressed that unpaid workers had made a 'great contribution' to the satisfactory operation of the NHS and recommended ways in which voluntary work might develop.[135]

The proponents of reorganization believed that profligate hospitals could be disciplined and inequalities between regions reduced by investing greater financial control in the Secretary of State. But rationalizing resources and getting value for money proved more difficult than the planners anticipated. Planning itself was not sophisticated enough to cope with the specific problems of administrative costs and financial management.[136] Furthermore, the 1974 oil crisis turned the Treasury's mind to retrenchment. When the government imposed cash limits on spending departments to combat inflation in 1976, a cry went up from the hospitals, which were still reeling from the effects of reorganization. 'Money' was now the principal worry, intoned the Fund's annual report for 1976, 'sharing resources fairly and according to real need has become the contested issue'.[137]

The proposals of the Resource Allocation Working Party (RAWP) heightened the anxieties in the Fund, and in the London hospitals, about reorganization. The working party was set up by the DHSS in 1975 to resolve the problem which had exercised generations of hospital administrators: how to reduce inequalities in the distribution of health provision. It delivered an interim report in 1975, which contained a population-based formula for redistributing both capital and revenue resources. The 'medium of control' was money, whose allocation turned on a scrutiny of budgets and expenditure.[138] On the face of it, a plan to produce an effective and equitable pattern of care across the country looked rational and sensible, especially in the provinces. But alarm bells sounded in London. The capital was not only well-endowed with hospitals and doctors, but its population was in decline numerically. It was soon obvious that the RAWP proposals did not mean that provision outside the capital was to be brought up to London standards.

The hospitals of London and their allies would have complained less had the government been in an expansionary mood. But in a recession the RAWP formula led to 'nothing short of panic in the four Thames regions'.[139] The question arose whether the working party's measurements were applicable to London, which had a high level of social deprivation and which attracted many patients from outside the capital. Sir Francis Avery Jones was among those who attacked the boffins in the DHSS: 'If London is to be carved up without an anaesthetic', he said in the *British Medical Journal*, 'the least the DHSS can do is to use a sharp knife and not the horribly blunt instrument devised by RAWP. Their use of mortality to measure morbidity, their failure to tackle social deprivation, and varying market costs will ensure the maximum pain and minimum justice.'[140]

The RAWP targets adopted by the NHS proved difficult to implement because of the level of cuts required within regions. But the London hospitals lost money to areas outside the capital and felt unjustly punished. There was especial concern for the prestige of the teaching hospitals, which trained so many overseas postgraduates. The RAWP report, *Sharing Resources for Health in England* (1976), which was imbued with a materialistic conception of health imposed by Treasury constraints, confirmed the limitations of a state service. It assumed 'that the resources available to the NHS are bound to fall short of requirements', and it concluded that there was 'no escaping the fact that one centre's "excellence" may be bought at the expense of another's "deprivation"'.[141] Sir Francis Avery Jones took this to be 'a miserable philosophy for the leading medical country in the world'.[142] His own hospital, St Mark's, had to close beds. In reaction to the cuts, it hired publicity agents and turned increasingly to charitable societies for support.[143] It was a pattern repeated in other hospitals across the capital.

The Fund trod uneasily through the NHS minefield in the late 1970s, offering support to the hospitals and advice to the government where it thought this appropriate. In general, its views reflected what it saw as the special problems of London provision. 'Strong representations' were made about the 'enormous strains' that RAWP had imposed on many hospitals in the capital. An internal report on future policy, undertaken by Sir Francis Avery Jones in 1979, argued that 'the extraordinary run down of primary care in the inner city zone at the same time as the weakening of the hospital support for acute work has been essentially due to these inner city zones being scheduled as losing areas under RAWP'.[144] Sir Francis recommended that the Fund should give Inner London priority in the light of the effects of RAWP, and that the Management Committee should consider a project to assist hospitals in raising local appeals. London's problems, he concluded, increased the scope for the Fund's usefulness.[145]

The effects of the 1974 reorganization on voluntary societies have yet to be explored. Lord Hayter said to the General Council in 1975 that reorganization had hit voluntary workers, and he included himself among them, especially hard.[146] Undoubtedly, he had the Fund in mind. As he was acutely aware, the changes and anticipated changes in the NHS from the late 1960s onwards had resulted in a constant and costly reshaping of its activities and facilities. On the most mundane level, there were few years in the 1960s and 1970s in which the Fund's officials were not scouring London to find new premises. One could argue that government enthusiasm for the reform of health provision reshaped the Fund more effectively than it did the NHS.

Roger Peers once compared the Fund to a fruit-tree, whose various branches drew their sap from the same parent trunk.[147] In a single decade most of the branches were pollarded. In 1967, the Fund had nine departments on six sites. By 1978, it had three departments on two sites: the headquarters and the Management College in Palace Court and the Centre in Albert Street.

In the late 1970s, one of the Fund's chief objects was to enlarge the scope of voluntary action in and around the hospitals. Lord Hayter and his colleagues embraced the idea of the Community Health Councils, those local consumer organizations which had been set up by the 1973 Act to oversee changes in health provision. In Hayter's mind they were 'substitutes for the individual layman's voluntary help in the context of the old set-up on the Management Committees' and represented the 'last remaining link between the volunteer and the reorganised health service'.[148] But as the NHS had little inclination to act on the views of its users, the Community Health Councils became, in the contemporary phrase, 'toothless watchdogs'. To bolster the Councils, the Fund provided facilities for an information service on their activities and assisted in setting up a national association. But as Hayter confessed, few people had heard of the Councils, and among those who had some thought they were responsible for street-cleaning.[149]

Despite the unhappy effects of reorganization on voluntarists, the future of medical charity was not in danger. In London, one could argue, reorganization and the effects of RAWP pointed to the need for greater charitable effort, not less, if only to make deteriorating state hospitals more acceptable to patients. Moreover, the integration of services brought about by reorganization had broadened the role of hospitals. It removed many volunteers from NHS management, but it also encouraged doctors and administrators to take a greater interest in preventive medicine and the facilities provided outside hospitals by local charities and educational centres. From the mid-1970s, the Fund made more money available to these agencies. Special attention was given to small groups which dealt with particular disabilities, such as the British Epilepsy Association, Combat Huntington's Chorea, and the Spinal Injuries Association.[150]

Although it set aside about 20 per cent of its grant-income to provide hospital buildings, equipment, and furnishings, the Fund preferred to make awards to NHS hospitals for the development of projects and ideas. But given the effects of reorganization and budget controls, the Fund could no longer indulge the view that the NHS would pay for maintenance costs or essential capital building. In 1977, to mark the Queen's Silver Jubilee, it decided to make special grants available for substantial capital projects. It set aside an initial sum of £1,000,000 to modernize wards in older general hospitals and consulted its adviser in hospital architecture, S. E. T. Cusden.[151] Such a small amount of money was unlikely to make a great impact, and some now doubt whether the Jubilee grants made the best use of the Fund's limited resources. But the project improved morale in the hospitals that were assisted and made a point which is now widely accepted: that well-built Victorian buildings could be brought up to acceptable standards at relatively low cost. The first Jubilee ward opened at Hackney Hospital. At the Hospital's request, it was named after Sir Francis Avery Jones.

In the late 1970s, the Fund thus returned to a role which it had expected to relinquish after 1948. Its 'Permanent Policy of Change' had brought it full circle. The point was not lost on the institution, for in its annual report of 1977, it quoted from its 1935 report, which described the purpose of grants in terms which echoed the current difficulties: 'the hospitals, with few exceptions, have by great efforts succeeded in raising sufficient funds to maintain their beds. But they have not been able to do as much as usual to bring their buildings and equipment up to date, and numerous urgent schemes of extension and improvement have had to be deferred'.[152] In 1979, the Fund's annual report quoted, with more than a hint of irony, the letter written by the Prince of Wales in 1897, which launched the society: 'The finances of hospitals in London have long been a source of anxiety and solicitude.'[153]

Civil servants ignored or manipulated charitable loyalties to the Health Service as it suited them. Still, the hospitals relied increasingly on charitable support, which successive governments, by oversight and design, had alienated through *dirigiste* policies. The irony for the central planners was that the more they extended central government control, the more the hospitals needed voluntarists to give them a human touch and a local identity. The more the planners pointed to the material limitations of state provision, as in the RAWP report, the more the hospitals needed assistance from those with a less utilitarian view of responsibility. Ives had said in the 1950s that the government must devise financial arrangements to provide a sound basic hospital service, while enabling voluntarists to extend its humanity. Only a philanthropist offers a helping hand to be bitten.

Unlike many of the hospitals it served, the Fund was secure as an institution, and it offered its hand with little expectation of gratitude or reward. It did not have to answer to government, to patients, or to subscribers. Constitutionally, it answered directly only to its Royal President or Governors. To some in the hospital world it was thus a bastion of privilege; to others, with hands outstretched, it was a 'marvellous anachronism'.[154] Whatever outsiders thought of the Fund, it remained committed to the hospitals and their patients. Its persistence in supporting an often exasperating NHS was the measure of its conscience. It could, after all, have pulled back from the Health Service in favour of a quiet life assisting independent hospitals, homes, and charities. Its old ally the Metropolitan Hospital Sunday Fund had largely taken this route after 1948.[155] By the end of the 1970s, there were one or two officers in the King's Fund who wished to do likewise.

The dilemma for the Fund was that it had chosen to enmesh itself in an elaborate hospital system whose bureaucracy it deplored but whose inadequacies and straitened finances invited more and more charitable involvement. It shared the ideals of the Health Service but felt out of sympathy with its undemocratic structure and many of its administrative policies and practices. There was, however, little the Fund could do about it all, despite contacts with the highest levels in the DHSS. In the face of successive governments determined to tighten their control over the Health Service, it did what good it could, in Geoffrey Phalp's phrase, by stealth. But while it prided itself on its resilience and pragmatism, it was not invariably defensive or reactive. On occasion, the charitable mouse could wag the lion's tail, or, as in Aesop's fable, gnaw through the net that bound the beast.

The Fund put the best possible face on its activities and incessant alterations, whether driven by government policy, medical advance, or cuts in hospital budgets. But in the 1970s, it was often reminded of just how volatile and intransigent a partner the State could be. Its object of 'maximising good and minimising mischief'[156] in the NHS was undergoing its severest test since the early 1950s. In July 1979, with the London hospitals in turmoil and a bitterly contested general election just concluded, Lord Hayter recalled the lines of Alexander Pope, which he proposed as a motto for the Fund:

> For forms of government let fools contest,
> Whate'er is best administered is best:
> For modes of faith let graceless zealots fight;
> His can't be wrong whose life is in the right.
> In faith and hope the world will disagree,
> But all mankind's concern is charity.[157]

9

The 1980s: Charitable Revival?

THE strategic planning in state welfare-provision which characterized the 1960s and early 1970s ended in doubts, reassessment, and recrimination. Though the planning-mentality had deep roots, social engineering was out of fashion by 1980. Following Mrs Thatcher's victory in 1979, central government became an increasingly reluctant patron of the Welfare State, and the emphasis in health and social services shifted to the pursuit of efficiency, private-sector expansion, and pluralism. Politics, it is said, is the organization of hatreds; and the 1980s witnessed a new-model Conservative Party taking its revenge on the public sector, which it equated with bureaucratic waste and national decline. The result for state health, education, and welfare was controversy and turmoil. For the NHS, there were portents of a possible change of direction, although there was no serious prospect of health provision ceasing to be primarily a government reponsibility.[1]

The drift of opinion away from statutory provision in the 1980s widened the public's awareness of philanthropic influences and stimulated voluntary campaigns. But the resurgence of charity was not invariably welcomed. On the Left, some commentators feared that it foreshadowed a return to the 1930s and the dismantling of the NHS. They tended to ignore just how much charity itself had changed since the war. Aneurin Bevan, who associated philanthropy with paternalism and social snobbery, would have found the voluntary sector much altered forty years on. Arguably, it had adjusted rather better to the post-war social economy than his own NHS. If charities were less snobbish and socially divisive than many had been in the 1930s, it was in part because of the rise of the Welfare State, which engendered egalitarian social aspirations. They were less amateurish in part because of their links with departments of state. Few, if any, of them could be found in the 1980s which were nostalgic about the 1930s. What they would have liked was a little less paternalism from politicians and civil servants.

With collectivism in retreat, voluntarism began to be taken much more seriously by politicians in the 1980s. Indeed, some Conservatives were more sanguine about what charity could achieve than charities were themselves. Innovation and cost-effectiveness were thought to be among the principal virtues of voluntarism, and these became increasingly apparent against the background of government economies and the spiralling costs of state provision. But while charities welcomed the publicity, they had to cope with greater pressure on their services. That distinctively 1980s word 'privatization' left them feeling decidedly nervous.[2] Just what privatization meant for welfare provision was unclear, but it suggested a primary role for voluntarism that it had largely abdicated. After decades of state supremacy in welfare, it was doubtful whether there was a cultural basis for a dramatic expansion of charity, or that charity was a suitable way of providing basic services according to need.

Whatever the outcome for philanthropists, the expectations of collectivists had not materialized. The vast expansion of state power in the social and economic spheres did not make voluntary institutions obsolete, as some socialists had predicted. On the contrary, the trends of greater government power and expanding democratic rights in the twentieth century had been accompanied by a proliferation of voluntary bodies 'unprecedented in British history'. The upshot, as a leading scholar has remarked, 'was that both government and individuals were in many ways more impotent than they had been under the traditional, restricted, imperfectly democratic system that had prevailed earlier in the century'.[3] Voluntarists, especially those in the hospital field, had done their best to limit the expansion of state power in the first half of the century. Once these attempts had largely failed, the virtues of democratic pluralism inherent in voluntary action became more apparent. In the second half of the century, campaigning charities turned their attention to government pretensions, deceits, and limitations.

Voluntarists had long recognized their own limitations. Various, divided, and parochial, they were ill-suited to move heaven and earth, certainly less suited than the State. But any residual belief that centralized state welfare might bring forth the millennium collapsed in the 1970s, if not earlier. Like philanthropy, government had made a massive contribution to reducing human misery, but it had failed to live up to expectations. This was partly because the public had ever greater expectations of personal and social life, which no government, however benevolent, could satisfy. Since the war, the public appears to have wanted both higher levels of welfare expenditure and lower levels of officialdom. Against the background of dependency and a desire for independence, the philanthropic pulse beats persistently, if erratically. In the 1980s, thousands of new charities were registered each year by the Charity Commissioners.[4] Many of them would amaze past philanthropists.

What would Lord Shaftesbury make of voluntary societies in aid of gay rights? What would Edward VII make of charities which received government money to assist nationalized hospitals?

As such rhetorical questions suggest, there has been a transformation in philanthropic attitudes since the nineteenth century. The change is perhaps most remarkable in regard to perceptions of the role of the State. Though they remain chary of state power, most voluntarists now look to government for greater expenditure on health and welfare and for leadership in tackling the causes of social deprivation.[5] The government, aware that voluntary bodies are an effective way of delivering a range of health and social services, increasingly contributes to charitable campaigns. Britain has reached a stage in the evolution of social policy in which the voluntary sector wants the State to do more and the State wants the voluntary sector to do more. There are signs that the long-standing ideological battle between voluntarists and collectivists, which many assumed to have been won by the latter, now appears to be heading for the ropes, with the combatants holding each other up.

The degree to which charities have become dependent on the State and enveloped in politics is a feature of British voluntarism that would alarm Victorian philanthropists. In the twentieth century, a central problem for charities has been to adapt to the complex and compromising world of state social provision without distorting their objectives and losing their way. Distinctions between public and voluntary assistance have become blurred as government regulation and funding have turned charities into beneficiaries of tax concessions and competitors for state money. In 1984, when annual philanthropic revenues had risen to an estimated £10,000 million, government funding had risen to about £1,000 million or 10 per cent of this figure.[6] In the 1980s, government became the largest single contributor to charitable causes in Britain. It is questionable whether those charities whose funds come largely from government can be described as 'partners' of the State. With few claims to autonomy, they are perhaps more appropriately called the government's agents or clients, their very survival subject to the vicissitudes of politics.[7]

The other side of the coin is the growing dependence of the Welfare State on charity. The Health Service in the 1980s is a signal, albeit ambiguous, example. Though income-generation and private-sector expansion were in vogue, voluntary support was rising sharply in the NHS. Some saw the trend as a return to the voluntary hospital ethos, where local fund-raising paid for services. As we have seen, there was nothing new in state hospitals appealing to charity. They reaped considerable advantages from doing so from the 1950s on. But as the health correspondent Nicholas Timmins argued in the *Independent* in 1987, charity was now 'moving to the very core of NHS activity'.[8] In terms of the overall needs of the NHS, the sums involved seemed like 'peanuts' to some, but as the manager of St Bartholomew's put it, 'at the moment peanuts are bloody useful'.[9]

The trust-fund assets of the NHS are the first charitable recourse for hard-pressed hospital managers. Valued at £609,000,000 in 1987–8, they provide an annual income of about £130,000,000.[10] Though small in relation to NHS expenditure as a whole, and sometimes put to doubtful uses by health authorities, much of this money continues to find its way into research and patient-welfare. (It is useful to recall that about 75 per cent of NHS expenditure is accounted for by salaries, so relatively small sums can be useful at the margins if spent on non-salary items.) Non-NHS health charities, many of which support research, have an annual income of something over £200,000,000.[11] The expenditure of the Association of Medical Research Charities reached the same level as the government-funded Medical Research Council in 1984.[12] In regard to cancer, the Imperial Cancer Research Fund and the Cancer Research Campaign between them contributed 79 per cent of all money spent on cancer research in Britain in 1985, up from 62 per cent in 1972.[13]

When we consider the further savings to the public purse represented by the innumerable medical charities dedicated to the care of virtually every disability from spina bifida to senile dementia, the degree to which the Health Service depends on voluntarism becomes more apparent. We must also include the six and a half million hours of voluntary service now provided each year by 1,300 Leagues of Friends, which represents thousands of extra full-time workers in the NHS.[14] And if we also consider the labours of millions of 'informal carers', who look after disabled relatives at home, the contribution of individuals to the nation's collective health-provision is clearly phenomenal. A recent report from the Family Policy Studies Centre estimated that informal carers saved the Exchequer up to £24,000 million a year, which is nearly the annual budget of the NHS.[15]

The division of responsibility between public and voluntary bodies has always been less distinct than is widely supposed, and not least in health provision. In the nineteenth century, distinctions centred on the 'deserving' and the 'undeserving' poor, or 'chronic' and 'acute' patients. In the twentieth century, these categories broke down, to be replaced by others in keeping with social and political change. In the hospitals since 1948, charitable money has been used largely for patient welfare, staff welfare, and research. The distinction between 'amenities' and 'essential' services, or between seed money and long-term support, provided the guide-line between charitable and government responsibilities. But the growing expectations of medical care and the deficiencies of state provision have made this division, in turn, increasingly artificial and misleading. The government has come to admit publicly that the resources available to the NHS are bound to be insufficient. As a mother whose son was undergoing treatment at the Royal Manchester Children's Hospital remarked, 'I thought charity paid for the frills. Here it pays for the basics.'[16]

While the boundaries between the voluntary and the statutory in the NHS were never altogether clear, the 1980 Health Services Act threatened to obliterate them. Before 1980, the health authorities had the power to accept and to administer trust funds, but they did not have the power to engage in fund-raising. In pursuit of the government's policy to encourage further charitable contributions to the NHS, Section 5 of the Act permitted health authorities to organize their own campaigns. Furthermore, it offered them interest-free Exchequer loans to pay for the costs of appeals. At a stroke, it gave what amounted to charitable status to statutory bodies and turned NHS administrators into fund-raisers.[17]

If this action had been taken by the government in 1948, many voluntarists, including those of the King's Fund, would have rejoiced. But in the 1980s, it stunned the charitable establishment. Those myriad societies which had struggled to find a place alongside the NHS as money-raisers for hospitals and related causes were now in direct competition with 'the largest, most heavily financed enterprise in the whole field of social welfare', whose fund-raising drives were to be financed by the Treasury.[18] By the end of the 1980s, Exchequer expenditure on fund-raising rivalled the money spent on appeals by leading independent charities. The Chairperson of the National Council for Voluntary Organisations, Sara Morrison, wanted to know what was to stop the government from giving the same advantages to education authorities and social services departments. She and the then Director of the NCVO, Nicholas Hinton, declared that the Act represented 'the most damaging blow suffered by the voluntary sector for many years'.[19]

But something more was at stake than statutory bodies competing with traditional charities for funds. Government had created many charitable agents through financial assistance, but now it threatened to distort the meaning of charity itself. 'The essence of voluntary action', as one authority puts it, 'is . . . independence and autonomy and its fundamental antithesis is statutory action.'[20] What then would be the result of statutory bodies being granted charitable status? Under Keith Joseph, the Conservatives had further centralized and bureaucratized the NHS. Did they now intend to do the same to the charitable sector by monopolizing it with statutory bodies transformed into quasi-voluntary institutions?

It would appear that the government, in an attempt to find additional funds to bail out a debilitated hospital service, did not consider the danger of undermining the traditional meaning of voluntarism as activity free from state control. If so, this was an inconsistency in the Conservative Party, which in the 1980s talked so much about Victorian values. In the ambiguous welfare-world of the 1980s, it became necessary to use the word 'independent' before the name of a non-governmental charity, for it was no longer obvious that a charitable institution was not a government body. Even the Medical Research Council, set up and funded by government, had charitable status.

Clearly, the Conservative governments in the 1980s were willing to undermine the assumption that the NHS was paid for entirely out of taxation and National Health Insurance payments. The long-term effects of highlighting the limitations of Treasury funding of the NHS are uncertain. Enoch Powell once famously remarked that 'the universal Exchequer financing of the [health] service endows everyone providing as well as using it with a vested interest in denigrating it, so that it presents what must be the unique spectacle of an undertaking that is run down by everyone engaged in it'.[21] The relative popularity of the NHS compared with other welfare services suggests the limitations of Powell's analysis. Still, state health-provision which is seen to be increasingly dependent on personal service and charitable gifts may generate stronger local loyalty (and even pride) than a monolithic, underfunded NHS. Sir Henry Burdett, it may be recalled, argued that people would always identify more closely with hospitals which they supported as individuals rather than with those which were paid for through taxation. But does a 'state' health service have much meaning when it cannot satisfy its basic aims without recourse to personal contributions?

The movement of health authorities into public appeals has contributed greatly to the growing muddle over the appropriate use of 'charitable' funds. Most of the money raised thus far by internal NHS appeals, which exceeds £100,000,000 a year, has been used to top up statutory funding rather than for charitable 'amenities' outside the statutory obligations of the NHS.[22] Without a clear separation between charitable and statutory obligations, as a writer in the *Lancet* recently argued, the more successful appeals may simply result in the government's reducing Treasury provision.[23] However worthy the cause, the public may question the desirability of their contributions being used to pay for NHS capital projects when 'independent' voluntary bodies, including hospitals, also have their hands outstretched. And it may question giving hard-earned cash to a service which is widely perceived to be badly managed by the government.

The issue of the appropriate use of charitable funds was brought up in the late 1980s by the Wishing Well Appeal, which raised £54,000,000 for the Great Ormond Street Children's Hospital. Although a separate charity was set up to work with the health authority, the proceeds of the appeal were to pay for rebuilding the hospital, not for additional services for patients. A deal had been struck between the Special Health Authority and government that a massive capital project could go ahead, so long as the hospital could raise much of the money from non-Exchequer sources.

Other institutions, from the Edinburgh Children's Hospital to London's Royal Marsden, have launched similar campaigns.[24] In a fresh departure, the local Health Authority in Worthing, West Sussex, has asked residents to pay for operations in order to cut waiting-lists.[25] The Director of the Directory of Social Change is among those who believe that such appeals are a 'singularly inappropriate' way of paying for hospital running-costs and that they will only exaggerate imbalances in provision. Obviously some communities are much more likely to raise money and some services are much more popular. But the Department of Health, anxious to control public expenditure, approves of any scheme which enables people to support their local hospital. The Shadow Health Secretary, Robin Cook, derided the experiment in Worthing as a sign of a 'flag day NHS'.[26]

In a welfare world seemingly turning itself upside down, traditional hospital charities, particularly those active in fund-raising, would have to adjust. The Secretary and Chief Executive Officer of the King's Fund, Robert J. Maxwell, who was appointed in 1980, is acutely aware of the financial woes of the NHS and the blurring of voluntary and statutory boundaries. He sees no 'quick fix' to the intractable problems of the NHS, but in regard to clarifying the relationship between medical charity and the State, he thinks two changes would be beneficial straight away. First, the NHS should admit its dependence on voluntary public service and philanthropy, and not see public donations simply as an easy way to top up Treasury funding. Secondly, in order to become more effective, charities themselves must put their own houses in order through better financial management and more selective intervention.[27]

Maxwell takes the view, reminiscent of that of his predecessor Ives, that given tax yields and Treasury commitments elsewhere, the British government will never be able to pay for the range of medical services increasingly desired by the public. Some things will thus be paid for by charges or by charity or not be done at all. It is possible, as Maxwell speculates, that the future boundaries of the State, the private sector, and voluntary action in health may be reminiscent of Victorian Britain. The State may increasingly concentrate its resources on the 'sick poor', once a preserve of philanthropy, while voluntarists, who now rarely think in terms of the 'sick poor', range across the spectrum of medical provision, addressing those problems which reflect their individual concerns. Alternatively the State could concentrate on essential, core services for everyone, topped up by the market for those who want (and can afford) more, with the voluntary sector seeking to offset the failings of both sectors. Either way, charity has a role but one that cannot sensibly be determined in isolation: how can it best intervene in the evolution of health provision, which is dominated by public services on the one hand and the market on the other?[28]

In the 1980s, the King's Fund itself adopted the line that its own grants and services would turn, not on the arbitrary division between 'amenities' and 'essentials', as in the 1950s, but on whether the NHS would pay for the project itself. But the problems of size and scale continued to bedevil planning in the Fund, and they pointed to the need to get the greatest leverage for the money spent. A comparison of the organization's expenditure for 1897 and 1985 illustrates just how dramatically things have changed for the Fund and for London's health provision generally in the twentieth century. With an expenditure of £3,200,000 in 1985, with £69,000,000 invested, the Fund's grants had risen by a factor of 145 and its capital by about four hundred times since 1897. But the expenditure of the London health districts and associated services had risen to £2,300 million or by three thousand times over the same period.[29]

The value of the Fund's investments, overseen by Robin Dent and his colleagues on the Finance Committee, rose impressively in the 1980s. With net assets of about £110,000,000 in 1989, up from £30,000,000 at the end of 1979, the Fund remained one of the leading charitable trusts in Britain.[30] In recent years it has dropped down the league table of trusts in terms of monies distributed, but its expenditure on grants and services came to £3,605,000 in 1989.[31] Given the pressure on its resources, some in the Fund have sought to raise new income from wealthy individual donors, but they have not had great success.[32] In 1988, the King's Fund Centre received a grant of £1,250,000 from the Sainsbury Family Charitable Trusts for the development of nursing, and similar grants from other trusts followed, demonstrating that the Fund continued to be held in regard by other charities.[33]

Still, further money-raising initiatives will be required if the level of the Fund's grants and services are to be maintained in the expanding voluntary sector. With so many other charities, including NHS hospitals, making their own appeals, there is some doubt whether the Fund's purposes can capture the public imagination. But in the present climate, charities inactive in money-raising may be said to have run out of ideas. As the Fund is not short of ideas, the issue of appealing to the public will not go away. It will probably be easier to do this for causes to which the Fund is committed—for example grappling with homelessness—than for the Fund itself.

Government departments have been an important source of financial assistance to the Fund since the early 1970s, and the payments continued throughout the 1980s. In 1989, contributions from the Department of Health and fees for conferences and courses brought in £2,800,000.[34] At the King's Fund Centre, contributions from the Department of Health alone provided over 35 per cent of overall expenditure. But it would be misleading to see the Fund, as some associated with its College of Management do, as simply an adjunct of the NHS. Its support for other voluntary causes and its substantial endowment provide some guarantee of independence. The phrase 'fragile partnership' continued to describe the Fund's relations with the NHS in the 1980s. Disputes were inevitable because the Fund's first loyalties (some on the staff might disagree) were not to the NHS but to the hospitals and their patients. Highly sensitive to interference in its operations, the Fund would probably withdraw services rather than be bullied into taking a particular line from the Department of Health.

The Fund's sensitivity about its independence increased in the 1980s, and it may be seen as a reflection of the wider anxiety in the charitable sector at a time of expanding government penetration of voluntary causes.[35] An illustration in the booklet *The King's Fund Yesterday, Today and Tomorrow* (1987), showed an NHS, here represented by a stupefied elephant, with its foot towering above the King's Fund mouse. The caption read 'How can I help you Mr Elephant? And look out where you put that great foot!'[36] In the adjoining text, Robert Maxwell pointed out that the Fund now paid for only about 60 per cent of the cost of its services, the balance coming from outside sources. 'The question must be asked', he added, 'how far should we continue to extend our activity while trying to retain a truly independent financial base.'[37]

But was there much point in retaining 'a truly independent financial base' if it meant that the institution was too small to be significant? A problem for the Fund was that without windfall profits from investments or successful public appeals, expansion would result in greater dependence on external sources, including government finance. Independence, as Maxwell put it, was there to be used. 'The only justification for [the Fund's] independence and for its privilege and relative wealth, is if its independence is used in areas that are difficult and controversial.'[38] In health provision in the 1980s, the principal area of controversy was government policy. Criticizing government policy would point out the Fund's independence, but it might alienate the very department of state which made the charity's expansion possible. An elephant may step on a mouse by oversight or by design.

Issues of size and influence preoccupied the Fund in part because of its commitment to staff, which numbered about 160 in 1990. Government support in the 1970s and 1980s had encouraged expansion; its withdrawal would bring contraction. In the shifting political terrain, it was not clear whether the drift away from statutory health-provision would result in an increase or a decrease in government grants and fees being paid to the Fund. In the circumstances, the Fund took what precautions it could. Most of the College faculty, for example, worked on short-term contracts, usually for three years. Consequently, many of them used the Fund as a stepping-stone to further their careers elsewhere. Those who wished to stay had to be adaptable. In the uncertain climate, institutional flexibility remained at a premium. In the late 1980s, there was a deliberate decision to move away from a salary base that was almost solely related to the NHS, to the creation of the Fund's own salary scale, which recognized market conditions.

The 1980s saw various changes to the Fund's honorary management. The retirement of Sir Francis Avery Jones at the end of 1979 was the most significant loss. Lord Hayter paid tribute to Sir Francis by quoting Pope's line, 'Who shall decide when doctors disagree?' The answer, Hayter pronounced, was Sir Francis! He added that 'if anyone came to write the history of the Fund over the last hundred years, he was certain that a lot of space would be devoted to the enormous contribution which Sir Francis had made in so many different ways. That was not to imply that he had been there for 100 years but that his contribution would be so marked.'[39] Not the least of his contributions had been his assiduous recruitment of capable men and women to serve on the institution's committees. Dr Anthony Dawson recalls being invited to sherry by Sir Francis one day and being invited to join the Fund the next.

Another loss was Lord Cottesloe, whose prominence in the arts world rather obscured his contributions to London's hospitals and charities. A long-standing member of the Fund's Management Committee (1957–73), he served as a Governor between 1973 and 1983. Lord Hayter, who replaced Cottesloe as a Governor, retired as Chairman at the end of 1982, having provided the Fund with firm leadership for eighteen years. The new Chairman was the Honourable Hugh Astor, JP. Astor had been Deputy Chairman of the Middlesex Hospital and was a well-known figure in the voluntary sector, having served on the councils or governing bodies of various charities. In 1989, he, in turn, retired. His successor was Marius Gray, a senior partner in a firm of accountants, who had served for ten years on the Fund's Management Committee. As a Governor and Treasurer of a medical school and a member of three Health Authorities, he has wide experience of NHS administration.[40]

The most important addition to the Fund's management was the appointment by the Queen of HRH Prince Charles as President. He took up his duties in January 1986, thus ending a fifteen-year period in which Governors, led by HRH Princess Alexandra, presided over the Fund's affairs. Princess Alexandra had maintained the royal connection with her own distinctive style. She had, as she put it, 'kept the seat warm' for the Prince of Wales, and was persuaded to remain as an honorary member of General Council to mark her continuing interest and the Fund's affectionate respect. Prince Charles was the fourth Prince of Wales to hold the presidency since the Fund's foundation but the first one for fifty years. Despite substantial philanthropic commitments elsewhere, he has shown himself to be a willing contributor to the Fund's activities; and through royal persuasiveness and gentle provocation, he has nudged the institution into areas, such as alternative medicine and hospital design, which are in keeping with his wider interests. The Prince fits well into the Fund's view of itself as an institution unafraid of controversy, spicing its traditions with radical initiatives.

The Secretary of the Fund, Robert Maxwell, has largely set the tone of the institution in the 1980s. An Oxford graduate with a First in English, winner of the Newdigate Prize for Poetry, his reflective temper has shown itself in recent policy reviews. A former consultant with McKinsey and Co., and latterly Administrator to the Special Trustees of St Thomas' Hospital, he has long experience in a variety of countries in health-services policy and management, subjects on which he has written extensively. Among his special interests are medical ethics and the assessment of quality in health care, which are in keeping with his intellectual leanings. As a manager, he has a way with committees and encourages staff initiative. He tells the story of himself that when he was on National Service, his commanding officer said of him that the troops would follow him 'if only out of curiosity'.

Among the other senior members of staff who joined the Fund in the 1980s are Iden Wickings, formerly an administrator in the Brent Health District, who became Deputy Secretary in 1986. He was already Director of CASPE (Clinical Accountability, Service Planning and Evaluation), which is based at the Fund, though paid for by the Department of Health and contracts with individual Health Authorities. Frank Jackson, Director of Finance, joined the Fund in 1987 from the North West Thames Regional Health Authority, where he was Director of Finance and Computing. He was also a former member of the Resource Allocation Working Party (RAWP). Barbara Stocking succeeded W. G. Cannon as head of the Centre in 1987 and adopted the title Director of Health Services Development. She came to the post from the King's Fund College, where she had been in charge of the Corporate Management Programme. At the College, Gordon Best became Director in 1986 after the untimely death of Tom Evans. With experience in health-service planning and management consultancy in Britain and abroad, he, like many others at the Fund, had closer links with the NHS than with the voluntary sector.

Partnership with the NHS encouraged diversity as well as resilience, and the 1980s saw the Fund developing a host of new ideas, while expanding its activities at the Centre and the College. A prominent theme was health care in inner London, which, in the Fund's view, the government was not adequately addressing. Among the most significant of the Fund's initiatives was the London Programme, which emerged from the recommendations of Sir

Francis Avery Jones at the end of the 1970s. A London Project Executive Committee was set up to steer the London Programme. Chaired by Professor Brian Abel-Smith and latterly Peter Westland, its aim was to encourage and to disseminate good practice in inner-city areas, with special reference to the disadvantaged. Several priorities were selected, including community hospitals and the improvement of the relationship between primary care and hospital services. In 1980, the London Programme allocated its first grants, worth £300,000.[41] Eventually the project developed into a national initiative in primary health care.

The London Project's distribution of money was only a portion of the total sum allocated to grant-making by the Fund. The overall object of distributing money would have been recognizable to Edward VII, though the language used to express it had moved on. 'Our main concerns remain the promotion of standards, the better management of health services and the delivery of health care in and for Greater London.'[42] In the late 1980s, there were six grant-making committees operating in parallel, which supported a vast array of projects, from fire precautions and cancer support centres to art in hospitals and this history of the King's Fund. One wonders whether Edward VII would see the latter as frittering away the Fund's resources on transitory objects.

The Management Committee, which itself provided grants, continued to determine the amounts to be distributed by the other committees. The best-endowed was the Grants Committee, which absorbed the work of the former Auxiliary Hospitals Committee in 1985. Applicants were sometimes confused by the intricacies of the Fund's administration, but most of them were aware of what it was unlikely to support: medical research, medical equipment, and contributions to running-costs. By the end of the 1980s, the Fund's various committees distributed a total of more than £2,000,000 a year in grants. While much of this money went to voluntary bodies, pressure was growing to give more of it to NHS hospitals in London because of the crisis in their finances. In 1985, the Grants Committee initiated a programme of major grants, with a ceiling of £250,000, for schemes designed to improve the quality of health care in the capital.

The 1980s saw a flowering of fresh initiatives in the Fund, many of them dealing with the disadvantaged or standards of care. In line with other charities, the accent in the Fund was on 'maximum autonomy for the patient, the family and the community'.[43] In addition to the London Project, an informal caring-support unit and a 'task force' on health and ethnic minorities was set up. More recently, homelessness has come to the fore, a trend encouraged by Prince Charles's interest in the issue. On standards, the publication of the *Report of a Confidential Enquiry into Perioperative Deaths*, jointly supported by the Fund and the Nuffield Provincial Hospitals Trust, monitored the quality of care provided by surgeons and anaesthetists in three pilot regions. The findings were surprising, and in some areas alarming. There were instances of surgeons performing operations for which they were not trained, and only 54 per cent of surgeons and 40 per cent of anaesthetists reviewed the results of their operations on a regular basis.[44]

The range of the Fund's interests and activities in the 1980s found expression in the many books and pamphlets produced by its publishing department, run by the urbane Victor Morrison. Publishing had enhanced the Fund's reputation since its foundation, but now most of the manuscripts came from outside the institution. Several stood out: *The Nation's Health: A Strategy for the 1990s* (1988), edited by Alwyn Smith and Bobbie Jacobson, studied patterns of disease and health-related behaviour. Brian Brooke's *The Troubled Gut* (1986) stylishly investigated the causes and consequences of diarrhoea (1986). *DRGs and Health Care: The Management of Case Mix* (2nd edition 1989) was put together by the productive CASPE Research Unit. It reviewed the applications of diagnosis-related groups (DRGs) and examined their potential in hospital budgeting and clinical performance. Numerous works on hospital management also appeared, some of them marred by an unhappy mix of graphics and sociological jargon. One that was not was Christopher Day's *From Figures to Facts* (1985), which showed the value of statistical information as a management tool. There was even a historical series, which included Lindsay Granshaw's splendid *St Mark's Hospital, London* (1985).

Such diversity and innovation, which the Fund's publishing and project work reflected, had disadvantages. The sheer variety of interests could be bewildering to outsiders, who were left with little impression of the Fund's corporate purpose. Its rather fragmented identity, as suggested earlier, had its roots in the institution's administrative reorganization of 1948, which gave greater autonomy to the respective branches. Many of the Fund's friends and allies only know the organization through one of its branches or projects, which operate from the separate sites in Camden Town and Palace Court. Bringing all the Fund's activities together on a single site has been much discussed, but it is not clear whether doing so would relieve or exacerbate the latent rivalries which can be aroused whenever there is pressure on resources. The forging of closer links between the Fund's disparate parts is now a priority.

The expansion of the King's Fund College in the 1980s threatened to unbalance the Fund's internal affairs. Though the demands of the NHS played a part in the College's rapid growth, it had more to do with the appointment of Tom Evans as Director in 1981.[45] Of Welsh mining-stock, he was a former student, and Chairman of the Labour Society, at the LSE. He came to the Fund from the London Business School, where he lectured on public-sector management. He convinced the Fund's Education and Management Committees of the virtue of radical developments, on the understanding that any expansion would be self-financing.[46] Given the Fund's anxieties about its finances at the time, it was no small achievement that he was able to increase the number of Fellows from three to nearly thirty in four years.[47]

Under Evans's persuasive leadership, there was also a notable transformation in the teaching methods and general approach to management in the College. Field work and consultancy grew in importance, and a 'manager-centred' philosophy emerged, which eschewed the College's traditional approach in favour of the 'personal development' of managers. 'The task of managers in the modern age', wrote Evans, 'is not one that can easily be reduced to identifiable bases of knowledge and technique.'[48] Not without a hint of 1960s radicalism, 'action learning' replaced 'structured training'.[49] The rapidity with which the College could now present fresh courses was remarkable, though it was made easier by dispensing with formal lectures. Flexibility was deemed essential to keep pace with the ever changing needs of the NHS. Clearly, the volatility of the NHS encouraged innovation, but, as Evans argued, it also suited his ambitions for the College. 'Turbulence in the NHS', as he remarked, should promote the development of management education and secure a more prominent role for the College.[50]

Such views betrayed a residual doubt that training health-service managers was, as yet, a profession. Traditionally, emerging professions have had, or at least have aspired to, a unique body of knowledge to develop and to exploit. The Fund's first Staff College, from its outset, had adopted a formal approach to knowledge and skills in its quest for professional status. But Evans and his colleagues, breaking with this tradition, did not wish to project any 'identifiable' body of knowledge in their teaching of health-service management. With a distinctive approach, the College provided an important management-training function for the NHS. But was perpetual innovation in reaction to NHS changes likely to constitute the foundation on which to build a teaching profession? And what would happen to the College, which identified itself so closely with what Evans called 'environmental turbulence', if NHS managers ever settled into more predictable routines? Given its philosophy, the College was more relevant to hospitals in turmoil than hospitals in tranquillity.

The 1980s were an exhilarating time in the College. But the death of Evans in 1985 from cancer, after a protracted illness, was a blow to morale. Expansion gave way to consolidation. And as financial pressures increased, consolidation gave way to thoughts of retrenchment. The College's strategy had been to increase earnings from the NHS. In this it had been successful, for in the five years 1981–6 the rise in income from course fees rose by 400 per cent. But the Fund's own expenditure on the College rose by 50 per cent in the same period.[51] This worried the Management Committee, which had expected the College 'to pay its own way'.[52] To make ends meet, the College became increasingly attuned to the market-place. One departing Fellow described it as a hybrid body, something between a business school and a consultancy firm, which happened to be housed in a charity. For their part, many NHS managers continue to see the College as their London club.

The King's Fund Centre, whose Committee was chaired by Professor Anthony Clare in the late 1980s, dealt with those who provided care or who were in direct contact with patients. It provided the administrative base for various projects, including those dealing with nursing, community care, and inner London. It also continued to host numerous conferences and seminars, which, combined with its extensive library services, attracted large numbers of visitors, 17,000 in 1985 alone.[53] Like the College, it geared itself to government initiatives, from NHS reorganization in 1982 to Sir Roy Griffiths's report, *Community Care: An Agenda for Action* (1988). And as at the College, the 'management of change' remained the priority, which encouraged a rapid turnover of projects and staff.

The Fund's most significant innovation in the 1980s was the King's Fund Institute. The idea of a think tank on health policy, free from government control, was prompted by an article, 'Does Britain Need an Academy of Medicine?', published in 1982 by Sir George Godber.[54] Impressed by the work of the Institute of Medicine in the United States, Godber argued that Britain should also consider setting up an agency that could take a broader view of health provision than could be provided by individual specialty groupings or the BMA. Though initially sceptical, Robert Maxwell thought that the idea merited further debate. With the approval of the Fund's Management Committee, he arranged an informal discussion-group in July 1983, on the proposal 'An Institute of Health?'. Led by Dr Anthony Dawson, Deputy Chairman of the Fund's Management Committee, twenty-five leading doctors, civil servants, and academics attended the seminar. As Dr Dawson put it, the upshot of the meeting was 'everyone thinks it's a good thing, but nobody knows what "it" is'.[55]

The Fund took the view that if it did not pursue the idea, no one else would; and after further internal discussion it decided to proceed. Of the various models considered, it opted for an institute of health policy analysis, which would face towards government and politicians. One reason for this choice was the belief that health policy had become, in Maxwell's words, 'increasingly partisan, narrow and short-term'.[56] What was needed was reliable data on health, impartial comment on trends in present policies, and cogent analysis of major policy issues.[57]

From the Fund's point of view, the chief argument against the proposal was financial, for the cost of setting up the unit was estimated at £1,250,000 over five years, with adjustments for inflation. Such an outlay of money would result in a financial commitment which might one day rival the expenditure on the Centre and the College. Once the Management Committee agreed to the costs, its object was to find a suitable Director. It appointed Ken Judge, who was Deputy Director of the Personal Social Services Research Unit at the University of Kent and formerly a lecturer in social policy at Bristol University. Under his direction, the King's Fund Institute opened in January 1986 in offices at the Centre in Camden Town. Dr Dawson was appointed to chair its Advisory Committee.

Since its foundation, the Institute's staff has taken on board a variety of tasks, including a submission to Sir Roy Griffiths's review of community care and the publication of numerous briefing papers on specific issues from health at work to medical negligence.[58] 'The cornerstone' of its activity was 'the conviction that health policy analysis, sponsored by a genuinely independent foundation, can make a significant contribution to the climate of informed opinion and that this in turn can help to change the direction of policy.'[59] It is rather too early to tell if the Institute has been or will be successful in changing the direction of policy, but its activities have attracted considerable attention. Indeed, most of the references in the press to the King's Fund in the last few years have been in regard to the Institute's operations. The signs are that the Institute has enhanced the Fund's intellectual respectability. And as it does not receive outside finance, it has helped to counter the notion that the Fund is simply an adjunct of the NHS.

The findings of the Institute added weight to the Fund's growing anxieties about health care in London. Government plans for the London districts during the 1980s were the latest in the long line of initiatives, both by the State and prior to it by the Fund, which sought to redress imbalances in hospital provision. Once again, 'rationalization' was on the agenda. As ever, the hospitals were reluctant to sacrifice themselves for what planners and politicians believed to be the national interest. The relative success of the teaching hospitals in frustrating the planners may be seen as remarkable, for all of those that existed in the late nineteenth century were still in London in the 1980s. Smaller institutions, still unfashionable and without political influence, were more vulnerable. Many were closed in the 1980s, including some long-associated with the Fund, such as the British Hospital for Mothers and Babies and the South London Hospital for Women and Children. In his day as Secretary, Ives considered the latter institution to be the best-managed hospital in London.[60]

The Fund was in the awkward position of having to balance national needs, as perceived by the NHS, against those of the London hospitals, whose services it wished to defend. It did not assume that simply spending more tax revenue on the hospitals was the solution, though it disapproved of government stinginess. In regard to London, with its particular social economy, it believed there was a strong case for providing additional money from the Treasury. But as in the inter-war years, when it was defending the voluntary hospitals, the Fund was willing to consider all the available financial options, including vouchers and charges. Though now better-described as an 'enabling' charity rather than an 'organizing' one, the Fund retained the co-ordination of hospital services as a goal. It still assumed that rationalizing hospital provision was necessary. What worried it was government heavy-handedness.

A report by the Fund for the Chairmen of inner London Health Authorities, *Planned Health Services for Inner London: Back to Back Planning* (1987), showed just how blunt an instrument government planning could be. It pointed out the contradictions between bed closures, increased workloads, and financial savings. But the study's key finding, which did not amuse the DHSS, was that it was impossible to draw a coherent and comprehensive picture of inner London's future health services from the data available.[61] 'National policy for health services in London', intoned the Fund's annual report for 1987, '... has been simplistic and extremely destructive.' To approach reform 'primarily through crude budget reductions over a relatively short timescale, without any positive incentives to change, was to invite disaster'.[62]

Planned Health Services for Inner London suggested that yet another round of 'strategic planning' was being implemented on the basis of incomplete information. The compilation and effective application of statistics has never been a strength of the Health Service. Captain Stone pointed out the deficiencies in hospital accountancy and information in the 1950s. So did the Guillebaud Committee, which censured the NHS for its failure to provide adequate knowledge of its workings. It singled out waiting-lists as 'notoriously unreliable'.[63] Enoch Powell was taken aback when he discovered that some of the statistics which he received as Minister of Health on waiting-lists and beds were, in his words, 'a conglomerated fiction'.[64] As numbers of beds were used as a basis for fixing certain staff pay-grades, any NUPE shop steward could have told him that in the NHS there were occupied beds, available beds, and *beds*.

In 1979, the Royal Commission on the NHS noted: 'the information available to assist decision-makers in the NHS leaves much to be desired. Relevant information may not be available at all, or in the wrong form. Information that is produced is often too late to assist decisions and may be of dubious accuracy.'[65] The limitations of statistical analysis were acute in London because of the variations in planning-data and the different methods used to collect it in the four Thames Regions.[66] Arguably, the marshalling of facts and figures for the London hospitals was less co-ordinated in the 1980s than it was in the 1930s, when the King's Fund produced its annual *Statistical Summary.*

Deficiencies in gathering information can lead to unfortunate social consequences. In anticipation of massive reductions in acute services in London, the DHSS imposed spending-restraints on the Districts in the mid-1980s. This was done just as up-to-date information began to show increased workloads in acute hospital services.[67] A hundred and fifty years after the 'statistical revolution', which gave rise to planning as a discipline, important discrepancies between government intentions and the actual changes taking place on the ground persisted. But the shortcomings of planning in the Health Service, not least its failure to consider social costs in its calculations, will rarely alter policies which are driven by politics. It is often said that planning is simply a mechanism by which the State gives legitimacy to its actions.[68] Reference to statistical 'truth' has the advantage of disguising the political culture behind the planner's art. As an accountant in the Fund puts it, statistics are true in the NHS if nobody complains about them.

According to a recent study, the NHS began in 'hopeful adhocery', but moved towards a planning-model with claims to rationality.[69] Its central dilemma in the early years was planning within the context of the tripartite division of the service. The 1974 reorganization eliminated the tripartite system, but created other problems in its place. In regard to London, the administrator and historian Geoffrey Rivett argues that 'the progressive reorganisations have attempted to mould the London authorities into a pattern which would make major change possible'.[70] But the preoccupation with financial targets, without reference to the radical changes in service utilization, staffing, and provision necessary to achieve them, does not inspire confidence.[71] Who can fault hospitals which resist 'rationalization' when the data used to justify reform cannot be believed and when government does not seem to worry about what happens to their patients? Conflict between the centre and hospitals on the periphery, which has been symptomatic of the NHS since its foundation, looks set to continue.

Many of the persistent maladies of NHS administration can be traced to the zeal to unify and to 'universalize' provision at the gestation of the service. Post-war governments and central planners wished to sweep away ideas and practices that were redolent of that 'low, dishonest decade', the 1930s. To them, voluntary and local-authority traditions were selective and demeaning. Consequently, they had little respect for the individual characteristics and pluralistic practices of the hospitals, which they sought to eliminate in the interests of integration. Integration was to be achieved by requiring institutions to conform to statistical norms and external authority. The King's Fund, it will be remembered, wielded the statistical stick to encourage hospital co-ordination before the war, but it was done with a respect for the peculiar constitutions and varying administrative practices of the institutions it served. Moreover, it argued that a uniform hospital service would create more problems than it resolved, for without variety within the system there would be no index of the relative efficiency of hospitals. Suddenly in the 1980s that was again a legitimate, even fashionable, point of view.

It is widely accepted that Bevan's NHS represented a compromise with vested medical interests and a pre-war hospital system often described, far too facilely, as defective and chaotic.[72] To many, including those responsible for the 'progressive reorganizations', its problems were a consequence of this compromise. It is implied that the problems of the Health Service would have been much reduced had the past been buried altogether. Given his ambition to create a unified service in a socialist society, Bevan himself was not disposed to salvage much from the past. With his faith in the power of the State to bring about social justice, he regarded traditional hospital practices as just so many anachronisms. Not all of them could be overcome at once, but when circumstances permitted, Bevan's successors excised most of the vestiges of independence and the distinctive practices that were associated with the former voluntary hospitals, including their long experience of internal administration, based on a tripartite system of checks and balances.

It is often thought that the planning-failures in the NHS were largely the result of a lack of government finance to eliminate inherited problems,[73] but it may also be argued that reforms were implemented without due regard for the best features of inter-war provision. It is certainly worth asking whether the shortcomings of NHS administration derived, not from too much compromise with past structures and practices, but from too little. Since 1948, the administration of the Health Service has shown itself to be increasingly centralist and paternalist; as Enoch Powell put it, the 1973 Act was an attempt to perfect the 'state monolith'. What is not so well appreciated is how profoundly ahistorical government planning has been. Statistics and coercion, not organic evolution, are the basis and measure of its success. The fact that a hospital has provided a distinctive service to its community for a century or more and is valued by residents will carry little weight with government officials, who are preoccupied increasingly with population shifts, land values, and cost accountancy.

An ahistorical planning-mentality, materialist and managerial in outlook, has become pervasive in British political culture, even in Conservative circles which appear to be hostile to social engineering. The voluntary sector too, despite its respect for inherited tradition, shows signs of losing touch with the past. This is most obvious in those societies which favour managerial solutions. In the King's Fund College, for example, many of the Fellows recruited in recent years describe themselves as planners or strategists and as specialists in management or organizational development. It may not have been a coincidence that the College dropped its lectures on the history of hospital administration, to make way for courses in keeping with the latest perceptions about public-sector management. It is said that Whitehall, despite its dependence on files, no longer has a collective memory, only a procedural memory. But where, without a sense of history, asks Peter Hennessy, an authority on the Civil Service, are we to get a perspective on public life, 'a kind of inoculating jab against what George Orwell called "the smelly little orthodoxies" of political fashion'?[74]

Whatever the explanation for failures in planning, they have led with unsettling regularity to further planning initiatives in the Health Service. Yet a coherent, balanced, and well-managed hospital system, which the NHS was brought into being to create, remained as elusive in the 1980s as in the 1940s or the 1920s.[75] The reorganization of the Health Service in 1982 was an admission that the 1974 reforms had failed to achieve their first purpose, which was effective management. The 1982 reform aimed to achieve value-for-money and higher performance. It eliminated the Area Health Authorities created only eight years before and encouraged further amalgamation and rationalization. But like the reorganization in 1974, it led to disruption, and 'the cost in human terms and hard cash was considerable'.[76] Most people accepted the need for planning in the Health Service, but they assumed that it was a means to an end and not the end itself. One former official of the Fund lamented in 1982 that the continual reorganization of the NHS was 'more than people can stand'.[77]

An awareness of the failings of the NHS grew apace in the 1980s, inside and outside the service. Less swayed by collectivist ideals than in the 1960s and 1970s, historians too are now beginning to have doubts about NHS management and doctrine, and they are turning a more critical eye on the original framework created by Bevan. They hope to discover whether 'the deficiencies of current National Health Service organisation and ideology, its hospital-dominated, undemocratic structure', were an inevitable consequence of the 1946 Act.[78] Put another way, were the continuing imbalances, turmoil, and low morale in the NHS the fault of meddling politicians and misguided planners, or did they result from flaws inherent in the dynamics of a centralized bureaucratic system?[79]

The answer to such questions may lie in the results of the latest Health Service reorganization, outlined in the White Paper, *Working for Patients*, published in 1989. In the Prime Minister's Foreword the White Paper promised, ominously, to be 'the most far-reaching reform of the National Health Service in its forty-year history'.[80] On the face of it, some of its objects were unexceptionable, such as the desire to make NHS management more flexible and less centralized. Its more contentious aspects had to do with the creation of a regulated market within the NHS, general practitioner budgets, and self-governing status for hospitals. (Given its traditions, one might have expected the King's Fund to be particularly enthusiastic about the latter.) 'Depending on one's preconceptions', Robert Maxwell argued, 'these ideas can be presented as an honest attempt to tackle long-standing problems of traditional NHS financing patterns, or as ideologically driven attempts to impose inappropriate market ideas, or as moves preparatory to dismantling the NHS.'[81]

The Fund had submitted papers to the Prime Ministerial Review of the Health Service in 1988. There was one on NHS financing from the Institute, and this concluded that 'partnership schemes between the NHS and the private sector can offer real benefits to both NHS and private patients. But care must be taken to ensure that they do not distort NHS objectives and priorities.'[82] The College submitted another paper, 'Reforming the NHS: Managed Experimentation', which argued that 'the use of incentives, competition and better management has already led to significant progress in improving efficiency, effectiveness and consumer responsiveness within the NHS'. The object was to build on these achievements through 'a managerially-orientated NHS Management Board, Regional agencies, organisation incentives and increased statutory freedoms'.[83] The College's submission was perhaps not entirely disinterested, for the further reform of NHS management would have benefits for a development agency so committed to experimentation.

The Fund's formal response to the 1989 White Paper was muted. This was in keeping with its tradition of adopting a wait-and-see attitude to government proposals. It did not wish to be seen to be allying itself with a particular political point of view. In any case, there was no unanimity of view among the members of the staff and the management. They spanned the political rainbow and saw the NHS from different perspectives. Having said that, the Fund gave a guarded welcome to the White Paper. Immediately after its publication, Maxwell called it a 'curate's egg', which had been published in haste; but he believed it 'a genuine attempt at reform, not destruction of the NHS and deserves to be treated as such. . . . The White Paper offers the opportunity to address problems in some potentially exciting ways. If we really can create within the NHS mechanisms that make the service more responsive, more flexible and more innovative, without sacrificing its fundamental decency and fairness, that will be a tremendous national accomplishment.'[84]

The Fund sought to maintain an open mind about the proposals and criticized the BMA for its head-on confrontation with the government.[85] One of its Fellows said the reforms constituted pebbles dropped in the Health Service pond. The ripples lapped against the Fund at once. The College offered new programmes for consultants and turned to 'comparative management'. At the Centre, clinical audit and quality in contracts moved up the agenda. The Grants Committee took the initiative and allocated £525,000 to projects which would monitor the application of the proposals. The King's Fund Institute published an analysis of the White Paper. It concluded that the proposals could make services more responsive to users but noted that the concentration on management of the acute-hospital sector and primary health care left 'many questions about public health, health services outside hospitals and the care of priority groups unanswered'.[86] It also sounded a note of alarm about the government's 'high-risk strategy', which, in its view, required additional resources and a slower timetable for implementation.

The National Health Service and Community Care Act received the royal assent in June 1990.[87] There was no certainty that the reforms would prove workable or beneficial. Given the history of social legislation in this century, there is every reason to suppose that they will have ambiguous effects. In any case, they would take time to show results. Meanwhile, the condition of the London hospitals, which had been subject to turmoil and financial uncertainty for over a decade, continued to deteriorate. The speed with which the latest reforms were to be carried into effect was a growing cause of concern. So was the incessant political wrangling. In an earlier era, Sir Henry Burdett called politicians 'the curse of the sick'. No one in the Fund speaks with such pungency today; its officials have chosen to work with the NHS, however politicized.

In response to the problems in the capital, the Fund decided to set up a Commission on London's Acute Services (see Plate 13). It appointed Marmaduke Hussey, a member of the Fund's Management Committee and Chairman of the Royal Marsden, as its Chairman, and Virginia Beardshaw, Director of the Fund's London Initiative, as Secretary. The Commission's terms of reference were to gather evidence and to develop a long-term strategy for London's acute services. A striking feature of the initiative was that it revived an investigative tradition in the Fund that dated to the early twentieth century. Tellingly, an inquiry into the state of the metropolitan hospitals would echo questions raised by the House of Lords select committee exactly a century earlier. Whether the present Commission will produce recommendations and results similar to that Victorian select committee remains to be seen; but, once again, it was asking the familiar question: what shape of hospital service does London need?[88]

In 1990, before the recommendations of the Commission were available, the Fund accepted that some 'shock' to the capital's hospital system might be in order. But it argued, with unusual solemnity, that the 'pace' of change across the four Thames Regions now threatened to make the shock 'terminal . . . by default'.[89] Yet again, as the Fund reported, government reforms were 'creating uncertainty and a serious loss of morale'.[90] Yet again, there were signs of the government 'trying to tackle so much in too little time with inadequate preparation'.[91] And yet again, changes were being implemented against a background of cash-shortages. The Fund's Secretary, Robert Maxwell, had long criticized the NHS for inconsistent management and a pervasive lack of communication. Along with persistent Treasury underfunding of pay awards, these characteristics made the Health Service 'virtually ungovernable'. Speaking personally in 1988, he concluded that 'the government seems barely to comprehend what managing the NHS means'.[92]

After forty-odd years under government control, the hospitals of London looked set for another decade of disorder and demoralization. Not since the 1950s had they needed charitable assistance so urgently; not since the 1930s had they received it so gratefully. The achievements of the NHS are undoubted; it continues to command the overwhelming support of the public; still, the voluntary sector's age-old prognosis of the failings of a bureaucratic hospital system enmeshed in party politics has proved broadly accurate. In the King's Fund, the successors of Edward VII and Sir Henry Burdett may be forgiven a twinge of irony as they look back on their past and forward to their centenary.

Notes to Chapter 1

1. The Fund paid Theodore Ramos 250 guineas in 1957 to copy the portrait. It was borrowed from Lady Mountbatten. In order to make it fit the wall in 2 Palace Court, the picture was reduced by omitting a strip on either side and at the top and bottom. See MS letters in KF, file labelled Portrait.

2. Sir James Stephen, *Essays in Ecclesiastical Biography* (2 vols.; London, 1849), i, 382. For an introduction to the history of philanthropy see David Owen, *English Philanthropy, 1660–1960* (London, 1964); Brian Harrison, *Peaceable Kingdom: Stability and Change in Modern Britain* (Oxford, 1982); F. K. Prochaska, *The Voluntary Impulse: Philanthropy in Modern Britain* (London, 1988); id., 'Philanthropy', in F. M. L. Thompson (ed.), *The Cambridge Social History of Britain 1750–1950* (3 vols.; Cambridge, 1990), iii. 357–93.

3. On this issue see F. K. Prochaska, *Women and Philanthropy in Nineteenth-Century England* (Oxford, 1980).

4. *The Times*, 9 Jan. 1885, cited in Owen, *English Philanthropy*, 469; *Hospital*, 5 Jan. 1895, 246.

5. From the chapter 'Podsnappery', quoted in a review by Michael Rose, *Social History of Medicine*, 3, (1), 114.

6. G. M. Young, *Portrait of an Age: Victorian England* (London, 1977), 25.

7. John Stuart Mill, *Principles of Political Economy* (Harmondsworth, 1970), 312–13.

8. See *Burdett's Hospitals and Charities*, an annual publication, which provides a wealth of information on London and provincial hospitals.

9. Harrison, *Peaceable Kingdom*, 240.

10. Brian Abel-Smith, *The Hospitals, 1800–1948* (London, 1964), 39, 44–5.

11. Linda Bryder, *Below the Magic Mountain: A Social History of Tuberculosis in Twentieth-Century Britain* (Oxford, 1988), 22–3, 44.

12. Abel-Smith, *The Hospitals*, 153, 156–7.

13. Ibid. 152–3.

14. Quoted in Lindsay Granshaw, '"Fame and Fortune by Means of Bricks and Mortar": The Medical Profession and Specialist Hospitals in Britain, 1800–1948', in Lindsay Granshaw and Roy Porter (eds.), *The Hospital in History* (London, 1989), 207.

15. Ibid. 214.

16. A. G. L. Ives, *British Hospitals* (London, 1948), 37.

17. E. W. Morris, *A History of the London Hospital* (London, 1910), 215.

18. F. B. Smith, *The People's Health 1830–1910* (London, 1979), 259. For an excellent recent survey of the social history of medicine see Virginia Berridge, 'Health and Medicine', in F. M. L. Thompson (ed.), *The Cambridge Social History of Britain, 1750–1950* (3 vols.; Cambridge, 1990), iii. 171–242.

19. Quoted in Heather Gilbert, 'King Edward's Hospital Fund for London: The First 25 Years', *Social and Economic Administration*, 8 (1) (Oxford, 1974), 52.

20. Frederick F. Cartwright, *A Social History of Medicine* (London, 1977), 164.

21. Quoted in Geoffrey Rivett, *The Development of the London Hospital System, 1823–1982* (London, 1986), 114.
22. Henry C. Burdett, *Hospitals and the State* (London, 1881), 5.
23. Abel-Smith, *The Hospitals*, 161.
24. Census of England and Wales 1901: County of London, Area, Houses and Population (HMSO, 1902), 102, 126.
25. Owen, *English Philanthropy*, 231–3. Somerset Maugham, *Of Human Bondage* (London, 1973), 396.
26. *The Times*, 15 Jan. 1883, 12.
27. Rivett, *The Development of the London Hospital System*, 131, 134–7.
28. *The Times*, 11 Nov. 1897, 6. He had called for a 'controlling authority' for hospitals in *Hospitals and the State*, 11.
29. *Third Report from the Select Committee of the House of Lords on Metropolitan Hospitals*, (HMSO, 1892), cvii.
30. See the articles entitled 'Central Hospital Board' in *Hospital*, 2, 9, 16, 30 May, 1896.
31. Ibid. 30 May 1896, 147.
32. Ibid. 5 Jan. 1895, 245.
33. *The Times*, 25 Dec. 1894, 7.
34. Ibid. 27 Dec. 1894, 8.
35. *Hospital*, 'Special Hospital Sunday Supplement', 15 June 1895, 15. Burdett's attendance-figures may have been overestimated, for hospitals often inflated the number of their patients in order to appear more efficient.
36. H. C. Cameron, *Mr Guy's Hospital* (London, 1954), 257.
37. Hilda Jennings, *The Private Citizen in Public Social Work* (London, 1930), 18.
38. *Hospital*, 5 Jan. 1895, 245; June 15 1895, 16.
39. Ibid. 13 June 1896, 181. On the Sunday Fund see Rivett, *The Development of the London Hospital System*, 121–3; *The Times*, 28 Dec. 1897, 5.
40. Abel-Smith, *The Hospitals*, 250–1.
41. *Rivett, The Development of the London Hospital System*, 122–3.
42. Reginald B. D. Acland, *The Work of the Hospital Saturday Fund: The Annual Address of the Chairman* (London, 1896), 12.
43. *Hospital*, 4 Jan. 1896, 229. Burdett had taken a dim view of the Saturday Fund for years. See *The Times*, 7 Nov. 1883, 12.
44. On Burdett, see Christopher Maggs, *A Century of Change: The Story of the Royal National Pension Fund for Nurses* (London, 1987), 13–22; Rivett, *The Development of the London Hospital System*, 124, 373–4. The obituaries in *Hospital*, May 1920 are invaluable. See also Norman Chaplin, 'Yearbook Centenary', *Health Services Management*, (Apr. 1989), 77–81.
45. Maggs, *A Century of Change*, 16.
46. *Hospital*, 8 May 1920, 130.
47. See Maggs, *A Century of Change*.
48. Henry C. Burdett, *Prince, Princess, and People: An Account of the Public Life and Work of their Royal Highnesses the Prince and Princess of Wales, 1863–1889* (London, 1889), 8.
49. Quoted in David Cannadine, 'The Context, Performance and Meaning of Ritual:

The British Monarchy and the "Invention of Tradition", *c.* 1820–1977', in Eric Hobsbawm and Terence Ranger (eds.), *The Invention of Tradition*, (Cambridge, 1984), 110.

50. Ibid. 119.
51. Ibid.
52. Ibid. 120.
53. Ibid. 122.
54. See, for example, Theo Aronson, *The King in Love* (London, 1988).
55. *Burdett's Hospitals and Charities* for 1902 gives a list of many of these charities under the prefix 'royal'.
56. *Hospital*, 14 May 1910, 193.
57. Prochaska, *The Voluntary Impulse*, 16.
58. Sir Sidney Lee, *King Edward VII: A Biography*, (2 vols.; London, 1925, 1927)), i. 566.
59. Ibid., i. 623–6.
60. *Hospital*, 14 May 1910, 192.
61. Burdett, *Prince, Princess, and People*, 345–6.
62. Georgina Battiscombe, *Queen Alexandra* (London, 1969), 258.
63. *The Times*, 25 Mar. 1887, 14.
64. Knollys to Burdett, 29 July 1914, Gwyer MS. Sir Savile Crossley, an initial Honorary Secretary, always said that Burdett was the 'founder of the Fund'. Fry to Maynard, 15 Jan. 1942, GLRO, A/KE/681/13.
65. Boulton to Crossley, 22 Oct. 1906, GLRO A/KE/573/42. Boulton was angling for a seat on the Fund's Management Committee, but it was not granted.
66. Frank Long, *King Edward's Hospital Fund for London: The Story of its Foundation and Achievements, 1897–1942* (London, 1942), 1. See also KF, *Annual Report for 1987*, across from title-page.
67. The best biography of the Countess of Warwick remains Margaret Blunden, *The Countess of Warwick* (London, 1967). Much of the correspondence of the Countess of Warwick, probably including material on the King's Fund, was destroyed by fire at Easton Lodge in 1918.
68. Frances Warwick to Burdett, 4 Dec. 1895, Gwyer MS.
69. Frances, Countess of Warwick, *Life's Ebb and Flow* (London, 1929), 210, 226.
70. Ibid. 213. Printed in the Countess's autobiography, this letter is dated 6 July 1895, but from internal evidence it is clear that the correct date is 1896.
71. Lee, *King Edward VII*, i. 620. Lee's information on the Fund for his biography of Edward VII came from Burdett.
72. *Hospital*, July 12 1919, 379.
73. *Punch*, 22 May 1897, 241.
74. Ibid. 13 June 1896, 182.
75. Cameron, *Mr Guy's Hospital*, 260–1.
76. Burdett memorandum, dated 1896, Gwyer MS.
77. The *Hospital*, 20 June 1896, 196.
78. Burdett memorandum, Gwyer MS.
79. Making way for the Prince of Wales, Lord Aldenham resigned 'through ill-health'. Indisposed, he did not attend the Festival Dinner. Lushington soon made way for

Cosmo Bonsor, a man admired by Burdett, as Treasurer. GLRO, H9/GY/A1/4/1, Minute Book of General Court, Guy's Hospital, ff. 178, 182–6. The Programme for the Festival Dinner, with seating arrangements, can be found in H9/GY/Y5/1.

80. Cameron, *Mr Guy's Hospital*, 261. Cameron drew his information from Cecil Roberts, *Alfred Fripp* (London, 1932), 77–82, 262. Fripp's role in the Fund was overplayed by Roberts and probably by Fripp himself. According to Frederick Fry, an Honorary Secretary of the Fund, who was around at the time, Fripp and the Guy's Appeal were not significant influences in the Fund's foundation. See GLRO A/KE/681/13, Fry to Maynard, 15 Jan. 1942.

81. GLRO, A/KE/573/42.

82. GLRO, A/KE/2/1/12.

83. Lee, *King Edward VII*, i. 620.

84. The full list of those in attendance at this meeting is given in a letter from Sir Francis Knollys to Sir Arthur Bigge, 22 Jan. 1897, *The Letters of Queen Victoria*, 3rd ser., edn. George Earle Buckle, iii, 1896–1901 (London, 1932), 123–4.

85. *Hospital*, 12 July 1919, 380.

86. See *The Letters of Queen Victoria*, iii. 124, note.

87. Long, *King Edward's Hospital Fund for London*, 4.

88. The Earl of Strafford died in 1898. Among his many hospital connections, he was President of the Tower Hamlets Dispensary.

89. *Hospital*, 30 Jan. 1897, 303.

90. *The Times*, 3 Feb. 1897, 11.

91. GLRO, A/KE/2/1.

92. *The Times*, 6 Feb. 1897, 11.

93. Lister to his niece, 16 Jan. 1897, GLRO, A/KE/681/1.

94. GLRO, A/KE/2/1; 27/1/6–8; 295/3A/B; 681/112; Long, *King Edward's Hospital Fund for London*, 4–5.

95. The letter was drafted by the Bishop of London, see A/KE/27/1/9.

96. A signed copy of this letter is in the GLRO, A/KE/641. It is also printed in KF, *First Annual Report*, 3–4, and in Long, *King Edward's Hospital Fund for London*, 5–7.

Notes to Chapter 2

1. From the *Pall Mall Gazette*, quoted in the *Hospital*, 13 Feb. 1897, 335.

2. Quoted in Frank Long, *King Edward's Hospital Fund for London: The Story of its Foundation and Achievements 1897–1942* (London, 1942), 10.

3. The Cancer Research Fund, founded in 1902, which received Edward VII's patronage in 1904, may have been influenced by the success of the financial policy of the King's Fund, for it too decided to build up a capital reserve. Several of the leading contributors and officers of the Imperial Cancer Research Fund were also attached to the King's Fund. See Joan Austoker, *A History of the Imperial Cancer Research Fund 1902–1986* (Oxford, 1988), 24–7.

4. Knollys to Burdett, 14 Nov. 1897, Burdett Papers, Bodleian Library, Oxford.

5. A. G. L. Ives to W. Hyde, 14 Dec. 1939, KF, Nuffield Provincial Hospitals Trust file.
6. See the extensive correspondence between Burdett and Knollys in the Burdett Papers, Bodleian Library.
7. I am grateful to Lord Somerleyton's family for these and other biographical details.
8. Beginning in 1923, the firm, now Freshfield, Leese and Munns, received payment from the Fund for its services. See GLRO, A/KE/40/1; KF, *Twenty-Sixth Annual Report*, 11.
9. GLRO, A/KE/293/80.
10. Total receipts for the years 1897–1906 were just under £1,700,000. Expenses were £22,783. See KF, *Tenth Annual Report*, 24–5.
11. Ibid.
12. GLRO, A/KE/27/4 f. 42. Miss Millns retired from the fund with 30 years service in 1945.
13. Baroness Burdett-Coutts (ed.), *Woman's Mission*, (London, 1893), 361–6.
14. GLRO, A/KE/572/33; A/KE/573/87b. On Maynard see also José Harris, *William Beveridge: A Biography* (Oxford, 1977).
15. For contributions see the KF annual reports.
16. For a heated exchange over this issue, see the Burdett–Holland correspondence in 1895 in the Burdett Papers, Bodleian Library.
17. Of the 26 medical visitors who worked for the Fund in 1905, for example, only 1 subscribed; of the 26 lay visitors 9 did.
18. The following figures can be found in the KF annual reports. In 1939 the Fund changed the format of its reports and the list of contributions of over £100, compounded from 1897, was discontinued.
19. John Aird, a member of the original Council, was also a Mason. In later years, other leading officials of the Fund who were Masons included the Earl of Donoughmore and Sir Ernest Peacock.
20. Burdett to Knollys, 10 Nov. 1897, Burdett Papers, Bodleian Library.
21. GLRO, A/KE/27/2; A/KE/40/2; A/KE/292/463.
22. Burdett to Knollys, 10 Nov. 1897, Burdett Papers, Bodleian Library.
23. GLRO, A/KE/292/463; A/KE/293/120.
24. Various senior officials of the King's Fund have had City Company connections, including Frederick Fry, an Honorary Secretary (1908–21), who was in the Company of Merchant Taylors; Sir Alan Anderson, an Honorary Secretary (1921–4), who was in the Company of Fishmongers; Sir Ernest Pooley, Chairman of the Management Committee (1948–56), who was in the Company of Drapers; and the Honourable Hugh Astor, Chairman of the Management Committee (1983–8), who is in the Company of Fishmongers.
25. Philip Magnus, *King Edward the Seventh*, (London, 1964), 407.
26. G. R. Searle, *Corruption in British Politics, 1895–1930* (Oxford, 1987), 24.
27. See the excellent entry on Cassel by Pat Thane in the David Jeremy (ed.), *Dictionary of Business Biography*, (5 vols.; London, 1984–6), 1. 604–14.
28. Searle, *Corruption in British Politics*, 245–6. For a critical contemporary assessment of Speyer see A. Moreton Mandeville, *The House of Speyer* (London, 1915).

29. Searle, *Corruption in British Politics*, 24. Burdett's role in Edward VII's invest-ments also deserves attention.
30. Ibid. See also Magnus, *King Edward the Seventh*, 389.
31. A useful guide to these connections can be found in Jeremy (ed.), *Dictionary of Business Biography*, see esp. Thane's entry on Cassel.
32. Philip Ziegler, *The Sixth Great Power: Barings 1762–1929* (London, 1988), 289.
33. Burdett to Sydney Holland, 18 Mar. 1895, Burdett Papers, Bodleian Library.
34. Ziegler, *The Sixth Great Power*, 278.
35. Mrs Bischoffsheim to the Prince of Wales, 22 Nov. 1906, RA GV C273/66.
36. Highly sensitive to the honours system, Burdett had declined a knighthood in 1896 on the grounds that it was not sufficient to extend his usefulness by adding to his authority. See Burdett to Marquis of Salisbury, 29 Dec. 1896, Gwyer MS.
37. Wernher's bequest was one-twelfth of the residue of his estate. For more information on the wealth of several of the Fund's principal benefactors see W. D. Rubinstein, *Men of Property* (London, 1981).
38. For a wider discussion of philanthropic motives see F. K. Prochaska, *The Voluntary Impulse: Philanthropy in Modern Britain* (London, 1988), 46–7.
39. See, for example, GLRO, A/KE/293/122.
40. These tags turn up among Burdett's papers in the Gwyer MSS and in the Samuel Lewis Trust Papers. I am indebted to Dr G. D. Black for information on Samuel Lewis and his wife, Ada.
41. Magnus, *King Edward the Seventh*, 91.
42. George Behlmer, *Child Abuse and Moral Reform in England, 1870–1908* (Stanford, 1982), 144; F. K. Prochaska, *Women and Philanthropy in Nineteenth-Century England* (Oxford, 1980), 27.
43. GLRO, A/KE/2/1; A/KE/293; A/KE/294; A/KE/567.
44. GLRO, A/KE/289/594.
45. GLRO, A/KE/292/366; A/KE/45; *Hospital*, 5 June 1897, 166–7; 17 July 1897, 275; *The Times*, 14 Sept. 1898, 4.
46. *The Times*, 12 Mar. 1898, 10.
47. *Daily News*, 27 Feb. 1899.
48. This figure is from a sampling of subscribers from the KF annual reports.
49. *The Times*, 2 Nov. 1899, 10; 9 Nov. 1899, 4.
50. Edward VII was hostile to female suffrage, see Magnus, *King Edward the Seventh*, 390.
51. British Library, Additional MS 47728, f. 97.
52. Ibid. 47728, f. 103.
53. Nightingale to Sir Harry Verney, 4 Aug. 1887, Claydon MS, Claydon House, Bucks.
54. KF, *First Annual Report*, 14.
55. *Burdett's Hospitals and Charities, 1898*, 1, 873.
56. Magnus, *King Edward the Seventh*, 254.
57. *Burdett's Hospitals and Charities* gives the annual figures for the various hospital funds.
58. See, for example, the *Daily Chronicle*, 2, Mar. 1899; *Nursing Record*, 11 Mar. 1899.

59. *Lancet*, 19 Feb. 1898, 519.
60. *BMJ*, 19 Feb. 1898, 511.
61. *Hospital*, 30 Dec. 1899, 205.
62. Ibid. 13 Feb. 1897, 335.
63. Quoted in *Hospital*, 13 Feb. 1897, 335.
64. Nothing has been written on the League of Mercy. The records of the League were passed to the Public Record Office after it was wound up in 1947 and are now included in the Ministry of Health files, MH/11/1–59. Further material on the institution is contained in the archives of the King's Fund, the Royal Archives, Windsor, and the Burdett Papers in the Bodleian.
65. Charles Loch to Dr Robert Lee, 20 June 1899, GLRO, A/FWA/C/D261/1.
66. GLRO, A/FWA/C/261/1.
67. Ibid., Holland to Loch, 23 Oct. 1898.
68. RA Add. A/4/89; A/4/101.
69. Burdett to King George V, 18 June 1915, RA GV 26296/208.
70. *Hospital*, 19 Mar. 1904, 456. For particulars of Burdett's speeches on behalf of the League in 1902–3 see the Gwyer MS.
71. The status of the Order of Mercy was not clear. In 1933 the Garter King of Arms took the view that it was a decoration and not an order and that the word 'order' was a misnomer. See E. F. Grove to A. F. Flatow, 18 July 1962, RA PP GVI 184.
72. *Hospital*, 9 Oct. 1909, 48.
73. See the Memorandum on Sir William Collins by Burdett in the Gwyer MS.
74. For details of the League's organization see Revd P. H. Ditchfield (ed.), *The Book of the League of Mercy* (London, 1907).
75. *BMJ*, 16 Nov. 1901, 1488.
76. PRO MH/11/53; MH/11/57. The annual contributions of the League to the Fund can be found in the Fund's annual reports.
77. KF, *Fifth Annual Report*, 15.
78. For early investments see GLRO, A/KE/2/1; A/KE/27/1. For details of the Fund's various deposit accounts after 1911, see English Client Account Ledgers, Baring Brothers and Co., Limited.
79. Quoted in Long, *King Edward's Hospital Fund for London*, 22.
80. Magnus, *King Edward the Seventh*, 279.
81. See, for example, GLRO, A/KE/569/7; A/KE/569/9.
82. For details of the Coronation Appeal see the folder in the entrance hall at the KF Centre, which contains numerous press cuttings. See also GLRO, A/KE/299; A/KE//750/1–36.
83. J. Blomfield, *St. George's, 1733–1933* (London, 1933), 90.
84. Knollys to Burdett, 25 Sept. 1902, Gwyer MS.
85. Revd H. G. Warner to Burdett, 31 May 1910, Gwyer MS. See also *Burdett's Hospitals and Charities, 1902*, 61–4.
86. Magnus, *King Edward the Seventh*, 279.
87. On Lord Mount Stephen and the Fund see Heather Gilbert, *The End of the Road: The Life of Lord Mount Stephen*, ii, *1891–1921* (Aberdeen, 1977), *passim*. See also id., 'King Edward's Hospital Fund for London: The First 25 Years', *passim*, and

her very useful 'Lord Mount Stephen and the King Edward's Hospital Fund for London', a copy of which is in GLRO, A/KE/751/17.

88. RA GV C273/20; C273/22.
89. RA GV C273/5.
90. RA GV C273/12.
91. Gilbert, *The End of the Road*, 236–7.
92. RA GV C273/67.
93. RA GV C274/3.
94. RA GV C273/3; C273/16–17.
95. KF, *Tenth Annual Report*, 8.
96. Bigge to Power, 18 Oct. 1906, GLRO, A/KE/573/17. The Lewis estate was not wound up until 1949. I am indebted to Dr G. D. Black for letting me look at a chapter of his life of Samuel Lewis.
97. Gilbert, 'King Edward's Hospital Fund', 45. For a list of the top individual contributors to the Fund see Long, *King Edward's Hospital Fund for London*, 25.
98. Bigge to Power, 8 Jan. 1907, GLRO, A/KE/574; RA GV C273/60.
99. RA GV C273/60. For further information on the Finance Committee see Gilbert, *The End of the Road*, 272–5.
100. RA GV C273/63.
101. RA GV C1578/7.
102. There are 270 items in the Royal Archives dealing with this issue. See RA GV C1578.
103. RA GV C1578/23; C1578/95.
104. RA GV C273/60.
105. GLRO, A/KE/572/17.
106. GLRO, A/KE/574.
107. Ibid.
108. GLRO, A/KE/27/2/165–6.
109. GLRO, A/KE/574.
110. Ibid.
111. Reported in *Hospital*, 8 June 1907, 269.
112. RA GV C1578/189.
113. *Parliamentary Debates*, 4th ser., vol. clxxii, 441–62. The Act is entitled *King Edward's Hospital Fund for London Act (7 Edward 7)*. A copy is in GLRO, A/KE/751/4.
114. GLRO, A/KE/27/2/179.
115. RA GV C273/22.
116. GLRO, A/KE/27/2/170, 217–19.
117. KF, *Fourteenth Annual Report*, 35.
118. See the relevant KF annual reports. These figures were still higher than the average annual yield on Consuls and on deposit accounts. See Forest Capie and Allan Webber, *A Monetary History of the United Kingdom, 1870–1982* (London, 1985) i. 494. For further information on the investments of the Fund see Gilbert: 'King Edward's Hospital Fund for London', *passim*.
119. GLRO, A/KE/29 f. 43.
120. Using the Retail Price Index figures provided by the Bank of England, it would

have required £174,000 in 1909 to buy the same amount of goods as could have been bought for £150,000 in 1897. We should use such figures with caution, for in hospital provision new goods and services were coming into use.

121. Gilbert, 'King Edward's Hospital Fund for London', 47.
122. *Hospital*, 14 May 1910, 186.

Notes to Chapter 3

1. For an introduction to these issues see Bernard Semmel, *Imperialism and Social Reform* (London, 1960), and J. R. Hay, *The Origins of the Liberal Welfare Reforms 1906–1914* (London, 1975).
2. *Burdett's Hospitals and Charities, 1902*, 62.
3. See, for example, KF, *Fourth Annual Report*, 6.
4. KF, *Sixth Annual Report*, 7.
5. Inaugural letter, quoted in Frank Long, *King Edward's Hospital Fund for London: The Story of its Foundation and Achievements, 1897–1942* (London, 1942), 5–6.
6. GLRO, A/KE/572/17.
7. RA GV C 1578/69.
8. King Edward's Hospital Fund for London Act, (7 Edward 7), GLRO, A/KE/751/4.
9. Ibid.
10. Lord Lister to the Prince of Wales, 16 Mar. 1898, GLRO, A/KE/751/2.
11. Knollys to Burdett, 14 Nov. 1897, Burdett Papers, Bodleian Library.
12. *The Times*, 23 Dec. 1897, 4; 27 Dec. 1897, 6.
13. KF, *First Annual Report*, 11–13.
14. Ibid. 8–11.
15. *Hospital*, 14 Jan. 1899, 267.
16. Ibid. 21 Jan. 1899, 287.
17. Holland to Burdett, 15 Jan. 1898, Burdett Papers, Bodleian Library.
18. *Lancet*, 7 Jan. 1899, 42.
19. GLRO, A/KE/292/333.
20. GLRO, A/KE/20/1 ff. 79, 88. When the Anti-Vivisection Hospital, Battersea General Hospital, was threatened with closure in 1935, a grant of £4,000 from the Fund kept the bankers at bay. See A/KE/40/4 f. 195; KF, *Fortieth Annual Report*, 32.
21. Lord Lister to the Prince of Wales, 16 Mar. 1898, GLRO, A/KE/751/2.
22. GLRO, A/KE/681/95.
23. Knollys to Burdett, 29 Sept. 1897, Burdett Papers, Bodleian Library.
24. These figures are compiled from the annual reports.
25. GLRO, A/KE/295/3b; KF, *Third Annual Report*, 11.
26. See Charlotte Knollys to Sir Arthur Bigge, 6 Apr. 1910, GLRO, A/KE/577.
27. Knollys to Burdett, 26 Dec. 1897, Burdett Papers, Bodleian Library.
28. KF, *Second Annual Report*, 7.
29. Ibid.
30. GLRO, A/KE/296/6.

31. KF, *Sixth Annual Report*, 12.
32. GLRO, A/KE/292/393.
33. *The Times*, 25 Mar. 1899, 3; see also Henry C. Burdett, *Pay Hospitals and Paying Wards throughout the World* (London, 1879).
34. GLRO, H9/GY/A1/4/1 ff. 246–9.
35. GLRO, A/KE/681/93.
36. A copy of this letter and the Prince's reply was published in *The Times*, 8 Mar. 1897, 14.
37. Ibid. 17 May 1901, 13; 19 Dec. 1901, 15.
38. See *Prince of Wales Hospital Fund. Memorial of the Metropolitan Radical Federation*, (1900). A copy of this pamphlet is in the British Library.
39. *BMJ*, 30 June 1900, 1598–9.
40. *The Prince of Wales Hospital Fund. Memorial of the Metropolitan Radical Federation*, (1900), 19.
41. Henry C. Burdett, *The Medical Attendance of Londoners* (London, 1903), 7. Burdett to Knollys, 19 Apr. 1898, Burdett Papers, Bodleian Library. See also, Geoffrey Rivett, *The Development of the London Hospital System, 1823–1982* (London, 1986), 153.
42. RA GV C273/29, quoted in Heather Gilbert, 'Lord Mount Stephen and King Edward's Hospital Fund for London', GLRO, A/KE/751/17, 18–19.
43. KF, *Ninth Annual Report*, 6–7; Rivett, *The Development of the London Hospital System*, 152–5; Gilbert, 'Lord Mount Stephen and King Edward's Hospital Fund for London', 21–2.
44. *The Times*, 21 Nov. 1910, 4.
45. See Burdett's correspondence with George V in the Gwyer MS.
46. RA GV C167/6. See also A/KE/579; A/KE/580; Rivett, *The Development of the London Hospital System*, 152–5.
47. Rivett, *The Development of the London Hospital System*, 342.
48. Long, *King Edward's Hospital Fund for London*, 18.
49. Memorandum by Burdett, GLRO, A/KE/45.
50. Lord Lister to the Prince of Wales, 16 Mar. 1898, GLRO, A/KE/751/2. See also Lawrence's obituary in the *BMJ*, 10 Jan. 1914, 121–2.
51. See the correspondence between Holland and Burdett in the Burdett Papers, Bodleian Library.
52. GLRO, A/KE/45. Burdett's list was quite different from Lister's. It contained only one visitor from St Bartholomew's.
53. *BMJ*, 5 May 1928, 778–80.
54. I have drawn this information from *The Medical Directory*.
55. For a summary of the changes in the Fund's area of operations see KF, *Forty-Fourth Annual Report*, 11.
56. Church to Crossley, 17 Feb. 1910, GLRO, A/KE/577.
57. GLRO, A/KE/27/2 f. 67; A/KE/27/3 ff. 122–3. See also Long, *King Edward's Hospital Fund for London*, 18–19.
58. GLRO, A/KE/45.
59. GLRO, A/KE/20/1.

60. There is an interesting letter on a visit from the point of view of the visited in *The Times*, 13 June 1899, 3.
61. GLRO, A/KE/45.
62. GLRO, A/KE/297/58.
63. GLRO, A/KE/61/85.
64. Lindsay Granshaw, *St Mark's Hospital, London: A Social History of a Specialist Hospital* (London, 1985), 174–5.
65. Crossley to Bigge, 30 Apr. 1907, GLRO, A/KE/574.
66. GLRO, A/KE/301 (1).
67. Ibid.
68. GLRO, A/KE/301 (2).
69. GLRO, A/KE/301 (1).
70. GLRO, A/KE/20/1, A/KE/571/29.
71. GLRO, A/KE/301 (1).
72. See App. II.
73. Ibid. See the figures compiled in KF, *Twentieth Annual Report*, 32–3.
74. *Burdett's Hospitals and Charities, 1902*, 113, 115.
75. Looked at from another point of view, in 1912 the Fund provided about 15 per cent of the total ordinary expenditure, which excluded capital expenditure, of 109 London hospitals. *Burdett's Hospitals and Charities* provides detailed information on income and expenditure of the London and provincial hospitals. See also KF, annual *Statistical Report*; Brian Abel-Smith, *The Hospitals, 1800–1948* (London, 1964), 185.
76. For figures on beds occupied in individual hospitals see KF, annual *Statistical Report*.
77. See App. III.
78. *Burdett's Hospitals and Charities, 1926*, xx.
79. GLRO, A/KE/27/3 f. 133.
80. Church to Crossley, 19 July 1908, GLRO, A/KE/575.
81. T. L. Devitt to Maynard, 25 Jan. 1910, GLRO, A/KE/577.
82. Burdett to Fry, 8 July 1910, GLRO, A/KE/577.
83. GLRO, A/KE/573/33.
84. See Power to Crossley, 14 July 1904, GLRO, A/KE/571/48.
85. GLRO, A/KE/297/184.
86. GLRO, A/KE/577. For details of conditions imposed on individual hospitals see the remarks of the Distribution Committee in the annual reports. See also Abel-Smith, *The Hospitals*, 184–5.
87. See the correspondence between Burdett and Perry in Oct. and Nov. 1907 in the Gwyer MS.
88. Quoted in Abel-Smith, *The Hospitals*, 184.
89. Cited in Rivett, *The Development of the London Hospital System*, 165–6.
90. Ibid. 161–6.
91. KF, *Seventh Annual Report*, 10, 13.
92. On this issue see Rivett, *The Development of the London Hospital System*, 166–70.
93. KF, *Sixth Annual Report*, 13.

94. GLRO, A/KE/279; Rivett, *The Development of the London Hospital System*, 169–70.
95. GLRO, A/KE/278; KF, *Eighteenth Annual Report*, 17; Rivett, *The Development of the London Hospital System*, 169–70.
96. GLRO, A/KE/277.
97. A. B. Masters to Alice Gregory, 24 Feb. 1913, GLRO, H14/BMB/A9/21.
98. GLRO, A/KE/277.
99. The fate of the British Hospital for Mothers and Babies is instructive. It was transferred from one health authority to another before being closed in 1984.
100. *Burdett's Hospitals and Charities, 1902*, 126; GLRO, A/KE/573/31.
101. Ibid. 101–2.
102. On this subject see S. Pollard, *The Genesis of Modern Management* (Harmondsworth, 1968).
103. Rivett, *The Development of the London Hospital System*, 129.
104. Sir Edward Cook, *The Life of Florence Nightingale*, (2 vols.; London, 1913, 1914), i. 433.
105. Burdett to F. C. Clayton, 10 Mar. 1910, Gwyer MS.
106. Rivett, *The Development of the London Hospital System*, 129–30.
107. Eason to Maynard, 28 Dec. 1925, GLRO, A/KE/582.
108. *Hospital*, 15 May 1915, 156.
109. Ibid. 29 Nov. 1913, 227; Long, *King Edward's Hospital Fund for London*, 26–7.
110. GLRO, A/KE/2/2 ff. 113, 206.
111. See the *Statistical Report . . . for the Year 1920*, 4.
112. E. W. Morris, *A History of the London Hospital* (London, 1910), 237.
113. *Hospital*, 31 Oct. 1914, 116.
114. Ibid. 29 Nov. 1913, 227.
115. For a list of publications see KF, typed article entitled 'Principal King's Fund Publications, 1903–1960'.
116. Charles Booth to Frederick Fry, 12 Nov. 1910, GLRO, A/KE/577.
117. RA GV C273/73. For a more thorough discussion of this issue see Gilbert, 'Lord Mount Stephen and King Edward's Hospital Fund for London', 47–52.
118. Morris, *A History of the London Hospital*, 10.
119. Heather Gilbert, 'King Edward's Hospital Fund for London: The First 25 Years', *Social and Economic Administration*, 8(1), (Oxford, 1974), 59.
120. KF, *Sixteenth Annual Report*, 7.
121. See B. B. Gilbert, *The Evolution of National Insurance* (London, 1966); Derek Fraser, *The Evolution of the British Welfare State* (London, 1973).
122. Abel-Smith, *The Hospitals*, 239–40.
123. Fraser, *The Evolution of the British Welfare State*, 155, 256–7.
124. GLRO, A/KE/298; The *Hospital*, 22 July 1912, 419.
125. *Hospital*, 22 July 1911, 417; 22 Mar. 1913, 679–82; 2 Aug. 1913, 533.
126. Ibid. 2 Aug. 1913, 534.
127. Receipts from the League of Mercy to the Fund dropped from £18,000 in 1912 to £14,000 in 1913. See the KF annual reports.
128. See the *Statistical Report* for 1912 and 1913; Abel-Smith, *The Hospitals*, 244–5.

129. Abel-Smith, *The Hospitals*, 248.
130. Crossley and Fry to Stamfordham, 6 Oct. 1911, RA GV C243/2.
131. A. M. McBriar, *An Edwardian Mixed Doubles: The Bosanquets versus the Webbs: A Study in British Social Policy 1890–1929* (Oxford, 1987), 233.
132. Abel-Smith, *The Hospitals*, 249–50.

Notes to Chapter 4

1. For more on the effects of the war on voluntarism see F. K. Prochaska, *The Voluntary Impulse. Philanthropy in Modern Britain* (London, 1988). ch. 5.
2. Brian Abel-Smith, *The Hospitals, 1800–1948* (London, 1964), 281.
3. In London alone, the voluntary hospitals treated 122,840 naval and military patients between the outbreak of war and the end of 1919. KF, *Statistical Report . . . for the Year 1919*, 4.
4. *Hospital*, 23 Dec. 1916, 244.
5. Ibid. 2 Nov. 1918, 84, quoted in Abel-Smith, *The Hospitals*, 280.
6. *Hospital*, 8 Nov. 1919, 118.
7. KF, *Nineteenth Annual Report*, 7.
8. Quoted in H. C. Cameron, *Mr Guy's Hospital* (London, 1954), 329.
9. Abel-Smith, *The Hospitals*, 282.
10. KF, *Statistical Report . . . for the Year 1918*, 4.
11. *Hospital*, 8 Nov. 1919, 118.
12. Cave Committee, *Final Report*, Cmnd. 1335 (1921), 34; KF *Statistical Report . . . for the Year 1920*, 10 put the figure at £515,000.
13. KF, *Twentieth Annual Report*, 13.
14. Abel-Smith, *The Hospitals*, 279.
15. GLRO, A/KE/27/4 ff. 98–9.
16. GLRO, A/KE/27/4, *passim*.
17. KF, *Twenty-Second Annual Report*, 6.
18. KF, *Eighteenth Annual Report*, 13.
19. For more on Tweedy, see *BMJ*, 12 Jan. 1924, 87–8; 19 Jan. 1924, 135.
20. Crossley to Fry, 10 May 1910, GLRO, A/KE/577.
21. Philip Ziegler, *King Edward VIII* (London, 1990), 108.
22. KF, *Twenty-Second Annual Report*, 16.
23. *Hospital*, 3 May 1919, 98. Anxious to encourage the Prince's voluntary impulses, Burdett sent him a copy of his *Hospitals and Charities* as a birthday present via Queen Alexandra. See Burdett to Queen Alexandra, 21 June 1912, Gwyer MS.
24. For Sunday Fund figures see *Burdett's Hospitals and Charities, 1926*, xxiii.
25. Abel-Smith, *The Hospitals*, 255.
26. See KF annual reports for the income and distribution figures. This inflation rate comes from figures provided by the Bank of England.
27. KF, *Statistical Report . . . for the Year 1920*, 9–10.
28. For more on John Baring, see David Jeremy (ed.), *Dictionary of Business Bio-*

graphy (5 vols.; London, 1984–6), i. 164–6, and Philip Ziegler, *The Sixth Great Power: Barings 1762–1929* (London, 1988), *passim.*

29. Heather Gilbert, 'Lord Mount Stephen and King Edward's Hospital Fund for London', GLRO, A/KE/751/17, 53. The Finance Committee Minutes for the war years are in GLRO, A/KE/29/1.
30. Heather Gilbert, 'King Edward's Hospital Fund for London: The First 25 Years', *Social and Economic Administration*, 8 (1) (Oxford, 1974), 61.
31. Ziegler, *The Sixth Great Power*, 326.
32. Gilbert, 'King Edward's Hospital Fund for London', 62.
33. KF, *Twentieth Annual Report*, 14.
34. Gilbert, 'Lord Mount Stephen and King Edward's Hospital Fund for London', 53.
35. KF, *Eighteenth Annual Report*, 8.
36. *Hospital*, 6 Dec. 1919, 220.
37. KF, *Twenty-Third Annual Report*, 21.
38. Ibid. 17.
39. Ibid.
40. Ibid. 15–16.
41. See particularly, *Hospital*, 8 May 1920.
42. E. W. Morris, *A History of the London Hospital*, (London, 1910), 226.
43. See letters from Knutsford to Stamfordham in Dec. 1919 in RA GV C1577.
44. Somerleyton to Stamfordham, 18 Dec. 1919, RA GV C1577/5.
45. Francis Watson, *Dawson of Penn* (London, 1951), 130. For an example of the First World War's effects on surgery in a particular hospital see Granshaw, *St Mark's Hospital, London: A Social History of a Specialist Hospital* (London, 1985), 219–20.
46. MH, Consultative Council on Medical and Allied Services, *Interim Report on the Future Provision of Medical and Allied Services* (Dawson Report), Cmnd. 693 (1920), 20.
47. John Stevenson, *British Society 1914–45* (Harmondsworth, 1984) 124.
48. David Owen, *English Philanthropy, 1660–1960* (London, 1964) 527.
49. KF, *Twenty-Fourth Annual Report*, 13.
50. Ibid. 14.
51. Ibid. 29.
52. Ibid. 29–35.
53. KF, *Twenty-Second Annual Report*, 19. The Woolwich and District War Memorial Hospital opened in 1927.
54. For the expenditure figures see KF, *Statistical Report . . . for the Year 1920*, 9. Not until 1979 did the Fund's grants exceed £700,000.
55. KF, *Twenty-Fourth Annual Report*, 22.
56. Quoted in Derek Fraser, *The Evolution of the British Welfare State* (London, 1973), 166.
57. *The Times*, 9 Dec. 1918, 10; see also the *Pall Mall Gazette*, 17 Mar. 1919.
58. D. Stark Murray, *Why a National Health Service?* (London, 1971), 6.
59. Geoffrey Rivett, *The Development of the London Hospital System, 1823–1982* (London, 1986), 186; On the setting-up of the Ministry of Health see Frank

Honigsbaum, 'The Struggle for the Ministry of Health 1914–1919', *Occasional Papers on Social Administration*, 37 (London, 1970).
60. See particularly Kenneth and Jane Morgan, *Portrait of a Progressive: The Political Career of Christopher, Viscount Addison* (Oxford, 1980).
61. Stamfordham to Somerleyton, 27 Feb. 1920; Stamfordham to Addison, 23 Apr. 1920. RA GV 30383.
62. Watson, *Dawson of Penn*, 159.
63. *Interim Report on the Future Provision of Medical and Allied Services* (the Dawson Report), *passim*.
64. Stamfordham to Somerleyton, 27 Apr. 1920, RA GV 30383.
65. See, for example, Stevenson, *British Society 1914–45*, 214; Abel-Smith, *The Hospitals*, 298; Watson, *Dawson of Penn*, 156.
66. Watson, *Dawson of Penn*, 156; Abel-Smith, *The Hospitals*, 290.
67. Frederick F. Cartwright, *A Social History of Medicine* (London, 1977), 166.
68. Abel-Smith, *The Hospitals*, ch. 18.
69. *Hospital*, 29 May 1920, 228–9; *The Times*, 9 Dec. 1918, 10.
70. Anne Crowther, *British Social Policy 1914–1939* (London, 1988), 22. See the interesting article by Pat Thane, 'Working Class and State "Welfare" in Britain, 1880–1914', *Historical Journal*, 27 (4) (1984), 877–900.
71. See Charles Webster, *The Health Services since the War. Problems of Health Care: The National Health Service before 1957* (London, 1988), 19. For an excellent introduction to the general political scene see José Harris, 'Society and the State in Twentieth-Century Britain', In F. M. L. Thompson (ed.), *The Cambridge Social History of Britain 1750–1950* (3 vols.; Cambridge, 1990), iii. 63–117.
72. *Interim Report on the Future Provision of Medical and Allied Services* (the Dawson Report), 20.
73. Abel-Smith, *The Hospitals*, 299–301.
74. In Cartwright, *A Social History of Medicine*, ample space is given to the Dawson Report but no mention is made of the Cave Committee. The same is true of Harry Eckstein, *The English Health Service: Its Origins, Structure, and Achievements* (London, 1959).
75. KF, *Twenty-Fifth Annual Report*, 12–14.
76. Ibid. The Fund's Proposals were published in the pamphlet *Resolutions on the Subject of the Policy to be Recommended for the Preservation of the Voluntary System of Hospital Management and Control* (1921).
77. Cave Committee, *Interim Report*, Cmnd. 1206 (1921), 2.
78. Cave Committee, *Final Report*, Cmnd. 1335 (1921), 9–10. See also the *Lancet*, 18 June 1921, 1311.
79. GLRO, A/KE/40/2, ff. 111–12.
80. Cave Committee, *Final Report*, 12.
81. KF, *Twenty-Fifth Annual Report*, 17.
82. Cave Committee, *Final Report*, 34.
83. *Hospital and Health Review*, Dec. 1921, 68–9.
84. Cave Committee, *Final Report*, 35.
85. GLRO, A/KE/40/1/126; A/KE/42/211.
86. KF, *Statistical Report . . . for the year 1921*, 6.

87. KF, *Twenty-Fifth Annual Report*, 9, 16.
88. Somerleyton to the Secretary of the London Labour Party, 2 Feb. 1922, RA GV PW/34.
89. On Cooper Perry see *The Times*, 19 Dec. 1938, 14; Cameron, *Mr Guy's Hospital*, 300–3.
90. KF, *Twenty-Fifth Annual Report*, 21.
91. Ibid. 19. In 1973 Lord Mount Stephen's surviving relatives requested that the Fund maintain the family grave, but after taking legal advice the Fund decided that such a course of action was outside its powers. KF, MCM, 1 Nov. 1973, 3.
92. Gilbert, 'King Edward's Hospital Fund for London', 62.
93. Frank Long, *King Edward's Hospital Fund for London: The Story of its Foundation and Achievements, 1897–1942* (London, 1942), 25.
94. KF, *Thirty-Seventh Annual Report*, 35.
95. See *Simplified Form of Accounts on a Cash Basis for Small Institutions* (KF, 1922).
96. Somerleyton to Godfrey Thomas, 17 Nov. 1921, RA GV PW/34.
97. Interview with A. G. L. Ives, Feb. 1988.
98. A copy of the telegram, dated 17 Mar. 1922, is in GLRO, A/KE/582.
99. Godfrey Thomas to Lord Somerleyton, 5 Apr. 1922, RA GV PW/34.
100. Ibid.
101. Watson, *Dawson of Penn*, 205.
102. Quoted in Sarah Bradford, *King George VI* (London, 1989), 78–9.
103. Copies of this letter can be found in the KF, file entitled '1922 Appeal'.
104. KF, *Twenty-Sixth Annual Report*, 20.
105. Ibid. 14.
106. GLRO, A/KE/58/7; for earlier relations with this charity see A/KE/579/5.
107. Minutes of the Policy Committee, 2 Dec. 1935, GLRO, A/KE/35.
108. *Hospital and Health Review*, Aug. 1922, 334.
109. GLRO, A/KE/298.
110. Lloyd George to Alan Anderson, 1 June 1922; a copy of this letter can be found in the KF, file entitled '1922 Appeal.' See also KF, *Twenty-Sixth Annual Report*, 47.
111. Lloyd George to Alan Anderson, 1 June 1922.
112. For details see KF, *Twenty-Sixth Annual Report*, 46–53; there are various files on the activities of the Combined Appeal in the KF. See also J. E. Stone, *Appeals for Funds and Hospital Publicity* (Birmingham, 1934), 29–36; *Hospital and Health Review*, July 1922, 298, Aug. 1922, 324–5.
113. E. F. Benson, *Final Edition* (London, 1988), 61.
114. The King's Fund has a copy drawn from the National Film Archive. It was also distributed under the title 'A Hundred Years of Progress'. See Stone, *Appeals for Funds and Hospital Publicity*, 24–5.
115. A. Delbert Evans and L. G. Redmond Howard, *The Romance of the British Voluntary Hospital Movement* (London, [1930]), 295.
116. GLRO, A/KE/58/55; A/KE/60/1/85.
117. KF, *Twenty-Sixth Annual Report*, 54.
118. Ibid. 53.
119. Stone, *Appeals for Funds and Hospital Publicity*, 29.

120. KF, *Twenty-Seventh Annual Report*, 18–19; on hospital deficits see also the leader in the *Hospital and Health Review*, May 1924, 127.
121. Owen, *English Philanthropy*, 527.
122. KF, *The Statistical Report . . . for the Year 1924*, 30–1.
123. Ibid. 5, 11.
124. KF, *Twenty-Eighth Annual Report*, 17.
125. Ibid.
126. MH, Voluntary Hospitals Commission, *Report on Voluntary Hospital Accommodation in England and Wales*, Cmnd. 2486 (1925), 5.
127. Ibid. 14.
128. KF, *Twenty-Ninth Annual Report*, 26.
129. *Report on Voluntary Hospital Accommodation in England and Wales*, 11.
130. Long, *King Edward's Hospital Fund for London*, 57.
131. KF, *Twenty-Sixth Annual Report*, 7.
132. Long, *King Edward's Hospital Fund for London*, 58. See also Christopher Maggs, *A Century of Change: The Story of the Royal National Pension Fund for Nurses* (London, 1987), 113–114.
133. Cave Committee, *Final Report*, 19–26. The *Lancet* recommended that the Sussex Provident Scheme, devised by Dr Gordon Dill, be applied to London. See *Lancet*, 14 May 1921, 1057; 16 July 1921, 141–2.
134. Abel-Smith, *The Hospitals*, 327.
135. GLRO, A/KE/584.
136. The words are those of the President of the British Hospitals Contributory Schemes Association, quoted in John Trevelyan, *Voluntary Service and the State: A Study of the Needs of the Hospital Service* (London, 1952), 119.
137. Abel-Smith, *The Hospitals*, 318.
138. Ibid. 327; Cartwright, *A Social History of Medicine*, 168.
139. KF, *Statistical Summary . . . for the Year 1929*, 44.
140. According to *Burdett's Hospitals and Charities, 1902*, 115, the 12 London teaching hospitals received 58 per cent of their ordinary income from investments in 1900. It was under 28 per cent in 1929. For details of individual hospitals and groups of hospitals see KF, *Statistical Summary . . . for the Year 1929*.
141. KF, *Statistical Summary . . . for the Year 1929*, 45.
142. Abel-Smith, *The Hospitals*, 322, 327.
143. *The Hospitals Year-Book, 1931*, 54.
144. *Lancet*, 13 Aug. 1921, 361.
145. *The Statistical Summary . . . for the Year 1928*, which reported a few months later, put the number of pay-beds at 1,069 and the total number of beds at 15,638, p. 80.
146. KF, *Pay Beds Committee 1927–1928: Summary of Report* (1928), 5–9.
147. Ibid. 10.
148. *Hospital*, 10 Jan. 1920, 328.
149. See the manuscript Travel Diaries (Japan) of Sidney and Beatrice Webb, in the British Library of Political and Economic Science, London School of Economics.
150. *The Hospitals Year-Book, 1931*, 55.
151. R. Pinker, *English Hospital Statistics 1861–1938* (London, 1966), 152–3. See also Webster, *The Health Services since the War*, 4.

152. It was 8 per cent in 1930. In that year the total from central funds, which included the Saturday and Sunday Funds, was 9.9 per cent of voluntary hospital income in London. KF, *Statistical Summary . . . for the Year 1930*, 46.
153. Eason to Maynard, 28 Dec. 1925, GLRO, A/KE/582.

Notes to Chapter 5

1. See KF, *Statistical Review . . . for the Year 1931*, 17.
2. Richard Crossman, 'The Role of the Volunteer in the Modern Social Service', in A. H. Halsey (ed.), *Traditions of Social Policy*, (Oxford, 1976), 265. I would like to thank Brian Harrison for this reference.
3. Margaret Brasnett, *Voluntary Social Action* (London, 1969), 69–71.
4. *Hospital*, 23 Dec. 1961, 243. Lord Dawson also took this political line, see Francis Watson, *Dawson of Penn* (London, 1951), 179.
5. *Lancet*, 18 Aug. 1921, 361.
6. G. A. Campbell, *The Civil Service in Britain* (London, 1965), 56, 69.
7. John Stevenson, *British Society 1914–45* (Harmondsworth, 1984), 462.
8. See F. K. Prochaska, *The Voluntary Impulse: Philanthropy in Modern Britain* (London, 1988), 73–4.
9. Geoffrey Rivett, *The Development of the London Hospital System, 1823–1982* (London, 1986), 198–200; Brian Abel-Smith, *The Hospitals, 1800–1948*, (London, 1964), chs. 22 and 23.
10. GLRO, A/KE/109; A/KE/110.
11. KF, *Thirty-Second Annual Report*, 17.
12. See Abel-Smith, *The Hospitals*, 364; Rivett, *The Development of the London Hospital System*, 196–7.
13. For figures on bed provision and bed occupancy see R. Pinker, *English Hospital Statistics 1861–1938* (London, 1966), chs. 10–12.
14. *The Hospitals Year-Book, 1932*, 13.
15. Ibid. 14.
16. The minutes of this committee are in the GLRO, A/KE/65; A/KE/66/1–2.
17. KF, *Thirty-Third Annual Report*, 10–11; *Thirty-Fourth Annual Report*, 11; A/KE/585.
18. KF, *Relations between Voluntary Hospitals and Municipal Hospitals under the Local Government Bill*, (London, 1929).
19. Ibid 3.
20. Ibid.
21. Rivett, *The Development of the London Hospital System*, 210. For further detail on the relations between the voluntary and municipal hospitals in the 1930s see PRO MH/58/165; MH/58/314; MH/58/321.
22. GLRO, A/KE/116.
23. Eason to Maynard, 12 Apr. 1930. GLRO, A/KE/117.
24. KF, interviews with A. G. L. Ives, 28 May and 23 July 1982.
25. Ibid.
26. On Manchester see John V. Pickstone, *Medicine and Industrial Society: A History*

of Hospital Development in Manchester and Its Region, 1752–1946 (Manchester, 1985), ch. 12.

27. *Time and Tide*, 9 Apr. 1932, 390.
28. GLRO, A/KE/117.
29. GLRO, A/KE/586.
30. Abel-Smith, *The Hospitals*, 367.
31. See, for example, KF, *Thirty-Second Annual Report*, 17.
32. John Sheldrake, 'The LCC Hospital Service', in Andrew Saint (ed.), *Politics and the People of London: The London County Council 1889–1965*, (London, 1989), 187–8. See also Charles Webster, *The Health Services since the War. Problems of Health Care: The National Health Service before 1957* (London, 1988), 20.
33. KF, *Thirty-Third Annual Report*, 48.
34. GLRO, A/KE/58.
35. GLRO, A/KE/40/2 f. 161. For more on 'Audax' and the Thank-Offering see A/KE/584 and A/KE/585.
36. KF, *Thirty-Third Annual Report*, 47–58.
37. Sir Sidney Lee, *King Edward VII. A Biography* (2 vols.; London, 1925, 1927), ii. 404; Philip Magnus, *King Edward the Seventh* (London, 1964), 398.
38. *Hospital*, 19 Aug. 1911, 521–3. The Radium Institute joined the Mount Vernon Hospital to become the Mount Vernon Hospital and Radium Institute, Northwood, Middlesex.
39. GLRO, A/KE/27/3 f. 226.
40. Joan Austoker, *A History of the Imperial Cancer Research Fund 1902–1986* (Oxford, 1988), ch. 3; Lindsay Granshaw, *St Mark's Hospital. A Social History of a Specialist Hospital* (London, 1985), 188–9.
41. Frank Long, *King Edward's Hospital Fund for London. The Story of its Foundation and Achievements, 1897–1942* (London, 1942), 64–5; see also KF, *Thirty-Second Annual Report*, 10; *Thirty-Third Annual Report*, 9–10.
42. For the guidelines associated with radium see *The Hospitals Year-Book, 1934*, 281–3.
43. See the various newspaper articles on the King's Fund and radium in GLRO, A/KE/589.
44. According to Ives, Cooper Perry in particular had no use for Dawson, 'who was too successful—and physician to the King'. See KF, interviews with Ives, 28 May and 23 July 1982. The reasons for Dawson's appointment to the Fund are discussed in GLRO A/KE/583.
45. KF, interviews with Ives, 28 May and 23 July 1982.
46. On Peacock see John Orbell's biography in David Jeremy (ed.), *Dictionary of Business Biography* (5 vols.; London, 1984–6), iv. 559–67; Philip Ziegler, *The Sixth Great Power. Barings 1762–1929* (London, 1988), *passim*.
47. KF, interviews with Ives, 28 May and 23 July, 1982.
48. See KF, annual reports for income figures. On prices see the Bank of England's Retail Price Index figures.
49. GLRO, A/KE/29/2.
50. KF, interview with Sir Andrew Carnwath, 20 July 1988. Carnwath, a Barings Director and Treasurer of the Fund, wrote the *DNB* article on Peacock.

51. GLRO, A/KE/583.
52. From the speech on the retirement of Ives by Roger Peers in KF, Ives's pension file.
53. KF, interviews with Ives, 28 May and 23 July 1982.
54. KF, MCM, 23 Sept. 1941, 2.
55. From job-interview notes in GLRO, A/KE/583; see also the speech made on Ives's retirement by Roger Peers in KF, Ives's pension file.
56. KF, interviews with Ives, 28 May and 23 July 1982.
57. Ibid. 10 Feb. 1988.
58. GLRO, A/KE/40/5
59. Long, *King Edward's Hospital Fund for London*, 78.
60. For a discussion of Peacock's role in the abdication crisis see Ziegler, *King Edward VIII* (London, 1990), ch. 18.
61. It has now been framed and hangs outside the board room in 10 Palace Court.
62. Ziegler, *King Edward VIII*, 219.
63. See RA GV PW/864.
64. GLRO, A/KE/589.
65. John W. Wheeler-Bennett, *King George VI* (London, 1958), chs. 2 and 3.
66. The Fund listed the names of those absent from its General Council and Distribution Committee meetings in the annual reports.
67. The activities of the Propaganda Committee were included in the annual reports, but there is a useful and amusing narration of them in an unpublished extract from the memoirs of Edward Jay, Secretary to the Committee, in GLRO, A/KE/751/13.
68. *Hospital and Health Review*, Oct. 1921, 16.
69. GLRO, A/KE/751/13, 11.
70. GLRO, A/KE/40/2 ff. 134, 160.
71. I have only been able to find the sound-track of this film, which, because of its title, found its way to the Imperial War Museum.
72. I would like to thank Clare Brown of the BBC Written Archives Centre, Caversham Park, for this information.
73. GLRO, A/KE/751/13, 13.
74. Lord Beveridge, *Power and Influence* (London, 1953), 228–33.
75. GLRO, A/KE/751/13, 36–9. See also KF, *The King's Fund Miniature Hospital* (London, 1934).
76. *The Times*, 30 Nov. 1929, 13.
77. *Parliamentary Debates* (Lords), vol. 75, 1929–30, 1490–1. KF, *Thirty-Fourth Annual Report*, 10.
78. 26 George 5, and 1 Edward 8, ch. 17; KF, *Fortieth Annual Report*, 12.
79. *Lancet*, 4 June 1938, 1283–4.
80. KF, *King Edward's Hospital Fund for London: Its Past History and Present Work. 1944* (London, 1944), 10.
81. John Langdon-Davies, *Westminster Hospital: Two Centuries of Voluntary Service, 1719–1948* (London, 1952), 221. On the Fund and redevelopment schemes see Rivett, *The Development of the London Hospital System*, 220–1.

82. The Westminster Hospital was awarded over £290,000 in grants from the Fund between 1897 and 1939. See App. II.

83. KF, *Thirty-Fourth Annual Report*, 9–10; *Thirty-Sixth Annual Report*, 10. See also KF, *Report of the Sub-Committee of Distribution Committee on Patients' Waking Hours in London Voluntary Hospitals* (London, 1931).

84. See KF, *Statistical Summary . . . for the Year 1930*, and later years.

85. KF, *Report of the Committee Appointed to Inquire into Out-patient Methods at London Voluntary Hospitals as Affecting Suitability of Patients and Time of Waiting* (London, 1932), 61.

86. KF, *Thirty-Seventh Annual Report*, 10.

87. See, for example, KF, *Time Saving Methods at Hospital Out-Patients Dispensaries* (London, 1935).

88. KF, Peers to Gordon McLachlan, 2 Sept. 1965, from file entitled 'Nuffield Provincial Hospitals Trust'.

89. *The Times*, 21 Jan. 1887, 6.

90. See GLRO, A/KE/7.

91. Rivett, *The Development of the London Hospital System*, 216.

92. GLRO, A/KE/25. See also KF annual reports and Sir Francis Avery Jones and A. J. Loewenthal, 'King Edward's Hospital Fund for London and the Emergency Bed Service,' *British Journal of Hospital Medicine*, (Mar. 1974), 393–9.

93. KF, *Forty-Second Annual Report*, 12. For in-patient attendance see the *Statistical Summary . . . for the Year 1939*, 86.

94. *Lancet*, 29 Sept. 1945, 410.

95. *Extracts from an Address by the Rt. Hon. Viscount Sankey . . . at the Annual Conference of the British Hospitals Association at Torquay, 28th May, 1937*, 2.

96. British Hospitals Association, *Report of the Voluntary Hospitals Commission*, para. 51, Apr. 1937. Summaries of the Sankey Report were published in *The Hospitals Year-Book, 1937*, 293–5 and *Lancet*, 8 May 1937, 1123–5. For further discussion of the Report, see Abel-Smith, *The Hospitals*, 412–23.

97. *Extracts from an Address by the Rt. Hon. Viscount Sankey*, 4.

98. *The Times*, 27 May 1938, 13.

99. *Sunday Pictorial*, 12 June 1938, 10.

100. 27 May 1938, included in GLRO, A/KE/589.

101. GLRO, A/KE/40/4.

102. KF, interviews with Ives, 28 May and 23 July 1982.

103. *Medical Press*, 31 July 1935.

104. KF, *Statistical Summary . . . for the Year 1938*, 47.

105. KF, *King Edward's Hospital Fund for London: Its Past History and Present Work*, 1.

106. KF, *Forty-Third Annual Report*, 20.

107. See the many articles published to celebrate the 40th anniversary of the NHS, for example, the *Guardian*, 1 July 1988, 4; 4 July 1988, 20; the *Independent,*, 4 July 1988, 2. There is a discussion of the tendency of post-war NHS reformers to disparage pre-war medical provision in John and Sylvia Jewkes, *The Genesis of the British Health Service* (Oxford, 1961), 46–8.

108. *Star*, 8 Dec. 1937, included in A/KE/589.

109. *Lancet*, 26 Jan. 1929, 193.
110. For a worthy exception see Pickstone, *Medicine and Industrial Society*, 266.
111. Pinker, *English Hospital Statistics*, 152–4. Pinker did not use the Fund's statistics but rather those supplied by the *Hospitals Year-Book, 1940*, 54, 60–4. These figures do not tally precisely with those of the Fund, for they deal with 154 hospitals rather than the Fund's 146, and they include Hospital Saturday Funds as receipts for services rendered. Pinker's figure for payments from patients and their societies comes to 39.4 per cent.
112. *Voluntary Service and the State*, 119.
113. KF, *Statistical Summary . . . for the Year 1938*, 46–7. The Fund always counted legacies and investments as voluntary income. See, for example, *Forty-Second Annual Report*, 18.
114. GLRO, A/KE/586/10.
115. See memo dated Feb. 1927 in GLRO, A/KE/42.
116. *The Hospitals Year-Book, 1941*, p. xlii.
117. KF, *Thirty-Sixth Annual Report*, 10. For details of the scheme offered by the British Provident Association for Hospitals and Additional Services see the *Hospitals Year-Book 1936*, 18–19. See also Sir Arthur Bryant, *A History of the British United Provident Association: BUPA, 1947–68* (London, 1968).
118. For details of the weekly costs of pay-beds at individual London hospitals see KF, *Statistical Summary . . . for the Year 1938*, 89–92.
119. GLRO, A/KE/69/1.
120. KF, *Statistical Summary . . . for the Year 1938*, 50, 86, 89–92.
121. See the press cuttings of the speech by Sir Bruce Bruce-Porter in GLRO, A/KE/589.
122. PRO, MH/80/24. See also MH/77/76.
123. D. Stark Murray, *Why a National Health Service?* (London, 1971), 43.
124. Webster, *The Health Services since the War*, 24.
125. See, for example, the *Leader*, 20 May 1939.
126. Note attached to the article in the *Leader*, 20 May 1939, GLRO, A/KE/589.
127. For further information on these meetings see PRO, MH/58/307; MH/80/24. See also Rivett, *The Development of the London Hospital System*, 222–5.

Notes to Chapter 6

1. C. L. Dunn (ed.), *The Emergency Medical Services* (2 vols.; London, 1952, 1953).
2. GLRO, A/AE/244; A/KE/589/17; see also W. R. Merrington, *University College Hospital and its Medical School* (London, 1976), 179–90.
3. The government agreed to pay for 70 per cent of the stuctural precaution schemes which it approved. See *The Hospitals Year-Book, 1939*, p. xliii.
4. KF, *Forty-Third Annual Report*, 26.
5. Brian Abel-Smith, *The Hospitals, 1800–1948* (London, 1964), 426.
6. For details see KF *Statistical Summary . . . for the Year 1944*, 41.

7. Abel-Smith, *The Hospitals*, 439.

8. Quoted ibid.

9. *The Hospitals Year-Book, 1942*, p. xliii.

10. At University College Hospital, for example, 200 beds were returned to civilian use before the raids in 1940. See Merrington, *University College Hospital and its Medical School*, 181.

11. The pre-war population of Greater London was 8,575,700. By the end of June 1941 it was 6,194,000 due to mass evacuation. See Dunn, *The Emergency Medical Services*, ii. 196.

12. KF, MCM, 8 Oct. 1940, 3.

13. For details see Richard M. Titmuss, *Problems of Social Policy* (London, 1950), pt. III; Dunn, *The Emergency Medical Services*, ii, pt. III, ch. 1.

14. Titmuss, *Problems of Social Policy*, 331, n.

15. Dunn, *The Emergency Medical Services*, ii. 221.

16. Titmuss, *Problems of Social Policy*, 462.

17. KF, *Forty-Fifth Annual Report*, 16. See also GLRO, A/KE/324, and George C. Curnock, *Hospitals under Fire* (London, 1941).

18. MH, *Hospital Survey: The Hospital Services of London and the Surrounding Area* (1945), 62. The archives of St. Thomas' Hospital contains a war diary, GLRO, H1/ST/Y6. See also *The Hospitals Year-Book, 1941*, liii–lvi.

19. GLRO, A/KE/243.

20. GLRO, A/KE/244.

21. Ibid.

22. GLRO, A/KE/243.

23. Victor Cornelius Medvei and John L. Thornton, *The Royal Hospital of Saint Bartholomew 1123–1973* (London, 1974), 88.

24. GLRO, A/KE/325; E. M. McInnes, *St Thomas' Hospital* (London, 1963), 186.

25. H. C. Cameron, *Mr Guy's Hospital* (London, 1954), 463. There is a war diary for Guy's Hospital in GLRO, A/KE/243.

26. I have been unable to find an estimate for the total cost of war damage to the London hospitals. But GLRO, A/KE/325 provides some useful detail on war–damage claims for the period up to Oct. 1943. For the aggregate surpluses see KF, *Statistical Survey . . . for the Year 1945*, 41.

27. Quoted in Titmuss, *Problems of Social Policy*, 449, n.

28. A. J. P. Taylor, *English History 1914–45* (Oxford, 1965), 455.

29. For a general discussion of war and social policy see Richard M. Titmuss, *Essays on 'The Welfare State'*, 2nd edn. (London, 1963), ch. 4.

30. The public support for state intervention has been exaggerated, for example by Derek Fraser, *The Evolution of the British Welfare State*, ch. 9. See José Harris, 'Society and the State in Twentieth-Century Britain' in F. M. L. Thompson (ed.), *The Cambridge Social History of Britain 1750–1950* (3 vols.; Cambridge, 1990), iii. 91–2.

31. GLRO, A/KE/58.

32. GLRO, A/KE/89.

33. GLRO, A/KE/364/3.

34. GLRO, A/KE/364/1.

35. GLRO, A/KE/242.

36. Ibid.

37. GLRO, A/KE/243; A/KE/244.

38. GLRO, A/KE/93.

39. Wernher had an interesting war. As a successful industrialist, he was appointed co-ordinator of port facilities and special shipping. See Sir Harold Wernher, *World War II: Personal Experiences* (London, 1950).

40. GLRO, A/KE/25.

41. For details see the KF annual reports.

42. GLRO, A/KE/57/1.

43. For details see the KF annual reports.

44. KF, interviews with Ives, 28 May and 23 July 1982.

45. GLRO, A/KE/44/1.

46. KF, *Forty-Fifth Annual Report*, 12.

47. I would like to thank Miles Hardie and Leslie Paine for this information.

48. Stone's books include *Hospital Organisation and Management*; *Law for Hospital Authorities*; *Hospital Accounts and Financial Administration*; *Hospital Appeals and Publicity*.

49. KF, interviews with Ives, 28 May and 23 July 1982. See also an article from the *Birmingham Mail*, 26 May 1936 in GLRO, A/KE/589/32.

50. KF, MCM, 22 Sept. 1941, 6.

51. See the leaflet, *Division of Hospital Facilities*, 1948, a copy of which is in RA, PP GVI 528.

52. *Lancet*, 4 Aug. 1945, 146.

53. Ibid. 6 Jan. 1945, 19–20.

54. Serbia, 'Patients on a Monument', 6, *Hospital Gazette*, June 1929, 115.

55. KF, *Second Memorandum on Hospital Diet for Consideration by Hospitals* (London, 1945). Miss M. C. Broatch, a dietician, acted as Secretary to the Committee.

56. GLRO, A/KE/31/1; KF, *Forty-Eighth Annual Report*, 8.

57. *Lancet*, 4 Aug. 1945, 147.

58. Charles Webster, *The Health Services since the War. Problems of Health Care: The National Health Service before 1957* (London, 1988), 22.

59. Frank Long, *King Edward's Hospital Fund for London. The Story of its Foundation and Achievements, 1897–1942* (London, 1942), 87.

60. Quoted ibid.

61. *Parliamentary Debates, House of Commons*, vol. 374, 1116–1118.

62. A. G. L. Ives, *British Hospitals* (London, 1948), 45.

63. GLRO, A/KE/19.

64. Geoffrey Rivett, *The Development of the London Hospital System, 1823–1982* (London, 1986), 249–50.

65. Webster, *The Health Services since the War*, 36. On the making of the Beveridge Report, see José Harris, *William Beveridge. A Biography.* (Oxford, 1977), ch. 16.

66. Harris, *William Beveridge*, 415–16.

67. Moses Abramovitz and Vera F. Eliasberg, *The Growth of Public Employment in Great Britain* (Princeton, NJ, 1957), 43. Of the 700,000, 464,700 were in civilian agencies and the rest were non-industrial defence staff.

68. Minutes of the Medical Sub-Committee, 6 Aug. 1942, 5, GLRO, A/KE/19.
69. Abel-Smith, *The Hospitals*, 457.
70. KF, *Coordination of Hospital Services: Statement issued by the Joint Committee of King Edward's Hospital Fund for London and the Voluntary Hospitals Committee for London* (London, 1943), 4–5. A copy of this document can be found in GLRO, A/KE/96.
71. Ibid. 7.
72. PRO, MH/80/25.
73. MH, *A National Health Service*, Cmnd. 6502 (London, 1944), 21. Webster, *The Health Services since the War*, 55–6.
74. Webster, *The Health Services since the War*, 58–9.
75. John and Sylvia Jewkes, *The Genesis of the British National Health Service* (Oxford, 1961), 3–4.
76. PRO, MH/77/76.
77. Ibid.
78. From 'First Reflections on the White Paper', quoted in Francis Watson, *Dawson of Penn* (London, 1951), 331. According to Webster, *The Health Services since the War*, 57, Lord Dawson privately called the White Paper 'a remarkable piece of work—well written and lucid—containing the principles on which a great new service could be built'.
79. Memorandum on the White Paper, GLRO, A/KE/355.
80. *A National Health Service*, Cmnd. 6502, 14.
81. GLRO, A/KE/355.
82. Dunn, *The Emergency Medical Services*, i. 173.
83. KF, MCM, 20 June 1944, 3.
84. PRO, MH/70/100.
85. There is a transcript of this meeting in GLRO, A/KE/98. See also PRO MH/80/27.
86. GLRO, A/KE/98.
87. Ibid.
88. MH, *Hospital Survey: The Hospital Services of London*, iv.
89. On the survey of the North-West, which was assisted by the King's Fund committee man Sir Ernest Rock Carling, see John V. Pickstone, *Medicine and Industrial Society. A History of Hospital Development in Manchester and its Region, 1752–1946* (Manchester, 1985), ch. 14.
90. MH, *Hospital Survey: The Hospital Services of London*, 78–9.
91. Rivett, *The Development of the London Hospital System*, 256.
92. PRO, MH/77/76.
93. Ibid.
94. The White Paper put the total cost to public funds at £132,000,000. See *A National Health Service*, Cmnd. 6502, 84. Another estimate in 1944 put the cost at £146,000,000, PRO, MH/80/27. On costings see also Webster, *The Health Services since the War*, 133.
95. *A National Health Service*, Cmnd. 6502, 23.
96. PRO, MH/77/76.
97. Abel-Smith, *The Hospitals*, 470.

98. Harry Eckstein, *The English Health Service: Its Origins, Structure, and Achievements* (London, 1959), 147–50.
99. The Fund had a further meeting with the Ministry on 16 Mar. 1945. See PRO, MH/80/34.
100. Webster, *The Health Services since the War*, 70.
101. John E. Pater, *The Making of the National Health Service* (London, 1981), 104. See also Abel-Smith, *The Hospitals*, 470–1.
102. KF, *Some Aspects of the Post-War Hospital Problems in London and the Home Counties* (London, 1945). See also *Lancet*, 15 Sep. 1945, 345–6.
103. KF, *Some Aspects of the Post-War Hospital Problems in London and the Home Counties*, 15.
104. Ibid.
105. *The Times*, 11 June 1945, 8.
106. Pater, *The Making of the National Health Service*, 106; Abel-Smith, *The Hospitals*, 452.
107. John Campbell, *Nye Bevan and the Mirage of British Socialism* (London, 1987), 111. Pater, *The Making of the National Health Service*, 106.
108. PRO, MH/80/29, dated 22 Aug. 1945.
109. Aneurin Bevan, *In Place of Fear* (London, 1952), 79.
110. Richard Crossman, *Planning for Freedom* (London, 1965), 66.
111. Ibid. 21.
112. Ibid. 58.
113. PRO, MH/80/29.
114. Webster, *The Health Services since the War*, 83.
115. Ibid. 85.
116. Ibid. 88; GLRO, A/KE/355.
117. From 'First Reflections on the White Paper', quoted in Watson, *Dawson of Penn*, 332.
118. PRO, MH/77/100.
119. See Lord Donoughmore's speech in *Parliamentary Debates, House of Lords*, vol. 143, 1946, 112–16.
120. Ives to Peacock, 9 Nov. 1945, GLRO, A/KE/355.
121. PRO, MH/77/77.
122. PRO, MH/77/76.
123. José Harris, 'Society and the State in Twentieth-Century Britain', 91–2.
124. Pater, *The Making of the National Health Service*, 117.
125. PRO, MH/80/34.
126. Quoted in Pater, *The Making of the National Health Service*, 122.
127. PRO, MH/80/34. See also KF, MCM, 12 Feb. 1946, 2.
128. PRO, MH/80/34.
129. KF, MCM, 12 Mar. 1946, 2.
130. KF, *Statement of Views Expressed by the King's Fund to the Minister of Health in Connection with the National Health Service Bill* (London, 1946), 1–4. See also KF, MCM, 31 Jan. 1946, 1–2.
131. PRO, MH/77/78; MH/77/79.
132. *Parliamentary Debates, House of Lords*, vol. 143, 9 Oct. 1946, 112–16 and *passim*.

133. GLRO, A/KE/41/21.
134. *The Times,* 9 Apr. 1946, 5.
135. PRO, MH/77/78.
136. PRO, MH/77/79.
137. This figure comes from a financial memorandum attached to the Bill. Webster, *The Health Services since the War,* 133, gives the estimate of the net cost, which excludes appropriations in aid from National Health Insurance, at £134,000,000.
138. Campbell, *Nye Bevan,* 180. See also Richard Crossman, *Paying for the Social Services* (London, 1969), 7.
139. Webster, *The Health Services since the War,* ch. 4. For a stimulating discussion of the role of the civil service in the creation of the National Health Service, see Frank Honigsbaum, *Health, Happiness, and Security: The Creation of the National Health Service* (London, 1989).
140. KF, interviews with Ives, 28 May and 23 July 1982.
141. *National Health Service Act, 1946,* 9 and 10 George 6, ch. 81, section 59.
142. Pickstone, *Medicine and Industrial Society,* 346.
143. Abel-Smith, *The Hospitals,* 487.
144. Ives, *British Hospitals,* 46.
145. See the article by Ives in *Lancet,* 30 Sept. 1950, 450–2; John Trevelyan, *Voluntary Service and the State* (London, 1952), 47–8.
146. *The Times,* 6 Jan. 1947, 5.
147. KF, *Today and Tomorrow: An Outline of the Work and Aims of the King's Fund* (London, 1947), 17.
148. *Voluntary Service and the State,* 32.
149. Quoted in Asa Briggs and Anne Macartney, *Toynbee Hall: The First Hundred Years* (London, 1984), 35–6.
150. KF, *Fiftieth Annual Report,* 8.
151. Peacock to Sir Ulick Alexander, 9 Jan. 1947, RA GVI PP 528.
152. KF, *Fiftieth Annual Report,* 8.
153. In addition to Frank Long's book, published in 1942, see KF, *King Edward's Hospital Fund for London: Its Past History and Present Work* (1944).

Notes to Chapter 7

1. See, for example, E. C. Midwinter, *Victorian Social Reform* (London, 1968) and Anne Crowther, *British Social Policy 1914–1939* (London, 1988).
2. David Owen, *English Philanthropy, 1660–1960* (London, 1964), 532. For a discussion of the effects of state policy on charities for child welfare, mental health, and the blind see Madeline Rooff, *Voluntary Societies and Social Policy* (London, 1957).
3. *Voluntary Service and the State,* 119–20. Between 1948 and 1981 the British Hospitals Contributory Schemes Association donated over £6,000,000 to NHS

hospitals and hospital charities. See Veronica Dawkins, *A Study of the Development of Hospital Contributory Schemes in England and Wales* (Bristol, 1982), 26–7.

4. *Daily Telegraph*, 1 May 1956. On relations between the King's Fund and the National League of Hospital Friends in the 1950s see KF, file entitled 'National League of Hospital Friends (Mr Wetenhall)'.

5. *Voluntary Service and the State*, 112–13.

6. Roger Silver, a public relations officer in the NHS, remembers attending several lavish functions paid for out of endowments in the 1960s and 1970s.

7. Luke FitzHerbert, *Charity and the National Health: A Report on the Extent and Potential of Charitable Funds within the NHS* (London, [1989]), 5.

8. HMC (48)25A.

9. KF, Lord Wigram to Pooley, 3 Feb. 1949, in file entitled 'National Council of Social Service'.

10. KF, MCP, 3716, 1965.

11. KF, Ives to John Trevelyan, 13 June 1950, in file entitled 'Social Service Enquiry (Trevelyan)'.

12. KF, memorandum to Peacock, 29 Oct. 1948, in file entitled 'National Council of Social Service'.

13. Ibid.

14. See App. II.

15. KF, MCM, 7 Nov. 1950, 4–5.

16. KF, *Select Committee on Estimates 1957: Memorandum from King Edward's Hospital Fund for London* (May 1957), 291. A printed copy of the Fund's evidence is in KF, file entitled 'Evidence for Select Committee (1957)'.

17. KF, 'Note for Mr Trevelyan's Enquiry', in file entitled 'Social Service Enquiry (Trevelyan)'.

18. KF, Ives to Trevelyan, 13 June 1950, in file entitled 'Social Service Enquiry (Trevelyan)'.

19. Charles Webster, *The Health Services since the War. Problems of Health Care: The National Health Service before 1957* (London, 1988), ch. 5.

20. Richard Crossman, *Paying for the Social Services* (London, 1969), 7.

21. See the draft of the Ministry of Health's Final Report of the Central Health Services Council Hospital Administration Committee, para. 41, a copy of which is in KF, file entitled 'Social Service Enquiry (Trevelyan)'.

22. KF, *Fifty-Second Annual Report*, 4–5.

23. KF, MCM, 16 Nov. 1948, 1–2. See also KF, file entitled 'Rockefeller Foundation Paris and New York'.

24. KF, MCM, 16 Nov. 1948, 1–2; *Fifty-Second Annual Report*, 6–8.

25. KF, *Fifty-First Annual Report*, 48.

26. See *Parliamentary Debates (Lords)*, vol. 163, 75–136.

27. KF, MCM, 8 Mar. 1949, 4. See also KF, file entitled 'Social Service Enquiry (Trevelyan)'.

28. From *On Liberty*, quoted in *Voluntary Service and the State*, 123.

29. *Voluntary Service and the State*, 121–2.

30. KF, MCM, 29 Nov. 1949, 5–6; 10 Jan. 1950, 4. KF, *Fifty-Third Annual Report*, 40–1.

31. KF, *Fifty-Third Annual Report*, 4–5. The Fund did compile and print a confidential *Statistical Summary* of the income, expenditure, work, and costs of convalescent homes from 1951 to 1974. Copies are in the King's Fund Centre Library.
32. KF, *Fifty-Second Annual Report*, 20.
33. Ibid. 19–21. For more detail on hospital income and expenditure for 1947 see *Statistical Summary . . . for the Year 1947*.
34. GLRO, A/KE/2.
35. KF, *Fifty-Second Annual Report*, 8.
36. KF, *Fifty-Sixth Annual Report*, 36.
37. KF, Edwards to Peers, 28 Apr. 1958, in file entitled 'Correspondence, Miss Edwards, 1959'.
38. KF, MCM, 7 Nov. 1950, 4–5.
39. KF, *Fifty-Third Annual Report*, 7.
40. KF, MCM, 12 Dec. 1950, 4.
41. Ibid. 7.
42. Quoted in KF, taped interview with David Halton, 19 Apr. 1982.
43. The Fund presented a special appendix on sanitary annexes in its evidence to the Guillebaud Committee in 1954.
44. KF, Distribution Committee Visitors' Reports, 1953–9.
45. Ibid.
46. For the details see KF, file entitled 'Correspondence with Miscellaneous Organisations, 1957–1967'.
47. For these and further details of grant allocations see the KF annual reports for relevant years.
48. *Medical Press*, 27 May 1953, 503.
49. Ibid.
50. MH, *Report of the Committee of Enquiry into the Cost of the National Health Service* (Guillebaud Report), Cmnd. 9663 (London, 1956), 137.
51. KF, *Fifty-Fifth Annual Report*, 70.
52. Ronald W. Clark, *A Biography of the Nuffield Foundation* (London, 1972), 186–7; A. R. Hall and B. A. Bembridge, *Physic and Philanthropy: A History of the Wellcome Trust 1936–1986* (Cambridge, 1986), 93.
53. Joan Austoker, *A History of the Imperial Cancer Research Fund 1902–1986.* (Oxford, 1988), 205–6, 317–18.
54. *The Times*, 29 May 1958, 14.
55. See Rooff, *Voluntary Societies and Social Policy, passim.*
56. KF, *Fifty-Fifth Annual Report*, 6.
57. *Manchester Guardian*, 22 Nov. 1954.
58. See the list of awards in the KF annual reports.
59. KF, *Fifty-Second Annual Report*, 38.
60. *The Times*, 10 Apr. 1951, 5. See also KF, MCM, 11 Feb. 1947, 4.
61. KF, *Fifty-Third Annual Report*, 9–17.
62. KF, *Sixtieth Annual Report*, 21–3. *Medical Press*, 27 May 1953, 504.
63. Details on the homes can be found in KF, *Fifty-Fifth Annual Report*, 17–20. See also KF, Minutes of the Auxiliary Hospitals Committee. The subsequent

histories of the homes can be traced in *The Hospitals and Health Services Year Book*.

64. KF, *Fifty-Ninth Annual Report*, 26–8.
65. KF, unsigned letter to Dame Enid Russell-Smith, 16 May 1961, in file entitled 'Correspondence with Miscellaneous Organisations, 1957–1967'.
66. Association of Chief Financial Officers in the Hospital Service in England and Wales. *Annual Conference... November 1956* ([1957]), 51.
67. KF, unsigned letter to Dame Enid Russell-Smith, 16 May 1961, in file entitled 'Correspondence with Miscellaneous Organisations, 1957–1967'.
68. KF, MCM, 14 June 1962, 5.
69. Quoted KF, *Sixty-Sixth Annual Report*, 9.
70. See Graham's obituary by Brian Dowling, *Independent*, 13 Apr. 1988.
71. PRO, MH 58/853, Rucker to Wernher, 16 Apr. 1947.
72. On the EBS see KF, taped interview with Valerie Peers, 25 June 1982.
73. KF, *Fifty-Third Annual Report*, 39.
74. KF, taped interview with Jack Langworthy, 2 June 1982.
75. KF, *Emergency Bed Service... Report for the Year ended 31st March 1954*. See also, KF, *Fifty-Eighth Annual Report*, 29.
76. On the Guillebaud Committee, see Webster, *The Health Services since the War*, 204–11.
77. KF, the 'Coiled Spring', 5, in file entitled 'Guillebaud Enquiry'.
78. Ibid. 4–5.
79. Ibid. 6.
80. Ibid. 6–8.
81. KF, *Fifty-Sixth Annual Report*, 5.
82. KF, Division of Hospital Facilities, Guillebaud Committee. First Draft Memorandum, section I, 1, in file entitled 'Guillebaud Enquiry'.
83. Ibid. Section I, 12.
84. Ibid. 10–11.
85. Ibid. 2–3.
86. Ibid. 5.
87. KF, MCM, 13 Apr. 1954, 3.
88. KF, copy of submission, dated 14 May 1954, is in KF, file entitled 'Guillebaud Enquiry'.
89. Ibid.
90. *The Times*, 31 Oct. 1952, 3.
91. Quoted, KF, *Fifty-Sixth Annual Report*, 58. See also *Lancet*, 24 Jan. 1953, 191–2.
92. KF, *Fifty-Seventh Annual Report*, 5.
93. MH, *Report of the Committee of Enquiry into the Cost of the National Health Service*, (Guillebaud Report), Cmnd. 9663, 135–6.
94. KF, *Fifty-Seventh Annual Report*, 6.
95. KF, *Fifty-Ninth Annual Report*, 8–15.
96. KF, *Fifty-Eighth Annual Report*, 5.
97. See MH, *Report of the Committee of Enquiry into the Cost of the National Health Service*, (Guillebaud Report), Cmnd. 9663.
98. On the reception of the Guillebaud Report, see *Parliamentary Debates, House of*

Commons, vol. 552, 7 May 1956, 851–966. See also Webster, *The Health Services since the War*, 207, 210.

99. KF, *Fifty-Ninth Annual Report*, 5.

100. MH, *Report of the Committee of Enquiry into the Cost of the National Health Service*, (Guillebaud Report), Cmnd. 9663, 121–32; *Parliamentary Debates, House of Commons*, vol. 552, 868–69; KF, *Fifty-Ninth Annual Report*, 5.

101. KF, *Fifty-Sixth Annual Report*, 30–2.

102. MH, *Report of the Committee of Enquiry into the Cost of the National Health Service*, (Guillebaud Report), Cmnd. 9663, 121–3. KF, *Sixtieth Annual Report*, 34.

103. KF, *Sixty-Third Annual Report*, 32.

104. *The Times*, 25 Oct. 1901, 5.

105. MH, *Report of the Committee of Enquiry into the Cost of the National Health Service*, (Guillebaud Report), Cmnd. 9663, 140–1.

106. KF, MCM, 9 Oct. 1945, 5.

107. The responsibility for training medical-records officers was eventually transferred to the Fund's Administrative Staff College.

108. The first Principal of the Staff College for Ward Sisters was Miss A. M. Downer, but she died in 1950 and was succeeded by Miss C. H. S. Dobie.

109. KF, *Fifty-Second Annual Report*, 31–2.

110. James Stirling Ross, *The National Health Service in Great Britain* (Oxford, 1952), 324.

111. KF, *Fifty-Third Annual Report*, 19.

112. For a profile of Mickelwright see *Hospital and Health Service Management*, Apr. 1962, 312–13.

113. For Jameson's important contribution to the Fund's post-war history see Neville M. Goodman, *Wilson Jameson, Architect of National Health* (London, 1970), ch. 9.

114. KF, taped interview with Frank Reeves, Apr. 20, 1982.

115. KF, *Fifty-Second Annual Report*, 44.

116. *Lancet*, 30 Sept. 1950, 450–2.

117. *Select Committee on Estimates 1957: Memorandum from King Edward's Hospital Fund for London*, 293–4.

118. MH, Central Health Services Council, *Report of the Committee on the Internal Administration of Hospitals* (the Bradbeer Report) (1954). The Fund's evidence to the Bradbeer Committee is in KF, file entitled 'Committee on Internal Administration of Hospitals'.

119. KF, *Fifty-Fourth Annual Report*, 24–5.

120. Ibid. 22.

121. KF, *Hospital Bed Occupancy: Report of the First Study Group set up by the Hospital Administrative Staff College of King Edward's Hospital Fund for London* (1954). See also *Lancet*, 7 Aug. 1954, 277–8.

122. KF, taped interview with Irene Warren, 30 Apr. 1982.

123. For further details of the activities of the Administrative Staff College see the KF annual reports. The manuscripts, photographic collection, and taped interviews dealing with the College are in the King's Fund. The British Library contains printed material on the early years of the College.

124. KF, MCM, 8 Apr. 1952, 3–4; KF, *Fifty-Sixth Annual Report*, 37–8; *Fifty-Seventh Annual Report*, 38.
125. *Lancet*, 6 Feb. 1954, 305.
126. Quoted ibid.
127. KF, *Fifty-Seventh Annual Report*, 39.
128. Rosemary White, *The Effects of the National Health Service on the Nursing Profession 1948–1961* (London, 1985), 258.
129. KF, MCM, 8 Apr. 1952, 4.
130. KF, *Fifty-Fourth Annual Report*, 36.
131. KF, typed MS, George Stormont, 'The Catering Advisory Service 1952–1973', 1. For further details of the Catering Advisory Service see the KF annual reports.
132. KF, *Sixty-Third Annual Report*, 51.
133. Ian McColl, 'The King's Fund and Quality of Medical Care', *Postgraduate Medical Journal*, 60 (November 1984), 825.
134. KF, *Sixty-Fourth Annual Report*, 6.
135. *The Times*, 29 May 1958, 14.
136. Richard Crossman, 'The Role of the Volunteer in the Modern Social Service', in A. H. Halsey (ed.), *Traditions of Social Policy* (Oxford, 1976), 259.
137. *The Times*, 10 July 1958, 11.
138. KF, Stephen Merivale to Ives, 5 Mar. 1957, in file entitled 'Evidence for Select Committee (1957)'.
139. *Manchester Guardian*, 19 Apr. 1955.

Notes to Chapter 8

1. David Owen, *English Philanthropy, 1660–1960* (London, 1964), 527.
2. Richard Crossman, 'The Role of the Volunteer in the Modern Social Service', in A. H. Halsey (ed.), *Traditions of Social Policy* (Oxford, 1976), 283.
3. Ibid. 279.
4. *Daily Telegraph*, 4 May 1961; *Sunday Telegraph*, 31 Jan. 1965.
5. I would like to thank Sir Andrew Carnwath and Sir Francis Avery Jones for this information.
6. KF, *Sixty-Fourth Annual Report*, 6.
7. *Daily Telegraph*, 13 Apr. 1962.
8. Nineteenth-century hospitals often had rigid disciplinary orders, but there were curious lapses, such as domestic pets being treated in receiving rooms. See E. W. Morris, *A History of the London Hospital* (London, 1910), 9.
9. *Daily Telegraph*, 1 June 1962.
10. *The Times*, 13 Feb. 1962, 11.
11. KF, *Sixty-Fourth Annual Report*, 6.
12. Ibid. 5.
13. Ibid. 10.
14. Pooley died in 1966. For a short obituary see the KF, *Sixty-Ninth Annual Report*, frontispiece.

15. KF, MCM, 27 July 1961, 2.
16. KF, taped interview with Derek Harington Hawes, Aug. 1982.
17. KF, MCM, 31 Mar. 1966, 3.
18. Ibid. 10 Dec. 1964, 1; 25 Mar. 1971, 1; 27 Jan. 1972, 1.
19. KF, GCM, 16 July 1971, 89.
20. KF, taped interview with David Halton, 19 Apr. 1982.
21. From the address given by Sir Francis Avery Jones at Phalp's memorial service, a copy of which is deposited in the King's Fund. I am also grateful to Sir Andrew Carnwath for information on Peers and Phalp.
22. For information on contributions see the KF annual reports.
23. KF, MCM, 22 July 1965, 2.
24. Ibid. 28 July 1966, 2.
25. KF, taped interview with David Halton, 19 Apr. 1982.
26. KF, MCM, 10 Dec. 1964, 4.
27. KF, GCM, 18 July 1972, 98.
28. KF, FCM, 14 June 1971, 44.
29. KF, GCM, 11 July 1974, 113.
30. Ibid.
31. MH, *A Hospital Plan for England and Wales*, Cmnd. 1604 (HMSO, 1962).
32. Ruth Levitt and Andrew Wall, *The Reorganised National Health Service*, 3rd edn. (London, 1984), 130.
33. *The Hospitals Year Book* contains a section on independent hospitals and thus permits comparisons.
34. KF, *Sixty-Fifth Annual Report*, 5.
35. KF, *Sixty-Sixth Annual Report*, 5.
36. KF, *Sixty-Fifth Annual Report*, 5.
37. KF, MCM, 22 Feb. 1962, 3.
38. KF, *The Shape of Hospital Management in 1980?* (1967), 22, 25. Paine, who received one of the first King's Fund bursaries, spoke to the General Council on the subject of hospital management in 1967. He later joined the Fund's Management Committee.
39. 7 and 8 Eliz. 2, ch. 72, 1.
40. KF, *Sixty-Third Annual Report*, 15–17.
41. Levitt and Wall, *The Reorganised National Health Service*, 157–8.
42. KF, MCM, 22 Nov. 1962, 4.
43. KF, *Sixty-Seventh Annual Report*, 27.
44. KF, *Sixty-Ninth Annual Report*, 42–6.
45. KF, *Annual Report 1974*, 7.
46. KF, *Sixty-Sixth Annual Report*, 8.
47. KF, MS, speech by Robert Maxwell, '25th Anniversary of the Kingston Medical Centre'. 1987.
48. The Nuffield Provincial Hospitals Trust set aside £250,000 to establish training centres outside London. See KF, *Sixty-Sixth Annual Report*, 7–8; *Sixty-Seventh Annual Report*, 15–16; KF, Distribution Committee Visitors' Reports, The Kingston Hospital, 1959; the *Guardian*, 4 Dec. 1962.
49. KF, *Annual Report 1974*, 7.

50. KF, *Sixty-Eighth Annual Report*, 7–10.
51. Olive Williams to P. W. Burton, 31 Oct. 1960, KF, file entitled 'National League of Hospital Friends (Mr Wetenhall)'.
52. I would like to thank Sir Francis Avery Jones for this information.
53. KF, *Annual Report 1974*, 7.
54. KF, MCM, 20 March 1975, 3.
55. KF, *Annual Report 1969*, 20
56. For further details on the work of the Division of Hospital Facilities see the KF annual reports and the Management Committee Papers.
57. KF, *Films for Hospitals* (1961), 8–9.
58. KF, *Sixty-Second Annual Report*, 27.
59. *Lancet*, 24 Jan. 1959, 203. See also *The Times*, 23 Jan. 1959, 8.
60. For some reason mental hospitals were an exception, HMC (52) 123.
61. *Lancet*, 24 Jan. 1959, 203.
62. *The Times*, 5 Feb. 1959, 11.
63. Ibid. 10 Feb. 1959, 9.
64. KF, *Sixty-Third Annual Report*, 28–9; *Sixty-Fifth Annual Report*, 21.
65. Frederick F. Cartwright, *A Social History of Medicine* (London, 1977), 184.
66. Crossman, 'The Role of the Volunteer in the Modern Social Service', 270–1.
67. KF, MCP 3469, 1961, copy in file entitled 'Hospital Centre'. Leslie Paine had also called for a Hospital Research Centre, which the King's Fund might provide.
68. KF, Peers to Jones, 2 Nov. 1961, in file entitled 'Hospital Centre'.
69. KF, MCM, 30 Nov. 1961, 3.
70. Ibid. 30 Nov. 1961, 4.
71. KF, file entitled 'Hospital Centre'.
72. Quoted in KF, *Sixty-Seventh Annual Report*, 7–8.
73. *Manchester Guardian*, 21 June 1963.
74. KF, *Sixty-Ninth Annual Report*, 22.
75. Ibid. 24.
76. See KF, *Design of Hospital Bedsteads* (1967).
77. KF, *Sixty-ninth Annual Report*, 21. See also 'Design of Hospital Beds', *Nursing Times*, 13 May 1966. Three further articles on the King's Fund Bed appeared in *Hospital Management Planning and Equipment*, May 1967.
78. A copy of the speech is in KF, file entitled 'Hospital Centre, Correspondence, 1966–1967'.
79. Jan Rocha, *Organisers of Voluntary Services in Hospitals* (KF, 1968), 37.
80. KF, Jane Hammond to Peers, 9 Aug. 1967, file entitled 'Hospital Centre, Correspondence, 1966–1967'.
81. Rocha, *Organisers of Voluntary Services in Hospitals*, 55.
82. Ibid. 54.
83. KF, Miles Hardie, 'The Work of the Hospital Centre, file entitled 'Hospital Centre, Correspondence, 1966–1967'.
84. KF, Miles Hardie, 'The Centre's Income'.
85. KF, *Annual Report 1969*, 20.

86. KF, MCP, 4051, 1971.
87. KF, MCM, 28 May 1970, 2.
88. KF, *Annual Report 1979*, 13.
89. KF, MCP, 4162, 1973; MCM, 23 Mar. 1972, 2–3.
90. For details and illustrations of the formal opening of the King's Fund Centre see KF, *Annual Report 1976, passim.*
91. KF, *Sixty-Seventh Annual Report*, 17–18.
92. KF, taped interview with Frank Reeves, 20 Apr. 1982.
93. I would like to thank Iden Wickings for this information.
94. KF, MCM, 23 Oct. 1975, 5.
95. KF, *Annual Report 1980*, 13.
96. See F. K. Prochaska, *The Voluntary Impulse: Philanthropy in Modern Britain* (London, 1988), 5–6, 67.
97. KF, MCP, 4071, 1971.
98. Ibid. 3774, 1966.
99. KF, *Annual Report 1967*, 15.
100. KF, MCM, 13 Dec. 1967, 3–4; MCP, 3841, 1967.
101. KF, Peers to Miss D. M. Cutcliffe, 18 Jan. 1968, file entitled 'Nursing Recruitment Service'.
102. KF, GCM, 11 July 1974, 117; *Annual Report 1973*, 9.
103. KF, taped interview with Tom Whatley, 30 July 1982.
104. KF, taped interview with Jack Langworthy, 1982.
105. KF, MCP, 4071, 1971; MCM, 21 Oct. 1971, 3.
106. Sir Francis Avery Jones and A. J. Loewenthal, 'King Edward's Hospital Fund for London and the Emergency Bed Service', *British Journal of Hospital Medicine* (1974), 399.
107. Ibid.
108. KF, Peers to George Godber, 31 Jan. 1968, file entitled 'Ministry of Health Correspondence'. See also KF, taped interview with Jack Langworthy, 1982.
109. KF, MCP, 4491, 4495, 1977; KF, taped interview with Jack Langworthy, 1982.
110. KF, Phalp to H. N. Lamb, 24 Mar. 1977, MCP 4495, 1977.
111. KF, taped interview with Jack Langworthy, 1982.
112. KF, *Working Together* (1968), 55.
113. Ibid. 57.
114. KF, *Annual Report 1968*, 2.
115. Ibid.
116. Quoted in Roger Hadley and Stephen Hatch, *Social Welfare and the Failure of the State* (London, 1981), 81.
117. David Widgery, *Health in Danger: The Crisis in the National Health Service* (London, 1979), 144.
118. I would like to thank Leslie Paine for this information.
119. KF, GCM, 21 July 1970, 87; 18 July 1972, 101.
120. Ibid. 10 July 1973, 108.
121. See, for examples, Levitt and Hall, *The Reorganised National Health Service*; R. G. S. Brown, *Reorganising the National Health Service: A Case Study of Administrative*

Change (Oxford, 1979); Keith Barnard and Kenneth Lee (eds.), *Conflicts in the National Health Service* (London, 1977); Geoffrey Rivett, *The Development of the London Hospital System*, 1823–1982 (London, 1986), chs. 13 and 14.

122. J. Enoch Powell, *Medicine and Politics: 1975 and After* (Tunbridge Wells, 1976), 75–6.

123. *The Future of Voluntary Organisations: Report of the Wolfenden Committee* (London, 1978), app. 4.

124. Hadley and Hatch, *Social Welfare and the Failure of the State*, 77.

125. Ibid. 82; Rivett, *The Development of the London Hospital System*, 324.

126. According to Widgery's figures, the number of administrative staff in the NHS expanded from 70,396 to 91,865 between 1971 and 1975, *Health in Danger*, 145. The *Royal Commission on the National Health Service*, Cmnd. 7615 (HMSO, 1979), 32, put the increase in the number of administrative and clerical staff in England between 1973 and 1977 at 28 per cent.

127. *Royal Commission on the National Health Service*, Cmnd. 7615, 165.

128. Brown, *Reorganising the National Health Service*, 217.

129. Widgery, *Health in Danger*, 144.

130. *Lancet*, 20 Nov. 1976, 1130–1.

131. *BMJ*, 1 July 1978, 5–9.

132. See KF, *Evidence to the Royal Commission on the National Health Service* (1977); KF, *Annual Report 1976*, 13.

133. KF, *Annual Report 1975*, 5.

134. *Evidence to the Royal Commission on the National Health Service*, 12, 20, *passim*.

135. Ibid., *passim*. A copy of the Fund's earlier submission to the Royal Commission can be found in KF, MCP, 4415, 1976.

136. Brown, *Reorganising the National Health Service*, 41.

137. KF, *Annual Report 1976*, 13. The Nuffield Provincial Hospitals Trust took a similar line on the 1974 reorganization. See its *Tenth Report*, 9–11.

138. Levitt and Wall, *The Reorganised National Health Service*, 116. See also the *Royal Commission on the National Health Service*, Cmnd. 7615, 344–6.

139. Widgery, *Health in Danger*, 145.

140. *BMJ*, 27 Nov. 1976, 1320. See also the article 'The London Hospital Scene' by Sir Francis Avery Jones in the *BMJ*, 30 Oct. 1976, 1046–9.

141. DHSS, *Sharing Resources for Health in England* (HMSO, 1976), 7, 47.

142. *BMJ*, 27 Nov. 1976, 1320.

143. Granshaw, *St Mark's Hospital, London. A Social History of a Specialist Hospital* (London, 1985), 306–12.

144. KF, MCP, 4650, 1979, 15–16.

145. Ibid. 15.

146. KF, GCM, 24 July 1975, 125.

147. KF, *Sixty-Seventh Annual Report*, 5.

148. KF, GCM, 12 July 1979, 158.

149. Ibid. 24 July 1975, 125.

150. For financial details of grants to specialized charities see KF, MCP, 4373, 1975.

151. KF, *Annual Report 1977*, 5, 15; MCP, 4526, 1977. I would like to thank Sir Francis Avery Jones for information on the Jubilee Project.

152. Ibid. 5.
153. KF, *Annual Report 1979*, 6.
154. This description of the Fund comes from a recent student at the College, who wishes to remain anonymous.
155. While the Sunday Fund provided the NHS with Samaritan Funds, its grants were heavily weighted toward independent hospitals, homes, and charities. See the *Metropolitan Hospital-Sunday Fund: Report of the Council for the Year Ended 31st Dec. 1989* ([London, 1990]), 3.
156. The phrase, drawn from *Lancet*, 1873, was used by Anthony Clare at the Fund's General Council Meeting in July 1990.
157. From Pope's *Essay on Man*, quoted in KF, GCM, 12 July 1979, 157.

Notes to Chapter 9

1. Robert Maxwell (ed.), *Reshaping the National Health Service* (New Brunswick and Oxford, 1988), ch. 12. Though he ignores the voluntary sector, there is a stimulating discussion of the rivalries between private- and public-sector professionals in Harold Perkin, *The Rise of Professional Society: England since 1880* (London, 1989).
2. See *Into the 1990s: Voluntary Organisations and the Public Sector*, a report by the NCVO and RIPA compiled by Marilyn Taylor (London, 1988), 3.
3. José Harris, 'Society and the State in Twentieth-Century Britain', in F. M. L. Thompson (ed.), *The Cambridge Social History of Britain 1750–1950* (3 vols.; Cambridge, 1990), iii. 63.
4. Just under 4,000 in 1986 alone. See *Report of the Charity Commissioners for England and Wales for the Year 1986* (HMSO, 1987), 8.
5. See article by Ruth Lister, 'Charity Cries Out for Justice', *Independent*, 18 May 1990, 21.
6. *The Times*, 17 Dec. 1984, 7.
7. F. K. Prochaska, *The Voluntary Impulse: Philanthropy in Modern Britain* (London, 1988), 4–6; Harris, 'Society and the State in Twentieth-Century Britain', 113–14.
8. *Independent*, 27 Nov. 1987, 19.
9. Ibid.
10. Luke Fitzherbert, *Charity and the National Health. A Report on the Extent and Potential of Charitable Funds within the NHS* (London, [1989]), 17.
11. Ibid. 11.
12. Tom Dean, 'Organising Medical Research: The Role of Charities and the State', in Alan Ware (ed.), *Charities and Government*, (Manchester, 1989), 140.
13. Joan Austoker, *A History of the Imperial Cancer Research Fund 1902–1986*, (Oxford, 1988), 318.
14. *Lancet*, 5 May 1990, 1085.
15. *Independent*, 4 July 1990, 6.
16. Ibid. 9 Apr. 1990, 17.
17. *Health Services Act 1980*, Eliz. II, ch. 53.

18. Quoted from Sara Morrison in Fitzherbert, *Charity and the National Health*, 6.
19. Ibid. 7.
20. F. J. Gladstone, *Voluntary Action in a Changing World* (London, 1979), 3.
21. J. Enoch Powell, *A New Look at Medicine and Politics* (London, 1966), 16.
22. Fitzherbert, *Charity and the National Health*, 7.
23. Malcolm Dean, 'The NHS Gets Out its Begging Bowl', the *Lancet*, 5 May 1990, 1086.
24. *Independent*, 9 Apr. 1990, 17.
25. *Guardian*, 11 Apr. 1990, 21.
26. Ibid.
27. KF, interview with Robert Maxwell, 20 July 1990.
28. Ibid.
29. KF, *The King's Fund Yesterday, Today and Tomorrow* (1987), 11.
30. In 1987 the King's Fund was the 11th largest British trust in terms of money distributed; in 1988 it was 22nd. See Charities Aid Foundation, *Charity Trends*, 12th edn. (Tonbridge, 1989), 64.
31. KF, *Annual Report 1989*, 19.
32. KF, MCP, 4765 (1981).
33. KF, *Annual Report 1988*, 4.
34. KF, *Annual Report 1989*, 19.
35. KF, MCM, 17 July 1980, 3–4: MCP 4714 (1980).
36. *The King's Fund Yesterday, Today and Tomorrow*, 15.
37. Ibid. 16.
38. Ibid. 18.
39. KF, GCM, 12 July 1979, 157.
40. For further information on Marius Gray see *KF News*, Mar. 1989.
41. See 'Development of the London Programme', KF Reports, and KF annual reports.
42. KF, *Annual Report 1984*, 8.
43. *The King's Fund Yesterday, Today and Tomorrow*, 13.
44. KF and NPHT, *The Report of a Confidential Enquiry into Perioperative Deaths*, ([1987]), vii; KF, *Annual Report 1987*, 13.
45. See Barbara Stocking (ed.), *In Dreams Begins Responsibility: A Tribute to Tom Evans* (KF, 1987). There is also a brief obituary of Evans in the *KF News*, Sept. 1985).
46. KF, MCP, 4866 (1982), 18; 4950 (1982), 4.
47. KF, *Annual Report 1985*, 10; KF, MCP 4714 (1980).
48. Tom Evans, 'An Intellectual Autobiography', in Stocking, *In Dreams Begins Responsibility*, 27.
49. For a further discussion of the College's approach to training see Laurie McMahon, 'Room at the Top'. *Management Process*, 1 (1) (July 1988), 18–20.
50. Evans, 'An Intellectual Autobiography', 31.
51. See KF annual reports.
52. KF, MCP, 4950 (1982), 4.
53. KF, *Annual Report 1985*, 7.
54. *Times Health Supplement*, 19 Feb. 1982, 9. See also *BMJ*, 1979 (2), 1611.

55. For background papers on the KF Institute see KF, MCP 4939 (1982); MCP 5055 (1985) includes a list of participants.
56. *KF News*, June 1985.
57. KF, MCP 5155 (1984), 5–6.
58. See KF annual reports. The Institute's briefing papers can be purchased at the KF Centre in Camden Town.
59. KF, *Annual Report 1987*, 7.
60. KF, interview with Ives, 10 Feb. 1988.
61. KF, *Planned Health Services for Inner London: Back to back planning* (1987), iii.
62. KF, *Annual Report 1987*, 12.
63. MH, *Report of the Committee of Enquiry into the Cost of the National Health Service* (Guillebaud Report), Cmnd. 9663 (1956), 233.
64. *The Times*, 5 May 1962, 5.
65. *Royal Commission on the National Health Service*. Cmnd. 7615 (HMSO, 1979), 350.
66. *Planned Health Services for Inner London*, iii.
67. Ibid. 21.
68. Neil Small, *Politics and Planning in National Health Service* (Milton Keynes, 1989), 126.
69. Ibid. 132.
70. Geoffrey Rivett, *The Development of the London Hospital System, 1823–1982* (London, 1986), 345.
71. Small, *Politics and Planning in the National Health Service*, 125–6. 136.
72. See John and Sylvia Jewkes, *The Genesis of the British National Health Service*, (Oxford, 1961), *passim*.
73. See Charles Webster, *The Health Services since the War. Problems of Health Care: The National Health Service before 1957* (London, 1988), 398.
74. See Peter Hennessy, 'History as an Antidote to the Knowledge Gap', *Independent*, 17 Sept. 1990, 6.
75. For a view from the Left on this issue see Gordon Best, 'NHS's Unhappy Returns', *Marxism Today*, July 1988, 20.
76. Ruth Levitt and Andrew Wall, *The Reorganised National Health Service*, 3rd edn., (London, 1984), 27.
77. KF, taped interview with Irene Warren, 30 Apr. 1982.
78. Virginia Berridge, 'Health and Medicine', in F. M. L. Thompson (ed.), *Social History of Britain 1750–1950* (3 vols.; Cambridge, 1990), iii. 236.
79. See *Independent*, 16 Dec. 1988, 20.
80. *Working for Patients* (HMSO, 1989), Foreword.
81. *KF News*, June 1989.
82. KF, *Health Finance: Assessing the Options* (1988), Institute Briefing Paper, no. 4, 4.
83. KF College, 'Reforming the NHS: Managed Experimentation', Executive Summary. Copies of this summary and the full submission are in the KF, file entitled 'NHS Review, Articles and Comments on the White Paper'.
84. *Observer*, 5 Feb. 1989.
85. *KF News*, June 1989.
86. KF, *Managed Competition: A New Approach to Health Care in Britain* (1989), Institute Briefing Paper, no. 4, 4.

87. See *National Health Service and Community Care Act* 1990, Eliz. II, ch. 19.
88. See KF, file entitled Commission on Acute Services; *The Times*, 28 May 1990, 6.
89. KF, *Annual Report 1989*, 16.
90. Ibid.
91. Ibid.
92. *BMJ*, 13 Feb. 1988, 496.

APPENDIX I

Officials of The King's Fund, 1897–1990

PATRONS

Edward VII, 1901–1910
George V, 1910–1936
Edward VIII, 1936
George VI, 1936–1952
Elizabeth II, 1952–

PRESIDENTS

Prince of Wales (Edward VII), 1897–1901
Prince of Wales (George V), 1901–1910
Prince of Wales (Edward VIII), 1919–1936
Duke of York (George VI), 1936
Duke of Kent 1936–1942
Duke of Gloucester, 1942–1970
Prince of Wales (Charles), 1986–

GOVERNORS*

Duke of Teck, 1910–1919
Viscount Iveagh, 1910–1919
Rt. Hon. James W. Lowther, MP, 1910–1919
HRH Princess Alexandra, 1971–1985
Lord Ashburton, 1971–1976
Lord Rosenheim, 1971–1972
Lord Cottesloe, 1973–1983
Sir Andrew Carnwath, 1976–1985
Lord Hayter, 1983–1985

* In accordance with the Fund's Act of Incorporation, the Sovereign appointed three Governors whenever a royal President was unavailable to serve.

TREASURERS

Lord Rothschild, 1897–1913
Lord Revelstoke, 1914–1928
Sir Edward Peacock, 1929–1954
Lord Ashburton 1955–1964
Sir Andrew Carnwath, 1965–1974
Robin Dent, 1975–

CHAIRMEN OF THE MANAGEMENT COMMITTEE

Lord Strafford, 1897
Hugh C. Smith, 1898–1906
Earl of Bessborough, 1907–1919
Lord Stuart of Wortley, 1920–1924
Earl of Donoughmore, 1925–1947
Sir Ernest Pooley, 1948–1956
Lord McCorquodale, 1957–1964
Lord Hayter, 1965–1982
Hon. Hugh Astor, 1983–1988
S. Marius Gray, 1989–

HONORARY SECRETARIES

Sir Savile Crossley (Lord Somerleyton), 1897–1934
C. Stuart Wortley, 1897
Sir John Craggs, 1898–1906
Viscount Duncannon (Earl of Bessborough), 1900
J. Danvers Power, 1904–1907
Sir Frederick Fry, 1908–1911, 1914–1921
John G. Griffiths, 1911–1920
Sir Alan Anderson, 1921–1924
Major General Sir Cecil Lowther, 1923–1926
Sir Harold Wernher, 1923–1948
Sir Leonard Cohen, 1925–1936
Lord Luke, 1928–1943
Sir Ernest Pooley, 1935–1948
General Sir Kenneth Wigram, 1940–1941
Sir Hugh Lett, 1942–1948

SECRETARIES

H. R. Maynard, 1906–1938
A. G. L. Ives, 1938–1960
R. E. Peers, 1960–1968
G. A. Phalp, 1968–1980
R. J. Maxwell, 1980–

APPENDIX II

King's Fund Grants Recommended to the General Hospitals with Medical Schools, 1897-1948 (£)*

Hospital	1897-1906	1907-1916	1917-1926	1927-1936	1937-1946	1947	1948	Total
Charing Cross	19,256	42,600	57,425	56,673	37,750	5,250	—	218,954
Guy's	62,913	86,200	132,600	135,818	104,650	8,230	600	531,011
King's	34,650	66,650	126,650	90,460	104,850	10,000	2,000	435,260
London	67,938	126,300	181,100	172,812	130,230	11,900	—	690,280
Middlesex	19,450	44,600	107,145	129,291	102,480	9,955	—	412,921
Royal Free	18,081	38,500	62,850	87,653	122,100	8,400	—	337,584
St Bartholomew's	—	—	67,100	77,521	49,900	5,500	—	200,021
St George's	12,856	23,750	71,200	83,815	63,645	6,500	4,000	265,766
St Mary's	19,106	48,650	60,000	84,661	80,050	8,000	1,000	301,467
St Thomas's	12,600	—	102,750	122,420	120,900	10,750	500	369,920
Westminster	17,844	35,310	70,500	74,802	89,700	8,800	1,080	298,036
University College	21,931	43,950	81,600	101,391	123,000	11,150	—	383,022

Total of grants recommended to the twelve above-mentioned hospitals   4,444,242

Grand total of grants recommended by the Fund 1897-1948   12,413,253

* The twelve hospitals included are those which were in existence at the time of the Fund's foundation. The figures, compiled from the Fund's annual reports, are for grants allocated. For various reasons, usually to do with the inability of a hospital to meet the conditions attached, they were not always taken up. These figures exclude the Fund's distribution of payments on behalf of the Bank of England, small grants, initiated in 1936, in aid of district nursing, and a few extraordinary grants.

APPENDIX III

Grants Recommended to a Few Other Selected Hospitals, 1897–1948*

	£
Cancer Hospital (Royal Marsden)	2,970
Dreadnought (Seamen's) Hospital	154,944
French Hospital	15,604
German Hospital	44,634
Hampstead General Hospital	142,462
Hospital for Consumption (Brompton)	134,225
Hospital for Sick Children, Great Ormond Street	185,965
Hospital for Women (Soho Square)	68,133
Italian Hospital	17,471
London Homoeopathic (Royal)	70,793
Miller General Hospital	185,997
National Temperance Hospital	127,595
Royal London Ophthalmic Hospital (Moorfields)	149,852
St Mark's Hospital	26,287
West London Hospital	265,950

* These figures, compiled from the Fund's annual reports, are for grants allocated. For various reasons, usually to do with the inability of a hospital to meet the conditions attached, they were not always taken up. These figures exclude the Fund's distribution on behalf of the Bank of England and small grants, initiated in 1936, in aid of district nursing.

SELECT BIBLIOGRAPHY

THIS book draws on manuscripts, printed sources, and interviews. The bulk of the records of the King's Fund for the years 1897 to 1965 and some material for the years 1965–85 have been deposited in the Greater London Record Office (GLRO). As much by accident as by design, the Fund itself holds material from its earlier history as well as most of the records after 1965. In my notes, the prefix A/KE is used for those records cited from the GLRO collection and KF for those cited from the Fund's holdings. Some items can be found in both institutions, in which cases I have usually used the Fund's copy. References to material in the Bodleian Library, the British Library, the Public Record Office (PRO), and the Royal Archives (RA) are given throughout in the notes. The Gwyer manuscripts which have been cited are now deposited in the archives of the Royal National Pension Fund for Nurses. See the List of Abbreviations at the beginning of the book.

Abel-Smith, Brian, *The Hospitals, 1800–1948* (London, 1964).

Abramovitz, Moses, and Eliasberg, Vera F., *The Growth of Public Employment in Great Britain* (Princeton, NJ, 1957).

Acland, Reginald B. D., *The Work of the Hospital Saturday Fund: The Annual Address of the Chairman* (London, 1896).

Aronson, Theo, *The King in Love* (London, 1988).

Association of Chief Financial Officers in the Hospital Service in England and Wales. *Annual Conference . . . November 1956* ([1957]).

Austoker, Joan, *A History of the Imperial Cancer Research Fund 1902–1986* (Oxford, 1988).

Avery Jones, Sir Francis and Loewenthal, A. J., 'King Edward's Hospital Fund for London and the Emergency Bed Service', *British Journal of Hospital Medicine* (March 1974), 393–9.

Battiscombe, Georgina, *Queen Alexandra* (London, 1969).

Behlmer, George, *Child Abuse and Moral Reform in England, 1870–1908* (Stanford, 1982).

Bernard, Keith, and Lee, Kenneth (eds.), *Conflicts in the National Health Service*, (London, 1977).

Berridge, Virginia, 'Health and Medicine', in F. M. L. Thompson (ed.), *Cambridge Social History of Britain 1750–1950* (3 vols.; Cambridge, 1990), iii. 171–242.

Best, Gordon, 'NHS's Unhappy Returns', *Marxism Today* (July 1988), 20–3.

Bevan, Aneurin, *In Place of Fear* (London, 1952).

Beveridge, William (Lord), *Power and Influence* (London, 1953).

—— *Voluntary Action* (London, 1948).

Blomfield, J., *St George's, 1733–1933* (London, 1933).

Blunden, Margaret, *The Countess of Warwick* (London, 1967).

Bradford, Sarah, *King George VI* (London, 1989).

Brasnett, Margaret, *Voluntary Social Action* (London, 1969).

Briggs, Asa, and Macartney, Anne, *Toynbee Hall: The First Hundred Years* (London, 1984).

British Hospitals Association, *Report of the Voluntary Hospitals Commission* (The Sankey Report) (1937).

British Medical Journal.

Brown, R. G. S., *Reorganising the National Health Service: A Case Study of Administrative Change* (Oxford, 1979).

Bryant, Sir Arthur, *A History of the British United Provident Association: BUPA, 1947–68* (London, 1968).

Bryder, Linda, *Below the Magic Mountain: A Social History of Tuberculosis in Twentieth-Century Britain* (Oxford, 1988).

Burdett, Henry C., *Hospitals and the State* (London, 1881).

—— *The Medical Attendance of Londoners* (London, 1903).

—— *Pay Hospitals and Paying Wards throughout the World* (London, 1879).

—— *Prince, Princess, and People: An Account of the Public Life and Work of their Royal Highnesses the Prince and Princess of Wales, 1863–1889* (London, 1889).

Burdett's Hospitals and Charities (London, 1890 etc.).

Cameron, H. C., *Mr Guy's Hospital* (London, 1954).

Campbell, G. A., *The Civil Service in Britain* (London, 1965).

Campbell, John, *Nye Bevan and the Mirage of British Socialism* (London, 1987).

Cannadine, David, 'The Context, Performance and Meaning of Ritual: The British Monarchy and the "Invention of Tradition", *c.*1820–1977', in Eric Hobsbawm and Terence Ranger (eds.), *The Invention of Tradition* (Cambridge, 1984).

Capie, Forest, and Webber, Allan, *A Monetary History of the United Kingdom, 1870–1982* (London, 1985).

Cartwright, Frederick F., *A Social History of Medicine* (London, 1977).

Cave Committee, *Final Report*, Cmnd. 1335 (1921).

—— *Interim Report*, Cmnd. 1206 (1921).

Chaplin, Norman, 'Yearbook Centenary', *Health Services Management* (Apr. 1989).

Charities Aid Foundation, *Charity Trends*, 12th edn. (Tonbridge, 1989).

Clark, Ronald W., *A Biography of the Nuffield Foundation* (London, 1972).

Cook, Sir Edward, *The Life of Florence Nightingale*, (2 vols.; London, 1913, 1914).

Coutts, Angela Burdett (ed.), *Woman's Mission* (London, 1893).

Crossman, Richard, *Paying for the Social Services* (London, 1969).

—— *Planning for Freedom* (London, 1965).

—— 'The Role of the Volunteer in the Modern Social Service', in A. H. Halsey (ed.), *Traditions of Social Policy* (Oxford, 1976), 259–85.

Crowther, Anne, *British Social Policy 1914–1939* (London, 1988).

Curnock, George, *Hospitals under Fire* (London, 1941).

Daily Chronicle.

Daily News.

Daily Telegraph.

Darlington, Ida, 'King Edward's Hospital Fund for London and its Records', *Journal of the Society of Archivists*, 2 (9), (1964), 423–30.

Dawkins, Veronica, *A Study of the Development of Hospital Contributory Schemes in England and Wales* (Bristol, 1982).

Department of Health and Social Security, *Sharing Resources for Health in England* (HMSO, 1976).

Ditchfield, Revd P. H. (ed.), *The Book of the League of Mercy* (London, 1907).

Dunn, C. L. (ed.), *The Emergency Medical Services* (2 vols.; London, 1952, 1953).

Eckstein, Harry, *The English Health Service: Its Origins, Structure, and Achievements* (London, 1959).

Evans, A. Delbert, and Redmond Howard, L. G., *The Romance of the British Voluntary Hospital Movement* (London, [1930]).

Extracts from an Address by the Rt. Hon. Viscount Sankey . . . at the Annual Conference of the British Hospitals Association at Torquay, 28th May, 1937 (1937).

Fitzherbert, Luke, *Charity and the National Health: A Report on the Extent and Potential of Charitable Funds within the NHS* (London, [1989]).

Fraser, Derek, *The Evolution of the British Welfare State* (London, 1973).

The Future of Voluntary Organisations: Report of the Wolfenden Committee (London, 1978).

Gilbert, B. B., *The Evolution of National Insurance* (London, 1966).

Gilbert, Heather, *The End of the Road: The Life of Lord Mount Stephen*, ii, 1891–1921 (Aberdeen, 1977).

—— 'King Edward's Hospital Fund for London: The First 25 Years', *Social and Economic Administration*, 8 (1) (Oxford, 1974), 43–63.

Gladstone, F. J., *Voluntary Action in a Changing World* (London, 1979).

Goodman, Neville M., *Wilson Jameson, Architect of National Health* (London, 1970).

Granshaw, Lindsay, *St Mark's Hospital, London: A Social History of a Specialist Hospital* (London, 1985).

—— and Porter, Roy, *The Hospital in History* (London, 1989).

Guardian.

Hadley, Roger, and Hatch, Stephen, *Social Welfare and the Failure of the State* (London, 1981).

Hall, A. R., and Bembridge, B. A., *Physic and Philanthropy: A History of the Wellcome Trust 1936–1986* (Cambridge, 1986).

Harris, José, 'Society and the State in Twentieth-Century Britain', in F. M. L. Thompson (ed.), *The Cambridge Social History of Britain 1750–1950* (3 vols.; Cambridge, 1990), iii. 63–117.

—— *William Beveridge: A Biography* (Oxford, 1977).

Harrison, Brian, *Peaceable Kingdom: Stability and Change in Modern Britain* (Oxford, 1982).

Hay, J. R., *The Origins of the Liberal Welfare Reforms 1906–1914* (London, 1975).

Health Services Act 1980, Eliz. II, ch. 53.

Honigsbaum, Frank, *Health, Happiness, and Security: The Creation of the National Health Service* (London, 1989).

—— 'The Struggle for the Ministry of Health 1914–1919', *Occasional Papers on Social Administration*, 37 (London, 1970)

Hospital.

Hospital and Health Review.

Hospital and Health Service Management.

Hospital Gazette.

Hospital Management Planning and Equipment.

The Hospitals and Health Services Year Book.

The Hospitals Year-Book.

Independent.

Ives, A. G. L., *British Hospitals* (London, 1948).

Jennings, Hilda, *The Private Citizen in Public Social Work* (London, 1930).

Jeremy, David (ed.), *Dictionary of Business Biography* (5 vols.; London 1984–6).

Jewkes, John and Sylvia, *The Genesis of the British National Health Service* (Oxford, 1961).

King's Fund, *Annual Reports* (London, 1897–1990).

—— *Coordination of Hospital Services: Statement issued by the Joint Committee of King Edward's Hospital Fund for London and the Voluntary Hospitals Committee for London* (London, 1943).

—— *Design of Hospital Bedsteads* (London, 1967).

—— *Emergency Bed Service . . . Report for the Year ended 31st March 1954* (London, 1954).

—— *Evidence to the Royal Commission on the National Health Service* (London, 1977).

—— *Films for Hospitals* (London, 1961).

—— *Health Finance: Assessing the Options* (London, 1988), Institute Briefing Paper, no. 4.

—— *Hospital Bed Occupancy: Report of the First Study Group set up by the Hospital Administrative Staff College of King Edward's Hospital Fund for London* (London, 1954).

—— *King Edward's Hospital Fund for London: Its Past History and Present work* (London, 1944).

—— *The King's Fund Miniature Hospital* (London, 1934).

—— *King's Fund News.*

—— *The King's Fund Yesterday, Today and Tomorrow* (London, 1987).

—— *Managed Competition: A New Approach to Health Care in Britain* (London, 1989), Institute Briefing Paper, no. 4.

—— *Pay Beds Committee 1927–1928: Summary of Report* (London, 1928).

—— *Planned Health Services for Inner London: Back to Back Planning* (London, 1987).

—— *Relations between Voluntary Hospitals and Municipal Hospitals under the Local Government Bill* (London, 1929).

—— *Report of the Committee Appointed to Inquire into Out-patient Methods at London Voluntary Hospitals as Affecting Suitability of Patients and Time of Waiting* (London, 1932).

—— *Report of the Sub-Committee of Distribution Committee on Patients' Waking Hours in London Voluntary Hospitals* (London, 1931).

—— *Resolutions on the Subject of the Policy to be Recommended for the Preservation of the Voluntary System of Hospital Management and Control* (London, 1921).

—— *Second Memorandum on Hospital Diet for Consideration by Hospitals* (London, 1945).

—— *Select Committee on Estimates 1957: Memorandum from King Edward's Hospital Fund for London* (London, 1957).

—— *The Shape of Hospital Management in 1980?* (London, 1967).

—— *Simplified Form of Accounts on a Cash Basis for Small Institutions* (London, 1922).

—— *Some Aspects of the Post-War Hospital Problems in London and the Home Counties* (London, 1945).

—— *Statement of Views Expressed by the King's Fund to the Minister of Health in Connection with the National Health Service Bill* (London, 1946).

—— *Statistical Reports*, (London, 1903–48).

—— *Time Saving Methods at Hospital Out-Patients Dispensaries* (1935).

—— *Today and Tomorrow: An Outline of the Work and Aims of the King's Fund* (London, 1947).

—— *Working Together* (London, 1968).

—— and Nuffield Provincial Hospitals Trust, *Report of a Confidential Enquiry into Perioperative Deaths* ([1987]).

Lancet.

Langdon-Davies, John, *Westminster Hospital: Two Centuries of Voluntary Service, 1719–1948* (London, 1952).

Leader.

Lee, Sir Sidney, *King Edward VII: A Biography* (2 vols.; London 1925, 1927).

The Letters of Queen Victoria, 3rd ser., ed. George Earle Buckle (London, 1932).

Levitt, Ruth, and Wall, Andrew, *The Reorganised National Health Service*, 3rd edn. (London, 1984).

Long, Frank, *King Edward's Hospital Fund for London: The Story of its Foundation and Achievements, 1897–1942* (London, 1942).

McBriar, A. M., *An Edwardian Mixed Doubles: The Bosanquets versus the Webbs: A Study in British Social Policy 1890–1929* (Oxford, 1987).

McColl, Ian, 'The King's Fund and Quality of Medical Care', *Postgraduate Medical Journal*, 60 (November 1984), 825–7.

McInnes, E. M., *St Thomas' Hospital* (London, 1963).

Maggs, Christopher, *A Century of Change: The Story of the Royal National Pension Fund for Nurses* (London, 1987).

Magnus, Philip, *King Edward the Seventh* (London, 1964).

Maxwell, Robert (ed.), *Reshaping the National Health Service* (New Brunswick and Oxford, 1988).

The Medical Directory.

Medical Press.

Medvei, Victor Cornelius, and Thornton, John L., *The Royal Hospital of Saint Bartholomew 1123–1973 (London, 1974).*

Merrington, W. R., *University College Hospital and its Medical School* (London, 1976).

Metropolitan Hospital-Sunday Fund: Report of the Council for the Year Ended 31st December 1989 ([London, 1990]).

Midwinter, E. C., *Victorian Social Reform* (London, 1968).

Mill, John Stuart, *Principles of Political Economy* (Harmondsworth, 1970).

Ministry of Health, *A Hospital Plan for England and Wales*, Cmnd. 1604 (1962).

—— *A National Health Service*, Cmnd. 6502 (1944).

—— Central Health Services Council, *Report of the Committee on the Internal Administration of Hospitals* (the Bradbeer Report) (1954).

—— Consultative Council on Medical and Allied Services, *Interim Report on the Future Provision of Medical and Allied Services* (Dawson Report), Cmnd. 693 (1920).

—— *Hospital Survey: The Hospital Services of London and the Surrounding Area* (1945).

—— *Report of the Committee of Enquiry into the Cost of the National Health Service* (Guillebaud Report), Cmnd. 9663 (1956).

—— Voluntary Hospitals Commission, *Report on Voluntary Hospital Accommodation in England and Wales*, Cmnd. 2486 (1925).

Morgan, Kenneth and Jane, *Portrait of a Progressive: The Political Career of Christopher, Viscount Addison* (Oxford, 1980).

Morris, E. W., *A History of the London Hospital* (London, 1910).

Murray, D. Stark, *Why a National Health Service?* (London, 1971).

National Health Service Act 1946.

National Health Service and Community Care Act 1990.

Nuffield Provincial Hospitals Trust, *Tenth Report 1975–1980* (NPHT, 1980).

The *Nursing Record.*

Nursing Times.

Owen, David, *English Philanthropy, 1660–1960* (London, 1964).

Observer.

Pall Mall Gazette.

Pater, John E., *The Making of the National Health Service* (London, 1981).

Perkin, Harold, *The Rise of Professional Society: England since 1880* (London, 1989).

Pickstone, John V., *Medicine and Industrial Society: A History of Hospital Development in Manchester and Its Region, 1752–1946* (Manchester, 1985).

Pinker, R., *English Hospital Statistics 1861–1938* (London, 1966).

Pollard, S., *The Genesis of Modern Management* (Harmondsworth, 1968).

Powell, J. Enoch, *Medicine and Politics: 1975 and After* (Tunbridge Wells, 1976).

—— *A New Look at Medicine and Politics* (London, 1966).

Prince of Wales Hospital Fund. Memorial of the Metropolitan Radical Federation (1900).

Prochaska, F. K., 'Philanthropy', in F. M. L. Thompson (ed.), *The Cambridge Social History of England 1750–1950* (3 vols.; Cambridge, 1990), iii. 357–93.

—— *Women and Philanthropy in Nineteenth-Century England* (Oxford, 1980).

—— *The Voluntary Impulse: Philanthropy in Modern Britain* (London, 1988).

Punch.

Report of the Charity Commissioners for England and Wales for the Year 1986 (HMSO, London, 1986).

Rivett, Geoffrey, *The Development of the London Hospital System, 1823–1982* (London, 1986).

Roberts, Cecil, *Alfred Fripp* (London, 1932).

Rocha, Jan, *Organisers of Voluntary Services in Hospitals* (KF, 1968).

Rooff, Madeline *Voluntary Societies and Social Policy* (London, 1957).

Ross, James Stirling, *The National Health Service in Great Britain* (Oxford, 1952).

Royal Commission on the National Health Service, Cmnd. 7615 (HMSO, 1979).

Rubinstein, W. D., *Men of Property* (London, 1981).

Searle, G. R., *Corruption in British Politics, 1895–1930* (Oxford, 1987).

Semmel, Bernard, *Imperialism and Social Reform* (London, 1960).

Sheldrake, John, 'The LCC Hospital Service', in Andrew Saint (ed.), *Politics and the People of London: The London County Council 1889–1965* (London, 1989), 187–97

Small, Neil, *Politics and Planning in the National Health Service* (Milton Keynes, 1989).

Smith, F. B., *The People's Health 1830–1910* (London, 1979).

Stephen, Sir James, *Essays in Ecclesiastical Biography* (2 vols.; London, 1849)

Stevenson, John, *British Society 1914–45* (Harmondsworth, 1984).

Stocking, Barbara (ed.), *In Dreams Begins Responsibility: A Tribute to Tom Evans* (KF, 1987).

Stone, J. E., *Appeals for Funds and Hospital Publicity* (Birmingham, 1934).

—— *Hospital Accounts and Financial Administration* (London, 1929).

Sunday Pictorial.

Sunday Telegraph.

Taylor, A. J. P., *English History 1914–45* (Oxford, 1965).

Taylor, Marilyn, *Into the 1990s: Voluntary Organisations and the Public Sector* (London, 1988).

Thane, Pat, *The Foundations of the Welfare State* (London, 1982).

—— 'Working Class and State "Welfare" in Britain, 1880–1914', *Historical Journal*, 27 (4), (1984), 877–900.

Third Report from the Select Committee of the House of Lords on Metropolitan Hospitals (HMSO, 1892).

Time and Tide.

The Times.

Times Health Supplement.

Titmuss, Richard M., *Essays on 'The Welfare State'*, 2nd edn. (London, 1963).

—— *Problems of Social Policy* (London, 1950).

Trevelyan, John, *Voluntary Service and the State. A Study of the Needs of the Hospital Service* (London, 1952).

Ware, Alan (ed.), *Charities and Government*, (Manchester, 1989).

Warwick, Frances, Countess of, *Life's Ebb and Flow* (London, 1929).

Watson, Francis, *Dawson of Penn* (London, 1951).

Webster, Charles, *The Health Services since the War. Problems of Health Care: The National Health Service before 1957* (London, 1988).

Wernher, Sir Harold, *World War II: Personal Experiences* (London, 1950).

Wheeler-Bennett, John W., *King George VI* (London, 1958).

White, Rosemary, *The Effects of the National Health Service on the Nursing Profession 1948–1961* (London, 1985).

Widgery, David, *Health in Danger: The Crisis in the National Health Service* (London, 1979).

Working for Patients (HMSO, 1989).

Young, G. M., *Portrait of an Age: Victorian England* (London, 1977).

Ziegler, Philip, *The Sixth Great Power: Barings 1762–1929* (London, 1988).

—— *King Edward VIII* (London, 1990).

INDEX